VANCOUVER PAST:
ESSAYS IN SOCIAL HISTORY

VANCOUVER PAST:
ESSAYS IN SOCIAL HISTORY

Vancouver Centennial Issue of *BC Studies*

Edited by

Robert A. J. McDonald and Jean Barman

University of British Columbia Press
Vancouver
1986

Vancouver Past: Essays in Social History

Vancouver Centennial Issue of *BC Studies*

© The University of British Columbia Press, 1986

This book has been published with the help of grants from the University of British Columbia, Simon Fraser University, the University of Victoria, the Social Sciences and Humanities Research Council of Canada, the Koerner Foundation, the British Columbia Heritage Trust and the Vancouver Centennial Commission.

Canadian Cataloguing in Publication Data

Main entry under title:
Vancouver past: essays in social history

   Also issued as BC studies, no. 69-70.
   Bibliography: p.
   ISBN 0-7748-0256-1

   1. Vancouver (B.C.) — Social conditions.
2. Vancouver (B.C.) — History. I. McDonald,
Robert A. J., 1944-   II. Barman, Jean,
1939-   III. BC studies.
FC3847.394.V35 1986   971.1'33   c86-091428-3
F1089.5.V22V35 1986

ISBN 0-7748-0256-1

Printed in Canada

To

MARGARET PRANG

Founding co-editor, *BC Studies*, 1968-83

Professor, Department of History, University of British Columbia, 1958-86

Head, Department of History, University of British Columbia,
1974-79 and 1982-83

President, Canadian Historical Association, 1976-77

Contents

BC STUDIES/Number 69-70

Illustrations

Maps

CREDITS

City of Vancouver Archives, 18, 50, 51, 80 top, 149 bottom, 192 top; Vancouver Public Library, 80 bottom, 262 top right and bottom, 263 top left, 306 top; Special Collections, University of British Columbia, 149 top; *Pacific Advocate*, 4 January 1946, 306 bottom; Sara Diamond, 263 bottom; Jane Fredeman, 192 bottom; Deryck Holdsworth, 19, 20; Patrick and Gloria Kerr, 263 top right; Louise Colley Tilton, 262 top left; Julia Sandquist, map, 17; Angus Weller, map, 135.

Preface

Vancouver's centennial of incorporation on 6 April 1886 has provided the impetus to this special issue of *BC Studies*. It seemed appropriate to bring together in a single volume research currently underway by academics, graduate students and other scholars on the history of Canada's third largest city.

The result has outdistanced its original, rather modest objective, the essays as a group demonstrating that the history of Vancouver is maturing. While previous work emphasized the city's early, formative years, the majority of essays in this volume treat the coast city as a dynamic, complex, urban place. Their concern is with the early and mid-twentieth century, thus pushing forward in time our knowledge of Vancouver's past. More importantly, perhaps, the political and economic focus of much of the previous work is here complemented by subtle and sustained analyses of Vancouver's social development. Emphasis on connections between the Burrard Inlet metropolis and its surrounding region, which as Patricia Roy points out in her essay has been a staple of writing about Vancouver, is giving way to discussion of the lives of ordinary citizens.

While the essays presented here do not attempt to establish a single interpretation of west coast life, together they touch on many aspects of the Vancouver experience, enriching our understanding of the city's history and opening numerous topics for further discussion. Deryck Holdsworth and Jean Barman explore the social significance of spatial arrangements. Holdsworth argues that, to 1929 at least, this low density, suburban city more readily fulfilled people's aspirations to live in detached houses than did the industrial centres of eastern Canada and Great Britain from which most residents came; Barman documents the social character of Vancouver neighbourhoods, concluding that, during the interwar years, the socio-economic distinctions separating East Side from West Side were lessened by the integrating ties of community. In an overview of working class life to 1914, Robert McDonald argues that, while capitalist economic relations fundamentally divided Vancouver's middle and working classes, several west coast influences lessened class tensions, creating in the city a relatively benign social environment.

Other articles explore basic components of many residents' lives. In an essay that examines aspects of both medical and women's history, Veronica Strong-Boag and Kathryn McPherson demonstrate that by the interwar years almost all women delivered babies in hospitals controlled by male doctors rather than in the more familiar setting of private homes. Recounting the experience shared by all young Vancouverites of going to school, Neil Sutherland utilizes oral history techniques to show that traditional educational practices continued to guide the conduct of teachers as late as the 1960s despite reformers' efforts to introduce a "progressive" educational system. In the most systematically structural of all the essays, James Huzel analyzes police court records to show tentatively that in the 1930s increased economic distress did correspond with higher levels of non-violent crime against property.

The remaining three authors approach the city's history somewhat differently, identifying the strategies by which particular groups responded to social and economic needs. Paul Yee describes the operations of a prominent Chinese business firm, documenting its surprisingly diversified range of activities and challenging our conventional view of orientals as the passive victims of discrimination. In contrast, Irene Howard looks at a group of white activists fighting for social justice. Her study of the Mothers' Council, a left-oriented organization intent on bettering the condition of the unemployed during the Depression, presents women as political actors and, in so doing, suggests ways of overcoming the problem of inadequate sources that often limits the writing of women's history. Canada's severe housing shortage during the Second World War evoked protests that in January 1946 culminated in the occupation by veterans of the Old Hotel Vancouver; Jill Wade sorts out the complex political and social forces that led to this striking assertion of popular will.

The innovative character of many of these essays makes it especially appropriate that this special issue of *BC Studies* should be dedicated to Margaret Prang. Dr. Prang, who retires in 1986 after a long and distinguished association with the University of British Columbia, was cofounder and longtime co-editor of *BC Studies*, as well as president of the Canadian Historical Association. Her efforts have guided the journal to success and have encouraged the study of both regional and national history in British Columbia.

ROBERT MC DONALD

JEAN BARMAN

Cottages and Castles for Vancouver Home-Seekers

DERYCK W. HOLDSWORTH

At the turn of the century Vancouver, like other west coast North American cities far from the main centres of population, developed a distinctively urban landscape. Plentiful and cheap land, an extensive streetcar system and the financial rewards of a resource-based boom economy expedited the acquisition of comfortable home settings for middle-class life in a low-density city. In the boom years working-class people were able to share in that prosperity, albeit modestly. Home-ownership was widely accessible. In time, the costs of land and of housing would increase, and the wage advantage of Vancouver over eastern cities would moderate.[1] Indeed, from the beginning, the uneven circumstances of capital and labour, of families and single men, and of racial minorities made Vancouver clearly part of, rather than distinct from, the industrial world.[2] Yet Vancouver was also special, a place different from the towns and cities in eastern Canada and Britain, whence most Vancouverites had come.[3] It was a place at a particular moment in time on the western North

---

[1] E. R. Bartlett, "Real Wages and the Standard of Living in Vancouver, 1901-1929," *BC Studies* 51 (Autumn 1981): 3-62, is ambiguous on housing costs, an issue that still needs a full analysis in light of the longer amortization of mortgages by the early twentieth century, and which made home acquisition a different matter than earlier. One attempt to focus the analysis is offered by D. McCririck, "Opportunity and the Workingman: A Study of Land Accessibility and the Growth of Blue Collar Suburbs in Early Vancouver" (M.A. thesis, Geography, UBC, 1981), who has argued that, in a small sample of residents in Grandview over a limited span of time, 25 percent of the people rented; therefore, opportunities were limited. Others might look at the other side of the coin and draw the more optimistic conclusion that 75 percent did not rent. An excellent analysis on the continental scale that points the way for future work is M. J. Doucet and J. C. Weaver, "Material Culture and the North American House: The Era of the Common Man, 1870-1920," *Journal of American History* 72, 3 (December 1985): 560-87. See also footnote 40 below.

[2] For class manifestation at the urban level, see R. M. Galois, "Social Structure in Space: The Molding of Vancouver, 1886-1901" (Ph.D. thesis, Geography, Simon Fraser University, 1979). For attitudes to oriental labour, see H. Glynn-Ward, *The Writing on the Wall* (Vancouver: *Sun*, 1921) reprinted by University of Toronto Press, 1974 and containing a useful introduction by P. E. Roy (pp. vi-xxxi).

[3] N. MacDonald, "Population Growth and Change in Seattle and Vancouver, 1880-1960," *Pacific Historical Review* 39 (1970): 297-321.

11

American frontier where a booming land market, the possibility of good wages in a number of industrial or service jobs, the ease and cheapness of building in wood, and the popularity of imported housing styles from which to execute charming settings for family life combined to encourage many Vancouverites to identify with their new city.[4]

In 1913 Frank Yeigh provided a typical observation of Vancouver's residential landscape:

> While the fine business section is steadily improving and building up, the excellent streetcar system is assisting in a rapid suburban expansion. The trolley line to Steveston, for instance, shows the battle that is being waged against forest and stumps by the makers of homes. On one lot will be seen a neat frame cottage, with a bit of lawn, a profusion of flowers, and a kitchen garden, while adjoining it the once fire-swept forest awaiting the more complete subjugation at the handle of man. More room, more homes for more people is the cry of Vancouver, and the homes of the new city are models of architectural style, all embowered with a wealth of flowers and vines.[5]

Such a description was common throughout Vancouver's first half-century. It described fringe locations up to six or eight miles from the city's original mill-town focus. The term "cottage" was broadly and warmly associated with "home" and could describe a cabin or a mansion, its "lawn" a 25-foot lot or a two-acre estate. Gradually, through a succession of building booms, the stump-filled spaces between the cottages were built upon, the earlier homes were joined by houses of different styles, and street frontages emerged in unusual, somewhat variegated wholes.

Vancouverites were convinced they were part of a unique urban landscape. And unique it was, by the standards of the day in the British Isles and eastern North America, because in most segments of Vancouver's society home-ownership levels were high and urban residential densities exceptionally low. A 1928 study revealed that 72 percent of the houses in the city of Vancouver were single-family, detached homes;[6] in the neighbouring municipality of South Vancouver single-family houses comprised 75 percent of all residential accommodation and 84 percent of

[4] P. E. Roy, *Vancouver: An Illustrated History* (Toronto: Lorimer, 1980), provides the best scholarly overview of the city's development. Another useful perspective is offered by W. G. Hardwick, *Vancouver* (Toronto: Macmillan, 1974). The residential landscape is the focus of D. W. Holdsworth, "House and Home in Vancouver: The Emergence of a West Coast Urban Landscape, 1886-1929" (Ph.D. thesis, Geography, UBC, 1981).

[5] F. Yeigh, *Through the Heart of Canada* (Toronto: Gundy, 1913), p. 303.

[6] H. Bartholomew, *A Plan for Vancouver Including Point Grey and South Vancouver* (Vancouver, 1929), p. 217.

houses were owner-occupied.[7] In the municipality of Point Grey owners prided themselves on being part of an exclusively residential suburb. (See map, page 17, for places mentioned in text.) While Vancouver had been touted as the "Glasgow of the North West" and the "Liverpool of the Pacific," it could hardly have borne such monikers. Over 60 percent of Glasgow's population lived in one or two rooms in tenements joined end-to-end in bleak rows, while Liverpool faced problems common to most English cities in trying to cope with housing inadequacy.[8] At the turn of the century, when Vancouver was an exuberant town of 25,000 and anticipated outstripping New York, Robert Hunter's seminal survey of poverty revealed that 94 percent of New Yorkers were renters.[9] At every turn Vancouver seemed a departure from old ways. It was defined by internal greenery and flowers as much as by sea and mountains. Its "models of architectural style" were almost entirely single-family houses, not the apartments, tenements, courts and row housing of other industrial cities.

Vancouverites, alert to their unique opportunities, rarely failed to appreciate the distinctive nature of their emerging city. The diary of J. J. Miller, resident and real estate agent in Vancouver's Grandview neighbourhood, is particularly graphic on the city's merits.[10] Miller arrived in Vancouver from Australia in 1905 on his way to establish himself in the Winnipeg wheat trade. Sidetracked by the opportunities in Vancouver, he stayed and prospered. In the spring of 1912 he embarked on a four-month trip to attend the coronation of King George V, and, while passing through Port Moody and into the Fraser Valley on the CPR, noted Vancouver's "vast possibilities for the workers and the home-seekers."[11] In his observations along the route, Vancouver was always the standard against which other places were measured. Between Winnipeg and Fort William, "snow was falling ... and we thought of our beautiful daffodils and hyacinths and green lawns at Grandview,

[7] *Ibid.*, pp. 311, 357.

[8] *Census of Scotland*, 1881, quoted in Loomis, *Modern Cities and their Religious Problems* (New York, 1887); see also J. Butt, "Working Class Housing in Glasgow, 1815-1914," in S. D. Chapman (ed.), *The History of Working Class Housing* (Newton Abbot: David and Charles, 1971), p. 64. On London, C. Booth, *Life and Labour of the People of London* (London: Macmillan, 1902); on York, B. S. Rowntree, *Poverty: A Study of Town Life* (London: Macmillan, 1901).

[9] R. Hunter, *Poverty* (New York: Macmillan, 1904); J. Riis, *How the Other Half Lives* (New York: Scribner, 1890).

[10] J. J. Miller, *Vancouver to the Coronation* (London: Watts, 1912).

[11] *Ibid.*, p. 3.

Vancouver and the lively spring weather there."[12] Of Toronto, he observed that

for miles and miles of suburbs nothing but substantial brick houses greet the eye. The only objectionable feature is the sameness of architecture. Evidently brick construction does not lend itself to the adoption of attractive architecture so well as the wooden buildings of Vancouver.[13]

New York stood in even greater contrast for him:

The main part of the city extends for miles upon miles of four and five-storey brick buildings. The life of the people is essentially a city life. Nowhere within easy reach of the city can be seen the beautiful suburban bungalows or private residences with flower gardens and lawns such as may be seen at Vancouver.[14]

Between Miller's west and his urban east there was no choice: Vancouver was in a league by itself.

For Harry Archibald, similar contrasts were evident. A civil engineer who had come to Vancouver from Nova Scotia, Archibald regularly sent letters to his father in Musquodoboit, where the family had lived and worked since arriving as Loyalists. He was fascinated by the pace of change, and from his stable Maritimes background could not help but observe:

Everything is raw, crude, and unfinished, as the work is still under progress. It is a very expensive operation — as stumps here cannot be pulled out with a yoke of oxen as back East. What do you think of clearing trees four feet in diameter and one hundred feet high off land to make room for a city residence?[15]

Some of his responses were cautious and tentative. The priorities of socialists were unfamiliar to him, and in his view somewhat un-Canadian. As he observed:

This Vancouver is full of Socialists. A peculiar thing is that the Socialists are nearly always foreigners — Englanders, Germans, Americans, etc. They have meetings nearly every evening and on Sundays. Their big meeting is on Sunday evening. Was there once, but do not think I will join for a while at least. Their ways are not my ways, and at present we have nothing in common. But nearly every evening at the street-corners one can see a crowd of them holding forth. Many of them remind me of the great unwashed.[16]

[12] *Ibid.*, p. 6.

[13] *Ibid.*, p. 12.

[14] *Ibid.*, p. 25.

[15] W. C. Archibald, *Home-Making and its Philosophy, as Recounted by a Nesting Branch of the Archibalds* (Boston: Archibald, 1910), p. 499.

[16] *Ibid.*, p. 498.

Yet for all his observations of an unfinished place and unfamiliar people (not only socialists but also remittance men and Chinese and Japanese workers), Archibald was a booster: "the land of Evangeline is a good country, but this is a long way ahead of it."[17]

The opportunity of owning a home in the city distinguished Vancouver from its eastern Canadian counterparts. Land was available to many more than in the east, and working- and middle-class people could either buy houses finished from developers or begin themselves to build a cottage on a cheap city lot. One such cottage is illustrated on page 18. A simple one-family house surrounded by a garden and fence typify working-class housing in Vancouver's east end; it was built in 1892 by one John Mason, a worker who settled about one mile from Hastings Sawmill. Such small cottages and cabins were common. One storey high, one room deep and balanced symmetrically around a central doorway, they presented a folk classicism as elegant as more expensive structures elsewhere in the city. The surroundings may have been chaotic, but the disorder of stumps testified to clearing done. Inside the picket fence was "home," the pivotal space of the family. While the house was like thousands built as temporary homes by farmers on the Canadian Prairies, or by companies in mining camps in the Rockies, here, in a city, the cabin had become a special castle. A Vancouver woman, writing of her childhood, noted that:

A picket fence ran around the whole from the backyard and separated it from a half-vacant lot on the other side. Through the fence one could see blackberry vines growing on the lot and one could hear birds chirping in the morning sunshine ... Up Powell St., about 2 houses from where we lived, stood a small and very white cottage behind a snowy white picket fence. Flowers grew in the front yard and green shrubbery banked the fence from the inside. A broad flight of steps, four or five in number led from the garden wall to the verandah of the cottage whose front door was often left open.[18]

Twenty blocks to the west the men who owned the sawmills and factories and who managed the docks and railway were building their own castles in a similar mould. For them too the same criteria of home as sought by the city's workers were being applied. In her somewhat autobiographical account of the construction of the family home of leading merchant W. H. Malkin, Vancouver novelist Ethel Wilson provided a colourful picture of the evolving landscape:

[17] *Ibid.*, p. 504.

[18] G. C. Schwesinger, *Recollections of Early Vancouver in My Childhood, 1893-1912* (Vancouver: Vancouver Historical Society, Monograph #4), p. 38.

Down came the forests. Chop. Chop. Chop. The blessed forests came down. The men of the chain gang were driven up in a wagon and with lumbering movements cleared away the fallen trees while their guard stood near, and interested passers-by watched and then speculated on their past and their future. The forest vanished and up went the city.

Aunt Topaz's nephew Stephen soon began to build a large house halfway between the town and English Bay. This was very pioneering of him, as there was yet no streetcar near there. . . . Stephen's house was painted red. It was with a doll's house kind of pleasure that Topaz, fresh from bricky England, saw painters painting little wooden houses red, white, green and even yellow among the standing cedars, fir trees and maples. The houses all had wooden trimmings and verandahs, and on the verandah steps when day was done the families came and sat and talked and counted the box pleats of the backs of fashionable girls' skirts as they went by, and visitors came and sat and talked, and idly watched the people too, and watched the mountains grow dark, and the stars come out above the mountains. And then they all went in and made a cup of cocoa.[19]

The early West End homes were built in a greater variety of Victorian styles than those of the East End, many of them designed by architects and featuring prominent turrets, broad verandahs and elaborate shingle or gingerbread decorations (page 18). Inside, dining and living rooms were used for formal social entertainment, including "At Home" afternoons,[20] as well as for private family life. For over twenty years the city's elite occupied streets of impressive home settings between the harbour and English Bay, adjacent to the city's premier open space, Stanley Park.[21]

Workers' cottages nestled among the castles, just as castles occasionally protruded above the cottages. Photographs of early Vancouver reveal many such arrangements within the cleared bush, built from similar sawmilled parts, covered with similar clapboard or shingle, and decorated with much the same gingerbread trim. As the city grew, a mix of one- and two-storey houses, speculatively built by contractors from a small range of pattern-book designs,[22] joined the extremes of owner-built cottage

[19] E. Wilson, *The Innocent Traveller* (Toronto: Macmillan, 1944), p. 124.

[20] A. E. Robertson, "The Pursuit of Power and Privacy: A Study of Vancouver's West End Elite, 1886-1914" (M.A. thesis, Geography, UBC, 1977), pp. 31-45; also D. W. Holdsworth, "House and Home in Vancouver: Images of West Coast Urbanism, 1886-1929," in G. A. Stelter and A. F. J. Artibise (eds.), *The Canadian City: Essays in Urban History* (Toronto: McClelland & Stewart, 1977), pp. 198-201.

[21] Robertson, *op. cit.*, pp. 12-31.

[22] Important pattern books at the time included *Palliser's Model Houses* (Bridgeport, 1878); *Shoppell's Modern Houses* (New York: Cooperative Building Plan Association, 1900); *Radford American Homes* (Chicago: Drake, 1903). These and other

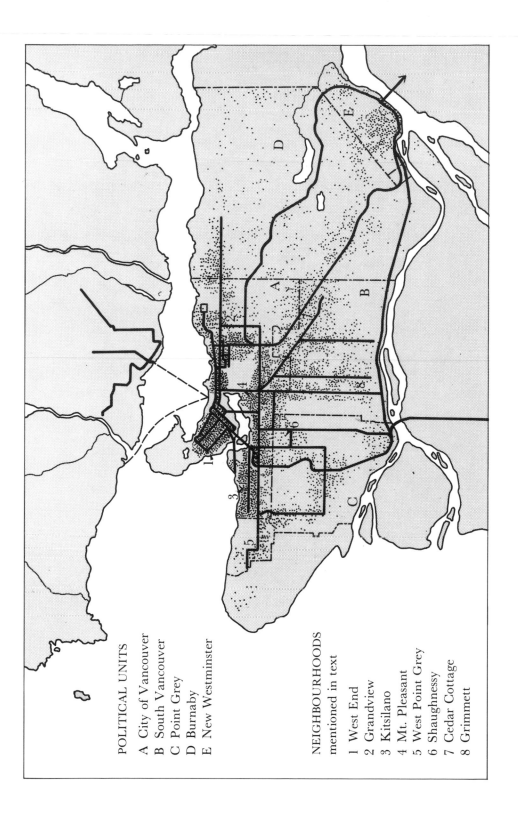

POLITICAL UNITS

A City of Vancouver
B South Vancouver
C Point Grey
D Burnaby
E New Westminster

NEIGHBOURHOODS
mentioned in text

1 West End
2 Grandview
3 Kitsilano
4 Mt. Pleasant
5 West Point Grey
6 Shaughnessy
7 Cedar Cottage
8 Grimmett

Cottage, Grandview, constructed 1892

Turreted house, West End, ca. 1890

*Designs for
workingmen's
homes from
Hodgson's
pattern book*

Half-timbered house, Third Shaughnessy, 1920s

California bungalow, 1920s

Stucco cottage, Point Grey, 1920s

and architect-designed mansion, as the West End, Yaletown and Strathcona districts filled up. Although there were shacks and cabins congested
near the sawmills and the railroad round-house, Vancouver had no close
counterpart to St. Henri in Montreal or to the back-to-back housing that
was still being built in Britain.[23] In large part this was because land was
available south and east of False Creek, and wood houses could be easily
built. Construction was relatively simple, and owner-built cottages were
possible. For the enterprising person, the low cost of land together with
high wages meant that a house could often be acquired rapidly.[24]

As in other developing cities of the North American west at the turn
of the century,[25] a broad swath of land was available in Vancouver for
suburban growth. Its dimensions had already been set by the initial
speculative steps taken to develop an interurban and suburban transportation system. Interurban Railway lines to New Westminster and later
Steveston and some 114 miles of electric streetcar tracks by 1928 would
make it possible to open up vast areas ahead of settlement, while competition between land speculators kept building lots affordable.[26] Some
people travelled out to the end of the streetcar lines and virtually into
the bush to reach their own piece of the world, a cheap suburban lot.
The following was noted of the behaviour of suburbanites:

pattern books are discussed in Holdsworth, 1981, pp. 109-61; see also Doucet and
Weaver, *op. cit.*

[23] See H. B. Ames, *The City Below the Hill* (1897) (Toronto: University of Toronto
reprint, 1972); also T. Copp, *The Anatomy of Poverty: The Condition of the
Working Class in Montreal, 1897-1929* (Toronto: McClelland & Stewart, 1974),
who observes: "the typical Montreal family in 1897 was made up of a husband,
wife and three children who lived in a five-room, cold-water flat located on a
narrow, densely populated side street in what is now the inner core of the city"
(p. 29). According to W. Beresford, in Leeds, England, poorly lit, cramped and
potentially unsanitary back-to-back houses were still being built in the early twentieth century: two-thirds of all new construction until 1903, still 49 percent in
1909, and 31 percent in 1912; "The Back to Back House in Leeds, 1787-1937,"
pp. 93-132 in Chapman, *op. cit.*

[24] H. J. Boam, *British Columbia: Its History, People, Commerce, Industry and Resources* (London: Sells, 1914), narrates the case of a carpenter who arrived in
March 1911 with $200 and had built a house worth $2,000 in nine months, only
owing the $200 cost of the site (p. 173).

[25] The impact of this land availability is summarized by studies of Los Angeles,
California. See, for example, S. B. Warner's essay "The New Freedom," in *The
Urban Wilderness: A History of the American City* (New York: Harper and Row,
1972), pp. 113-49. That this new urban realm was a product of the streetcar
rather than the freeway is amply illustrated by R. M. Fogelson, *The Fragmented
Metropolis: Los Angeles, 1850-1930* (Cambridge, Mass.: Harvard University Press,
1967).

[26] Holdsworth, 1981, pp. 59-108; see also Roy, *op. cit.*, on streetcars (p. 38) and on
South Vancouver Island (p. 68).

It is a trait noticeable in the people of Vancouver that the homemaker would rather live in a large comfortable residence a few miles out of town than exist in a shack in the heart of the city. The best, even if he has to go to some daily trouble to get it, is an aim characteristic of the Vancouverite. This idea he carries out in his everyday insistence on the best in the way of homes that has brought about the rapid upbuilding of the suburban districts tributary to Vancouver.[27]

Step by step outward from the core of the city, suburban home building was typified by the process of seeking "the best."

Immigrants arriving in large numbers before 1914, many from Britain, brought with them memories of the industrial city of their past. Before they emigrated, the prospect of home-ownership was beyond the imagination of clerks and artisans in British cities. Most had rented, and only long-term membership in a building society, backed by secure employment and sound domestic management, could make the prospect of independence from landlords even a remote possibility. For the majority, a suburban alternative to terraces or tenements would materialize only as local governments intervened to purchase land and construct estates.[28] Canadians who moved to Vancouver from Toronto often brought similar residential experiences, having lived as tenants in "flats," in rooms within subdivided brick houses or in frame and rough-stucco cottages in Cabbagetown or "the Ward." There too attempts at garden city-style reform housing were often too expensive for the people who needed it most.[29] Yet what was only a dream in such older cities seemed a reality in the "fresh" new city on the Pacific.

If the supply of cheap land in Vancouver was the product of competitive land speculation, the hope of home-ownership lay behind much of the demand for land. Real estate interests in the city skilfully played upon

[27] "Vancouver Today Hallmarked by Capital," Vancouver *Province*, Saturday Magazine, 18 June 1910, p. 8.

[28] A. A. Jackson, *Semi-Detached London* (London: Allen and Unwin, 1973) describes the circumstances of railway clerks in Edwardian London who were advised to be earning £90 (sterling) a year before marrying, and then only being able to rent: "a difference of a shilling or two in a white collar worker's weekly outgoings really mattered" (p. 42). The critical changes in salary and transport costs are traced through into house accessibility for an earlier period of London housing by H. J. Dyos, *Victorian Suburb: The Growth of Camberwell* (Leicester: Leicester University Press, 1962), especially pp. 114-37. See also J. Burnett, *A Social History of Housing, 1815-1970* (Newton Abbott: David and Charles, 1978).

[29] R. F. Harney (ed.), *Gathering Places: Peoples and Neighbourhoods of Toronto, 1834-1945* (Toronto: Multicultural History Society of Ontario, 1985). On attempts to develop low-cost housing, see S. Spragge, "A Confluence of Interests: Housing Reform in Toronto, 1900-1920," pp. 247-67, in A. F. J. Artibise and G. A. Stelter (eds.), *The Usable Urban Past: Planning and Politics in the Modern Canadian City* (Toronto: Macmillan, 1979).

the immigrants' desire to own a home. "Rent" conjured a specific set of unequal associations and unpleasant memories; "home" evoked dreams. A house owned was the safest form of security — so argued the land and housing industry. One advertisement for suburban land included a sketch of a mother kneeling beside her baby's crib, and suggestively asked: "Try and figure out what the land values of Point Grey will be when your boy or girl becomes of age. Do you not think a piece of property in this beautiful locality would lighten their path along life's highways?"[30] Such advertising played on the hopes for the future and on the doubts of the undecided. In a city where "the future was guaranteed" (as every booster maintained), a purchase when the opportunity was "right" ensured security later when the city filled and its land would be expensive. A building lot purchased would lead to a house being built and a home begun. Mercilessly, the hype for land was parlayed into immigrants' hopes for homes and their fears of the future, not to mention tidy profits for the speculators.

Oftentimes, the company selling land was also selling houses, and consequently boosting the ideal of home-ownership was doubly needed. In one article Vancouver was hailed as a "City of Beautiful Homes":

> The measure of a city's stability, financial soundness and attractiveness to the newcomer is not to be found in its palatial hotels, skyscraper office buildings and apartment houses. The dweller in flats is an uncertain and unsettled quantity. The man in the office may be a foot-loose adventurer. Homes alone indicate the extent and quality of citizenship. The home is the heart, the life and the index of a city. Vancouver may well be proud of her beautiful homes, and of her great industries that are directly concerned with the promotion of home-building — sawmills, sash and door factories, and home-building companies. Among those who have come here from the great schools of older lands and from the great republic to the south of us are many brilliant young architects who have brought to us their genius, unfettered by effete convention and worn-out tradition. They have evolved new and attractive types of bungalows and mansions that are a revelation to the town dweller from the east or from overseas, where they are familiar with terraced rows of cottages that seem to have been made by the gross to one dreary pattern. The immigrant has brought with him a deeply implanted love of home life.[31]

The design being promoted in this case was a California Bungalow, to be set on a lot spacious enough to be free of neighbourly nosiness and no

[30] Vancouver *Province*, 28 April 1910, p. 17 (advertisement for Highbury Park, D.L. 320, Point Grey. Marriott and Fellows, Real Estate agents).

[31] F. Pemberley, "Vancouver, a City of Beautiful Homes," *British Columbia Magazine* VII, 12 (December 1911): 1313-15.

doubt appointed with roses and other blooms. Other firms promoted the historic and bucolic associations of a stuccoed cottage with half-timbered trim. Both were visual contrasts to the brick and grimy rows in cities to the east and overseas, and both exploited the imagery of openness as the antidote to industrial life.

The distinction between residential densities in working-class Vancouver and other industrial cities was recognized, valued and defended. In the Vancouver *World* of 1912 it was insisted that

there will be no slums in South Vancouver, no tenement district, and the living factories that grace themselves with the name of apartment houses dare not enter where there is room for neat cottages and gardens and chicken yards; where the working man may bring his family up in the fresh air; and the rays from the sun in Heaven may enter without restraint.[32]

Here was a residential image that had characterized parts of Vancouver for more than twenty years — gardens for fruit, vegetables and poultry, detached houses in healthy, almost rural settings. The real estate interests, promoting for their own profit an image of contented home-ownership in a garden setting, could not easily be condemned for their self-interest given that the workers of Vancouver might benefit by attaining standards of life well beyond those of their old industrial world cousins.

The case history of Jesse Enefer, labourer, highlights some of the benefit working men could derive in Vancouver's cheap suburban land market. In 1908 Jesse lived in rooms near the docks while working for McDonald Marpole Coal. His neighbours included many like him, all part of an unskilled labour pool close to the waterfront.[33] Two years later, now working for a plumbing contractor digging pipe-lines, he moved a mere half block to another set of rooms, but also in 1910, just two years after coming to Vancouver, Jesse made the transition to the city's suburban ideal of home-ownership. He moved three-and-a-half miles south to East 48th Avenue in South Vancouver. Three years later he had moved eleven blocks further south to the Grimmett area at the south end of Main Street, where five other house-owning Enefer kin also lived. All

[32] "South Vancouver: Where the Renter Ceases Trembling and the Landlord is at Rest," Vancouver *World*, 1912, Progress and Building Education, p. 92.

[33] Prior Street three blocks east of Westminster (later Main Street) in 1907 listed: teamster, motorman, Italian, labourer, waiter, junk store, labr., logger, 2nd-hand store, clerk, labr., longshoreman, stonecutter, dress-maker, widow, labr., grocer, teamster, feed lot, boat builder, insurance, stoves, laundry, manager, hotel keeper, engineer, 2nd-hand store, grocer, motorman, machinist, inspector, painter, janitor, engineer, gasfitter, millman, conductor, labourer.

the Enefers were listed in the directory as labourers.[34] Their achievement in obtaining homes in the suburbs was repeated by many others in the Grimmett district.

The area was scantily settled. There was just one person per acre,[35] and, between houses, forest and scrub mixed with the gardens, orchards and cow pastures of city workers. Most of the occupants of the isolated houses were unskilled labourers or artisans — sawmill workers, teamsters and carpenters — yet they were close to downtown employment by street-car and as close to sawmills at Eburne and New Westminster via the Interurban Railway. Here, at a time when English planners were experimenting with Garden City alternatives to high density working-class housing, Grimmett had already been created as a residential environment that fitted South Vancouver's confident boast of being the "Garden Suburb of the West."[36]

Grimmett homes were far different than the consciously "arts and crafts" cottages being contrived for the British garden cities.[37] Very few of the houses in this neighbourhood, or in South Vancouver as a whole, developed from blueprints that had an architect's signature. Most incorporated the innate design sense of contractors or owner-builders, assisted by a newer generation of pattern books than those that had influenced late nineteenth-century contractor-built houses.[38] Many were designs for "workingmen's cottages" (page 19). Most were simple rectangular structures, usually oriented gable-on to the road with a verandah across the front, or else variants of the cabin shown on page 18. Setbacks were irregular; some houses stood in the middle of several lots, surrounded by a nascent orchard, while others were placed at a roughly standard dis-

[34] Holdsworth, 1981, table 1, "The Enefer Clan: Residential and Occupational Mobility," p. 13.

[35] For a 22-block, 180-acre area bounded by Ontario Street, 58th Avenue, Prince Edward Street and River Road, 160 dwellings, occupied land at a density of less than one per acre (*Henderson's Vancouver Directory*, 1913, 1922, 1926). Grimmett took its name from a pioneer settler whose name was used for that of the local post office.

[36] Municipality of South Vancouver, Publicity Bureau, "Garden Suburb of the West," 3 pages, 1924 (City of Vancouver Archives Pamphlet Collection). South Vancouver as a whole had a density of nine persons per acre in 1928: Bartholemew, *op. cit.*, p. 357.

[37] W. L. Creese, *The Search for Environment: The Garden City, Before and After* (New Haven: Yale University Press, 1966).

[38] These included *Hodgson's Low Cost American Homes* (Chicago: Drake, 1906), *Hodgson's Practical Bungalows and Cottages* (Chicago, 1912), *Radford's Artistic Bungalows* (Chicago, 1908), H. Wilson, *The Bungalow Book* (Chicago, 1911), J. Yoho, *Craftsmen Bungalows* (Seattle, 1913).

tance back from the sidewalk, as if nominally acknowledging the urban
order that would gradually follow. In many cases houses grew in stages
around a kitchen and bedroom, additions being the product of the
owner's "sweat equity" or his participation in the "informal economy" of
neighbourly help. Cottages were raised to provide a deeper or sounder
basement or expanded by raising the roof to add an upper storey, and
such changes were sometimes associated with moving the house to a
different lot. Some houses were totally prefabricated — such as the cottages made at the B.C. Mills factory on False Creek largely for construction on the lumber-scarce prairies, but also popular on Vancouver's east
side.[39] By middle-class standards, these suburban fringe developments
were little more than "shacktowns," but for their occupants architectural
conformity was secondary to the sense of a private realm, of arcadia,[40]
that Jesse Enefer undoubtedly felt in contrast to the dockside rooms he
had occupied during his early days in the city.

The upper-class counterpart of Jesse Enefer's search for the suburban
ideal was exemplified by the move of Edward P. Davis, a prominent
lawyer who left the West End in 1912 for a house at the tip of the Point
Grey peninsula. Pressures of change prompted by the expansion of downtown had begun to erode the West End's earlier exclusiveness. Davis had
lived on Seaton Street (now Hastings), very close to the waterfront but
in circumstances quite different from Jesse Enefer's. Originally part of
the area of CPR executives' homes, Seaton Street in 1905 included the
residences of Davis; F. C. Wade, later proprietor of *The Sun* newspaper;
Ed Mahon and W. Nichols, two of the city's leading real estate figures;

---

[39] E. G. Mills and D. W. Holdsworth, "The B.C. Mills Prefabricated System: The
Emergence of Ready-Made Buildings in Western Canada," Canadian Historic Sites:
Occasional Papers in Archaeology and History, no. 14, Ottawa, 1974, pp. 127-69.

[40] R. Knight, *A Very Ordinary Life* (Vancouver: New Star, 1974), pp. 209-10 and
225-31, contains a fascinating portrait of a small cabin on Wall Street, in Vancouver's East End, acquired after World War II. Although minimal, it was a step
up from the two decades of mobility and seasonal work across Canada; indeed, it
became home for a life in post-war Vancouver.

Such experiences should not be overlooked in the search for more objective
measures of home-ownership or of standards of living as discussed in footnote 1
above. In many cities the "informal sector" housing supply, with shacks and cabins
gradually turning into houses, was a critical element of working-class independence
and self-worth. On the fringes of London, England, for example, they become the
subject of an important book by D. Hardy and C. Ward, *Arcadia For All: The
Legacy of a Makeshift Landscape* (London: Mansell, 1984); for the same phenomenon in Paris, France, see N. Evanson, *Paris: A Century of Change, 1878-1978*
(New Haven: Yale University Press, 1979), pp. 226-38. For Canadian examples,
see J. T. Saywell, "Housing Canadians: Essays on the History of Residential Construction in Canada," Economic Council of Canada, Discussion Paper No. 25,
1975, pp. 114-36.

T. O. Townley, a past mayor; and several bankers and merchants. But the change underway meant that by 1908 the street also included a brewery, and the conversion of large private houses to apartment functions had begun. The visual amenities had been altered too by expansion of port and rail facilities that interrupted the view of the harbour and mountains. Davis withdrew to a location with a dramatic view of the coast mountains where he built a half-timbered mansion set in one and a half acres of garden.[41] Others of his profession and class also left the West End, most moving to Shaughnessy Heights, where estate-lots along treed crescents were marketed by the Canadian Pacific Railway.

In Shaughnessy, as in Grimmett, society tended to be comfortably homogeneous, the neighbourhood being especially favoured by barristers, managers, owners and company directors as well as by leading public service professionals. Restrictive covenants and high real estate prices for large lots helped codify exclusivity amid acceptable architectural variation. The dominant house style echoed English Tudor manors. Their aged appearance belied their newness and provided a sophisticated and "rooted" setting for families to enjoy their position in society. The drawing rooms were larger than those used for "at Homes" in the West End, and the central hallways were sometimes impressively two storeys high with open staircases and galleries in the manner of medieval halls; an inglenook seating area provided cosy corners within such voluminous spaces. Tudor Revival houses shared treed streets with revivalist interpretations of rough-stuccoed English farmhouses, smooth-stuccoed and red-tiled Spanish Missions, gambrelled-roof Dutch Colonial farmhouses or even flamboyantly porticoed mansions modelled after those in the American South.[42]

Such structures were built in Shaughnessy for over twenty years as the CPR opened further segments of the subdivision to the south. One of the most impressive half-timbered houses from the 1920s was the residence of Alvah Hager, an American from Boston who came west, built up a

[41] Davis's house, initially called "Kanakla," is now known as the Cecil Green Park and is the home of the University of British Columbia Alumni Association; as such it is one of the most accessible houses of that class in Vancouver. Other Tudor Revival mansions along the Point Grey shoreline that are also publicly accessible include one built for J. S. Rear (later called "Aberthau" and now the home of the West Point Grey Community Centre) and "Thorley Park" (now the Brock House seniors' centre). These houses receive treatment in J. Bingham, *Samuel Maclure, Architect* (Ganges: Horsdal and Shubert, 1985), pp. 79-82. Similar mansions were built on prominent sites in the East End and near Burnaby Lake.

[42] H. D. Kalman and J. H. Roaf, *Exploring Vancouver* (Vancouver: University of British Columbia Press, 1974), pp. 145-64.

fortune and then enjoyed it in one of the most emphatically English houses anywhere in the city (page 19). Several reasons may explain why a Bostonian chose to live in Third Shaughnessy in an imitation thatched cottage near Vancouver's school superintendent, who resided in a Dutch Colonial-style house, and near a wholesale grocer in a stuccoed English farmhouse. Possibly Vancouver was merely replicating what Cleveland's Shaker Heights, Philadelphia's Main Line or developments in other eastern cities had already achieved — gracious rustic homes as a foil for work in the industrial city — but on a more modest scale as befitted its location on the fringe of a continental economy.[43] Alternatively, the litmus of success for a largely English city was the country house and not an urban townhouse,[44] and so the informal and bucolic Tudor Revival set in a pastoral subdivision was more apt than the streets of denser Victorian housing in the West End. Whatever the reason, the frequency and apparent ease with which these successful men changed residence, many of them having at least two distinguished addresses within a decade, suggests a restlessness in the "city of homes." Grimmett and Shaughnessy shared a great deal, albeit at the opposite ends of the social scale.

Grimmett and Shaughnessy, two homogeneous but socio-economically distinct residential areas, illustrate the spatial sorting of Vancouver's suburban population that developed as suburban sites became available. The distinction between east-side and west-side Vancouver, noted as early as 1891 ("the West End is the home of the merchant and professional, the East that of the lumber king and mechanic"), clearly persisted as the suburbs developed. Yet the city was not totally compartmentalized on rigid class or occupational lines.[46] In Kitsilano, Mount Pleasant,

[43] E. Johannesen, *Cleveland Architecture, 1876-1976* (Cleveland: Western Reserve Historical Society, 1979), pp. 101-09; for similar grandiose housing in Philadelphia and other east coast settings, see V. Scully, *The Shingle Style* (New Haven: Yale University Press, 1955).

[44] This preference is explored by M. J. Weiner, *English Culture and the Decline of the Industrial Spirit, 1850-1980* (Cambridge: Cambridge University Press, 1981); see also J. S. Duncan and N. G. Duncan, "A Cultural Analysis of Urban Residential Landscape in North America: The Case of the Anglophone Elite," pp. 255-76, in J. A. Agnew, J. Mercer, D. E. Sopher (eds.), *The City in Cultural Context* (Boston: Allen and Unwin, 1984).

[45] *Williams Vancouver Directory* (1891), p. 128.

[46] E. M. Gibson, "Lotus Eaters, Loggers and the Vancouver Landscape," pp. 57-74, in L. J. Evendon and F. F. Cunningham (eds.), *Cultural Discord in the Modern World* (Vancouver: Tantalus, 1973), suggests some of the broad patterns of segregation. A more precise analysis of working-class fractions is offered by R. M. Galois, *op. cit.*

Cedar Cottage and Grandview — all neighbourhoods beyond False Creek but still within the limits of the pre-1929 city of Vancouver — socio-economic strata overlapped. The juxtaposition within a single neighbourhood of people in different economic circumstances led to complex residential landscapes in this belt of "middle-suburbs" two or three miles from downtown. A range of pioneers — some farmers, others labourers, yet others professionals — provided widely different initial housing stock, and a variegated cadastral plat of 25, 33 and 50 foot lots created a range of density options for subsequent booms that filled the blocks with a variety of contractor-built bungalows and cottages.[47]

Both the California Bungalow and the English Cottage shared the aesthetic inspiration of the Arts and Crafts Movement then prevalent in Britain and North America,[48] and both found popularity with middle-class as well as working-class purchasers. Bungalows and stucco cottages were built with many variants of decoration and volume, and their rusticity and garden settings made them comfortable neighbours on many city streets.

The California Bungalow was typically a one-storey wooden house with broad verandahs, decorative brick porch supports, exposed rafters and shingled siding (page 20). The sense of spaciousness was reinforced by an informal indoor-outdoor floor plan. It was a pattern-book interpretation of elegant wood houses designed by the Pasadena, California, architectural firm of Greene and Greene.[49] In Vancouver, as in other more northern settings, a high basement for the furnace made it look taller than its southern cousin.[50] Larger and more expensive variants were known as "Swiss Chalet" bungalows, which incorporated a large upper-floor dormer and balcony. In Vancouver contractors specialized in building one or two plans from these California design books, and their interpretations brought distinctive variants of the style to different

[47] For a case study of Grandview, see Holdsworth, 1981, pp. 17-24; for Kitsilano, the range of houses is recorded in D. W. Holdsworth, "Vernacular Form in an Urban Context" (M.A. thesis, Geography, UBC, 1971).

[48] William Morris was central to this movement: see E. P. Thompson, *William Morris: Romantic to Revolutionary* (London: Lawrence and Wishart, 1955); also A. Briggs (ed.), *William Morris: Selected Writings and Designs* (London: Pelican, 1962). For the leading American exponent, see M. A. Smith, *Gustav Stickley, The Craftsman* (Syracuse: Syracuse University Press, 1983).

[49] R. Winter, *The California Bungalow* (Los Angeles: Hennessey and Ingalls, 1980); C. Lancaster, *The American Bungalow, 1880-1930* (New York: Abbeville, 1985).

[50] D. W. Holdsworth, "Regional Distinctiveness in an Industrial Age: Some California Influences on British Columbia Architecture," *American Review of Canadian Studies* XII, 2 (1982): 64-81.

Vancouver neighbourhoods.[51] Few really expensive bungalows were built in the "pure" Greene and Greene style, however, since the Vancouver elite preferred the more traditional Revivalist styles. Most bungalows, copied from pattern books, were built by small-scale contractors. By the 1920s only the single-storey versions were being built, both in the west-side suburbs and in less elaborate manner on the east side. In its least expensive form the bungalow was little different than John Mason's cabin of the 1890s, with perhaps the addition of stone or pebble piers supporting the verandah and a few exposed rafter-ends.

The other popular house-type connected with the Arts and Crafts Movement was a stucco cottage that featured some half-timber trim.[52] It was a vernacular cousin of the Tudor Revival mansions found in Shaughnessy Heights, and its broad pattern-book popularity led to its adoption in suburbs of quintessentially American cities such as Minneapolis[53] as well as the Anglo-Canadian Vancouver suburb of Point Grey (page 20). Typically a half-hip (or jerkin) gable suggested thatched-cottage roofing, an illusion reinforced by asphalt tiles curved around the eave and also by small eye-lid dormers. The front facade might also utilize fake end-buttresses that suggested a thick cob wall, or an exaggerated sloping gable (a "cat-slide" roof) whose lines were inspired by the designs of the English architect C. F. A. Voysey.[54] Half-timber trim was added in lesser or greater amounts, although only architect-designed cottages went so far as to add pargetting, nogging or other infill material for the "authentic" vernacular touch.[55] Most were built on the western flanks of Shaughnessy, in Kerrisdale, West Point Grey and Dunbar Heights during the 1920s. Very few had the spacious hallways or inglenook detail associated with the architect-designed versions. In its more minimalist form, the cottage approximated the early cabin, only now with a jerkin roof and stuccoed walls.

Whether a cottage, a bungalow or a mansion, housing for Vancouver home-seekers developed in response to urban images that had been

[51] Holdsworth, 1981, pp. 162-205.

[52] J. D. Kornwolf, *M. H. Baillie Scott and the Arts and Crafts Movement* (Baltimore: Johns Hopkins University Press, 1972); B. Palmer, "Development of Domestic Architecture in British Columbia," *Journal of the Royal Architectural Institute of Canada* (November 1928): 405-16; also Holdsworth, 1981, pp. 206-48.

[53] T. Harvey, "Mail Order Architecture in the Twenties," *Landscape* 25, 3 (1981): 1-9.

[54] D. Gebhard, *Charles F. A. Voysey, Architect* (Los Angeles: Hennessey and Ingalls, 1975).

[55] A. W. Jackson, *The Half Timbered House: Its Origins, Design, Modern Plan and Construction* (New York: McBride Nast, 1912).

framed elsewhere and experiences that pre-dated Vancouver. The sense that here was a world apart came not just from the boosterism of the place itself, but most strikingly from a common appreciation of the distinctive opportunities in Vancouver. Miller and Archibald, Mason and Enefer, Davis and Hager each reveal something of the specific links between Vancouver and a prior world. Emotionally and experientially, the reference points were largely eastern Canadian or British. Vancouverites looked back to other remembered places and saw a measure of themselves. They looked at the landscape of Vancouver and enlarged their vision of what was possible in a city. The detached single-family house as home — an external object set within a garden world and an internal space where family developed — was at the heart of that vision.

In 1929 the city of Vancouver amalgamated with its two suburban municipalities, South Vancouver and Point Grey, to confirm legally a spatial reality that had existed for the previous quarter century. This period had seen the skeleton of the modern metropolis laid out, neighbourhoods defined and stabilized social gradients developed. Throughout this process, there had been little reform rhetoric. In the minds of civic leaders and embryonic planners there were few tenements and few areas of abject poverty, overcrowding and disease.[56] For nearly all men and women the city seemed to offer adequate shelter together with the hint of further affluence. Little reformist planning was thought to be needed, because the vision of an appropriate future for Vancouver, originating in the attitudes of landowner/developers and embraced willingly by immigrant home-seekers, seemed to be realized in the landscape.

To a large extent this optimism was justified. Vancouver on the eve of the Depression was emphatically suburban.[57] Patches of land (indeed, building lots on most streets) were still available on the Burrard Peninsula, and the urban fringe extended clear into the Fraser Delta and Fraser Valley to the south and west, and north across the harbour to the lower slopes of the North Shore mountains. Then so too was there a sense that housing was still accessible. Second and Third Shaughnessy might seem beyond reach, but its western flanks offered more affordable homesites on serviced and landscaped streets. While the east side was a more chaotically developed region of smaller houses, it was nonetheless

---

[56] For the broader Canadian context, see J. C. Weaver, *Shaping the Canadian City: Essays on Urban Politics and Policy, 1890-1920* (Toronto: Institute of Public Administration of Canada, 1977); P. Rutherford (ed.), *Saving the Canadian City: The First Phase 1880-1920* (Toronto: University of Toronto Press, 1974).

[57] Hardwick, *op. cit.*, pp. 36-40; Roy, *op. cit.*, p. 113; and J. Barman, "Neighbourhood and Community in Interwar Vancouver," this issue of *BC Studies*.

well away from occupants' workplaces. If there was not a uniform suburbia, Vancouver was still a city of predominantly single-family homes — some tiny, others small, yet others comfortable and even palatial. Together they shared a peninsula on the edge of the Pacific and at the foot of coastal mountains. The perception that Vancouver provided a unique urban opportunity in a magnificent natural setting, and in a verdant landscape of parks and treed streets, was not always to be confirmed for everyone, and the essentially conservative notion that the best city was a low-density suburban region would create mounting problems for planners and later generations of home-seekers; but for those who were part of the city's first half-century of growth, the dream of a "neat frame cottage, with a bit of lawn," seemed realizable.

Working Class Vancouver, 1886-1914:
Urbanism and Class in British Columbia*

ROBERT A. J. McDONALD

Conventional wisdom holds that in the early years of the twentieth century British Columbia workers expressed a relatively high level of class feeling. Travellers of the period identified relations between capital and labour as British Columbia's distinguishing feature. Once west of the Rockies an easterner "finds himself confronted with a new set of moral and social problems," Rev. S. D. Chown, a leading social critic from Ontario, commented during a west coast visit in 1904; the "most insistent question of the common people is not, what have you to say about temperance or prohibition, but, what is your message in respect to capital and labor; what is your scheme for bettering the material conditions of the people, and producing peace and good will between the employer of labor and his employees."[1] British writer J. A. Hobson concurred: "Nowhere else in Canada is the labour question so prominent, nowhere else is class sentiment of employer and employed so much embittered."[2] Scholarly assessments of British Columbia politics and labour relations during the early 1900s corroborate these contemporary observations. One author characterizes British Columbia as the "company province," where a unique political system based on competing class interests emerged; two others describe it as the "militant province," marked by a higher than average level of strikes; and still another portrays it as the radical province, where workers, led by miners and railroad navvies, embraced revolutionary forms of socialism.[3]

* I would like to thank Jeremy Mouat, Allen Seager, Peter Ward, Logan Hovis, Jean Barman and Keith Ralston for their helpful comments on an earlier draft of this paper and Douglas Cruikshank for generously assisting in the generation and analysis of strike data.

1 S. P. Mosher, "The Social Gospel in British Columbia: Social Reform as a Dimension of Religion, 1900-1920" (M.A. thesis, University of Victoria, 1974), p. 64.

2 J. A. Hobson, *Canada To-day* (London: T. F. Unwin, 1906), p. 32.

3 Martin Robin, *The Rush for Spoils: The Company Province, 1871-1933* (Toronto: McClelland & Stewart, 1972); essays by Stuart M. Jamieson and Emil Bjarnson in Jamieson et al., *Militancy in the British Columbia Labour Movement* (Vancouver: The Institute of Industrial Relations, University of British Columbia, 1977), pp.

BC STUDIES, nos. 69-70, Spring-Summer 1986

While agreeing that British Columbia's unstable resource economy accounts for working class militancy and radicalism, writers are less clear about Vancouver's role. Except for a brief discussion of the subject by David Bercuson, the urban dimension of British Columbia's class system is either ignored or seen to reflect the regional pattern.[4] According to Ross McCormack, workers in Winnipeg and across the prairie provinces expressed their class identity through "labourism," a moderate form of labour radicalism; by contrast, British Columbia workers espoused revolutionary socialism.[5] Yet this interpretation distorts B.C. history by overlooking the dissimilarity between metropolitan centre and surrounding region. The following paper aims to investigate this difference by examining working class Vancouver from 1886 to 1914. It argues that the city's economy created an urban working class more complex and more moderate than that of the highly polarized mining communities of Vancouver Island and the Kootenays. Vancouver workers, like their Winnipeg counterparts, expressed class feeling more through moderate labourism than doctrinaire socialism. In addition, the city's strike record more closely approximated the pattern of capital-labour strife in Toronto and Saint John than the chronicle of strident conflict in Rossland and Nanaimo.

For the turn-of-the-century period discussed in this essay, class is defined in the Marxist sense as the product of capitalist society's fundamental division between those individuals who owned the means of production (such as land and capital), or whose interests and aspirations (such as professionals and managers) led them to identify with the owners, and those who did not, and who thus had to sell their labour.[6] Wage labour, sold as a commodity in the marketplace, characterized the system. Two types of class relationships resulted. One was an "experienced objective relationship" between capital and labour, a "concrete, material,

---

3-8 and 9-11; and A. Ross McCormack, *Reformers, Rebels, and Revolutionaries: The Western Canadian Radical Movement 1899-1919* (Toronto: University of Toronto Press, 1977).

[4] David Jay Bercuson, "Labour Radicalism and the Western Industrial Frontier: 1897-1919," *Canadian Historical Review* 58 (June 1977).

[5] McCormack, *Reformers, Rebels, and Revolutionaries*, passim.

[6] See Rennie Warburton, "Race and Class in British Columbia: A Comment," *BC Studies* 49 (Spring 1981): 79-85; Leonard Beeghley, *Social Stratification in America: A Critical Analysis of Theory and Research* (Santa Monica, Cal.: Goodyear Publishing Co., 1978), chap. 1; and Michael B. Katz, Michael J. Doucet and Mark J. Stern, *The Social Organization of Early Industrial Capitalism* (Cambridge, Mass.: Harvard University Press, 1982), chap. 1. The quotations are from Warburton.

lived" relationship defined by one's place in the productive system. The second was class-motivated action based on a subjective perception of mutual interests, evident when people who shared common interests, experiences and aspirations acted in a class-conscious manner to distinguish themselves from others who did not share these attributes.[7] While accepting the assertion of sociologist Rennie Warburton that the working class must be viewed through its relationship with the property-owning "bourgeoisie," the following paper concentrates on wage earners primarily and the middle class only secondarily. It asks what influences encouraged or retarded the development of an objective condition of class into a subjective state of class consciousness among Vancouver workers. It suggests that urban influences (or urbanism) significantly moderated the thrust toward militancy and radicalism emanating from British Columbia's mining hinterland.

*　*　*

Born as a service and lumber mill community on tree-lined Burrard Inlet, Vancouver blossomed from village to city within a few months of its incorporation in 1886. News of the CPR's impending arrival sparked a real estate and construction boom that lasted to the early 1890s, generating a wide range of subsidiary business activities typical of urban places. Construction, lumber manufacturing and the CPR's rail and steamship services dominated the economy, accounting directly for 45 percent of the city's labour force in 1891 and indirectly for many more. As early as the 1890s the bulk and perishability of many consumer products and the simple technology required to make them had induced local production of candy, canned fruit, bakery goods, beer and tailored clothing. The severe depression of the mid-1890s reversed economic growth and reduced the size of Vancouver's work force. But prosperity returned with the Klondike gold rush, renewing the process of economic diversification and establishing Vancouver as British Columbia's metropolitan centre for commerce, lumber manufacturing, transportation and business services. Sustained urban growth to 1907 and another highly inflated real estate and building boom from 1909 to 1913 created thousands of additional construction jobs. By the First World War, then, Vancouver had emerged as a characteristic mid-sized city, offering a wide range of business functions and boasting a varied and complex work force. A January 1891 statistical survey of Vancouver's economy listed 5,016 employees out of a

[7] W. Peter Ward, "Class and Race in the Social Structure of British Columbia, 1870-1939," *BC Studies* 45 (Spring 1980) : 17-35; quotation from p. 18.

city population of about 13,000; twenty years later the work force had grown to 50,628 out of 100,401. Two-thirds of the 1911 labour force, or approximately 33,000 employees, formed the wage-earning core of Vancouver's pre-war working class.[8]

TABLE 1

Urban Growth in Vancouver: Selected Occupational Categories Compared for Eight Canadian Cities, 1911

City	Total work force	% Population increase over previous decade	Construc-tion	Commerce: trade & merchan-dising	Trans-porta-tion	Manu-factur-ing
Vancouver	50,628	271.7	17.6	15.4	9.7	18.5
Calgary	21,320	893.7	20.8	14.4	12.6	15.1
Winnipeg	62,265	221.3	17.2	22.1	13.7	17.6
Toronto	169,520	81.9	12.2	19.2	7.1	34.9
Montreal	183,257	75.7	13.4	17.9	14.3	33.2
Hamilton	37,428	55.7	10.8	12.5	6.5	50.7
London	19,615	21.9	7.6	16.9	9.2	42.2
Halifax	17,909	14.2	9.5	18.3	12.3	20.7

[1] The population statistics for Vancouver refer to Vancouver proper and do not include N. and S. Vancouver and Point Grey.

SOURCE: *Census of Canada, 1911,* vol. I, table 13 and vol. VI, table 6.

Table 1 places Vancouver's labour force in comparative perspective. It suggests that Vancouver's employment structure in 1911 approximated

[8] See Robert A. J. McDonald, "City-Building in the Canadian West: A Case Study of Economic Growth in Early Vancouver, 1886-1893," *BC Studies* 43 (Autumn 1979): 3-28 and "Victoria, Vancouver, and the Evolution of British Columbia's Economic System, 1886-1914," in *Town and City,* ed. Alan F. J. Artibise (Regina: Canadian Plains Research Centre, University of Regina, 1981), pp. 31-55; L. D. McCann, "Urban Growth in a Staple Economy: The Emergence of Vancouver as a Regional Metropolis, 1886-1914," in *Vancouver: Western Metropolis,* ed. L. J. Evenden (Victoria: Department of Geography, University of Victoria, 1978), pp. 17-41; and *Census of Canada, 1911,* vol. VI, table 6, pp. 286-97. In calculating the wage-earning proportion of Vancouver's work force, I defined typists and stenographers as working class but included commercial and office "clerks" in the middle class. My findings correspond closely to Michael Piva's conclusion that blue-collar workers constituted 66.3 percent of Toronto's work force in 1911; see Piva, *The Condition of the Working Class in Toronto, 1900-1921* (Ottawa: University of Ottawa Press, 1979), p. 15.

that of other Canadian cities but departed fundamentally in the area of manufacturing. Vancouver had emerged as B.C.'s principal trade, shipping and railway centre, with commerce and transportation employing one-quarter of the city's workers. Because of the Terminal City's relatively small hinterland market, trade and transportation industry employees formed a slightly less important part of Vancouver's working class than they did of Winnipeg's or Montreal's. Urbanization generated employment for thousands of construction workers across Canada during the Laurier years, with the demand for builders in the rapidly growing west exceeding that in the more settled east.

Industrial production differentiated central from western Canada more sharply. British Columbia enjoyed a comparative advantage in national and international markets for its primary resources, to which only limited value had been added. The huge Hastings Sawmill on Burrard Inlet and the several saw, shingle, and sash and door mills lining False Creek testified to the pervasive influence of forest wealth on Vancouver's economy. But as a thinly populated region far removed from major markets, British Columbia did not experience the scale or locational economies required to manufacture highly processed items competitive beyond provincial boundaries. B.C.'s industrial pattern shaped Vancouver's work force. Small by national standards, the city's consumer goods plants, engineering works and clothing shops met only local and regional needs. Consequently, in 1911 proportionately more than twice as many Vancouver workers as their Toronto counterparts toiled in wood manufacturing and lumber plants, a reflection of the obvious importance of forest-related production in the coast city. By contrast, a Toronto worker was three times as likely to labour in clothing and related industries and twice as likely to find employment in metal-manufacturing firms.[9] Table 1 indicates that, overall, industrial jobs in Toronto and Montreal exceeded manufacturing work in Vancouver by a margin of almost two to one.

In addition to diversifying the city's occupational structure, urbanization differentiated workers by economic condition. Without manuscript census or tax assessment rolls it is impossible to determine accurately economic differences among workers, but census statistics that document the annual earnings of family heads in a select number of occupations (table 2) offer some insight into employment stratification.

Work skills furnished the most obvious source of difference. Highly trained members of the railway running trades, led by locomotive engi-

[9] Calculated from *Census of Canada, 1911*, vol. VI, table 6 and Piva, *Condition of the Working Class in Toronto*, pp. 15-25.

neers, formed the working class elite in Vancouver, as elsewhere in Canada, earning almost double per year that of unskilled labourers. Skilled trainmen and electricians earned more than salesmen, despite the latter's higher status as white collar workers. Experiencing less competition from novices learning their trade on the job, bricklayers and plumbers accumulated higher yearly incomes than did carpenters. At the bottom of the income hierarchy were labourers: lacking specialized skills they had to accept lower hourly wages and lower annual incomes than skilled craftsmen.

TABLE 2

Average Annual Earnings of Heads of Vancouver Families in Specified Occupations, 1911

Trainmen	$1,213.59
Electricians	1,022.64
Salesmen	1,022.44
Bricklayers, Masons, and Stonecutters	973.82
Plumbers and Gas Fitters	963.67
Chauffeurs	955.38
Bakers	927.11
Carpenters	914.75
St. Ry. Employees	895.47
Domestic and Personal Workers	868.36
Painters and Decorators	857.24
Labourers	629.30

SOURCE: *Census of Canada, 1921*, vol. III, xx.

Job regularity also influenced total earnings. Certainly, tradesmen could usually expect greater job security and thus higher annual incomes than unskilled workers, but the relationship was not always straightforward. For example, in 1911 carpenters commanded an hourly wage of fifty cents compared to thirty-five cents for street railway conductors and motormen.[10] Yet their annual incomes, as documented in table 2, were almost identical. The difference is explained by the more secure and less seasonal employment offered by the paternalistic British Columbia Electric Railway Company.[11]

[10] Canada, Department of Labour, *Wages and Hours of Labour in Canada, 1901-1921* (Ottawa: 1921), pp. 5 and 18.

[11] Patricia E. Roy, "The B.C.E.R. and its Street Railway Employees," *BC Studies* 16 (Winter 1972-73): 3-24.

Seasonal influences created a pattern of differentiation that overlapped with but did not entirely match that defined by skill. Winter unemployment plagued Canadian workers from Montreal's docks to Cornwall's cotton mills to British Columbia's logging camps. The building trades were especially vulnerable to unemployment, even in Vancouver where rain hampered large street, sewer and water line projects. During a period of four months in 1903 wet conditions restricted Vancouver construction workers and machinists to twelve days' employment in thirty.[12] Both skilled tradesmen and unskilled labourers endured layoffs. Vancouver's status as a regional employment centre intensified these seasonal variations. By 1900 new railroad and shipping ties had solidified Granville's earlier function as a labour distribution and service hub. The Terminal City became the "centralization point for all men seeking work" on the transcontinental railway,[13] as well as the place from which workers headed to coastal fish canneries and logging camps. As Eleanor Bartlett notes, the "province's resource industries were active primarily in spring, summer and early fall. When winter closed these operations, the workers flocked to Vancouver to find other work or to spend their unemployment."[14] Vancouver's mild climate and terminal location further enhanced the city's image during winter as a "mecca of the unemployed."[15] Spring and summer brought their own employment rhythm, with many men leaving for resource jobs while others arrived for construction work. Of the latter the seasonal influx during the pre-war boom of Italian labourers — as many as 4,000 in 1911 — to take up well-paying street excavation jobs offers the most notable example.[16]

Geographic mobility marked the employment histories of most urban workers during the industrial era, with evidence from American cities showing that only 40 to 60 percent of all adult males persisted in the

---

[12] *Labour Gazette* (hereafter *LG*) 3 (January 1903): 517 and *Daily News-Advertiser* (hereafter *N-A*), 4 June 1892, p. 8.

[13] *Vancouver Daily Province*, 6 August 1912, p. 1.

[14] Eleanor A. Bartlett, "Real Wages and the Standard of Living in Vancouver, 1901-1929," *BC Studies* 51 (Autumn 1981): 8.

[15] Patricia E. Roy, "Vancouver: 'The Mecca of the Unemployed,' 1907-1929," in *Town and City*, pp. 393-413.

[16] *N-A*, 6 September 1911, p. 1 mentions 5,000-6,000 Italians in Vancouver whereas the 1911 census lists 1,922. I have assumed that most of the difference is accounted for by summer transients. Also see British Columbia, Commission on Labour, 1912-1914, *Transcripts of Evidence* (hereafter B.C., C. on L., *Evidence*), 11 March 1913 [J. H. McVety], vol. 3, file 10, p. 332, RG684, Provincial Archives of British Columbia.

same community for as long as a decade.[17] Preliminary evidence suggests the same pattern for Vancouver.[18] But transiency itself was a complex phenomenon, with seasonal workers experiencing a regular and ongoing pattern of movement not characteristic of others with more stable, if far from permanent, city jobs. The seasonal pattern of regional resource industries and urban construction generated through Vancouver a flow of single, mobile workers who, when in the city, lived in a relatively self-contained world defined by waterfront-area rooming houses and saloons. By contrast, families, detached cottages in residential neighbourhoods and a variety of associational affiliations characterized the lives of more stable urban workers.[19] Whether skilled loggers or unskilled Italian labourers, seasonal wage earners joined Vancouver's work force for only a portion of each year. Seasonally determined transiency meant irregular employment, fluctuating income and marginal integration into the city's working class.

Also poorly integrated were Asians. In 1911, 6 percent of Vancouver's population claimed Asian ancestry; most were single, male and of working age. They included 3,364 Chinese, 1,841 Japanese and fewer than 1,000 Indians, mainly Sikhs.[20] The deeply entrenched racism then pervading white society forced Asians to the margins of Vancouver's economy. Here they sold their labour at one-half to two-thirds the value of white labour or engaged in petty commerce.[21] Probably more than half worked as labourers in resource extractive industries. Some, such as the Chinese cannery workers who butchered salmon prior to canning, had

[17] Stephen Thernstrom, *The Other Bostonians: Poverty and Progress in the American Metropolis, 1880-1970* (Cambridge, Mass.: Harvard University Press, 1973), pp. 221-27.

[18] David Darling, "Patterns of Population Mobility in Vancouver, 1891-1931" (M.A. extended essay, Simon Fraser University, 1979).

[19] Very little has been written about the daily lives of Vancouver workers before 1914. For a brief glimpse of loggers' society see M. Allerdale Grainger, *Woodsmen of the West*, New Canadian Library No. 42 (Toronto: McClelland & Stewart, 1964), pp. 13-17. Deryck Holdsworth discusses working-class housing, emphasizing the residences of more advantaged urban workers, in "House and Home in Vancouver: The Emergence of a West Coast Urban Landscape, 1886-1929" (Ph.D. thesis, University of British Columbia, 1981). A somewhat less sanguine view of working class housing is offered in Donna McCririck, "Opportunity and the Workingman: A Study of Land Accessibility and the Growth of Blue Collar Suburbs in Early Vancouver" (M.A. thesis, University of British Columbia, 1981). Also see interviews with several pre-war Italian immigrants in "Opening Doors: Vancouver's East End," *Sound Heritage* 8 (1979).

[20] Patricia E. Roy, *Vancouver: An Illustrated History* (Toronto: James Lorimer and Company, 1980), pp. 169-70.

[21] W. Peter Ward, *White Canada Forever* (Montreal: McGill-Queen's University Press, 1978), pp. 17, 81 and 112.

acquired considerable skill; most Asians laboured doggedly at routine and unsophisticated tasks. The Asian proportion of Vancouver's lumber industry work force appears to have increased from the 1890s to the First World War; according to one worker, by 1913 they had "practically driven white labour out of the mills."[22] The Chinese became especially prominent as small businessmen, providing service as grocers, laundrymen, pedlars, shopkeepers and restaurateurs either to the white community or exclusively to a Chinese clientele.[23] While ethnocentrism and the single, sojourner status of most Asians undoubtedly helped separate them from white workers, segregation ultimately rested on the hardpan of racial prejudice. The existence of a dual class structure defined by race marked one of the features that most distinguished Vancouver from other Canadian cities.

Women too comprised a distinct part of Vancouver's work force, exhibiting employment characteristics both common in other cities and particular to the west coast. According to widely held middle-class perceptions of the period, women belonged in the home, where they were to support the principal bread-winner and nurture the children. If economic necessity required that women work for wages outside the family, suitable job choices extended from this domestic role into health care and education, personal service, clerical labour and certain kinds of manufacturing.[24] Based on the assumption that "men and women were suited to different types of employment," wage-earning women were segregated into a very few occupations characterized by "low wages, irregular work and dull, dead end tasks."[25] Women also enjoyed few opportunities for promotion to skilled or managerial positions.

This familiar pattern of economic discrimination determined job choices for Vancouver women. Of the 6,452 female wage earners documented for Vancouver in the 1911 Canadian census, the largest portion worked in domestic and personal service (2,720), the professions (1,484) and trade and merchandising (1,075). "Professional" women, numbering 604 stenographers and typists, 357 teachers and 242 nurses, were little

[22] B.C., C. on L., *Evidence*, 20 January 1913 [T. Turnbull], vol. 1, file 2, p. 162. Also see *The Independent* [Vancouver], 22 September 1900, p. 3 and *Province*, 26 April 1901, p. 3.

[23] Ward, *White Canada Forever*, p. 16.

[24] Terry Copp, *The Anatomy of Poverty: The Condition of the Working Class in Montreal, 1897-1929* (Toronto: McClelland & Stewart, 1974), chap. 3 and Paul Phillips and Erin Phillips, *Women and Work: Inequality in the Labour Market* (Toronto: James Lorimer and Company, 1983), chap. 1.

[25] Veronica Strong-Boag, "The Girl of the New Day: Canadian Working Women in the 1920s," *Labour/le Travailleur* 4 (1979): 135 and 137.

better off than the others, holding positions of relatively limited status and pay.[26] As with Chinese workers, employers valued women's labour at 40 to 50 percent below that of white males. For example, before the First World War the David Spencer department store paid female clerks an average of $8.60 per week compared to $14.50 for salesmen.[27] Young women in Ramsay's biscuit factory earned from $5 to $8 per week, the equivalent of ten to sixteen cents an hour; unskilled male builders' labourers commanded three times that amount.[28]

While approximating a national pattern, Vancouver's female work force also exhibited regional influences. Table 3 suggests the degree of distinctiveness: women constituted a substantially smaller portion of the work force in Vancouver than in Toronto or Winnipeg. One reason was the greater gender imbalance in British Columbia, where in 1911 working-age men outnumbered women by a ratio of 2.3 to 1. British Columbia was a society of immigrants, and the employment opportunities that attracted immigrants in turn shaped the west's demographic structure. Since the region's resource extractive, construction and transportation sectors required labouring men rather than whole families or women, British Columbia appealed particularly to male immigrants of working age.[29] Furthermore, B.C.'s comparative disadvantage as a location for end product manufacturing — the result of a remote location, small population, and discriminatory Canadian tariff and freight rate policies — particularly affected Vancouver, where such industrial activity would have centred. Consequently, clothing, textile, tobacco and food processing industries, which employed large numbers of women in eastern cities and a growing number in Winnipeg, offered limited job opportunities for women on the west coast. As table 3 indicates, women comprised only 9.6 percent of Vancouver's manufacturing work force, compared to 17.2 percent in Winnipeg and 25.5 percent in Toronto. These figures correspond closely to the overall distribution of female wage earners in the three cities.

26 Star Rosenthal, "Union Maids: Organized Women Workers in Vancouver 1900-1915," BC Studies 41 (Spring 1979): 41.

27 Eleanor Anne Bartlett, "Real Wages and the Standard of Living in Vancouver, 1901-1929" (M.A. thesis, University of British Columbia, 1980), Appendix 1, "Vancouver Wage Data from Transcripts of the Commission on Labour, 1912-1914," p. 113.

28 B.C., C. on L., Evidence, 7 March 1913 [Miss H. R. Gutteridge], vol. 3, file 2, p. 126 and Canada, Wages and Hours of Labour, p. 10.

29 W. Peter Ward, "Population Growth in Western Canada, 1901-71," in The Developing West, ed. John E. Foster (Edmonton: University of Alberta Press, 1983), pp. 163-72.

TABLE 3

*Wage-Earning Women: Vancouver
Compared to Winnipeg and Toronto, 1911*

	Women as % of total city work force[1]	Women as % of manufacturing portion of work force[1]	Women as % of urban population[2]
Toronto	25.3	25.5	50.6
Winnipeg	18.3	17.2	45.3
Vancouver	12.7	9.6	39.9

[1] Percentages calculated from *Census of Canada, 1911*, vol. II, table 6; includes females 10 years of age and older.

[2] Percentages calculated from *Census of Canada, 1911*, vol. I, table 1; takes into account women of all ages, including children.

Vancouver's trade union movement exhibited the consequences of internal working class stratification. Unlike British Columbia miners, who joined industry-wide "industrial" unions, Vancouver workers characteristically formed more exclusive "craft" organizations limited to individuals with similar skills. Vancouver's earliest trade unionists belonged to locals of the Knights of Labor, a movement that attempted to join together all workers regardless of skill into units organized by industry. But by the mid-1890s the Knights had disappeared, victims of employers' opposition, jurisdictional disputes with unions of skilled tradesmen, and a visionary idealism many years ahead of its time. In the spring of 1887 bricklayers and typographers formed Vancouver's first craft unions. Two years later, in November 1889, the carpenters, plasterers, painters and Knights of Labor established a city-wide Trades and Labor Council (VTLC).[30] Skilled workers continued to lead the movement. From 1889 to 1913 typographers, machinists and carpenters contributed 75 percent of all VTLC presidents, with various construction unions providing half this total. In addition, building tradesmen comprised the VTLC's most active regular members.[31]

[30] For the early years of Vancouver's labour movement see George Bartley's "Twenty-five Years of Labor Movement in Vancouver," in *The British Columbia Federationist* (hereafter cited as *Federationist*), 6 May 1912, p. 3 and 27 December 1912, pp. 14-15, 24 and 27-32.

[31] For Trades Council presidents see the Vancouver Trades and Labour Council Minutes (hereafter VTLC Minutes), 1889-1914. The role of building tradesmen is suggested in attendance reports published in *The Western Wage-Earner* (Vancouver), February 1909, p. 21 and the *Federationist*, 20 January 1912, p. 1.

Less skilled workers played a more peripheral role. The mid-1890s depression almost destroyed Vancouver's infant labour movement, but starting in 1897 renewed prosperity stimulated a trade union renaissance, giving new life to suspended union locals and generating even among less skilled workers, such as retail clerks, teamsters, civic employees and laundry employees, the enthusiasm and market strength required to organize.[32] However, despite broadening the movement's social base, prosperity failed to shake the dominance of skilled craftsmen. The collapse in 1903 of the United Brotherhood of Railway Employees (UBRE), an industrial union of semi- and unskilled ticket agents, clerks, and freight handlers, re-affirmed that Vancouver's trade union movement would remain fragmented by occupation and dominated by advantaged tradesmen.[33]

Several factors explain the movement's structure, of which the labour market is pre-eminent. Specialized skills protected craftsmen from the competition of unskilled labourers and the opposition of employers.[34] For example, the economic roles assigned to women greatly limited their ability to organize[35] while transiency and job insecurity hampered the unionization of lumber workers. In addition, skilled workers strongly believed in advancement according to merit and thus insisted on wage differentials that "recognized their exalted status over helpers and labourers... in this sense they were quite willing to accept some limited degree of hierarchical stratification."[36] This consciousness of economic privilege blunted their enthusiasm for organizing the unskilled; in one instance, the UBRE conflict of 1903, the elite railway brotherhoods actively opposed the less skilled railway strikers.[37] Social attitudes towards

[32] Eugene Forsey, *Trade Unions in Canada 1812-1902* (Toronto: University of Toronto Press, 1982), p. 276; *Federationist*, 27 December 1912, p. 24; *Independent*, 17 May 1902, p. 4 and 5 September 1903, p. 5; and VTLC Minutes, 4 December 1902, p. 99.

[33] For the 1903 United Brotherhood of Railway Employees strike, see McCormack, *Reformers, Rebels, and Revolutionaries*, pp. 44-48 and Paul Phillips, *No Power Greater: A Century of Labour in B.C.* (Vancouver: B.C. Federation of Labour, 1967), pp. 39-41. The unions of semi and unskilled workers, such as clerks and civic workers, often did not survive long; for the clerks' union see *The Independent*, 16 June 1900, p. 1 and *LG* 6 (September 1905), p. 276, and for civic employees, *N-A*, 22 April 1911, p. 1.

[34] Bercuson, "Labour Radicalism and the Western Industrial Frontier," pp. 171-73.

[35] Despite structural difficulties, women's attempts to organize were not entirely futile; see Rosenthal, "Union Maids," passim.

[36] Craig Heron, "Labourism and the Canadian Working Class," *Labour/le Travail*, 13 (Spring 1984): 59.

[37] J. Hugh Tuck, "The United Brotherhood of Railway Employees in Western Canada, 1898-1905," *Labour/le Travailleur*, 11 (Spring 1983): 82-83.

women had the same divisive effect. Consequently, unionized men either ignored women workers or relegated them to "auxiliaries" on the outer edge of the labour movement.[38] And racism segregated Orientals from white workers and their institutions. Together these influences restricted union membership to 15 percent of the city's work force at the movement's peak in 1912,[39] with virtually all Asians, most seasonal migrants and women, and many unskilled workers excluded.

To summarize, then, Vancouver's working class exhibited a number of traits distinctive to the region: the exaggerated importance of construction work, the relative weakness of industrial employment, the seasonal labour flow to and from hinterland mining, logging, construction and fishing sites, the unusually low number of women wage-earners, and the divisive force of race. Yet these west coast peculiarities only modified an employment structure that was fundamentally urban, replicating among Vancouver workers the labour functions and economic differentiation evident in other major centres. This structural base influenced the urban character of another feature of working class life in pre-war Vancouver: labour militancy.

*   *   *

"Militancy" infers "a propensity to act," "a willingness or propensity to fight and struggle."[40] In studies of class relations the term is often employed to indicate workers' readiness to strike — that is, to withdraw their labour in an attempt to extract concessions from bosses; in this sense it is viewed as a subjective measure of class feeling. Contrarily, capitalists could pressure workers by refusing to allow them to work. Labour conflicts in early Vancouver took the form almost entirely of strikes rather than lockouts, though many strikes were instigated by employers.

Strikes reflected fundamentally different views within the middle and working classes about the economic role of labour. Employers urged that

[38] Elaine Bernard, *The Long Distance Feeling* (Vancouver: New Star Books, 1982), p. 18 and "Last Back: Folklore and the Telephone Operators in the 1919 General Strike," in *Not Just Pin Money*, ed. Barbara K. Latham and Roberta J. Pazdro (Victoria: Camosun College, 1984), pp. 279-86; and Marie Campbell, "Sexism in British Columbia Trade Unions, 1900-1920," in *In Her Own Right*, ed. Barbara Latham and Cathy Kess (Victoria: Camosun College, 1980), pp. 167-86.

[39] This figure, calculated from the number of unionized Vancouver workers in 1912 as a percentage of the city's 1911 work force, undoubtedly over-represents the proportion of organized workers. See *LG* 14 (July 1913): 46 and *Census of Canada, 1911*, vol. VI, table 6, p. 286.

[40] Stuart M. Jamieson, "Militancy in the British Columbia Labour Movement," in Jamieson et al., *Militancy*, p. 3.

an ample supply of cheap labour be available to ensure economic growth. Of particular concern to managers were labour shortages during periods of rapid growth; these favoured workers, allowing them a choice of jobs and driving up wages. Thus in 1901 and 1906 industrialists lamented the dearth of cheap labour for B.C.'s resource industries, claiming that a tight labour market slowed the influx of capital and made local products uncompetitive.[41] By contrast, a plentiful labour supply favoured employers. Even more threatening for some middle-class observers was the shortage of inexpensive domestic workers, which menaced "the stability of the home" and retarded the "physical and social development of white residents."[42] A reserve labour supply would keep the wheels of industry turning smoothly and maintain middle-class social standards.

Essential to preserving a competitive labour market was an open immigration policy. From the time of CPR construction in the 1880s, Asians had provided the most readily available pool of semi- and unskilled workers, and controversy about their role in British Columbia's development continued to resonate through the province's history. In 1890 Vancouver alderman James Fox, a contractor, articulated the assumptions that underlay the capitalist class's demand for Asian labour:

We have an extensive province without a population. Shall it remain in its primeval state . . . , with its forests of wealth rotting, with its vast treasures of riches lying hid(den), with its pastoral lands arid wastes, with its waters stinking with fish undevoured . . . ? Shall we linger along ambitionless . . . and pass away without employing that power that Heaven has placed in our hand . . . (?)[43]

Certainly not, asserted Fox. But the province lacked sufficient labour to carry out this development. He suggested as the solution an influx of up to two million Chinese workers who would open B.C.'s treasure house and generate untold wealth. CPR president William Van Horne similarly supported an open immigration policy and sharply criticized anti-Oriental legislation that prevented it. Looked at from "a practical and selfish point of view," he argued, restricting competition from Chinese labour retarded development of British Columbia's resources "to the material disadvan-

[41] *Province*, 25 April 1901, p. 1; *N-A*, 10 October 1906, p. 2; and R. H. H. Alexander to Sir T. G. Shaughnessy, 20 November 1906, Canadian Pacific Railway (CPR) Archives, RG2 [Correspondence Inward], File 82481.

[42] May Fitz-Gibbon to Sir T. G. Shaughnessy, 21 November 1907, CPR Archives, RG2 [Correspondence Inward], File 85132.

[43] *N-A*, 12 February 1890, p. 3.

tage of the very working-men it is intended to help . . . It is sad to see our laws prostituted to a race prejudice."[44]

In addition, owners demanded complete control over the work process. For them capital's economic role superseded labour's. Consequently, the owners of capital should be left alone to determine whom they would employ, the level of remuneration, and working conditions. Whether the proprietor of a small tailoring shop or the manager of an American-controlled fishing company, capitalists iterated that they refused to be dictated to by workers.[45] In the words of a Vancouver sheet metal shop owner, "we have a right to run our own businesses along lines to suit ourselves."[46] They especially opposed trade unions, which challenged their economic authority.

On the other hand, workers recognized that capitalism had reduced labour to a commodity to be bought and sold for its exchange value. For this reason they strongly rejected the owners' demand for an open and unregulated labour market and forcefully opposed the immigration of unskilled workers. In 1913 J. W. Wilkinson, secretary of the Vancouver Trades and Labour Council, explained why market vulnerability led workers to oppose immigration:

We are working men and the only way we have of getting our livelihood is by selling ourselves from day to day, wherever we can find someone to hire it . . . the price we can get will determine to a large extent the standard of living we shall enjoy.[47]

Whether comprising Asians arriving on their own resources or "the industrial garbage of the Old Country" sent by benevolent societies, an influx of unskilled labour threatened to undermine the job security and living standard of settled white workers. This attitude may seem selfish, Wilkinson conceded, "but in the struggle for existence matters are very often reduced to the ethics of the jungle."[48]

Some wage-earners, particularly the more advantaged skilled tradesmen, articulated a sharply different role for labour than that advanced by

[44] W. C. Van Horne to [Francis Carter] Cotton, 6 October 1896, Public Archives of Canada, Canadian Pacific Railway Collection, Letterbook 51 [Correspondence Outward], Microfilm, no. M2287.

[45] *Vancouver World*, 12 April 1899, p. 4 and Canada, Department of Labour, Strikes and Lockouts Files, Public Archives of Canada, [hereafter cited as Strikes and Lockouts], RG27, Microfilm, Roll 3, file 3159A. These files were later revised; the latter are hereafter cited as Strikes and Lockouts, RG27 (revised).

[46] Strikes and Lockouts, RG27, Microfilm, Roll 3, file 3235.

[47] B.C., C. on L., *Evidence*, 7 March 1913 [J. W. Wilkinson], vol. III, file 8, p. 180.

[48] Quotations in last two sentences are from *loc. cit.*

employers. Reflecting the influence of their artisanal past, they argued that it was not the capitalist who supported the worker, but rather the worker who supported the capitalist.[49] Workers contributed as much to the economy as capitalists. Consequently, workingmen wanted to "be on equal terms with their employers."[50] This required that wage-earners be protected from undue competition for their jobs, that they be paid "fair" and "proper" wages determined by traditional payment practices, and that they retain substantial control over the work process.[51] Crucial to attaining this relationship with capital was the owners' recognition of trade unions, through which workers could voice their concerns and protect their interests.

The substantial number of strikes in early Vancouver testifies that the objective reality of class relations differed markedly from the workers' ideal. The inherently antagonistic condition of capital and labour generated a recurring pattern of labour conflict. The city's strike history remains cloudy to 1901, before the federal government began systematically to record strikes and lockouts. But for the 1901-14 period, federal Department of Labour data and local newspapers reveal seventy-six strikes, ranging in duration from one-half hour to more than a year and engaging from a mere half-dozen to more than 5,500 workers (table 4).

Vancouver's strike pattern is explained first by fluctuations in the provincial labour market, which it closely followed. The four strikes in 1889 came at the peak of the city's early construction boom. Unable to find substitute workers, contractors and sash and door factory owners were forced to accept the carpenters' demand that nine hours constitute a normal working day. But already by June 1891 40 percent of city carpenters and 20 percent of bricklayers were without work, and the full onset of depression in 1893 further eroded job security and wages.[52] Local newspapers record only seven strikes during the bleak years from 1890 to 1898, with no strikes in five of them. Yet improved conditions in the late 1890s soon produced a labour shortage in B.C., leading a local labour journal to proclaim in May 1902 that "so far as demand for men and wages go things were never better in Vancouver."[53] An improved

---

[49] *Independent*, 31 March 1900, p. 3.

[50] *Ibid.*, 12 April 1902, p. 2.

[51] *N-A*, 10 May 1894, p. 1 and 16 January 1897, pp. 4-5.

[52] For the carpenters' strike see the *N-A*, 5-17 July 1889 and the *World*, 5-11 July 1899; on advancing unemployment see the *N-A*, 25 June 1891, p. 1 and 2 December 1894, p. 3.

[53] *Independent*, 3 May 1902, p. 8.

TABLE 4

Yearly Level of Strikes in Vancouver, 1901-1914

Year	No. of strikes	No. of strikers[1]	Striker-days[2]	Largest strikes (and striker-days)[3]
1901	3	165	1,773	3 strikes (unknown)
1902	11	524	3,782	tel. linemen/operators (420)
1903	10	1,311	51,719	UBRE [sympathy] (38,075)
1904	3	99	2,324	halibut fishermen (1,300)
1905	5	189	2,873	painters (1,425)
1906	4	159	5,709	tel. operators/elect. linemen (4,082)
1907	5	1,440	30,585	carpenters (27,000)
1908	0	0	0	—
1909	6	428	5,896	longshoremen (2,700)
1910	7	627	12,077	machinists/engineers (7,170)
1911	6	6,046	257,112	bldg. trades [sympathy] (241,216)
1912	9	1,168	78,818	halibut fishermen (74,200)
1913	5	416	5,864	granite cutters (2,500)
1914	2	80	691	sheet metal (100)
TOTALS	76	12,652	459,223	

SOURCE: Canada, Department of Labour, Strikes and Lockouts Files (original and revised), Public Archives of Canada, RG27; *Labour Gazette* 1-15 (1901-15); and local newspapers and labour papers.

[1] These yearly figures are based on hard data for 53 strikes and a statistical average of 55 workers for each of the remaining 24 for which no information was available. In calculating the average I deleted the 10 largest strikes (each involving more than 199 workers) and averaged the number of strikers in the remainder.

[2] I employed the same technique for 26 strikes for which striker-days information was unavailable, calculating an average of 591 striker-days for the 40 conflicts that resulted in the loss of no more than 2,499 striker-days of work.

[3] Only hard data, not the calculated averages, are listed.

labour market and higher expectations triggered renewed demands from workers for better wages, hours and working conditions. Local tailors, whose union was broken in an unsuccessful strike in 1893, regained recognition from master tailors in 1899[54] and initiated a period of labour struggles that peaked with eleven strikes in 1902 and another ten the following year. The economic downturn of 1907-08 ended the labour

[54] Forsey, *Trade Unions in Canada*, pp. 262-63 and *World*, 12 April-27 May 1899.

Printers' picnic, Gibson's Landing, ca. 1894

Carpenters' gathering, 1890

Dupont
[Pender] Street,
ca. 1899

Rev. George R. Maxwell

Louis D. Taylor

market conditions that for several years had favoured workers; not surprisingly, no strikes were recorded for 1908. But renewed prosperity once
again gave workers the confidence and market power to challenge
employers. Consequently, the pre-war years featured an increased number
of labour conflicts, including a huge construction workers' walkout in
1911 and a substantial halibut fishermen's strike in 1912.[55] By 1914 the
familiar pattern of bust following boom had once more drained Vancouver's workers of the economic strength to confront employers on the
picket line.

Changes in the structure of Canadian capitalism also shaped relations
between capital and labour in Vancouver. The trend towards increased
capitalization of companies, greater concentration of ownership and
further centralization of control reduced the influence of small, regional
entrepreneurs while increasing that of more highly bureaucratic and
powerful corporations in metropolitan cities such as Toronto, Montreal
and New York. The trend to capital concentration extended to British
Columbia, especially to the province's resource industries. The Kootenay
mining boom of the 1890s opened a whole new region to heavily capital-
ized corporations, and the resulting tension between managers and miners
turned the Kootenays into a centre of labour militancy at the century's
turn. Even in Vancouver evidence of capitalism's new structure came
after 1900 in a series of takeovers of local businesses by outside firms. The
1902 consolidation of much of the coast salmon canning industry into one
large Vancouver-based corporation exemplified the trend.

Accompanying the emergence of large-scale, or "monopoly," capitalism
was a new management offensive to curb the growth of trade unions.
Strikebreaking represented the most obvious denial of workers' claim to
equal status with capital. All workers were affected, whether skilled
machinists and tailors or unskilled longshoremen and street labourers.
Companies recruited strike-breakers externally as well as locally, finding
Puget Sound cities a particularly convenient source of labour. Longshoremen in 1889 and 1900, tailors in 1899, ship carpenters and caulkers in
1901 and electrical workers in 1909 shared the experience of facing strike-
breakers imported from Port Townsend or Seattle.[56] The transcontinental
railway broadened the labour market and increased the area from which

---

[55] For the construction workers' strike see Strikes and Lockouts, RG27 (revised), files
3335, 3356 and 3378; for the halibut fishermen, *ibid.*, file 3637.

[56] *World*, 27 September 1889, p. 2, 12 April 1899, p. 4 and 3 May 1899, p. 7;
Forsey, *Trade Unions in Canada*, pp. 263, 340 and 342; and Strikes and Lockouts, RG27, Microfilm, Roll 2, File 3123 and Roll 3, File 3152.

large companies could draw substitute workers. In 1903 during the UBRE strike the CPR imported workers from eastern Canada to replace striking freight handlers.[57] In July 1910 an employing contractor forced Italian street construction labourers back to work by threatening to import Galician replacements from the east.[58]

To diminish trade union influence, city capitalists in May 1903 formed the Employers' Association of Vancouver.[59] Fraser River salmon canners had anticipated the Vancouver organization in the late nineties, establishing associations to lobby the federal government for favourable fish licensing arrangements and to control the price and production of salmon. By 1905 B.C. employers had formed twenty-six associations.[60] The coincidental appearance of similar bodies in eastern Canada and the United States, including Pacific Coast organizations with which the Vancouver Employers' Association became affiliated, seems to support the view of local trade unionists that employers had launched a broadly based attack on unionized workers.[61]

The Employers' Association proposed to return managerial power to the owners and representatives of capital. To achieve this goal they aimed to terminate "closed shop" agreements, thus opening unionized firms to both unorganized and organized workers. In each case where the unions have secured the closed shop they have driven up wages and "imposed numerous working conditions which are very unpalatable to the employers," argued R. H. Sperling, general manager of the British Columbia Electric Railway Company.[62] To end this condition the Employers' Association vowed to import and subsidize strikebreakers, lobby governments in opposition to union demands, and pursue legal action against "the leaders of mobs" and people who threatened business property.[63] In 1904 the Association listed 103 members, all of whom employed five or

---

[57] Phillips, *No Power Greater*, p. 40. In "Strikes in the Maritimes, 1901-1914," *Acadiensis* 13 (Autumn 1983): 21-28, Ian McKay describes the labour market transformation that accompanied the consolidation of Canadian capitalism.

[58] *N-A*, 22 July 1910, p. 4 and 23 July 1910, p. 15.

[59] *Independent*, 11 April 1903, p. 2 and 9 July 1904, p. 1 and *LG* 4 (July 1903): 8.

[60] Harry Keith Ralston, "The 1900 Strike of Fraser River Sockeye Salmon Fishermen" (M.A. thesis, University of British Columbia, 1965), pp. 83 and 92-96 and Phillips, *No Power Greater*, p. 41.

[61] *N-A*, 26 May 1911, p. 2; *Federationist*, 9 December 1911, p. 1; and Piva, *Condition of the Working Class in Toronto*, pp. 150-56.

[62] R. H. Sperling to Hiram Williams, 12 April 1911, British Columbia Electric Railway Papers, Special Collections, University of British Columbia, General Managers' Letter Books, A x B 3-4 (January-June 1911).

[63] *Independent*, 9 July 1904, p. 1.

more "hands," and in 1911 it claimed as members "ninety percent of the representative business houses in the city."[64] While the latter figure may be questioned, the Employers' Association clearly represented a broad consensus of middle-class opinion about organized labour. Starting in 1903, this attitude further strained relations between "the two great classes"[65] and increased the number and intensity of labour conflicts in Vancouver.

Perhaps the best-known Vancouver example of employer intimidation is the UBRE strike of 27 February - 27 June 1903, which precipitated formation of the Employers' Association. While the strike has been documented elsewhere, its importance as an example of the objective reality of class relations deserves emphasis. The UBRE, which had formed a Vancouver local in 1902, represented an attempt to broaden the labour movement to include less skilled workers and to organize all wage-earners by industry. This the CPR refused to accept. Vowing to limit unionization on the railway to the more elite skilled tradesmen,[66] the CPR in early 1903 embarked on a form of secret warfare against the UBRE using the tactics of wholesale intimidation and discrimination against union members.[67] It eventually forced the union to strike in defence of an unfairly dismissed worker. Not even the concurrent walkouts of long-shoremen, messengers, teamsters and steamshipmen, constituting B.C.'s first sympathetic strike, could limit the force of corporate power. Faced with the CPR's aggressive tactics, including espionage, the importation of strike-breakers and the killing of labour leader Frank Rogers, the Vancouver-centred strike collapsed, destroying the UBRE with it.

Trade union militancy might also be seen as a source of increased strike activity after 1900. The growth of socialism produced a new group of ideologically motivated trade union leaders, including Will MacClain and Frank Rogers, who organized the Fraser River fishermen's strikes of 1900 and 1901 respectively. In addition, the Industrial Workers of the World (IWW), a union essentially of unskilled workers intent on fundamental social change through direct confrontation with capital, also exerted some influence in Vancouver. Its lumber handlers and longshoremen's union, which embraced men of eighteen different nationalities, was

[64] VTLC Minutes, 19 May 1904 and *Federationist*, 9 December 1911, p. 1.

[65] *Independent*, 2 November 1901, p. 1.

[66] Tuck, "United Brotherhood of Railway Employees," pp. 77-78 and 88.

[67] *The Daily Columbian* [New Westminster], 3 March 1903, p. 1. Other sources for the UBRE strike include: references in note no. 33, cited above; the monthly reports of the *Labour Gazette*; Strikes and Lockouts, RG27 (revised), vol. 2333; and Tuck, "United Brotherhood of Railway Employees."

"the first IWW local to conduct a strike in western Canada."[68] And during the July 1910 walkout of unorganized street construction workers, the strikers' spokesmen proudly wore IWW buttons.[69] However, to say that "agitators" were mainly responsible for labour disputes, as businessmen and their political friends were quick to do,[70] would be to miss the fundamental source of strikes: different class perceptions about the economic role of labour.

Table 5, which documents the issues at stake in sixty-eight strikes for which causes are known, clearly illustrates the objective reality of class

TABLE 5

Issues in Vancouver Strikes, 1901-1914[1]

Category I: Economic	
For higher earnings	34
Against wage reductions	3
Category II: Control	
For recognition of union	10
For shorter hours	14
Sympathy	4
Apprenticeship control	4
Objection to new work system	0
Change in work conditions	2
Demand for, or defence of, the closed shop	19
Adjustment of wage payment procedures	2
Against dismissal of worker or supervisor	1
Other/unknown	9

[1] The number of times strike issues are recorded (102) exceeds the number of strikes for which causes are known (68) because individual strikes often centred on more than one major issue. Consequently, some strikes are recorded in the table more than once.

conflict in early twentieth-century Vancouver. Over half the strikes centred on economic issues, with the two sides contending in an ongoing struggle about the value of labour. Countervailing pressures constantly

[68] McCormack, *Reformers, Rebels, and Revolutionaries*, p. 102.

[69] *N-A*, 22 July 1910, p. 4.

[70] Paul Craven, *'An Impartial Umpire': Industrial Relations and the Canadian State 1900-1911* (Toronto: University of Toronto Press, 1980), pp. 246-52.

threatened hard-won wage increases, the product of employer intransi-
gence and cyclical growth. As one Vancouver carpenter observed:

In 1907 we had a strike and settled for $4.25 under an agreement which
lasted until 1908. Conditions got bad and the contractors gave notice that
wages would be reduced to $3.50, but things were in such shape with men
out of work so long during the winter and trade affairs so bad in general
that men had to accept this. They got $4.00 (per day) in 1909 and $4.25
in 1911,[71]

the latter resulting from a major strike. By 1913 renewed depression had
again reversed the fortunes of city carpenters.

Perhaps more revealing are the larger number of strikes, almost three-
quarters of those for which causes are known, that involved control of
the labour process. "Control" is defined broadly to include all aspects of
the nature of work.[72] The subject of working hours endured throughout
the pre-war period, with the issue of nine and then eight hour daily
maximums for civic workers providing a popular focus.[73] Issues more
specific to the work process, such as the control and training of appren-
tices or alterations to working conditions, were less important, both
absolutely and comparatively. The reason is to be found in Vancouver's
economic structure: the smaller proportion of secondary manufacturing
workers and greater demand for semi- and unskilled labour in Vancouver
than in Toronto or Montreal made the scientific techniques of labour
management then being applied in the East less attractive to employers
in the west. By contrast, control over entry to the labour market was
controversial in Canada from the Atlantic to the Pacific coasts. Employers
and workers in Vancouver battled persistently over the issue of the exclusive employment of union members: in November 1902 building trades
workers struck briefly against contractors Robertson and Hackett to preserve the "closed shop" at a hotel construction site; their success contrasted with the failure in 1904 of unionized boilermakers and machinists
to prevent the Vancouver Engineering Works, backed by the newly

[71] B.C., C. on L., *Evidence*, 17 January 1913 [J. A. Key], vol. 1, file 1, p. 69.

[72] The issue of workers' control of the work process is discussed in McKay, "Strikes
in the Maritimes"; Craig Heron and Bryan D. Palmer, "Through the Prism of the
Strike: Industrial Conflict in Southern Ontario, 1901-14," *Canadian Historical
Review* 58 (December 1977): 423-58; and Palmer, *A Culture in Conflict: Skilled
Workers and Industrial Capitalism in Hamilton, Ontario, 1860-1914* (Montreal:
McGill-Queen's University Press, 1979), chap. 3.

[73] *N-A*, 17 August 1890, p. 8, 19 April 1892, p. 3, 1 May 1892, p. 8, 23 February
1909, p. 2, and 11 April 1909, p. 8; *Independent*, 12 May 1900, p. 2; and *Province*, 26 November 1908, p. 18.

formed Employers' Association, from opening its plant to non-union tradesmen.[74]

While Vancouver's pre-war labour record reveals a society inherently divided by class, does it also show that Vancouver wage earners defended and promoted their class interests more aggressively than urban workers elsewhere in Canada? A comparison of strike statistics for other urban centres, though at best very tentative, suggests that the frequency and scale of strikes in Vancouver were not unusual. Based on strike data published for Ontario cities by Craig Heron and Bryan Palmer,[75] the number of strikes between 1901 and 1914 per 1,000 members of the work force in 1911 indicates a ratio of 2.46 for Hamilton and 1.16 for Toronto. Vancouver's 76 strikes produce a ratio of 1:50 per 1,000 people employed. The lesser number for Toronto can be accounted for in part by the different sources used; Heron and Palmer included only strikes listed in the *Labour Gazette*, a much less complete source of information than the updated records of the Canadian Department of Labour utilized for Vancouver. Consequently, the incidence of strikes in Toronto per 1,000 members of the work force was probably no less than that in Vancouver; the proportion in Hamilton was far greater. In addition, a comparison of employment lost by strikers in Saint John and Halifax (examined by Ian McKay)[76] and in Vancouver suggests a similar conclusion: for the period 1901-14 the total number of striker-days of work lost when divided by each 1,000 persons employed in 1911 produces ratios of 12,088 in Saint John, 9,071 in Vancouver and 3,584 in Halifax. Again, despite the rough nature of this statistic, the data's general thrust clearly indicates that Vancouver wage-earners, when compared with workers in other Canadian cities, were militant but not exceptionally so. Nor were they particularly radical.

*　　*　　*

"Radicalism" implies a commitment to "fundamental or extreme change," specifically "a design for modifying society . . . based ultimately on a Marxist analysis of capitalism."[77] The term is a relative one that can be employed to describe either the essentially moderate "labourism" or more

---

[74] *LG* 3 (December 1902): 430, 4 (April 1904): 1002, and 4 (May 1904): 1140-41; and *Independent*, 9 July 1904, p. 2.

[75] Heron and Palmer, "Through the Prism of the Strike," p. 425.

[76] McKay, "Strikes in the Maritimes," p. 14.

[77] Bercuson, "Labour Radicalism and the Western Industrial Frontier," p. 155 and McCormack, *Reformers, Rebels, and Revolutionaries*, p. ix.

doctrinaire forms of socialism. According to Craig Heron's summation of existing historical literature, before 1920 labourism had evolved as the main ideological current in independent working-class politics east of the Rockies.[78] By contrast, radicalism in British Columbia history is usually associated with the Marxist-based socialist movements that emerged at the turn-of-the-century.[79] Whereas labourists accepted capitalism but sought to reform it, B.C. socialists aimed to destroy it. One socialist group tried to achieve this through direct confrontation with capital, organizing workers into revolutionary industrial unions and employing strikes as political weapons. This approach is associated with the IWW. While having some influence in Vancouver, the Wobblies found their support primarily among unskilled itinerants in hinterland logging, mining and construction camps. The other socialist group worked through the political system to educate workers about the need for fundamental social change. Represented by the Socialist Party of Canada, which was founded as the Socialist Party of British Columbia in 1901, the B.C.-centred movement was "one of the most starkly revolutionary organizations on the continent."[80] Because it advocated a highly theoretical and completely uncompromising approach to capitalism, critics viewed its aims as unrealistic and branded its philosophy as "impossiblist." Electoral support for doctrinaire socialism, represented by the election in mining areas of three MLAs in each of 1903, 1907 and 1909 and two in 1912, is seen as the principal evidence of class sentiment in British Columbia. To summarize, historians have concluded that the Marxist socialism of the IWW and the Socialist Party of Canada constituted radicalism in the Pacific province; labourism and more pragmatic forms of socialism belonged to other areas of the country.

In this literature urban places are divided into two groups: the "closed and polarized" mining communities where "class divisions were stark," few restraints mediated relations between workers and companies, and the Socialist Party gained substantial electoral support; and larger western Canadian cities where class tensions found more moderate expression.[81] According to Ross McCormack,

[78] Heron, "Labourism and the Canadian Working Class," p. 45.
[79] McCormack, *Reformers, Rebels, and Revolutionaries*, chaps. 2-4 and 6; Ross Alfred Johnson, "No Compromise — No Political Trading: The Marxist Socialist Tradition in British Columbia" (Ph.D. thesis, University of British Columbia, 1975); and Ronald Grantham, "Some Aspects of the Socialist Movement in British Columbia, 1898-1933" (M.A. thesis, University of British Columbia, 1942).
[80] Ross McCormack, "Socialism and Militancy in the British Columbia Labour Movement," in Jamieson et al., *Militancy*, p. 19.
[81] Bercuson, "Labour Radicalism and the Western Industrial Frontier," passim.

impossiblism was directly relevant to the experience of BC coal and hard-rock miners and, given this power base, had a general relevance in a largely proletarian province experiencing a rapid transition to industrial capitalism. But these conditions were peculiar. Not confronted with the same ruthless capitalism which B.C. miners faced, workers in places such as Calgary, Edmonton, and Winnipeg did not develop a similar degree of class consciousness.[82]

Missing from this analysis are west coast cities. Did Vancouver workers respond to capitalism in the radical manner of B.C. miners or in the more moderate style of their prairie counterparts?

Early in Vancouver's history labourism emerged as an ideological form of political expression sharply at odds with the philosophy of British Columbia's governing elites. Initially labourism united both working- and middle-class reformers. The movement began when a middle-class group, led by newspaper editor Francis Carter-Cotton, formed to oppose David Oppenheimer in the December 1889 mayoralty election and the provincial government, with which Oppenheimer and his supporters had close ties, in 1890.[83] The Trades and Labor Council (VTLC) endorsed a carpenter in January 1892 and a bricklayer one year later for aldermanic office, establishing an independent voice for working people in civic affairs. Both candidates were elected, as were two other carpenters later in the decade.[84] Labourism blossomed in 1894 when the Nationalist Party, British Columbia's "first real 'labor party'," was formed.[85] Its nominee for the British Columbia election that year, Robert Macpherson, won his contest. So too did party member Rev. George Maxwell, elected in 1896 to the House of Commons with the help of federal Liberals and the Labor Council. Macpherson, a carpenter, and Maxwell, formerly a British coal miner and now an eastside Presbyterian minister, were re-elected in 1898 and 1900 respectively. Ironically, principal labourists in the nineties, including Nationalist Party leaders, came mostly from the

---

[82] McCormack, *Reformers, Rebels, and Revolutionaries*, p. 75.

[83] For the 1889 civic election see the *N-A*, 24 November-24 December and the *Province*, 15 November 1924, p. 24. For the 1890 provincial contest, see the *N-A* and *World*, 30 May-14 June 1890.

[84] VTLC Minutes, 8 January 1892, p. 166, 6 January 1893, p. 283, and 21 December 1894, p. 422 and *N-A*, 4 January 1895, p. 7 and 15 January 1898, p. 5.

[85] For the Nationalist Party's history, see Thomas Robert Loosemore, "The British Columbia Labor Movement and Political Action, 1879-1906" (M.A. thesis, University of British Columbia, 1954), pp. 64-66 and 71-87, quotation from p. 64, and VTLC Minutes, 1 March 1895, p. 433, 10 April 1896, pp. 495-96, and 8 November 1895, pp. 460-67.

middle rather than working class. The decade's severe depression had driven away many of the city's best workers,[86] stunting the full development of working-class institutions and limiting organized labour's role in politics to an essentially secondary one of support for middle-class reformers.

Class collaboration gave way to class conflict after 1900. The same economic prosperity and consolidation of capital that had accompanied growing labour tension in mining communities also inspired new confidence among Terminal City workers.[87] The important legislative victories of pro-labour MLAs in Victoria after 1898 may have had a similar short-term effect. Working-class activists repudiated their earlier alliance with middle-class reformers, sharpening labourism's focus as a vehicle of class expression. Unlike 1894, when he ran as a Nationalist Party candidate, Robert Macpherson in 1900 strongly asserted his working-class identity and promised to serve as a "straight Labor man."[88] Another leading labourist of the period, Francis Williams, urged that the Vancouver Labor Party (VLP), founded in 1900 as the political arm of the Trades and Labor Council, "be out and out for class legislation."[89] Even the intensely anti-socialist J. H. Watson, an American Federation of Labor union organizer, encouraged workers to recognize that they had "certain distinctly class interests."[90] Reflecting this new aggressiveness, the VTLC nominated two candidates for the 1900 provincial election, endorsed Macpherson in 1901, and, through the VLP, ran three additional labour candidates in 1903. Working-class feeling received its strongest political expression in Vancouver before the 1930s when, offended by the CPR's role in the UBRE strike, electors in the October 1903 provincial contest cast more than one in five votes for labour and socialist candidates.[91] Labourists then disappeared from provincial and federal slates in Vancouver until the war years.

Displacing labourists were socialist candidates who in 1900 first challenged the formers' right to speak for workers electorally. Soon radicals and moderates had split openly, with an articulate and aggressive cadre

[86] *N-A*, 28 March 1896, p. 6.

[87] Loosemore, "British Columbia Labor Movement," p. 99 and *Federationist*, 27 December 1912, p. 24.

[88] *Independent*, 24 November 1900, p. 1.

[89] *Ibid.*, 7 July 1900, p. 1 and 26 September 1903, p. 1.

[90] *Ibid.*, 12 May 1900, p. 6.

[91] Loosemore, "British Columbia Labor Movement," pp. 193-94.

of socialist leaders coming to dominate working-class institutions.[92] They edited the *Western Clarion* from 1901, the *Western Wage-Earner* from 1909 to 1910 and the *British Columbia Federationist* thereafter. They presented the only distinctly "leftist" candidates in regional and federal, but not municipal, elections and participated actively in the Labor Council, despite Socialist Party of Canada policy to the contrary. Socialists James McVety and Parm Pettipiece dominated the VTLC from 1905 to the war, while Jack Kavanagh and Victor Midgely played supporting roles. Socialists in the Council also promoted industrial unionism, thus challenging the conservative "business unionism" philosophy that dominated the national labour movements in Canada and the United States. Socialists led the VTLC out of the Trades and Labour Congress of Canada in 1903 and "sponsored the Vancouver resolution that sparked the second B.C. campaign for industrial unionism in the years before World War I."[93] This multi-faceted activity has led most historians to suggest, either implicitly or directly, that the doctrinaire radicalism characteristic of the region also typified working-class politics in Vancouver. For several reasons, this notion should be questioned.

To begin with, this impression of Socialist Party strength in Vancouver is based more on organizational influence than on popular appeal to urban workers. As British Columbia's metropolitan centre, Vancouver served, in the words of the *Western Clarion* in 1916, as "the nerve centre from which Socialism radiates" throughout the region,[94] providing a convenient location for the national party headquarters and for party conventions. The small cadre who worked from Vancouver thus exerted inordinate influence over labour institutions within it. Yet the party's electoral support, ranging to 10 percent of the votes cast in Vancouver before 1914, while respectable, was not substantial. Ross Johnson points out that the party faced "a constant struggle (in Vancouver) to inspire the membership to action and to increase the size of the membership body." Its regular Sunday night meetings for the study of Marxist economics drew large numbers of transient workers "during the winter months of logging and construction camp shut-downs." But like the party's electoral strength, this support came mainly from hinterland workers who, while spending time in Vancouver, were only marginally

[92] For example, see *ibid.*, pp. 138, 157, 190-92; the *Federationist*, 27 December 1912, p. 24, and the *Independent*, 4 April-6 June 1903.

[93] McCormack, "Socialism and Militancy in the British Columbia Labour Movement," p. 21.

[94] *Western Clarion*, October 1916, p. 1.

integrated into the city's work force. As Johnson suggests, evidence hardly supports the view long held by revolutionary socialists that Vancouver "was the cradle of socialism in Canada."[95]

In addition labourism, the political expression of skilled wage-earners, did not disappear from Vancouver but continued to thrive at the civic level. The Socialist Party's ascendancy after 1903 had put moderates on the defensive and ended labourism in its institutionalized form. In this sense B.C. radicalism extended into Vancouver. But lack of party organization, which historians have taken to mean the disappearance of non-Marxist labour politics, did not, in fact, preclude the continued influence of labourism as an expression of working-class attitudes and values. Rather, aldermen John MacMillan, a builder, John Morton, a carpenter and contractor, Robert Macpherson, a carpenter, and Francis Williams, a tailor, worked together as an identifiable pro-labour clique on city council for a total of sixteen council years from 1903 to 1911.[96] Sitting for wards distinguished by upper working- and lower middle-class voters, they provided an opposition minority to council's pro-business majority.

The four articulated a distinctively labourist view of civic affairs, reiterating policy positions publicized a decade earlier by the VTLC and the Nationalist Party.[97] Drawing on the long established culture of British skilled artisans, they defined work very differently from employers. As noted earlier, their ideas centred on notions of "just" employment practices and "fair" compensation. The idea of honest labour, fairly recompensed, accounts in part for the racist tone of their criticism of Chinese immigrants who willingly accepted low wages and deplorable conditions. Labourists expressed faith especially in what Craig Heron calls the "full promise of liberal democracy."[98] Hoping to transform society's institutions through the universal application of democratic principles, they called for the widest acceptance of free speech, free assembly and a universal franchise, including the vote for women.[99] Labourists on city council in both the 1890s and 1900s argued in vain that all property qualifications be removed from the civic franchise and that aldermen be paid for their work. Otherwise only the elite could afford to participate in local govern-

---

[95] Quotations in this paragraph are from Johnson, "No Compromise — No Political Trading," pp. 236 and 378.

[96] MacMillan was elected for Ward 6 in 1906, 1908 and 1909; Morton for Ward 5 in 1903-06 and 1908-09; Macpherson for Ward 4 in 1903-04 and 1910-11; and Williams for Ward 6 in 1904-06.

[97] VTLC Minutes, 8 November 1895, pp. 460-67.

[98] Heron, "Labourism and the Canadian Working Class," p. 55.

[99] N-A, 25 March 1894, p. 3 and Independent, 3 November 1900, p. 1.

ment.[100] Economic privilege was as unacceptable as political inequality, and concentrations of economic power, whether through land monopolies or large corporations, were against the public interest. The CPR consti- tuted a favourite target of criticism.[101] The single tax would remove unearned profits from land speculators while the public ownership of urban utilities, including the street railway and electric light companies in the 1890s and telephone company in the following decade, would limit the unjust concentration of economic influence.[102] Labour aldermen fought particularly hard to stop large private companies from controlling street ends and water lots on False Creek.[103] The same egalitarian impulse conditioned sharp criticism of social privilege. Working people's contempt for the social elite found expression in demands that Vancouver's City Hospital be managed by elected officials and not by charitable "Lady Beautifuls" to whom nurses and hospital officials "would be expected to bow and smile and smirk." The poor needed real jobs, not "insulting and degrading charity."[104] Education should be as "free as the air," not a privilege of the rich.[105] And recreational space, such as the beach at English Bay, should be made freely available to the masses.[106]

Wage-earners also expressed their class interests by voting for candi- dates affiliated with, or members of, the federal Liberal Party. Leading Vancouver labour leaders around 1900 were invariably Liberals, among them Robert Macpherson, Harry Cowan, J. H. Watson, George Bartley and Chris Foley.[107] In addition, George Maxwell had Liberal Party support in 1896 and ran as a joint Liberal-labour candidate in 1900. For the provincial contest that year Macpherson had joined the provincial faction of Joseph Martin, a federal Liberal who openly promoted labour causes in B.C. Macpherson's nomination came from a meeting of 200 to

[100] VTLC Minutes, 31 January 1896, p. 480 and *N-A*, 18 February 1902, p. 5.

[101] *Ibid.*, 1 October 1898, p. 7, 5 April 1907, p. 4 and 9 February 1909, p. 5.

[102] *Ibid.*, 16 March 1895, p. 5, 21 February 1904, p. 2, and 17 August 1906, p. 4; VTLC Minutes, 4 July 1891, p. 135; and *Independent*, 6 October 1900, p. 1.

[103] *N-A*, 10 December 1895, p. 3 and *Independent*, 8 February 1902, p. 1 and 14 February 1903, p. 3.

[104] *Ibid.*, 22 February 1901, p. 1. Also see VTLC Minutes, 8 November 1895, p. 466 and *World*, 28 August 1909, p. 12.

[105] *Independent*, 7 May 1902, p. 1. Also see *ibid.*, 19 January 1901, p. 2 and 22 August 1904, p. 10.

[106] Robert A. J. McDonald, " 'Holy Retreat' or 'Practical Breathing Spot'?: Class Perceptions of Vancouver's Stanley Park, 1910-1913," *Canadian Historical Review* 65 (June 1984) : 127-53.

[107] *N-A*, 26 September 1897, p. 5; *Province*, 16 November 1900, p. 9 and Loosemore, "British Columbia Labour Movement," pp. 165-66.

300 unorganized workers.[108] Except for division of the working-class vote between Martinites, labourists and socialists, Macpherson would have won re-election handily. A decade later the mayoralty campaigns of another federal Liberal, Louis D. Taylor, again emphasized working-class issues. Described as "the dominant power in the local liberal camp,"[109] Taylor challenged C. S. Douglas, a prominent member of Vancouver's business and social elites, in 1909 and 1910, failing the first time but succeeding the second. Taylor's campaigns centred on such popular labour issues as the eight-hour day for civic workers, the exclusion of Orientals from city jobs, and the need to retain public control of waterfront street ends.[110] Douglas and his principal supporter, the business-oriented *Vancouver Province*, concluded that he owed his 1910 victory to "the solid Socialist vote" from eastern and southern wards; the *Western Wage-Earner* agreed that "Taylor's victory was due in no small measure to the support of . . . members of organized labor."[111]

In other words, the extent to which Vancouver politics expressed class feeling among wage-earners went beyond the minority of electors, ranging after 1903 from 12 to 18 percent in federal and provincial elections, who voted for third party labour or socialist candidates.[112] Together with evidence of labourist strength at the civic level and the Socialist Party's rather tenuous political base in the city, it suggests that moderate expressions of class identity far surpassed radical ones in extent and significance. From the broader perspective of political support, then, labour radicalism in Vancouver appears little different from that in Winnipeg. Just as the careers of Arthur Puttee, Fred Dixon and Dick Riggs have become synonymous with Winnipeg's "reform" tradition of working-class politics, so too should the careers of Rev. George Maxwell, Robert Macpherson, Francis Williams and L. D. Taylor symbolize the strong labourist presence in the coast city. Generalizations about labour radicalism in Vancouver, as about labour militancy, must emphasize big city rather than resource hinterland parallels.

*   *   *

[108] *Independent*, 28 April 1900, p. 1.

[109] S. J. Gothard to Richard McBride, 20 October 1909, Provincial Archives of British Columbia, Premiers' Papers, Private Correspondence, Doc. 892/1909. Also see *N-A*, 13 November 1908, p. 1 and 17 March 1912, p. 28.

[110] *Ibid.*, 30 December 1908, pp. 1-2 and 13 January 1909, pp. 1-2 and *World*, 11-12 January 1910.

[111] Quotations from *Province*, 10 January 1910, p. 6 and 14 January 1910, p. 1 and *Western Wage-Earner*, February 1910, p. 12.

[112] Ward, "Class and Race," p. 23.

One issue remains unresolved. The urban patterns of militancy and radicalism described here indicate a dichotomy between objective and subjective manifestations of class. Workers defended their class interests through actions that accepted the continued existence of capitalism. Most workers struck in small units defined by skill or occupation; only rarely did they confront capital by joining together across occupational lines. In addition, most expressed political support either for leftist candidates who advocated evolutionary rather than revolutionary change or for candidates of the two main national parties. In other words, the fundamental contradiction within the productive system between those who owned or managed capital and those who sold labour did not generate among workers a commensurate level of class-based economic or political action. Workers' subjective perception of class relations differed from the objective reality of Vancouver's economic structure. Several factors limited the evolution of class condition into class consciousness.

First is what Rev. Dr. Alfred Garvie, a British "social activist," referred to as "the universal materialism of Canada."[113] Signs of the untrammelled quest for individual economic betterment were especially obvious during the Laurier period in western Canada, nowhere more so than in rapidly growing western cities. On the prairies speculation in real estate, the most obvious manifestation of exaggerated growth, was mainly limited to urban centres but in British Columbia the whole province experienced a "wild orgy of speculation."[114] Vancouver businessmen directed much of the commerce in hinterland mining claims, land and timber limits, fueling real estate hysteria in the metropolitan area. Between 1909 and 1913 a highly inflated real estate boom engulfed the entire lower mainland.

Fragmentary evidence suggests that Vancouverites on both sides of the class line embraced the materialist ethos of the boom. In 1909 the booster element captured the local government of suburban South Vancouver, a working-class community described as "home of the industrial classes." In the words of one contemporary observer, "From the artisan who owned a 33 foot lot, to the large speculator who owned 50 and 100 acres, the slogan (in South Vancouver) was progress."[115] In 1912 the *British*

---

[113] George Feaver, " 'Self-Respect and Hopefulness': The Webbs in the Canadian West," *BC Studies* 43 (Autumn 1979): 59.

[114] W. G. Cameron and Thos. Kidd, "First Report," in Robert M. Haig, *Reports of the Board of Taxation With A Report on Taxation in the Province of British Columbia by Robert Murray Haig* (Victoria: Wm. H. Cullin, 1919), p. Q6.

[115] Alfred H. Lewis, *South Vancouver: Past and Present* (Vancouver: Western Publishing Bureau, 1920), pp. 16 and 18.

Columbia Federationist reported that the "fever of speculation has seized the workers as well as the rest, many of them having invested their scant savings in a house and lot."[116] As owner of the *World* newspaper, L. D. Taylor headed one of Vancouver's shrillest booster organs, forcing working-class voters who supported his pro-labour policies to accept, if not actively embrace, his concurrent role as advocate of speculative capitalism. In addition, hourly wages in Vancouver during the pre-war boom were among the highest in Canada, approximating those in other major western Canadian cities but exceeding those in central Canada and the Maritimes by one-third and two-thirds respectively.[117] The resulting expectation of economic improvement undoubtedly explains the pre-war migration of thousands of workers into Vancouver. It may also account for the political apathy of wage-earners at the peak of the boom, an apathy noted by labour observers[118] and reflected in the labour clique's temporary disappearance after 1911 from city council. The myth of prosperity appears to have united many middle- and working-class Vancouverites in a common belief that capitalism offered a realistic hope for material advancement. By making economic and social improvement appear attainable through individual effort, the myth retarded collective action by working people.

So did evidence of upward social mobility, of which rapidly growing cities, in contrast to one-industry mining and lumber towns, furnished numerous examples. In Vancouver new office towers sprouted from the business district, an exclusive residential neighbourhood for business and social leaders sprang from the soil of Shaughnessy Heights, and the rich flaunted their wealth as never before, leaving the impression of widespread opportunity for economic gain. More influential in lessening class consciousness among wage-earners, however, may have been examples of social movement upward from the working class into the petit bourgeoisie.[119] Many carpenters became contractors, among them Aldermen Morton and Hepburn. Several skilled workers prominent in the local labour movement established their own shops: typographer Harry Cowan formed a printing business; cigarmaker John Crow founded a cigar factory; and Joseph Dixon advanced from carpenter to contractor to office and store fixtures manufacturer. Even an unskilled laundry worker,

---

[116] *Federationist*, 5 April 1912, p. 1.

[117] Calculated from *Census of Canada, 1921*, vol. III, pp. xix-xx.

[118] *Western Wage-Earner*, June 1909, p. 12 and *Federationist*, 6 December 1912, p. 2.

[119] Social mobility is defined here as movement from a wage labour to wage employer position; occupations were traced through city directories.

C. N. Lee, was able to finance an English Bay tea and refreshment parlour. Contemporaries could easily have interpreted such experiences, whether typical or not, as demonstrable evidence of a society open to success.

Urbanism impeded the emergence of class consciousness in another way: rather than being internally uniform, Vancouver's working class was a large, economically differentiated entity characterized by significant occupational divisions. As noted earlier, the interrelated factors of skill, geographic persistence, gender and race sorted workers into a hierarchy defined by varied incomes, market power and status. These economic distinctions in turn acquired social and cultural expression. The skilled worker who was raising a family, belonged to a craft-organized trade union, took part in union picnics, baseball games and balls, had joined the Odd Fellows Lodge, owned or rented a small cottage in Mount Pleasant and voted in provincial and municipal elections lived in a very different social world than the single loggers for whom cheap hotels, "skidway saloons," shooting galleries, prostitutes and Sunday evening Wobblie meetings constituted Vancouver society. Ethnicity and race erected even larger barriers between Italian or Asian minorities and the British-born majority. Reinforced by rampant materialism and examples of social mobility, these differences precluded a widely shared feeling of community among Vancouver wage-earners.

In turn, a social environment that compared favourably with B.C. resource towns and large Canadian cities alike lessened the conditions that might exacerbate class tensions. Despite the presence of significant ethnic and, especially, racial minorities, Vancouver's population was predominantly Anglo-Saxon.[120] The west coast city's social geography did not include the teeming immigrant ghettoes of Winnipeg's North End, Toronto's "Ward" or New York's Lower East Side. Ironically, by segregating Vancouver's Asian population physically, politically and economically, racism reduced social anxiety by removing from the mainstream of Vancouver life the city's most clearly recognizable foreign element. Deryck Holdsworth argues that housing conditions also marked Vancouver "as a somewhat benign example of an industrial city."[121] A suburban environment of detached residences with surrounding gardens rather than a dense concentration of tenements characterized Vancouver housing; so did the lack of harsh residential segregation, despite an over-

[120] Norbert MacDonald, "Population Growth and Change in Seattle and Vancouver, 1880-1960," *Pacific Historical Review* 39 (1970): 297-320.
[121] Holdsworth, "House and Home in Vancouver," p. 261.

all spatial division of the city by class.[122] Health conditions appear to have
been better in Vancouver than in comparable Canadian cities as well.
Margaret Andrews has demonstrated that Vancouver's death rate — "a
measure of the state of health of the whole population" — was relatively
low.[123] The city's liberal expense of money and effort on health services
and readily available supply of fresh water conspired to check disease.
However, such generalizations apply less to one section of the city than to
the others: the higher incidence of death from disease and the deplorable
tenement and rooming conditions in the eastside waterfront area[124]
emphasize again the need to differentiate between the domestic circum-
stance of seasonal migrants and that of more stable urban workers.

The preceding analysis corroborates Peter Ward's conclusion that
several influences, including the pervasiveness of individualistic and
materialistic values, the geographic mobility of the labour force and
broadly held perceptions of upward social and economic mobility, muted
class feeling in British Columbia at the turn of the century.[125] But it
departs from his conclusion in one fundamental way. Ward emphasizes
the subjective, intellectual dimension of class, concentrating on elements
that constrained class awareness while neglecting its persistent, structural
features. Yet the experience of Vancouver workers shows that only by
examining both objective and subjective elements can historians fully
appreciate the process of class formation. While recurrent cycles of prosperity may have sustained for Vancouver's ordinary people the myth of
economic and social improvement, the reality of their essential powerless-
ness was never far distant. The 1913-16 economic collapse that drove
almost one-quarter of Greater Vancouver's population, especially wage
earners, from the area illustrates clearly the ongoing social contradiction
of British Columbia's capitalist system.

The Vancouver experience also suggests that, for too long, labour
historians have generalized for the whole province from the history of

122 *Ibid.*, chaps. 1 and 7.

123 Margaret W. Andrews, "Medical Services in Vancouver, 1886-1920: A Study of
the Interplay of Attitudes, Medical Knowledge, and Administrative Structures"
(Ph.D. thesis, University of British Columbia, 1979), pp. 1, 3-7, 17-18, and 33 and
Roy, *Vancouver*, p. 176, n. 43. For comparative purposes see Copp, *Anatomy of
Poverty*, p. 100 and Alan F. J. Artibise, *Winnipeg: A Social History of Urban
Growth, 1874-1914* (Montreal: McGill-Queen's University Press, 1975), p. 231.
Medical health officials and others often commented on Vancouver's plentiful
supply of fresh water: *N-A*, 21 August 1891, p. 12; and 31 October 1912, p. 2.

124 Andrews, "Medical Services in Vancouver," pp. 20-22 and *N-A*, 14 October
1911, p. 9 and 26 May 1912, p. 1.

125 Ward, "Class and Race."

coal and hardrock miners. Vancouver's work force, in 1911 equalling 25 percent of the provincial total,[126] constituted British Columbia's largest single concentration of wage-earners, yet this group has been virtually ignored in the existing literature. The foregoing discussion shows that a variety of urban characteristics, including the appearance of greater economic opportunity and the reality of a more complex occupational structure, distinguished working-class history in Vancouver from that elsewhere in the province. In studying British Columbia's past, then, historians must consider more fully the role of local factors in giving varied expression to regional patterns of labour militancy, labour radicalism and social structure.

[126] *Census of Canada, 1911*, vol. VI, table 5, p. xv and table 6, p. 286.

Sam Kee: A Chinese Business in Early Vancouver*

PAUL YEE

Canada's reception of the early Chinese migrants was characterized by vicious hostility and antagonism at legislative and popular levels of society. Politicians, journalists, housewives and workers alike sought to exclude and restrict the Chinese. Yet the Chinese remained and settled, attracted by the economic opportunities open to them as wage-labourers and self-employed businessmen. This paper explores the pre-1916 activities of the Sam Kee Company 三記號, one of the wealthiest merchant firms of early Vancouver's Chinatown, in order to look at the Chinese-Canadian past from a perspective different from those traditionally used in viewing Chinese-Canadian history. It looks at how one Chinese firm conducted its affairs and how the institution of business contributed to the process of immigrant adjustment.

In the writing of Chinese-Canadian history, one group of scholars has looked extensively at the roots and agitators of the racism that surrounded the Chinese during their early settlement in Canada.[1] These studies have explained the politics, the economics and the psychologies of what remains essentially a white phenomenon the victims and targets of which are the Chinese. Other scholars have examined the voluntary associations established by the Chinese to meet various community and social needs.[2] These studies have commented on how the social bases of organization

* I wish to acknowledge the comments of W. Peter Ward on earlier drafts of this article and the assistance of Mrs. Yat Leong Chang and Dr. Theodore Chang in providing personal information on Chang Toy.

[1] See, for examples, James Morton, *In the Sea of Sterile Mountains* (Vancouver: J. J. Douglas, 1974) and W. Peter Ward, *White Canada Forever: Popular Attitudes and Public Policy Towards Orientals in British Columbia* (Montreal: McGill and Queen's University Press, 1978).

[2] A large volume of literature has emerged on the topic of voluntary associations. For examples, see: Chuen-yan Lai, "The Chinese Consolidated Benevolent Association in Victoria: Its Origins and Functions," *BC Studies* 15 (Autumn 1972): 53-67; Edgar Wickberg, editor, *From China to Canada* (Toronto: McClelland & Stewart, 1982); William E. Willmott, "Chinese Clan Associations in Vancouver," *Man* 64 (1964): 33-37.

came from China as part of the immigrants' cultural baggage to provide familiar points of reference and support for new immigrants.

But white racism and community organizations are only two aspects of the immigration experience of the Chinese in Canada. This article explores a third realm of that past: business activity. The records of Vancouver's Sam Kee Company, while incomplete and unclear, allow a rare look inside the immigrant world. To date, studies of the Chinese-Canadian past have hardly used primary documentation from within the Chinese community. Studies of anti-Asian agitation, for example, have rarely explored racism's psychological impact upon the Chinese people, nor have organizational studies investigated the internal workings of a clan or county-based association. Business records, on the other hand, document Chinese firms and individuals as active participants in the immigrant past, as people responding to a New World context.

Furthermore, business history explores an area of primary concern to the Chinese migrants themselves. After all, the Chinese, like other immigrants to North America, came to make money, not to stir up racism nor to establish clubs and meeting halls. By looking through the frame of business history, it is possible to begin to think more seriously about how the Chinese adjusted to the New World with regard to their own economic motivations and expectations.

Vancouver's Chinese community grew from the lumber industries of the region and from the completion of the Canadian Pacific Railway to nearby Port Moody. After the city's incorporation in 1886, the Chinese worked there as land-clearers, ditch-diggers and farmers, and as cooks and servants in homes, hotels and logging camps. As Vancouver developed, the Chinese established laundries, merchant tailor operations, and other businesses to meet consumer demands from the white population. Merchants inside Chinatown provided the growing Chinese community with a full range of essential services. With the trans-Pacific steamships docking at Vancouver's harbour, Chinatown firms channelled the burgeoning import trade from China into the British Columbian interior, where the majority of the province's Chinese lived. Vancouver's Chinatown soon overtook Victoria's as the leading commercial and social centre of the Chinese in Canada.[3]

The Sam Kee Company was one of the four firms in Vancouver's Chinatown that grossed over $150,000 in 1907, a figure six times greater

---

[3] Information of Chinese activities in early Vancouver is taken from Paul R. Yee, "Chinese Business in Vancouver, 1886-1914" (M.A. thesis, University of British Columbia, 1983), pp. 28-41.

than the average income of two-thirds of Chinatown's businesses.[4] The wealthier merchants of Chinatown filled many roles and functions within the immigrant community while enriching themselves. They provided the essentials of food, housing and employment (directly and indirectly through labour contracts) to their fellow countrymen. They helped the community attain a high degree of self-sufficiency in a hostile environment. Because wealth was one important determinant to leadership inside and outside of Chinatown, these merchants often acted as the community's spokesmen. They organized two early chambers of commerce in 1898 and 1899 and also formed the backbone of the Chinese Benevolent Association, nominally the highest ranking body within Chinatown.[5] Merchants were the most outspoken segment of the community and defended their interests in court and at city hall to demonstrate a confident understanding of western legal and political institutions.[6]

In many respects the merchants helped to recreate in the overseas settlement a semblance of a Chinese social order. Migrants accustomed to the flourishing market towns and county centres of rural South China encountered a familiar free market economy in Canada, complete with limited prospects of upward mobility as they toiled at whatever jobs they found. Peace and order were needed for the smooth functioning of the economy, and this impelled Chinatown's merchants to deal with the vagaries of the New World by shouldering the traditional welfare and mediary duties of the gentry and lineage elders of China. Since wealth and financial acumen were highly respected, business activity helped transform the social and economic values brought from China into a familiar, functional hierarchical system where migrants could labour patiently at realizing their own dreams.

Chang Toy (陳才, Chen Cai, also known as Chen Dao-zhi 陳道之 and 陳長僅 Chen Chang-jin) was the founder and guiding force of the

4 Public Archives of Canada, William Lyon Mackenzie King, Memoranda and Notes 1887-1921, vol. C41, Royal Commission to Investigate into Losses Sustained by the Chinese Population of Vancouver, B.C., 1908, Resultant Claims (1) and (2), pp. C32537-C32719. (Hereafter King Papers)

5 David T. H. Lee, [A History of Chinese in Canada] (Taipei, 1967), pp. 208-09; King Papers, p. C31560; Doe Chuen Lee, Inside the Chinese Benevolent Association (Taipei, 1969), pp. 12-13.

6 Chinese laundrymen, for example, carried on a prolonged battle with civic officials in Vancouver over licensing and bylaw regulations, while land-owning merchants complained about the condition of streets and sidewalks and about police raids into Chinatown. Other merchants sued the city for damages incurred during razing and lobbied for licence reductions. See Paul Yee, "Chinese Business in Vancouver, 1886-1914" (M.A. thesis, University of British Columbia, 1983), pp. 33-35, 47, 49-50 and 51.

Sam Kee Company. According to family sources, he was born in 1857 to poor peasant Hakkas (客家) in Poon Yue (番禺) county of Guangdong (廣東) province. His father died when Chang Toy was three years old, but the boy managed to acquire three years of education after the age of ten. In 1874 Chang Toy came to Victoria, B.C. His passage had been paid by a fish canner, for whom Chang was to work one season in repayment. However, due to contrary winds, the boat arrived late, and only one month's work remained.

Chang then went to New Westminster to work in a sawmill. After two years he came to the Vancouver area and began a laundry business. In subsequent years he gradually moved into imports and exports, retail sales, charcoal and fuel sales, labour contracting in the timber, fishing and sugar industries, steamship ticket sales and real estate development. The Sam Kee store emerged as a gathering place for migrants of Hakka and Poon Yue origins who came to purchase goods and look for work. The firm's name, Sam Kee, was used by the company and customers alike as a person's name, although no such person ever existed.

The company's earliest surviving records document the sale of Chinese goods to local Chinese. Import-export firms shipping goods to and from China have been identified as the earliest businesses of the Chinese immigrants to North America. These firms did not require large amounts of initial capital because they relied extensively on credit and good business contacts in Canton and Hong Kong. Many of these firms were private partnerships between one or more owners, while others were attached to locally formed home-county associations, where officers acted as owner-managers and carried on the business. The primary imports were rice, tea and dry goods such as clothing and food items, while exports to China included gold, wheat, barley, mercury, salt and dried seafoods.[7]

The Sam Kee Company's retail endeavours started with goods shipped from Victoria's Wing Chong Company (永祥號), owned by Chang Toy's good friend Chu Lai (徐禮). Chang Toy was involved from the outset, employing two helpers in 1888. Shum Moon (沈滿) later emerged as his comptroller. For 1888, sales totalled $4,356.45, and the net profit was $374.81.[8] The company stocked a wide range of goods: a 1901 inventory listed over 350 different kinds of items including all types of Chinese

---

[7] L. Armentrout Ma, "Big and Medium Businesses of Chinese Immigrants to the United States, 1850-1890: An Outline," *Bulletin of the Chinese Historical Society of America* 13 (September 1978): 1-2.

[8] City of Vancouver Archives, Add. MSS 571, Sam Kee Company Papers (hereafter cited as Sam Kee) vol. 15 file 6 " 光緒十四年吉日計記來貨 " [Record of Goods on Hand], 1888.

foods (rice, preserved fruits, dried seafoods, salted goods, beans, pastes, spices, and oil), Chinese medicines and wines, and a variety of dry goods such as thread, writing brushes, envelopes, matches, fish-knives and hand-kerchiefs.[9] The firm's retail sales climbed in the 1890s from $7,740.25 in 1893 to $8,660.44 in nine months of 1898.[10] A tally of daily cash-book entries shows that $13,831 was received and $14,891 expended in 1891,[11] while $19,540 was received and $18,471 expended in 1896.[12] Clearly Sam Kee had sources of income other than retail sales of imported Chinese goods.

Sam Kee relied on connections to China and abroad for supplies and for credit. It purchased goods from firms in Hong Kong and Yokohama, chief of which was the Sun Tong Chong Company (新同昌) of Hong Kong. Sun Tong Chong acted as the company's agent in China, purchasing goods both outright and on credit for shipment to Canada. In payment, Sam Kee sent funds and Canadian goods to Sun Tong Chong which were then sold to Chinese buyers. Between 1902 and 1907, Sam Kee's purchases from Sun Tong Chong climbed from 9,810 taels ($6,180.30) to 22,735 taels ($17,960.65).[13] Sun Tong Chong levied interest charges of between 6 and 8 percent on annual outstanding balances.[14] As table 1 shows, Sam Kee relied heavily on credit purchases, owing amounts that ranged from 2,453 taels ($1,545) to 9,314 taels ($7,358) during the 1902-07 period.

In the 1890s the Sam Kee Company was shipping goods to Chinese stores in Kamloops, Lillooet and Ashcroft, and in the 1900s it supplied smaller towns such as Extension on Vancouver Island and Enderby in the interior.[15] Until 1902 the store was located on the south side of the unit block East Pender Street, and the back of the store overlooked the waters of False Creek, which facilitated the shipping of goods. In Vancouver credit from Sam Kee was readily available to Chinatown individuals and firms, and even Japanese and a few whites had accounts

---

[9] Sam Kee, vol. 15 file 1 " 雜貨成本簿 " [Cost of Goods On Hand], 1901.

[10] Sam Kee, vol. 15 file 9, " 光緒十九年春月立記現沽數簿 " [Record of Sales, 1893]; vol. 15 file 12 " " [Record of Sales, 1898].

[11] Sam Kee, vol. 14 file 1 " 光緒十七年抄進支總簿 " [Journal, 1891].

[12] Sam Kee, vol. 14 file 2 " 光緒二十二年立記進支總簿 " [Journal, 1896].

[13] Sam Kee, vol. 3 file 6 [List of Goods Shipped to Vancouver], 1905-06; and vol. 3 file 11 [List of Goods Shipped to Vancouver], 1908.

[14] *Ibid.*

[15] See letters in Sam Kee, vol. 3 files 2, 3, 8 for correspondence with camps and towns throughout British Columbia.

TABLE 1

Sam Kee Company Payments and Purchases from Sun Tong Chong Company

Year		Total sent to Sun Tong Chong	Interest allowed by Sun Tong Chong	Total held by Sun Tong Chong	Total purchases from Sun Tong Chong	Interest charged by Sun Tong Chong	Total owing	Balance
1902	T	10,241.3.6	570.9	10,712.1	9,810.0.8		9,810.0.8	902.0.9
	$	6,451.83	359.10	6,748.56	6,180.30		6,180.30	586.26
1903	T	9,361.0.9	737.2.5	10,098.3.4	11,757.9.8	793.4	12,551.3.8	2,453.0.3
	$	5,991.04	471.68	6,462.72	7,524.48	507.52	8,032.64	1,569.92
1905	T	18,462.2.0	1,204.8.8	19,667.0.8	20,896.4.3	1,623.8.6	22,520.2.9	2,853.2.1
	$	13,477.26	878.92	14,356.91	15,254.08	1,184.79	16,439.60	2,082.69
1906	T	9,932.4.1	643.1.7	10,575.5.9	14,656.4.4	916.2.5	15,572.6.9	4,997.1
	$	7,945.60	522.40	8,460.00	11,724.80	732.80	12,457.60	3,995.20
1907	T	13,650.1.6	1,093.5.1	14,743.6.9	22,725.0	1,332.8.6	24,057.8.7	9,314.1.8
	$	10,783.50	863.47	11,646.97	17,952.75	1,052.28	19,005.03	7,358.06

SOURCE: City of Vancouver Archives, Add. MSS 571, Sam Kee Papers, vol. 3 file 6 [List of Goods Shipped to Vancouver 1905-1906], vol. 3 file 11 [List of Goods Shipped to Vancouver, 1908].

CURRENCY CONVERSION: Average value of Haikwan tael for 1902 — 63¢; 1903 — 64¢; 1904 — 66¢; 1905 — 73¢; 1906 — 80¢; 1907 — 79¢. Source: Canada. House of Commons. Report of the Department of Trade and Commerce, *Sessional Papers* No. 10 (1903), p. 137; Canada. House of Commons. Report of the Department of Trade and Commerce, *Sessional Papers* No. 10a (1908), p. 189.

with the company.[16] Chinese imports such as rice, soya sauce and fire-crackers were sold to white wholesale firms in Vancouver and in Revel-stoke,[17] and prior to 1908 the firm handled occasional shipments of opium, forwarding goods from a Victoria firm to white customers in Vancouver.[18]

As well, a network of communication existed between Sam Kee and individual Chinese immigrants scattered throughout British Columbia in small towns and isolated camps. Most Chinese immigrants had come to Canada expecting to earn enough money for an eventual retirement back in China. In the meantime, for purposes of ongoing household main-tenance, they regularly sent funds home to their relatives. Sam Kee Com-pany acted as a clearing-house for cash remittances. After receiving the money from migrants, Sam Kee forwarded the funds by personal carriers or by mail to Sun Tong Chong in Hong Kong and to other business associates in Canton. These firms then arranged to distribute the funds to the appropriate recipients. In the 1890s Sam Kee arranged for monthly dispatches of remittances containing individual amounts ranging from $10 to $200.[19]

In Sam Kee's import-export trading, rice was one major import which the company promoted extensively. In 1900 it brought in at least ten tons of rice from China.[20] These supplies may have been insufficient to meet local demands, since a year later Sam Kee purchased additional quantities of rice from local wholesale grocers such as F. C. Davidge and W. A. Anderson.[21] By 1908, however, Sam Kee had gained better con-trol of its Chinese rice supplies and was selling rice directly to the major wholesale firms of Victoria and Vancouver including Kelly, Douglas and Company and the W. H. Malkin Company,[22] as well as indirectly to other customers through local food broker J. E. Chipman.[23]

16 Sam Kee, vol. 12 file 1 " 三記光緒二十七年賣客薄 " [Ledger of Customers Accounts, 1901]; vol. 12 file 2 " 光緒二十八年客報總薄 " [Ledger of Customers Accounts, 1902]; vol. 12 file 3 " 光緒二十九年客報總薄 " [Ledger of Customers Accounts, 1903].

17 Sam Kee, vol. 1 Book 1, p. 54, Sam Kee to McLennan and McFeely, 30 July 1908; vol. 6 file 7, Woolsey, LeFeaux and Co. to Sam Kee, 15 May 1906.

18 Sam Kee, vol. 6 file 4, Shon Yuen and Co. to Sam Kee, 19 December 1904, 18 December 1904.

19 Sam Kee, vol. 18 file 6 " 代寄銀信薄 " [Record of Cash and Letter Remittances], 1891; file 7 " 匯銀寄信薄 " [Record of Cash and Letter Remittances], 1896.

20 Sam Kee, vol. 5 file 6, Customs declarations, 9 March 1900, 21 May 1900.

21 Sam Kee, vol. 5 file 9, F. C. Davidge to Sam Kee, 22 March 1901, 26 March 1901; W. A. Anderson and Co. to Chang Foy [sic], 28 March 1901.

22 Sam Kee, vol. 1 Book 1, p. 120, Sam Kee to Kelly Douglas and Co., 31 May 1908; vol. 1 Book 1, p. 33, Sam Kee to W. H. Malkin, 18 January 1908.

In 1908 Sam Kee Company set up its own rice mill in Vancouver to process uncleaned rice, but this venture appears to have failed since a year later the firm was attempting to sell the milling equipment.[24] The company proved to be an aggressive seller of its rice, sending samples and prices to white wholesale firms across western Canada in Calgary, Edmonton, Lethbridge, Regina and Winnipeg.[25] It was a canny bargainer too, admitting in one instance that the firm could meet any lower price of competitors because it had purchased its rice too early in the season and was therefore anxious to sell.[26] The company also sold rice to local Japanese wholesalers including the Japan Rice Mill.[27]

Fish was the Sam Kee Company's major export. British Columbia's massive overseas shipments of canned salmon had helped to consolidate the province's staples-based economy in the 1870s. In 1899 Sam Kee sent thirty-five cases of canned crab to Hong Kong and thirty tons of salted dogfish to Yokohama.[28] In 1901 over five tons of pickled salmon, canned salmon and dried salt salmon were shipped to Chinese firms in Hawaii.[29] Then the development of a salt herring industry in British Columbia, matched with a powerful consumer demand from across the Pacific for salted fish, led Sam Kee to export large quantities of this fish to Asia beginning in 1903. Most of the early shipments of salt herring went to the Sun Tong Chong Company in Hong Kong, but by 1907 considerable amounts of the fish were being consigned to Shanghai.[30] Table 2 shows that the volume of salt herring exports almost tripled from at least 521 tons in 1905 to at least 1,544 tons in 1915.[31]

---

[23] Sam Kee, vol. 6 file 12, J. E. Chipman to Sam Kee, 2 January 1907, 10 January 1908.

[24] Sam Kee, vol. 8 file 1, Sam Kee to V. E. Roberts, 18 February 1909.

[25] Sam Kee, vol. 6 file 12, Sam Kee to Campbell Bros and Wilson, Calgary, Georgeson and Co., Calgary, Hudson's Bay Company, Winnipeg, et al., 22 January 1908; vol. 1 Book 1, pp. 67-70, Sam Kee to various firms, 19 March 1908.

[26] Sam Kee, vol. 1 Book 1, p. 52, Sam Kee to Rat Portage Lumber Co., Harrison River, 6 March 1908.

[27] Sam Kee, vol. 1 Book 1, p. 89, Sam Kee to Japan Rice Mill, 31 March 1908.

[28] Sam Kee, vol. 5 file 4, Bills of Lading, Sam Kee to Wing Lee Chun, 25 February 1899, 28 December 1899; Sam Kee to J. Hori, 27 February 1899.

[29] Sam Kee, vol. 5 file 9, Bills of Lading, Sam Kee to Chin On, 1 November 1901; 11 December 1901.

[30] Sam Kee, vol. 9 file 2, Bills of Lading, 1906-08.

[31] The export figures are modified by "at least" because the compilation may be affected by missing records.

TABLE 2

Sam Kee Company Salt Herring Exports to China, 1904-1915

Year	Exports
1904 - 1905	573.29 tons
1905 - 1906	321.55 tons
1906 - 1907	587.59 tons
1908 - 1909	638 tons
1910 - 1911	1,005.8 tons
1912 - 1913	1,649.2 tons
1914	,1,544.25 tons

SOURCE: City of Vancouver Archives, Add. MSS 571, Sam Kee Company, vol. 9 file
1, Bills of lading and insurance certificates, 1904-05; vol. 9 file 2, Bills of
lading and insurance certificates, 1906-08; vol. 9 file 3, Bills of lading and
insurance certificates, 1911; vol. 9 file 5, Insurance policies, 1912-13; vol. 9
file 6, Bills of lading and insurance certificates, 1914-15.

The rapid growth of this export trade led to Sam Kee's direct participation in the processing side of the industry. Its plants were centred at
Nanaimo, on Vancouver Island, where the herring was caught in nearby
waters and immediately salt-packed for export. Local Japanese firms had
exported the fish to Japan prior to 1903, when both the Sam Kee and
Wing Sang companies of Vancouver began shipping the fish to Hong
Kong.[32] At the outset, Sam Kee merely purchased the fish from white
and Japanese packers, but soon it began to advance funds to packers to
ensure sufficient supplies for itself.

Sam Kee's role as supplier of capital and buyer of the finished products
relieved the cash shortages and marketing problems of early fish packers.
During the 1903-04 season the company advanced funds to Nanaimo
packer H. M. McCrae, charging him 7 percent interest per annum.[33]
When McCrae delivered his shipment of fish to Sam Kee, the company
paid cash for one-half the shipment and was allowed to defer the balance
for sixty days.[34] Sam Kee then received a 10 percent commission from
McCrae for helping to sell the fish.[35] In the early days of the trade, when

[32] Leung, p. 6.

[33] Sam Kee, vol. 6 file 4, H. M. McCrae to Sam Kee via E. W. MacLean, 19 February 1904.

[34] Sam Kee, vol. 6 file 4, Agreement between H. M. McCrae and Sam Kee, 14
December 1903.

[35] Sam Kee, vol. 6 file 4, H. M. McCrae to Sam Kee via E. W. MacLean, 19
February 1904.

there was little regulation or quality control over salting and packing procedures, Sam Kee also withheld part of its payment as indemnity against any weight loss or damage resulting from improper salting.[36]

By 1908 Sam Kee was dealing with several Japanese packers, principally Charlie Okuri and U. Makino. For the 1908-09 season both Okuri and Makino agreed to supply Sam Kee with one thousand tons of salt herring.[37] But still these two packers supplied only a portion of Sam Kee's total export volume, and the company purchased 800 tons of fish from another Japanese firm in the same season.[38] The firm's relationship with different Japanese packers varied over the years, with Okuri and Makino operating independent salteries on waterfront land owned by Sam Kee. Okuri and Makino received fish from Japanese fishermen, and their workers drained the herring and salted and packed it for shipment. Other Japanese packers later rented buildings and equipment owned by the Chinese firm, but earlier operators had rented only the waterfront land and put up their own buildings.[39]

Sam Kee's dealing with the Japanese packers also involved the lending of money. In March of 1908 Charlie Okuri borrowed $300 from Sam Kee for a six-month term, promising to pay interest at $2 a month and offering his saltery buildings and fishing outfit as security.[40] In turn, Sam Kee guaranteed to the William Hoggan General Store in Nanaimo that it would buy Okuri's fish upon packing and would pay Okuri's account at the store in the meantime.[41] Sam Kee was a demanding money-lender and did not hesitate to order its lawyers to threaten foreclosure over the Japanese fish-boats and fishing gear on which it held a chattel mortgage.[42] Sam Kee was a ruthless manager too. When it became displeased with Okuri's slow packing and his fishermen's sale of herring to other firms, it threatened to default on Okuri's account at the general store.[43] Similarly,

[36] Sam Kee, vol. 6 file 4, M. Komatsu and Co. to Sam Kee, 7 April 1904.

[37] Sam Kee, vol. 7 file 6, C. Okuri to Sam Kee, 22 September 1908; U. Makino to Sam Kee, 31 October 1908.

[38] Sam Kee, vol. 7 file 6, Awaya, Ikeda and Co. to Sam Kee, 21 September 1908.

[39] Sam Kee, vol. 1 Book 1, Sam Kee to Red Fir Lumber Co., Ladysmith, B.C., 15 November 1909.

[40] Sam Kee, vol. 1 Book 1, p. 54, C. Okuri to Sam Kee, 13 March 1908.

[41] Sam Kee, vol. 1 Book 1, p. 56, Sam Kee to C. Okuri, 13 March 1908.

[42] Sam Kee, vol. 1 Book 2, p. 24, Sam Kee to MacNeill, Bird, Macdonald and Banfield, 2 October 1912.

[43] Sam Kee, vol. 1 Book 1, pp. 312, 315, Sam Kee to C. Okuri, 10 December 1908, 12 December 1908.

Chang Toy,
founder of
Sam Kee Company

Sam Kee Company, 433 Carrall Street, ca. 1905

Sam Kee began to charge Makino ground rent of a dollar per ton of salt fish when it discovered that he was also selling fish to other buyers.[44]

In overseeing the Japanese packers, Sam Kee arranged for the purchase and delivery of all supplies. Salt was purchased from several Vancouver wholesale dealers including Colin F. Jackson and Company and Evans, Coleman and Evans to be shipped to Vancouver Island. It also bought salt for export to China.[45] Sam Kee bargained determinedly and demanded prices that it wanted.[46] For instance, in October 1908 it bluntly told A. R. Johnston that its price was too high,[47] and in May it rejected Evans, Coleman and Evans' offer of a December delivery on 100 tons of salt and insisted upon a November delivery.[48]

As backer and purchasing agent to the Japanese packers, Sam Kee made the most of its intermediary position in dealing with suppliers. The Hoggan general store in Nanaimo gave the firm a 5 percent discount for settling Okuri's account on a monthly basis.[49] Sam Kee then took a similar discount, without asking, on its own account at a local lumber firm, reasoning that it deserved to earn something for bringing its Japanese business there.[50] With another supplier, Sam Kee demanded that wholesale prices apply to its purchases.[51]

Sam Kee was a careful buyer of supplies. When it came time to purchase 10,000 wooden boxes for shipping, the company invited quotations from nine lumber mills on the mainland and on Vancouver Island.[52] Hardware wholesalers were also asked to submit quotations for nails and other supplies.[53] When rumours hinted that purse-seining for herring

[44] Sam Kee, vol. 1 Book 1, p. 388, Sam Kee to U. Makino, 15 February 1908.

[45] Sam Kee, vol. 7 file 1, Evans, Coleman and Evans to Sam Kee, 16 May 1908.

[46] See, for example, Sam Kee, vol. 6 file 11, Colin F. Jackson and Co. to Sam Kee, 7 June 1907. C. F. Jackson and Company subsequently reduced their price by ten cents a ton. Sam Kee, vol. 1 Book 1, p. 232, 27 October 1908.

[47] Sam Kee, vol. 1 Book 1, p. 232, Sam Kee to A. R. Johnston, 27 October 1908; vol. 1 Book 1, p. 245, Sam Kee to A. R. Johnston, 3 November 1908.

[48] Sam Kee, vol. 1 Book 1, p. 113, Sam Kee to Evans, Coleman and Evans, 18 May 1908.

[49] Sam Kee, vol. 7 file 2, W. Hoggan to Sam Kee, 19 October 1908.

[50] Sam Kee, vol. 1 Book 1, p. 758, Sam Kee to Red Fir Lumber Company, 15 April 1910.

[51] Sam Kee, vol. 1 Book 2, p. 40, Sam Kee to M. Furuya and Co., 25 November 1911.

[52] Sam Kee, vol. 1 Book 1, pp. 160, 186, 187, Sam Kee to various mills, 18 August 1908; pp. 198-200, Sam Kee to various mills, 12 October 1908.

[53] Sam Kee, vol. 1 Book 1, p. 163, Sam Kee to Wood, Vallance and Leggatt Ltd., 19 August 1908; vol. 1 Book 1, p. 164, Sam Kee to McLennan and McFeely Ltd., 19 August 1908.

might be prohibited by government regulation, Sam Kee quickly cancelled its salt orders and urged its supplier Evans, Coleman and Evans to verify the rumour,[54] and when the company declined a salt purchase from C. Gardiner Johnston in August 1908, it alleged that the cancellation had arisen due to the inability of Japanese fishermen to secure fishing licences.[55]

Pressures to restrict the number of licences issued to Japanese fishermen were an ongoing concern to Sam Kee. The company usually paid a white agent in Nanaimo to obtain the necessary licences for its Japanese packers.[56] In July 1909 Sam Kee was sufficiently concerned to instruct agent H. J. Simpson to interview the Fisheries Commissioner with regard to hostile protests about the Japanese fishermen.[57] Next year Sam Kee discovered that white saltery owners were attempting to manipulate the number of licences issued, and it requested that Simpson handle the matter.[58] Things worsened in 1911 when only fifteen licences were granted, and the firm had to send discreet funds to its Nanaimo agent to sway the situation in its favour.[59] In 1910 Sam Kee had approached Furuya and Company, a major Seattle-based herring exporter, about jointly setting up an arrangement to control the salt herring industry, noting that the white packers had tried to do so already but without success.[60] No further details on this matter were found in the company's records, but it would appear that Sam Kee wanted either to set up a buyers' syndicate to obtain fishing licences en bloc or to stop competing buyers from bidding up the price of herring and cornering the supplies of fish.

During 1909 Sam Kee contemplated exploiting new sources of herring located at Swanson Bay and in the Queen Charlotte Islands farther up the coast. In March the company informed local agents for the major trans-Pacific steamship lines that it would be receiving salt herring from northern British Columbia for shipment to China, and it wanted to ship

54 Sam Kee, vol. 1 Book 1, p. 129, Sam Kee to A. E. Planta, 18 June 1908; vol. 1 Book 1, p. 130, Sam Kee to Evans, Coleman and Evans, 18 June 1908.

55 Sam Kee, vol. 1 Book 1, p. 170, Sam Kee to C. Gardiner Johnston, 27 August 1908.

56 Sam Kee, vol. 1 Book 1, pp. 646, 747, Sam Kee to J. H. Simpson, 18 June 1909, 11 March 1910.

57 Sam Kee, vol. 1 Book 1, p. 659, Sam Kee to J. H. Simpson, 3 July 1909.

58 Sam Kee, vol. 1 Book 1, pp. 750, 753, Sam Kee to J. H. Simpson, 18 March 1910, 20 March 1910.

59 Sam Kee, vol. 7 file 7, George Hannay to Sam Kee, 6 September 1911.

60 Sam Kee, vol. 1 Book 1, p. 748, Sam Kee to M. Furuya, 14 March 1910; vol. 1 Book 1, p. 755, Sam Kee to M. Furuya, 28 March 1910.

directly out of Victoria rather than out of Vancouver or Seattle.[61] The NYK, Waterhouse and Blue Funnel lines responded positively and offered to discount the cost of transfers between Victoria and Seattle if Seattle shipments were necessary.[62] At this stage Sam Kee was shipping such large volumes of fish that coastal steamship companies and agents such as the Coast Shipping Company and Evans, Coleman and Evans would send Sam Kee their sailing schedules well in advance of the herring season.[63]

The northern shipments did not materialize, however, and Sam Kee continued to rely on Nanaimo for most of its herring and added new Japanese packers to its list of suppliers. The export volume expanded through the 1910 decade, and competition from other Chinese exporters arose.[64] The firm considered buying more waterfront property in Nanaimo to expand its operations, but no frontage with a deep enough moorage could be found.[65] For the 1909-10 season, Makino supplied Sam Kee with 292 tons of salt herring, Nakaji and Modokoro 374 tons, and Takeda 528 tons.[66] Sam Kee instructed its agent to watch that these three suppliers did not sell any herring to its competitors, noting that if Makino misbehaved, the company would move to have the Inspector of Fisheries cancel his licence immediately.[67] To meet the export demand, Sam Kee continued to buy salt herring elsewhere, from the Nanaimo Fish and Bait Company and through A. R. Johnston.[68]

By 1911 Sam Kee's investments in the Nanaimo salt herring industry included waterfront land and a wharf, two gasoline launches worth $3,500, fish tanks, a mess hall, a bunkhouse and other saltery buildings.[69] All were rented to Japanese packers under agreements closely resembling labour contracts. Takeda, for example, applied to Sam Kee in 1912 for some operating capital and for use of the company's facilities. Rent was

[61] Sam Kee, vol. 1 Book 1, pp. 497-499, Sam Kee to Dodwell and Co., K. J. Burns, and Greer, Courtney and Skene, 5 March 1909.

[62] Sam Kee, vol. 1 Book 1, p. 535, Sam Kee to Coast Steamship Co., 10 March 1909.

[63] Sam Kee, vol. 7 file 2, Evans, Coleman and Evans to Sam Kee, 22 August 1908; vol. 7 file 6, Coast Shipping Company to Sam Kee, 15 September 1908.

[64] Leung, p. 6.

[65] Sam Kee, vol. 1 Book 1, pp. 561, 584, Sam Kee to A. E. Planta, 18 March 1909.

[66] Sam Kee, vol. 1 Book 1, p. 767, Sam Kee to E. G. Taylor, no date.

[67] Sam Kee, vol. 1 Book 1, pp. 736, 812, Sam Kee to George Hannay, 30 January 1910, 23 November 1910.

[68] Sam Kee, vol. 1 Book 1, p. 726, Sam Kee to Nanaimo Fish and Bait Company, 8 January 1910; vol. 1 Book 1, p. 700, Sam Kee to A. R. Johnston and Co., 25 November 1909.

[69] Sam Kee, vol. 9 file 4, Insurance Policies, 1911.

charged for the use of the wharf and the boat, and Takeda had to agree to sell his catch solely to Sam Kee at specified prices and to purchase all nets, food, fishing gear and packing supplies exclusively from the firm.[70]

The Sam Kee Company's salt herring exports led it to extensive dealings with white business institutions and their representatives. This included the general stores, lumber mills and hardware and commission firms that supplied the salteries, marine insurance and steamship agents who arranged for local and export shipments, and the company's own agents in Nanaimo. In all these dealings, Sam Kee's actions and positions were guided by market demands and profit-seeking. At no point did it behave differently from any other astute business operation of the period. Sam Kee was not placed at a disadvantage because of its Chinese background. It behaved aggressively, secure in the knowledge that its volume of production and trade gave it advantages and power. Its middleman role was made possible by the shortage of operating capital among local packers, by the demand in China for salt fish, and by the existence of a viable transportation system over the Pacific.

The success of the herring trade did not hinge upon the Chinese immigrants' disadvantaged position in the general economy. By contrast, Sam Kee's work as a labour contractor did help to lock the Chinese into low-paying, semi-skilled work in other areas. The early economy of British Columbia was one reliant on using ready sources of cheap labour to exploit the various natural resources of the land, and middlemen contractors such as Sam Kee were an essential link to the pools of immigrant workers. Labour contracting pre-dated the company's entry into the herring trade and may have exposed it to a wider range of business practices that it used later to its own advantage. Certainly the business acumen that characterized Sam Kee's herring trade strategies surfaced in its labour marketing activities.

Contract labour and the Chinese have been studied with reference to the salmon canning industry,[71] but its key features also apply to the areas in which Sam Kee plied its trade. In the salmon industry, a cannery operator and a Chinese labour contractor drew up an agreement whereby the contractor agreed to supply men at a specified price to can a certain quota of fish. The canner provided a cash advance, which the contractor

[70] Sam Kee, vol. 8 file 6, Agreement between Sam Kee and O. Takeda, 18 November 1912.

[71] Paul Yee, "The Chinese in British Columbia's Salmon Canning Industry," in Garrick Chu, et al., editors, *Inalienable Rice: A Chinese and Japanese-Canadian Anthology* (Vancouver: Private Printing, 1980), pp. 9-11.

TABLE 3

Sam Kee Company Sawmill Contract Labour Accounts, 1906

Year 1906	Number of men	Wages	Expenses: food and supplies	Expenses as percentage of wages	Net wages received	Net wages as percentage of total wage	Average wage
Crew A							
June	16	$ 371.95	$ 57.05	15%	$ 314.90	85%	$19.68
July	14	288.05	81.85	28	206.20	72	14.72
Aug.	9	241.43	43.60	18	197.83	82	21.98
Sept.	10	207.50	48.60	23	158.90	77	15.98
Nov.	11	401.70	86.10	21	315.60	79	28.69
Crew B							
July	69	1,493.45	390.95	26	1,102.24	74	15.97
Aug.	96	2,154.19	563.76	26	1,590.43	74	16.56
Sept.	74	1,935.90	602.90	31	1,333.00	69	18.01
Oct.	58	2,025.95	648.00	32	1,377.95	68	23.75
Nov.	61	1,978.75	542.50	27	1,436.25	73	23.54
Dec.	64	1,975.40	590.40	30	1,385.00	70	21.64
Jan. 1907	57	1,312.37	498.00	38	814.37	62	14.28

Source: City of Vancouver Archives, Add. MSS 571, Sam Kee Papers, vol. 11 file 3 [Payroll], 1906-07.

used to entice men to take the job. Crews were then sent to the canneries
where they worked and were boarded by the contractor. At season's end
the contractor received the final payment and paid his crew their wages
less amounts deducted for the advance, room and board.[72]

However, if the salmon run for that season was low, or if any other
reason prevented the workers from filling the quota of fish stated in the
contract, the canner could refuse to pay the balance of the contract. The
contractor too could pass his loss onto his workers by inflating the costs of
provisions and food he had supplied. Thus workers could emerge from a
cannery having been fed and housed but denied their expected wages.
In short, the contract system shifted the risks of an unstable industry onto
the contracted workers and their contractor.

Sam Kee's many cannery customers included William Hickey, John
Wallace, William Hill and J. H. Todd, as well as such firms as the Burrard Inlet Packing Company, Malcolm and Windsor, Wurzburg and
Company and the Imperial Cannery.[73] Sam Kee's dealings revealed one
other way in which the middleman was vulnerable to the losses suffered
by the canner. In August 1905 the Canadian Canning Company sued
Sam Kee Company, charging that the firm's foreman had lost control
over his men and that the crew had failed to produce the required 1,200
cases a day.[74]

Yet, since they controlled the vital supply of labour that cannery owners
needed, the contractors were not entirely powerless. Canners were constantly demanding full and skilled crews of workers from Sam Kee.[75] In
two instances canners guaranteed in writing to Sam Kee that workers'
wages would be paid.[76] In 1901 Sam Kee's lawyers successfully issued a
garnishee against one canner for non-payment of its account,[77] but it
appears that the competition between the many Chinese contractors of

[72] *Ibid.*

[73] For a sample of his clients, see Sam Kee, vol. 1 Book 1, p. 96, Sam Kee to John
Wallace, Naas River, 15 April 1908; vol. 6 file 5, W. Hickey Canning Co. to Sam
Kee, 5 September 1905; vol. 5 file 1, Burrard Inlet Packing Company to Sam
Kee, 1897; vol. 5 file 4, Sam Kee to Wurzburg and Co., 9 November 1899; vol.
5 file 9, Imperial Cannery to Sam Kee, 12 April 1901.

[74] Sam Kee, vol. 6 file 5, Russell and Russell to Sam Kee, 11 August 1905.

[75] For example, see Sam Kee, vol. 1 Book 1, p. 645, Sam Kee to John Wallace, 15
June 1909.

[76] Sam Kee, vol. 6 file 5, W. Mowat to Sam Kee, 9 September 1905; vol. 6 file 7,
J. O. W. Brown to A. Desbrisay, 22 March 1906.

[77] Sam Kee, vol. 5 file 9, Cowan, Kappele and McEvoy to Sam Kee, 18 May 1901,
30 June 1901.

Chinatown precluded any possibility of their united action to improve bargaining and working conditions.[78]

The contract system functioned in similar fashion in the sawmill industry. Sam Kee supplied men for packing, jointing, knot-sawing and other jobs in sawmills, shingle mills and planing mills. The mills were quick to complain about inexperienced labour crews, about their late arrival, and about their insufficient numbers.[79] The contractor's vulnerability was exposed again when the Spicer Shingle Mill informed Sam Kee that if sufficient men were not on hand when needed, then the mill would hire additional men and charge their wages to Sam Kee's account.[80]

Two sets of tallies kept by Sam Kee for its sawmill workers in 1906 yield additional information on the nature of contract labour. Table 3 shows that the number of men employed fluctuated from month to month; in some months over twenty men were taken on or discharged. The amounts deducted for food and supplies ranged from 15 to 38 percent of the total wages calculated, so that workers eventually received on average 75 percent of the original wage. The average monthly wage also fluctuated, from a low of $14.28 to a high of $28.69, reflecting the different grades of wages paid for different tasks.

In 1902 Sam Kee began supplying workers to the newly established Knight Sugar Company of Raymond, Alberta.[81] Sam Kee furnished crews of "good, healthy and practical" workers under the supervision of an English-speaking boss to cultivate and harvest 800 acres of sugar beets for sale to the sugar company.[82] Contract terms, like those in other labour agreements, specified that if Sam Kee defaulted on the work it would have to pay Knight Sugar the cost of labour that the sugar company would subsequently engage.[83]

With the sugar beet contracts, Sam Kee protected its own position wherever it could. In 1904 it successfully changed the contract to have Knight Sugar accept the beets in good condition regardless of saccharine content or purity.[84] Earlier contracts had specified a 12 percent sugar

[78] Duncan Stacey, "The Iron Chink," *Material History Bulletin* 12 (Spring 1981): 105.

[79] For examples, see Sam Kee, vol. 5 file 9, E. H. Heaps and Co. to Sam Kee, 13 July 1901; Spicer Shingle Mill to Sam Kee, 13 May 1901.

[80] Sam Kee, vol. 5 file 1, Spicer Shingle Mill to Sam Kee, 22 March 1898.

[81] Sam Kee, vol. 6 file 2, Knight Sugar Co. to Sam Kee, 27 June 1902.

[82] Sam Kee, vol. 6 file 2, Agreement between Knight Sugar Co. and Sam Kee, 2 December 1903.

[83] *Ibid.*

[84] Sam Kee, vol. 6 file 4, E. P. Ellison to Sam Kee 17 November 1904.

content and an 80 percent purity in the beets.[85] Sam Kee also arranged
with the Canadian Pacific Railway Company for a guaranteed return
fare for the workers,[86] even though transportation costs were refunded by
Knight Sugar.[87] Sam Kee purchased land near Raymond in 1904[88] to
cultivate beets to sell to another sugar company[89] but had left the sugar
trade by 1907 without explanation.[90]

Sam Kee's ready access to Chinese labourers also led it to work in
logging and timber sales. Lumber mills, brickyards, woodyards and other
small manufacturers needing wood for fuel or for production contracted
with Sam Kee to purchase cut timber, paying according to the amount of
wood purchased.[91] In some cases the buyers held timber leases or owned
land which they wanted logged, but in other cases Sam Kee had to find
its own source of wood. Most sites were situated around Vancouver, but
some were located as far away as Ruskin, Stave Lake and Chilliwack.[92]
The wood products included shingle bolts, cordwood, long bolts and logs
suitable for use as pilings and telegraph or telephone poles.[93]

The contract terms varied according to the owner of the uncut wood.
One mill paid for towing costs while Sam Kee paid for stumpage; another
customer paid for a road to be built to remove the timber.[94] Yet another
buyer of timber supplied a horse for loading the wood and even promised
to pay for wood not delivered by year's end.[95] When Heaps and Company neglected to have the shingle bolts cut at Stave Lake promptly mea-

[85] Sam Kee, vol. 6 file 2, Agreement between Knight Sugar Co. and Sam Kee, 2
December 1903.

[86] Sam Kee, vol. 6 file 4, E. P. Ellison to Sam Kee, 17 November 1904.

[87] Sam Kee, vol. 6 file 2, Agreement between Knight Sugar Co. and Sam Kee, 15
October 1903.

[88] Sam Kee, vol. 6 file 4, E. P. Ellison to Sam Kee, 23 April 1904.

[89] Sam Kee, vol. 6 file 5, Agreement between Union Stock Company and Shum
Moon, 13 May 1905.

[90] Sam Kee, vol. 6 file 10, E. P. Ellison to Sam Kee, 20 February 1907; vol. 6 file
11, E. P. Ellison to Sam Kee, 13 April 1907.

[91] Sam Kee, vol. 1 Book 1, p. 29, Sam Kee to Douglas and Thomas, 3 September
1907; vol. 6 file 4, Harold Burnet to Sam Kee, 12 January 1904; vol. 7 file 1,
John Coughlan and Co. to Sam Kee, 25 June 1908; vol. 7 file 2, Joseph Chew
Lumber and Shingle Manufacturing Co. to Sam Kee, 3 September 1908; vol. 6
file 10, E. H. Heaps and Co. to Sam Kee, 28 February 1907 and 6 March 1907.

[92] Sam Kee, vol. 5 file 9, Dean Brothers to E. H. Heaps and Co., 1 August 1907;
vol. 1 Book 1, Sam Kee to Henry Fitzgerald, 17 November 1910.

[93] Sam Kee, vol. 6 file 2, Brown and Vanostrand to H. H. Chow for Sam Kee, 9
April 1903.

[94] Sam Kee, vol. 5 file 9, E. H. Heaps to Sam Kee, 8 March 1901.

[95] Sam Kee, vol. 6 file 11, Cascade Wood Co. to Sam Kee, 26 September 1907.

sured, Sam Kee was quick to remind them of their contract obligations.[96] When no satisfactory action resulted, the fallers hired a lawyer, and Sam Kee hastened to set up a meeting to avoid a lawsuit.[97]

Sam Kee subcontracted some of the logging work and once again acted as capital supplier. In November 1907 it entered a "partnership" with W. H. Chow to cut timber on 340 acres of CPR land. Chow undertook to fell and dispose of the timber with all sale proceeds to be submitted to Sam Kee's bookkeeper.[98] Sam Kee's cash advance to Chow was to be repaid from the profits, with interest set at 10 percent per annum. In another situation Sam Kee sold its contract for supplying timber and its camp outfit outright to a Chinese sub-contractor.[99]

Sam Kee proved once again to be an aggressive dealer in buying and selling its wood products. When the CPR invited tenders for cutting shingle bolts and timber on its land, Sam Kee argued that it should win the contract because it had already worked the site under another lessee and had spent some one thousand dollars putting in roads. Sam Kee bid $1.10 per cord, with instructions that an additional ten cents could be added if any firm should outbid it.[100] In August the firm purchased the timber standing in several sites in the Hastings Townsite[101] and later approached Arthur McEvoy, a prominent Vancouver solicitor, to tender the wood for quick sale to city hall, the City Hospital, schools, churches and "any other big buildings" to clear its stock before the summer.[102] When necessary, Sam Kee knew how to use the appropriate middleman.

In its business dealings Sam Kee encountered problems that any firm might have faced. Lumber mills accumulated unpaid debts to Sam Kee for contracts completed.[103] Other customers complained about the quality

[96] Sam Kee, vol. 1 Book 1, p. 529, Sam Kee to E. H. Heaps and Co., 8 March 1909.

[97] Sam Kee, vol. 1 Book 1, p. 648, Sam Kee to E. H. Heaps and Co., 19 June 1909.

[98] Sam Kee, vol. 6 file 11, Agreement between Sam Kee and W. H. Chow, 13 November 1907.

[99] Sam Kee, vol. 6 file 11, Agreement between Chow Mew and Sam Kee, 20 February 1908.

[100] Sam Kee, vol. 6 file 11, Sam Kee to CPR Land Department, 25 April 1907.

[101] Sam Kee, vol. 6 file 11, Edward Donlan to Sam Kee, 25 August 1907 re: timber on NW¼ of Section 47; Townsend Brothers to Sam Kee, 17 August 1907 re: NE and NW¼ of Block 44; H. Farlow to Sam Kee, 28 August 1907 re: NW¼ of Block 46.

[102] Sam Kee, vol. 1 Book 1, p. 13, Sam Kee to A. McEvoy, 5 February 1908.

[103] See, for examples, Sam Kee, vol. 6 file 7, C. W. Brown to Sam Kee, 8 May 1906 re: $950 debt; Fred A. Shore of Foss Lumber to Sam Kee, 8 August 1906.

of Sam Kee's shingle bolts and refused full payment.[104] The company pursued sales with other customers by guaranteeing good timber in its shipments.[105] Transportation posed a problem too, and Sam Kee complained to the B.C. Electric Railway Company about the lack of cars available for carrying wood into town. Sam Kee pointed out that it had built a spur line for one area and therefore deserved better service.[106]

The company's work in the lumber and logging industries may have grown from its charcoal manufacturing and woodyard operations which were running by 1898[107] and possibly as early as 1889.[108] Newspaper reports had noted that a "syndicate" of Chinese was making charcoal from the refuse of the Moodyville sawmill in an oven built by themselves.[109] By 1900 Sam Kee was running the Quick Delivery Coal and Woodyard at 48 Dupont Street, selling coal, coke, charcoal and wood to businesses such as chandleries, small foundries, restaurants, hotels, homes and other fuel dealers.[110] Charcoal was sold as far away as Calgary.[111]

Conveniently, the major charcoal customers were the salmon canneries, many of which Sam Kee also supplied with labourers. These buyers were located nearby along the Fraser River and at Steveston and further away at sites on the Skeena and Nass Rivers, Quathiaski Cove and Smith's Inlet.[112] Charcoal shipments averaged between 200 and 250 bushels and were shipped on the many steamships servicing the British Columbia coast. By 1907 Sam Kee may have had difficulties in supplying charcoal as it investigated purchasing the product from another manufacturer in town.[113]

In another retail venture that involved steamship tickets, Sam Kee combined its intermediary role between Chinese and whites with its mer-

[104] Sam Kee, vol. 7 file 2, Joseph Chew Lumber and Shingle Manufacturing Co. to Sam Kee, 3 September 1908.

[105] Sam Kee, vol. 1 Book 1, p. 129, Sam Kee to John Coughlan, 16 June 1908.

[106] Sam Kee, vol. 1 Book 1, p. 274, Sam Kee to General Superintendent, B.C.E.R., 14 November 1908.

[107] Sam Kee, vol. 5 file 2, Sam Kee to T. Dunn and Co., 1898 no date; Sam Kee to W. H. Morton Mining and Milling Supplies, 25 November 1898.

[108] City of Vancouver Archives, James Skitt Matthews Newsclipping Collection file M1765 "Charcoal," *World* clipping dated 22 April 1889.

[109] City of Vancouver Archives, James Skitt Matthews Newsclipping Collection file M1765 "Charcoal," clipping dated 6 January 1898.

[110] Sam Kee, vol. 5 file 5, Delivery lists, 14 February 1900.

[111] Sam Kee, vol. 1 Book 1, p. 114, Sam Kee to C. D. Taprell, Calgary, 20 May 1908.

[112] For examples, see Sam Kee, vol. 5 file 9.

[113] Sam Kee, vol. 6 file 11, Electric Turpentine Company of Canada to Sam Kee, 12 October 1907.

chant role of supplying goods and services demanded by the immigrants. By 1905 Sam Kee was acting as the Chinatown agent for the Blue Funnel Line and the Japan Mail Steamship Company through Dodwell and Company, a local broker. Sam Kee sold the tickets to Chinese travellers and boarded them locally as they came to town to await their ship's departure.[114] The competition among the various trans-Pacific steamship lines was fierce, with each having Chinese agents based in Chinatowns all across Canada. In 1909 Sam Kee appointed twenty-seven Chinese sub-agents for the Blue Funnel Line in thirteen cities including Montreal, Ottawa, Hamilton, Winnipeg, Swift Current and Moose Jaw.[115]

The pre-eminent firm in the industry was the Canadian Pacific Steam-ship Company with its fleet of Empress liners. In compiling information on this competitor, Sam Kee reported to Dodwell that just over 2,000 Chinese had departed from Vancouver aboard CPR ships in 1907.[116] The CPR's advantage, of course, lay in its ability to sell its steamship tickets at the same time that eastern travellers purchased train passage to reach the west coast. To counter this, Sam Kee and the Blue Funnel Line offered trans-Pacific passage at the same price charged by the CPR and offered its eastern agents a $2 commission if they sold these Blue Funnel passages together with the CPR railway fare without informing CPR officials.[117]

As the Chinese agent, Sam Kee publicized the advantages of the Blue Funnel Line carefully. It pointed out to its Chinese customers that there were no first or second class accommodations on board the eight steamers of the line, thus allowing all passengers to walk freely about and avoid being racially segregated.[118] The 1908 fare of $43.50 included passage, cartage and board.[119] The Blue Funnel Line, in line with its competitors, offered a discounted ticket to indigent Chinese, and Sam Kee was held responsible for verifying the applicants' neediness.[120]

Sam Kee was also quick to report passengers' complaints to Dodwell, noting that bad publicity not only injured the Blue Funnel Lines traffic but also gave the CPR a better chance to regain its share of the busi-

[114] Sam Kee, vol. 18 file 17 " 代理藍烟通輪船寫位記 " [Record of Writing Seats on Behalf of Blue Funnel Line], 1905.

[115] Sam Kee, vol. 1 Book 1, pp. 611-13, Sam Kee to Dodwell and Co., 7 May 1909.

[116] Sam Kee, vol. 1 Book 1, p. 148, Sam Kee to Dodwell and Co., 30 May 1908.

[117] Sam Kee, vol. 1 Book 1, p. 203, Sam Kee to Dodwell and Co., October 1908.

[118] Sam Kee, vol. 1 Book 1, p. 443, Translation of Advertisement, no date.

[119] *Ibid.*

[120] Sam Kee, vol. 1 Book 1, p. 239, Sam Kee to Dodwell and Co., 2 November 1908.

ness.[121] In 1908 the indigent rate was raised by all the steamship lines to $30 from $25.[122] In 1910, when Dodwell considered raising the passage to match the CPR's higher fares, Sam Kee advised against doing so because the Chinese would prefer to travel aboard the Empresses if steamship prices were identical.[123]

In the land-owning arena, Sam Kee became one of the first Chinese to buy land in Chinatown, then centred around the unit block of East Pender (then Dupont Street) at Carrall and extending east towards the 100 block East Pender.[124] Originally the lots had formed part of the land grant used to entice the Canadian Pacific Railway Company to locate its terminus in Vancouver instead of in Port Moody. These lots had passed quickly into the hands of a succession of white speculators who rented the property to the Chinese for use as stores and dwellings. In some cases the Chinese tenants were authorized to erect their own buildings.[125] Not until the early 1900s did the Chinese purchase most of the remaining Chinatown lands. For its part, Sam Kee held some ten lots in the Chinatown area,[126] but its acquisitions elsewhere in the city were far more extensive.

Outside Chinatown, the company purchased two corner sites in Gastown and another at the downtown intersection of Pender and Richards Streets.[127] Residential hotels and apartment buildings containing commercial space existed or were erected on these lots, which were then leased to non-Chinese hotel operators or turned over to white real estate agents for

[121] Sam Kee, vol. 1 Book 1, p. 799, Sam Kee to Dodwell and Co., 25 October 1910.

[122] Sam Kee, vol. 7 file 8, Dodwell and Co. to Sam Kee, 7 December 1908.

[123] Sam Kee, vol. 1 Book 1, p. 810, Sam Kee to Dodwell and Co., 19 November 1910.

[124] British Columbia. Ministry of the Attorney General. Land Titles Office. Absolute Fees Book, Volume 21, Folio 280, Henry Town to Chang Toy, 25 September 1889.

[125] For two examples see Land Titles Office (hereafter LTO), Charge Book Volume 12, folio 424, lease dated 15 February 1893 between John M. Spinks and Hing Kee. This was a fifteen-year lease, with the lessee agreeing to pay rent of $20 per month, to remit one-half of the amount of assessed taxes, and to erect a building. A twenty-year lease is contained in LTO Applications Series, #4772E. The lessors were W. J. Bowser and George I. Wilson, the lessees were Yip Yen and Yip Sang. The lease is dated 4 August 1902, and the lessees agreed to erect a two-storey brick building within five years of the signing of the lease.

[126] Sam Kee, vol. 10 file 7, List of taxes due, 1905, and vol. 10 file 9, List of taxes due, 1911.

[127] The Gastown sites were Lots 9-11, Block 2, DL 196, and the south 55 feet of Lot 15, Block 2, DL 541. Sam Kee vol. 10 file 7, City of Vancouver to Sam Kee, 23 September 1910; vol. 10 file 5, Mortgage between Shum Moon and Francis Walter Hall, 1 August 1906. The downtown site included Lots 19-20, Block 25, DL 541. Sam Kee, vol. 10 file 6, City of Vancouver to Sam Kee, 30 August 1904.

rent collection. Sam Kee owned five hotel sites and buildings in central Vancouver and leased from German entrepreneur Edward Stolterfoht two sites on which it then constructed hotels for sub-leasing.[128]

In managing its hotels, the firm dealt firmly with civic officials through its lawyers R. R. Parkes and W. A. Macdonald, K.C. In March 1911 the city health inspector condemned Sam Kee's Oriental Hotel and ordered it demolished. The company, however, argued that its solicitor and architect had consulted earlier with two civic aldermen and the building inspector, and they had all agreed to let the building stand for another five years. Sam Kee ordered its lawyer to appeal the decision, but in vain.[129] In another instance, when the city expropriated one of Sam Kee's Pender Street lots, the firm instructed its lawyers to start negotiations at $70,000 to reach the desired price of $62,000.[130]

Elsewhere in Vancouver, Sam Kee bought land fronting on Burrard and on Hastings Streets, both of which became major thoroughfares in the city.[131] Sam Kee also held water frontage on the industrial south shore of False Creek,[132] as well as land in what later became the southeast sector of Vancouver.[133] More land was acquired in the neighbouring districts of Burnaby, North Vancouver, Steveston, Caulfield (later West Vancouver) and the Hastings Townsite.[134] Land, of course, represented

[128] Sam Kee, vol. 1 Book 1, p. 133, Sam Kee to Ed. Stolterfoht, 22 June 1908; Sam Kee to R. R. Forshaw, 10 October 1910.

[129] Sam Kee, vol. 2 Book 1, p. 16, Sam Kee to R. R. Parkes, 31 March 1911.

[130] Sam Kee, vol. 2 Book 1, p. 15, Sam Kee to W. A. Macdonald, K.C., 30 March 1911.

[131] These were Lots 9 and north ½ of Lot 10, Block 40, DL 541 and Lots 4, 5, Block 100, DL 541. Sam Kee vol. 10 file 9, typescript list of property taxes due to City of Vancouver, 1911. Also Lots 9 and 10 Block 8 DL 183D in Sam Kee vol. 10 file 9, typescript list of property taxes due to City of Vancouver, 1911.

[132] These were Lot 23, Block 2, DL 200A in Sam Kee vol. 10 file 7, City of Vancouver to Sam Kee, 23 September 1910; and Lot 12, Block 9 DL 200A, Sam Kee, vol. file 9, typescript list of property taxes due to City of Vancouver 1911.

[133] These were the following: DL 394, Block 15, Subdivision 5-9 in Sam Kee, vol. 10 file 7, Municipality of South Vancouver to Sam Kee, 26 June 1907; DL 714, East ½, Southwest ¼ in Sam Kee, vol. 10 file 7, Municipality of South Vancouver to Sam Kee, 26 June 1907; DL. 648, East ½, Subdivision 5, Lots 6-9 in Sam Kee, vol. 10 file 7, Municipality of South Vancouver to Sam Kee, 1908 Tax Statement; DL 335, L½, East ¼ in Sam Kee, vol. 10 file 7, Municipality of South Vancouver to Sam Kee, Tax Statement, 1 November 1911; DL 335, South ½, Southeast ½, Sam Kee, vol. 10 file 7, Municipality of South Vancouver to Sam Kee, Tax Statement, 18 October 1910; DL. 14, Lots 1-4, 7-22, Sam Kee, vol. 10 file 11, Municipality of South Vancouver to Sam Kee.

[134] Sam Kee, vol. 10 file 7, Richmond Municipality to Sam Kee, 12 December 1908 for Steveston Block 2, Lot 3; vol. 10 file 7, District of North Vancouver to Sam Kee, 15 November 1911 re DL. 887, Block 4; vol. 10 file 7, W. L. Fagan to Sam Kee, 24 June 1907 re: Hastings Townsite Section 45, East Pt. SW½.

the most permanent of assets, prized in China for its ability to generate food, rental income and loans.

As one of Chinatown's merchant princes, Chang Toy showed interest in the development of Chinese education in the community. In 1905, Toy added a third floor to his Carrall Street building to serve as a Chinese language school and as a hostel for visiting scholars. The school (愛國學堂) was closely associated with the Chinese Empire Reform Association. The hostel contained a living room, kitchen, warm air and hot water heaters and washing facilities. Also consistent with the custom of wealthy Chinese men, Chang Toy took several wives. At least two of his five wives provided him with many Canadian-born children. Chang Toy died in 1920.

*   *   *

The slice of company life presented in this paper attests again to the importance of business in facilitating immigrant settlement in the New World. Other studies have noted how the institution of business carried Italian migrants over the ocean, helped them find work and shelter and, in the case of boarding houses, re-established familiar Old World social patterns.[135] Elsewhere, the prominence of commerce and trading in South China peasant life has been noted, as well as the cross-over of credit devices from China to Canada.[136] The Sam Kee Company, while not operating at a level of trade shared by average entrepreneurs, did play its own distinct role in immigrant adjustment.

The success of the Sam Kee Company reflected upon both immigrant initiative and host society tolerance. The firm stood out as an enterprise ably surviving in the local economy with regional and international linkages. It bought and sold herring, salting supplies, charcoal and transportation services like any merchant and invested in real estate, making money in areas quite separate from the servicing of immigrant needs. In these matters, race did not interfere with doing business as the industrial interests of Vancouver and Sam Kee seemed to share mutual needs met by the trading of goods and services. The scale and diversity of Sam Kee's operations, of course, placed it into an elite class of Chinese merchants, and the small number of these firms allowed whites to see them as nonthreatening operations worthy of trade.

[135] Robert F. Harney, "Boarding and Belonging: Thoughts on Sojourner Institutions," *Urban History Review* 2 (1978): 8-37.

[136] Paul Yee, "Business Devices from Two Worlds: The Chinese in Early Vancouver," *BC Studies* 62 (1984): 44-67.

Sam Kee, of course, did not conduct business to test white racism. Its aim was to pursue profits by seizing all available opportunities to market goods and services. The firm's growth followed a logical chain of interconnected activities. Labour contracting and retail sales attracted Chinese customers to the store, where steamship tickets were later sold. The firm's shipping connections to China facilitated its remittance function and herring exports. Products from contract logging were channelled into its charcoal manufactory and woodyard sales. Charcoal sales then reinforced contacts with salmon canneries where labour was supplied.

While the company's activities demonstrated fundamental business acumen and aggressiveness, they also reflected upon Sam Kee's unique role as middleman between two cultures. Certainly the company profited as remittance agent, steamship ticket seller and importer, but under its labour contractor hat it had to acknowledge the limited power of the Chinese labourers in the workplace. The extra obligations that the firm (and workers) shouldered over quotas of cans, sugar and lumber were terms dictated by white employers who knew that job opportunities for the Chinese were limited.

Studies of immigrant middlemen have commented upon their exploitative nature, but the limited evidence presented here does not reveal how much profit Sam Kee was deriving from its contract workers. Doubtless a profit was made, but this was accepted by the immigrant community because a cultural and linguistic gap precluded direct communication between employer and employee. The middleman broker was a familiar model to the Chinese as well, having functioned in the treaty ports of Hong Kong and Canton.

The company's many middleman activities facilitated the adjustment of early migrants and reduced the trauma of settlement in a foreign land. Amid the adverse racial setting, the company helped newcomers realize their migration ambitions by providing jobs, food and contact with the mother country. The company's efforts did not alter the racial climate or directly promote greater acceptance of the Chinese minority. Instead, it merely helped the newcomers co-exist peacefully beside their inhospitable hosts. In some functions, the company brought Chinese into greater contact with other Canadians, while in others it helped the Chinese retain their self-sufficiency.

Importantly, Sam Kee's activities reveal how the institution of business encouraged newcomers to act and behave as economic men without concern about colour. These non-racist encounters were limited to a small circle of businessmen and did not generally affect race relations, but the viability and impressive wealth of the Sam Kee Company demonstrated clearly to the immigrant community that there was indeed room in the host society economy for them to work and prosper.

It was in the business arena that host society acceptance of the Chinese was the greatest. Thus, the success of firms such as Sam Kee stimulated the hopes of smaller operators that they too might enjoy comparable success and similarly bring their families over. Indeed, it can be observed that the continuing settlement of the Chinese community in Canada was founded largely upon family and business stakes. Finally, despite the common language of the Chinese as victims of racism and industrial capitalism, their business ambitions and endeavours prove them far from powerless.

Neighbourhood and Community in Interwar Vancouver: Residential Differentiation and Civic Voting Behaviour

JEAN BARMAN

For a quarter century after incorporation in 1886, Vancouver experienced rapid growth. Its population approached 14,000 within five years, despite depression doubled over the next decade, and then almost quadrupled to surpass 100,000 by 1911. Concurrently, settlement pushed out from an enclave on Burrard Inlet westward along the water's edge, east as far as neighbouring Burnaby, and south to the two residential suburbs of South Vancouver and Point Grey. The inevitable concomitant was, as numerous historians have detailed, residential diversity.[1] As new arrivals sought out suitable living arrangements, so they congregated in neighbourhoods reflecting their socio-economic status and possibly also their racial and ethnic background. By the time of the First World War Vancouver's

[1] I am grateful to Bob McDonald and Pat Roy for their perceptive critiques of this essay. On the early history of Vancouver, see Norbert MacDonald, " 'C.P.R. Town': The City-Building Process in Vancouver, 1860-1914," pp. 382-412 in *Shaping the Urban Landscape: Aspects of the Canadian City-Building Process*, ed. G. A. Stelter and A. F. J. Artibise (Ottawa: Carleton University Press, 1982); Robert A. J. McDonald, "The Business Elite and Municipal Politics in Vancouver, 1886-1914," *Urban History Review* 11 (February 1983): 1-14; McDonald, "Business Leaders in Early Vancouver, 1886-1914" (Ph.D. thesis, Department of History, University of British Columbia [UBC], 1977); Angus Everett Robertson, "The Pursuit of Power, Profit and Privacy: a Study of Vancouver's West End Elite, 1886-1914" (M.A. thesis, Department of Geography, UBC, 1977); Deryck Holdsworth, "House and Home in Vancouver: The Emergence of a West Coast Urban Landscape, 1886-1929" (Ph.D. thesis, Department of Geography, UBC, 1981); Edward M. H. Gibson, "The Impact of Social Belief on Landscape Change: A Geographical Study of Vancouver" (Ph.D. thesis, Department of Geography, UBC, 1971); Robert M. Galois, "Social Structure in Space: The Making of Vancouver, 1886-1901" (Ph.D. thesis, Department of Geography, Simon Fraser University, 1979); Donna McCririck, "Opportunity and the Workingman: A Study of Land Accessibility and the Growth of Blue Collar Suburbs in Early Vancouver [1886-1914]" (M.A. thesis, Department of Geography, UBC, 1981); and Patricia E. Roy, "The British Columbia Electric Railway Company, 1897-1928" (Ph.D. thesis, Department of History, UBC, 1970). Also of interest are Patricia E. Roy, *Vancouver: An Illustrated History* (Toronto: James Lorimer and National Museum of Man, 1980); Walter G. Hardwick, *Vancouver* (Don Mills: Collier-Macmillan, 1974); Chuck Davis, ed., *The Vancouver Book* (North Vancouver: J. J. Douglas, 1976), esp. "Neighbourhoods," pp. 45-116; Harold Kalman, *Exploring Vancouver 2* (Vancouver: UBC Press, 1978 rev.); and Michael Kluckner, *Vancouver The Way It Was* (North Vancouver: Whitecap Books, 1984).

BC STUDIES, nos. 69-70, Spring-Summer 1986

98   BC STUDIES

socio-demographic framework was essentially in place, particularly since growth henceforth moderated. During the 1920s increase in numbers came as much from the amalgamation of South Vancouver and Point Grey as it did from new arrivals, and thereafter the decennial growth rate has not exceeded 25 percent.

Compared to early Vancouver, much less is known about the interwar city and, more specifically, about the nature and extent of residential differentiation. What was the legacy of extraordinarily rapid growth? What had Vancouver become? A community? Or a city of neighbourhoods? An examination of two complementary contemporary sources, the federal censuses for 1931 and 1941 and annual civic electoral returns for school trustees, suggests that, despite the existence of geographical areas with distinctive demographic characteristics and voting preferences, most residents were at the same time bound together by common attributes and priorities. Neighbourhood and community were not mutually exclusive in interwar Vancouver.[2]

I

The residential diversity which characterized interwar Vancouver had its origins in the city's earliest years. From the 1860s a tiny lumbering community existed on the south side of Burrard Inlet between First and Second Narrows. At first it seemed as if this settlement at Hastings Saw Mill and nearby businesses at Granville about a mile to the west would form the nucleus of the incorporated city brought into being by the extension of the transcontinental railroad to the coast in 1886, but it very soon became clear that Canadian Pacific's management intended to attract newcomers to its large landholdings further to the west and south.[3] The immediate consequence was the emergence of the West End, as it was dubbed, as the city's most prestigious residential area.[4] Stanley Park, created shortly after Vancouver's incorporation, bordered the West End on one side; on the other lay the Business District, into which Granville

[2] The general literature on urban demography and residential differentiation and the emergence of neighbourhoods and suburbs distinguished by socio-economic, or class, characteristics is too extensive to be detailed here. For an overview of Canadian demographic structure, see Warren E. Kalbach and Wayne W. McVey, *The Demographic Bases of Canadian Society*, 2nd ed. (Toronto: McGraw-Hill Ryerson, 1979).

[3] For the railroad's precise holdings, see MacDonald, p. 384.

[4] See Robertson; MacDonald; and McDonald, "Elite" and "Leaders." Information on Vancouver neighbourhoods taken from Holdsworth, Roy, *Vancouver*, Davis, Kluckner, and J. P. Nicolls, *Real Estate Values in Vancouver: a Reminiscence* (Vancouver: City Archives, 1954), unless otherwise specified.

was subsumed, and beyond that the original area of settlement, known as the East End.

Other residential options became feasible as soon as public transportation made it possible to live apart from place of employment.[5] While difficult economic conditions dashed the original expectation that another West End would immediately follow the railroad's stimulation of streetcar service to its more southerly holdings in 1891, residences gradually began to appear on Fairview Slopes and at Mount Pleasant. While some homes, particularly those set on the bluff looking north over False Creek, were, to quote a contemporary, among "Vancouver's most striking residences," the majority were far less imposing. Their owners were more often clerks, small businessmen, artisans or others of "everyday means" unable to afford the West End.[6] Also made accessible by public transportation was Yaletown, on the edge of the Business District next to the Canadian Pacific works yards and home to many of its manual employees.[7]

During these early years additional pockets of settlement grew up in areas that would eventually become part of Vancouver. In the 1860s a seaside resort hotel had been constructed east of Hastings Mill at the north end of the trail linking New Westminster to Burrard Inlet. Movement into this area, to become known as Hastings Townsite, was encouraged by the creation of an adjacent park in 1888 and, more generally, by Vancouver's expansion eastward. In 1892, a year after interurban service was initiated with New Westminster, the intervening land mass was incorporated. The eastern section became Burnaby, which would remain a separate municipality, the area lying south of Fairview and Mount Pleasant becoming — with the exception of a small parcel of land subdivided about 1890 as District Lot 301 — South Vancouver.[8] South Vancouver appealed both to farmers and to working people eager to acquire their own homes but unable to afford property elsewhere, and settlements soon grew up around the interurban's stops at Cedar Cottage, southeast of

[5] Roy, "Railway," and McCririck, pp. 13-51.

[6] "Fairview and Other Suburban Districts," *Province*, 21 September 1907; Gibson, pp. 82-83; and Gladys Schwesinger, *Recollections of Early Vancouver in My Childhood, 1893-1912* (Vancouver: City Archives, c. 1964), p. 35.

[7] In 1901, according to Galois (313), virtually three-quarters of its male residents (72.6 percent) held working-class occupations. Yaletown was apparently named after the previous home of many of its residents, the railroad construction camp at the town of Yale in the Fraser Canyon.

[8] On District Lot 301, see Reuben Hamilton, *Mount Pleasant Early Days* (Vancouver: City Archives, 1957), and McCririck, pp. 88-100.

Mount Pleasant, and further along at Collingwood.[9] Other South Vancouver neighbourhoods developed near places of work, as with the quarry on Little Mountain and sawmills at Eburne along the Fraser River. By 1901 the municipality's population reached 1,500, whereas 27,000 people lived in Vancouver itself, another 900 in Hastings Townsite and District Lot 301.[10]

The years between the turn of the century and the First World War saw the population of Vancouver and its environs quadrupling and possibly quintupling consequent to a federal immigration campaign launched in 1896. Newcomers needed homes or, at the least, places to live. As the West End filled in, Canadian Pacific looked to its landholdings in South Vancouver as the best location for an equally prestigious residential development. Concerned that the municipality was taking on a visibly working-class character, property developers including company officials used their influence to have its western half separately incorporated in 1908 as Point Grey. Shaughnessy Heights was then opened up two years later as the intended home "of the coming smart set." Subdivided with an elegant park-like atmosphere, lots were especially large and the homes constructed on them by "Vancouver's richest and most prominent citizens" — about 250 in total by 1914 — visibly intended to display owners' status.[11]

Even as Vancouver residents with social pretensions and the money to effect their realization were achieving residential differentiation, so those at the other extreme of the socio-economic scale were becoming clustered in the city's East End. Many of its large residences from which Vancouver's earliest entrepreneurs fled to the West End had become boarding houses offering a refuge to the poor, to the transient and to "foreigners, Italians, Greeks and Russians." Particularly in the neighbourhood known as Strathcona, other forms of housing similarly intended for new arrivals of modest status or for males seasonally employed in resource extraction had also grown up, including "two-roomed tenement cabins that have practically no light or ventilation" and "rooms in blocks, where whole

9 Jeremy Barford, "Vancouver's Interurban Settlements: Their Early Growth and Functions — the Changes and Legacy Today" (B.A. essay, Department of Geography, UBC, 1966), pp. 5-10.

10 *Census of Canada*, 1911, v. 1, pp. 38-39.

11 Henry J. Boam, comp., *British Columbia: Its History, People, Commerce, Industries and Resources* (London: Sells Ltd., 1912), p. 175. Purchasers of Shaughnessy property were required to construct a house worth at least $6,000 and conform to designated style requirements, R. J. McDougall, "Vancouver Real Estate for Twenty-Five Years," *B.C. Magazine* 7, no. 6 (June 1911): 606; and Gibson, pp. 86-87 and 95-96.

families are crowded into one dark room without ordinary conveniences."[12]

For new arrivals who were neither very rich nor very poor, various residential options existed, both in and near Vancouver. Grandview, the stop immediately east of Strathcona on the interurban line to New Westminster, appealed to tradesmen, shopkeepers and workers at nearby dockside industries.[13] The provision of streetcar service to Hastings Townsite in 1909 heralded a steady influx of working men and women and, two years later, a successful local initiative by its 2,300 residents to amalgamate with Vancouver. Also in 1911 District Lot 301, with about 2,750 inhabitants, joined its much larger neighbour to the north. New streetcar lines made South Vancouver accessible to employees of False Creek's growing number of mills and businesses, while the dredging of the Fraser River in 1910-14 brought new industries and residential development to the southern reaches of the municipality. According to a 1912 description of South Vancouver, "the houses are mostly of an unpretentious though useful type, the population mainly consisting of the working classes of Vancouver."[14]

Other neighbourhoods took on a middle-class flavour. As Mount Pleasant and Fairview Slopes filled in, Canadian Pacific negotiated to extend streetcar service to its holdings further westward. Two years after Kitsilano opened up in 1905, it and neighbouring Fairview were being termed "better-class suburbs of the Terminal City."[15] A few years previous, interurban service had been initiated through Point Grey to Eburne to carry workers to Fraser River mills and canneries. Stops along the way, such as the farming community of Kerrisdale, acquired appeal. So did Eburne itself, to be renamed Marpole. As streetcar lines crisscrossed Point Grey, neighbourhoods grew up at West Point Grey and Dunbar Heights. The promise of residential exclusivity was a prime component of many developers' strategies, being underpinned by requirements to construct houses

---

12 Vancouver Board of School Trustees, *Annual Report*, 1911, pp. 59 and 63, and 1913, p. 40. For the variety of ethnic backgrounds in the East End, see the survey reported in *British Columbia Federationist*, 13 October 1913. See also Daphne Marlatt and Carole Itter, *Opening Doors: Vancouver's East End*, vol. 8, nos. 1-2 (1979) of *Sound Heritage*, and Patricia E. Roy, "Vancouver: 'The Mecca of the Unemployed,' 1907-1929," pp. 393-413 in Alan F. J. Artibise, ed., *Town and City* (Regina: Canadian Plains Research Centre, 1981).

13 McCririck, pp. 100-11.

14 Boam, p. 175. See also "The Making of South Vancouver," *B.C. Magazine* 7, no. 6 (June 1911): 645; and "Vancouver, a City of Beautiful Homes," *B.C. Magazine* 7, no. 12 (December 1911): 1315.

15 "Fairview" in *Province*.

of a certain minimum value. As a Point Grey developer explained to prospective owners, "this restriction is your protection and is ample assurance that your neighbours will be desirable."[16]

The parameters of residential expansion are evident from census data for 1911 and 1921, with the latter also suggesting the situation in 1914 when mass immigration ceased.[17] Over the first decade of the century, the original core of settlement extending from the East to West Ends through the Business District had filled in, its population of just over 60,000 remaining relatively constant for the next several decades.[18] The core's special appeal was to immigrants who as late as 1921 comprised 58 percent of inhabitants, with just over half born in Britain, the remainder in either Europe, the United States or Asia. Vancouver's residential periphery, extending from Hastings Townsite southwest across District Lot 301, Mount Pleasant and Fairview to Kitsilano, continued to grow, from 40,000 in 1911 to 56,000 a decade later. Unlike the core, most inhabitants were Canadian by birth and, of the 44 percent born elsewhere, three-quarters came from Britain. Growing at a yet faster pace were Point Grey and South Vancouver, the former's population tripling from just over 4,000 in 1911 to almost 14,000 by 1921, the latter's doubling to 32,000. While Point Grey's population in 1921 paralleled that of Vancouver's periphery, South Vancouver was much more a British immigrant society: 54 percent of its residents came from outside of Canada, fully 88 percent of them from Britain. In other words, in the periphery and Point Grey about one in three residents were British-born, compared with almost half in South Vancouver. Conversely, everywhere excepting the core about one in ten were non-British, or "foreign," born, and there they

<hr/>

[16] See Holdsworth, pp. 80 and 102, and Barford, pp. 12-18.

[17] Of British immigrants resident in Vancouver city in 1921, 90.3 percent of males and 82.3 percent of females had come to Canada prior to 1914; of immigrants from elsewhere 80.4 percent of males and 73.6 percent of females had arrived in Canada prior to 1914. No data is available for South Vancouver and Point Grey. *Census of Canada*, 1921, v. 2, pp. 418-19. The 1921 census utilized the federal electoral divisions, as well as city boundaries. The electoral district of Vancouver Centre comprised the West End, Business District, and East End, which equated both with city wards 2, 3 and 4 and the original core of settlement. The electoral district of Burrard took in the remainder, or periphery, of Vancouver city, and the district of Vancouver South, the municipalities of South Vancouver and Point Grey plus a small Indian reserve. See *Electoral Atlas of the Dominion of Canada, According to the Redistribution Act of 1914 and the Amending Act of 1915* (Ottawa: Department of the Interior, 1915).

[18] Comparable totals were 60,104 in Vancouver Centre in 1911, 60,879 in 1921, 65,537 in wards 1-3 in 1931, and 65,609 in social areas 1-3 in 1941. *Census of Canada*, 1911, v. 1, pp. 29-30; 1921, bulletin VI, p. 3; 1931, bulletin XL, pp. 16-17; and 1941, bulletin A-16, p. 2.

reached one in four. By 1921 Vancouver and its two municipalities contained a total of 163,220 residents.[19]

Thereafter growth moderated. Over the 1920s the combined population of Vancouver, South Vancouver and Point Grey increased by half to 245,593, due principally to buoyant economic conditions as Vancouver took advantage of its new strategic location consequent on the completion of the Panama Canal in 1914 to become a major terminus for the shipment of prairie grain. Between 1922 and 1928 real wages climbed by about 12 percent, twice that in Canada as a whole.[20] Neighbourhoods like Dunbar and Kerrisdale first opened up for settlement before the war once again became hives of building activity. Superseded by Shaughnessy Heights as the city's most prestigious residential district, the West End took on a new personality as its large homes became converted into or replaced by rental accommodations.[21] Then came the depression and stagnation, Vancouver's population edging upward to 273,354 by 1941.

Residential expansion during the interwar years centred in Point Grey, whose population quadrupled to almost 60,000, and to a lesser extent South Vancouver and the city's periphery, which expanded by two-thirds and three-quarters to almost 55,000 and 100,000 respectively. By 1941 the majority in each of the four areas were Canadian-born, their numbers ranging from just over half in the core upwards to two-thirds in Point Grey. Conversely, the British-born now comprised just a quarter of inhabitants everywhere excepting South Vancouver, where they held at 30 percent.[22] The parameters of Vancouver's population in 1941 strongly reflected the city's prewar origins.

[19] *Census of Canada*, 1921, v. 1, pp. 338-39.

[20] Eleanor Bartlett, "Real Wages and the Standard of Living in Vancouver, 1901-1929," *BC Studies* 51 (Autumn 1981): 53 and 57. The quantity of grain dispatched via Vancouver grew from just over a million bushels in 1921 to almost a hundred million in the bumper crop year of 1928.

[21] Harland Bartholomew, *A Plan for the City of Vancouver, Including Point Grey and South Vancouver* (Vancouver, 1929), p. 26. The transition appears to have begun even before the war: McCririck (73) found that 48 percent of West End voters in the 1911 voters' list were tenants. The debate generated by a 1926 bylaw provides much information on West End conditions. See esp. series A-1, v. 22, file 2, in Vancouver City Archives and press coverage, for instance *Province*, 21 October and 5 November 1926.

[22] This data is approximated from *Census of Canada*, 1941, bulletin A-16, pp. 16-17, by equating the core with "social areas" 1-3, the periphery with 4-5, 7-10 and ½ of 16, Point Grey with 6, 11-13, 17 and ½ of 18, and South Vancouver with 14-15, ½ of 16, ½ of 18 and 19. Based on this approximation, the core contained in 1941, 65,609 inhabitants, the periphery 98,112, Point Grey 57,765 and South Vancouver 53,925. The four areas had respectively 52.3, 63.2, 65.9 and 60.7 Canadian born and 22.5, 25.4, 24.5 and 29.4 British born, the remainder being "foreign" born.

II

The internal dynamics of interwar Vancouver, as opposed to its overall structure, are revealed in census and electoral data. Based on the units utilized by these two sources, Vancouver can for the purposes of analysis be divided into nine geographical areas which, while much larger than single neighbourhoods, for the most part possess some rough correspondence with the city's development as it occurred historically. Electoral boundaries changed repeatedly prior to the amalgamation of South Vancouver and Point Grey in 1929, when the eight wards used previously to elect aldermen became twelve.[23] The core retained its status as three separate wards, as did Hastings Townsite. By contrast, the large residential area extending from False Creek south to the Fraser River was divided into eight strips running north to south so that no part of the two former municipalities formed a separate ward. These divisions remained electoral units even after 1935, when voters opted for a completely at-large system for civic elections. Unfortunately, while the 1931 census utilized these twelve wards, the 1941 census classified Vancouver into nineteen "social areas" and the 1921 census had only divided the area between the core, periphery, South Vancouver and Point Grey.[24]

Nonetheless, post-amalgamation wards provide the most consistent basis for the city's division into geographical areas of approximately equal population and some residential coherence. The WEST END (ward 1) extends from Stanley Park to Burrard Street. The adjoining BUSINESS DISTRICT (ward 2) runs east to Carrall Street, and the EAST END (ward 3) east to Victoria Drive and south to Terminal Avenue. Contained within the Business District is Yaletown and within the East End both Strathcona and most of Grandview. The six remaining areas have here been named, for convenience of identification, after a longstanding area of settlement. HASTINGS (wards 4-5) takes in the area east of the East End extending south, primarily along Nanaimo Street, to the Fraser River and east to Burnaby. It thus includes not only Hastings Townsite but

[23] In January 1920 Vancouver voters abandoned the existing eight-ward system used to elect aldermen in favour of proportional representation based on twelve electoral units, whereby each voter ranked candidates for civic office in order of preference. The complexities of the system, including ballot tabulation also in order of voter preference, contributed to its replacement in a plebiscite of June 1923 by eight redesigned wards, which then held until amalgamation. On proportional representation, see *Province*, 9 January 1920 and 15 January 1921; *Sun*, 10 and 15 January 1921, and 17 June 1923; and Roy, *Vancouver*, p. 119. For boundary divisions between wards, see ward maps 5-8, Vancouver City Archives, and Barry W. Mayhew, *A Regional Atlas of Vancouver* (Vancouver: United Community Services, 1967).

[24] *Census of Canada*, 1931, bulletin XL, and in 1941, bulletin A-16.

Collingwood and extreme eastern Grandview. Southwest of Hastings is CEDAR COTTAGE (ward 6) and beyond Knight Street MOUNT PLEASANT (ward 7), extending west to Ontario Street and containing Little Mountain. Hastings, Cedar Cottage and Mount Pleasant together include the eastern half of Vancouver's periphery and almost all of the municipality of South Vancouver, whose western boundary was a bit further west along Cambie Street. The area as a whole was generally known as the East Side, just as the three remaining areas, together taking in the western half of the periphery and Point Grey, were referred to as the West Side. FAIRVIEW, bordered on the west by Burrard and Arbutus Streets and Angus Drive (wards 8-9), includes Shaughnessy and Eburne/Marpole, while KITSILANO, extending west to Trafalgar Street (ward 10), contains Kerrisdale. Beyond lies WEST POINT GREY (wards 11-12), also including Dunbar. Pre-1928 electoral divisions and the 1941 census have been accommodated so far as possible between these divisions, the former extending south only to Vancouver's pre-amalgamation boundary, which for the most part ran along Sixteenth Avenue.[25] See map, page 135.

When the censuses for 1931 and 1941 are broken down by these nine geographical areas, it becomes clear that the demographic communality which characterized Vancouver as a whole did not for the most part extend to two of the three core areas: the East End and, probably as a consequence of residential spillover, the Business District. Both areas were dominated by ageing males from non-English-speaking countries, many almost certainly long-time residents but others possibly recent arrivals due to the depression.[26] In 1931, as indicated by table 1, fully seventy-nine out of every hundred adults in the East End and seventy-four of one hun-

[25] In 1920, West End (ward 1), Business District (2), East End (3 and 4), Hastings (7), Cedar Cottage and Mount Pleasant (each ½ of 5 and 8), Fairview, Kitsilano and West Point Grey (each ⅓ of 6); in 1921-22, West End (district 1), Business District (2), East End (3 and 4), Hastings (5 and 6), Cedar Cottage (7), Mount Pleasant (8), Fairview (9 and 10), Kitsilano (11), and West Point Grey (12); in 1923-27, West End (ward 1), Business District (2), East End (3), Hastings (7), Cedar Cottage (4), Mount Pleasant (8), Fairview (5), Kitsilano (½ of 6), West Point Grey (⅓ of 6); and in the 1941 census, West End (social area 1), Business District (2), East End (3), Hastings (4, 5, 16 and ½ of 19), Cedar Cottage (½ of 10, ⅔ of 15 and ½ of 19), Mount Pleasant (½ of 10, ½ of 14, ⅓ of 15 and ¼ of 18), Fairview (9, 13, ½ of 14 and ¾ of 18), Kitsilano (8, 12 and ⅔ of 17), and West Point Grey (6, 7, 11 and ⅓ of 17).

[26] According to Roy, *Vancouver*, p. 100, "during the summer of 1931, a number of men established 'jungles' " in various areas of the East End. On the other hand, the number of male residents recorded in the census may have been lessened by virtue of its being taken in early June (1 June 1931 and 2 June 1941), when many winter-time residents may well have been away at seasonal work in lumbering, fishing or other resource industries. *Census of Canada*, 1931, v. 1, p. 29; 1941, administrative report, p. 3; and Roy, *Vancouver*, p. 26.

TABLE 1

Demographic Profile of Vancouver Population, by
Sex and Geographical Area, 1931

	West End	Business District	East End	Hastings	Cedar Cottage	Mount Pleasant	Fairview	Kitsilano	West Point Grey	Total
Male total	9,422	10,841	21,829	15,163	11,977	18,846	19,147	8,875	15,373	131,473
Mean age	36	41	38	28	27	30	31	30	30	34
Female total	10,393	4,658	8,394	14,459	11,685	18,376	20,757	9,767	16,631	115,120
Mean age	35	31	23	26	27	29	29	29	30	28
MALES' AGES										
% 0-4[1]	3.3	2.3	4.0	8.4	7.7	7.1	6.5	6.5	7.1	6.0
% 5-14	8.7	4.9	8.6	20.0	19.7	18.8	16.1	17.7	18.7	15.0
% 15-24	16.7	9.9	9.6	16.3	18.5	19.5	18.0	17.8	16.5	17.0
% 25-34	18.9	17.3	15.0	12.8	12.2	12.4	13.1	12.8	12.8	13.9
% 35-44	17.1	22.7	26.5	15.1	13.8	13.8	14.8	15.2	17.4	17.7
% 45-54	17.8	25.0	23.3	15.7	15.8	15.3	16.6	16.4	16.2	18.1
% 55-64	10.8	12.0	9.3	7.2	7.9	8.1	8.9	8.2	7.2	8.7
% 65 +	6.8	5.8	3.7	4.5	4.4	5.0	5.9	5.4	4.2	4.9
FEMALES' AGES										
% 0-4	2.7	5.1	10.4	8.3	8.0	7.5	5.5	5.7	6.8	6.7
% 5-14	7.8	11.5	21.7	20.1	19.7	18.7	14.2	16.1	15.7	16.5
% 15-24	19.6	20.9	19.3	18.2	19.2	19.4	21.6	19.3	17.6	19.4
% 25-34	18.5	18.4	16.3	14.4	13.5	13.2	15.4	15.3	16.6	15.3
% 35-44	18.5	17.3	14.2	13.9	14.5	14.7	15.9	16.1	17.6	15.9
% 45-54	16.3	14.5	10.5	15.3	14.0	13.8	14.0	14.3	14.0	13.9
% 55-64	9.7	8.0	4.5	6.3	6.5	7.1	7.3	7.6	6.7	7.1
% 65 +	7.0	4.4	3.1	4.1	4.5	5.5	6.0	5.5	5.0	5.1
MALE ADULTS' STATUS[2]										
% of all adults	47.4	73.5	78.7	51.5	50.0	50.7	47.2	47.0	46.8	54.7
% single	37.5	48.5	41.5	21.6	19.8	24.6	26.8	23.8	20.0	30.4
% married	57.4	46.2	55.1	74.3	76.4	71.2	69.2	72.4	77.3	65.6
% widowed	4.3	4.4	3.0	3.9	3.6	3.9	3.7	3.6	2.5	3.6
% divorced	0.8	0.9	0.4	0.2	0.3	0.4	0.3	0.3	0.1	0.4
FEMALE ADULTS' STATUS										
% single	32.7	22.3	14.6	12.0	14.1	16.8	29.0	22.1	20.9	21.2
% married	52.0	62.1	75.1	78.4	75.5	71.3	59.5	65.6	68.4	67.1
% widowed	14.4	14.4	9.8	9.3	10.0	11.3	11.2	11.9	10.4	11.2
% divorced	0.9	1.1	0.6	0.3	0.4	0.7	0.4	0.5	0.4	0.5

[1] All percentages exclude individuals about whom information not given.

[2] Adults defined as individuals aged 20 and over.

dred in the Business District were male, as were eighty-two and seventy-one a decade later. In 1931 the average male was respectively four and seven years older than the citywide mean of 34. By 1941, as detailed in table 2, mean age across the city had risen a year, but climbed three years in the East End to 41 and fully five years in the Business District to 46. The two areas also contained by far the greatest proportions of single adult males, in 1931 42 and 49 percent, compared with 30 percent in Vancouver generally.

East End and Business District males were further set apart, as made clear in tables 3-6, by their birthplace and ethnicity, and here the two areas differed significantly not only from Vancouver as a whole but from each other. Even though the East End took in most of Grandview, whose residents were not distinguished in the eyes of contemporaries from those of other similarly modest areas of the city, just over a quarter of East End males in 1931 and a third a decade later were British by ethnic origin, compared with three-quarters citywide. Conversely, almost 40 percent in 1931 had been born in China, another 6 percent in Japan, as had 9 and 2 percent across Vancouver. Proportions from northwestern and southeastern Europe were double city means at 8 and 7 percent. As well, 1 in every 250 males was black, a proportion which, while small, was four times greater than in Vancouver as a whole. The largest differential between birthplace and ethnicity in 1931 was among the Japanese, suggesting that many of the area's relatively small number of male children, those aged 14 and under, were Nisei. While proportions of East End males born in Europe and Japan grew marginally during the 1930s, that born in China more than halved to just 16 percent, due probably to a combination of age and Canada's restrictive immigration policy.

The sole census data which even hints at socio-economic status relates to illiteracy in 1931 and school attendance in 1941, the latter figures summarized in table 2. Only in the East End did the total deemed illiterate in 1931 surpass the number of residents aged 0 to 6½. By this rough measure, approximately one out of every twelve East End adult males could not read or write.[27] Similarly, whereas across Vancouver one in twelve males aged 10 and above possessed four or fewer years of schooling in 1941, one in four, or three times as many, were so limited in the East End. Conversely, one in ten Vancouver males aged 10 and above had 13 or more years of schooling, but just one in twenty-five had reached that milestone in the East End.

[27] *Census of Canada*, 1931, bulletin, pp. 16-17 and 31.

TABLE 2

Demographic Profile of Vancouver Population, by
Sex and Geographical Area, 1941

	West End	Business District	East End	Hastings	Cedar Cottage	Mount Pleasant	Fairview	Kitsilano	West Point Grey	Total
MALES' AGES										
% 0-4	3.1	2.3	4.6	7.4	7.2	7.0	6.0	5.9	6.3	5.7
% 5-14	6.3	4.3	11.1	14.6	13.7	13.3	12.0	12.3	13.2	11.6
% 15-24	14.1	7.7	11.8	17.1	17.8	17.6	16.5	17.6	16.9	15.6
% 25-34	20.3	13.5	11.5	16.5	16.9	17.6	18.0	16.2	15.6	16.3
% 35-44	14.3	17.8	14.8	13.3	11.9	12.1	12.7	12.5	14.1	13.6
% 45-54	14.7	20.6	17.2	12.1	11.8	11.8	13.0	13.5	14.6	14.1
% 55-64	15.5	20.8	17.8	11.7	12.2	12.3	12.7	13.3	12.2	13.9
% 65+	11.6	13.0	11.1	7.2	8.4	8.2	9.0	8.7	7.1	9.1
Mean age	38	46	41	30	30	30	32	32	32	35
FEMALES' AGES										
% 0-4	2.4	5.0	8.1	7.3	6.9	6.8	5.4	5.0	5.8	5.8
% 5-14	5.0	9.1	17.2	14.9	13.9	13.5	10.8	10.3	11.5	11.7
% 15-24	17.4	18.0	19.7	17.3	17.8	17.6	18.2	18.3	16.4	17.6
% 25-34	20.8	21.5	17.0	18.1	17.3	18.0	18.8	17.5	17.6	18.4
% 35-44	14.5	15.0	13.6	12.8	11.9	12.1	12.8	13.5	15.0	13.4
% 45-54	14.9	13.3	11.3	12.4	12.5	12.5	13.1	14.7	14.8	13.5
% 55-64	13.5	10.2	8.0	10.5	11.3	11.1	11.4	11.8	11.1	11.2
% 65+	11.5	7.9	5.2	6.7	8.3	8.3	9.4	8.9	7.7	8.3
Mean age	37	32	27	29	30	30	32	33	33	32
MALE ADULTS' STATUS										
% of all adults[1]	44.3	71.2	81.9	51.1	50.0	49.8	47.0	45.7	46.6	50.9
% single	33.8	46.4	39.1	23.2	23.4	23.7	27.2	24.6	21.9	28.7
% married	59.9	45.2	54.9	72.8	72.0	71.5	68.1	71.2	74.8	66.3
% widowed	5.1	6.5	5.4	3.6	4.2	4.3	4.3	3.9	3.0	4.4
% divorced	1.3	1.9	0.6	0.4	0.4	0.5	0.5	0.3	0.3	0.6
% 0-4 yrs of schooling[2]	3.0	16.1	24.6	7.3	6.6	9.3	6.7	6.3	4.0	8.3
% 13+ yrs	13.0	5.7	4.3	5.3	5.3	6.6	11.8	18.9	20.7	10.6
FEMALE ADULTS' STATUS										
% single	32.3	22.1	16.2	14.1	16.3	17.0	26.0	24.7	21.8	22.1
% married	48.9	58.8	70.1	75.4	71.6	70.2	59.0	58.0	66.2	64.0
% widowed	16.8	15.7	12.8	10.3	11.4	12.1	14.3	16.3	11.3	12.9
% divorced	2.0	3.4	0.9	0.2	0.7	0.8	0.7	1.0	0.7	1.0
% 0-4 yrs of schooling	2.0	9.5	20.1	6.9	5.5	7.4	4.4	2.7	3.1	5.0
% 13+ yrs	11.2	5.7	4.1	5.0	5.2	6.2	12.3	16.1	17.8	10.7

[1] Actual population figures not given since divisions only approximate those in 1931 census due to different units used as basis for 1941 census.

[2] Due to nature of original data, calculations perforce presume that individuals aged 15-19 possessed at least four years of schooling: to extent they did not, these percentages **are high.**

Only some of the minorities which congregated in the East End spread into the Business District. While the proportion born in British Columbia was by far the lowest in the city, a consequence of relatively few children, proportions born elsewhere in Canada and in Britain approached city-wide means. At the same time, one in five Business District males did come from China in 1931, one in six a decade later. One in 100 was from Japan, one in 300 black. The area had special appeal to north-western Europeans, who comprised one in ten male residents in 1931. Probably concurrently, as summarized in tables 7 and 8, one in ten was Lutheran, a proportion more than double the Vancouver average. As in the East End, males' mean years of schooling in 1941 were markedly below the city mean.

To be female in the East End or Business District was a very different matter, the relative paucity of females due primarily to the virtual absence of Chinese-born: in 1931 the East End contained 233 females born in China alongside 7,973 males. Proportions born in Europe were also smaller, especially in the Business District. The few females who lived in the two areas probably did so for quite different reasons, in the case of the Business District possibly due to proximity to employment. Mean age was three years above the city mean. As well, the area contained over twice as many females aged 20 to 24 as were 10 to 14, suggesting movement into the area in adulthood rather than residence from childhood.[28] Acceptability in the work force was probably assisted by 72 percent being British by ethnic origin in 1931, a proportion not that much lower than the city mean of 82 percent. Although the proportion dropped by twelve percentage points over the decade, while falling across the city by just three, the new "foreign" element consisted primarily of prairie migrants, who doubled to a quarter of the Business District's female population by 1941, and whose experience with Canadian life prior to arrival in Vancouver probably made them equally employable.

East End females were much more likely to be members of family groupings as spouses or children. Adult females, virtually three-quarters of whom were married compared with 60 percent in the Business District, shared their male counterparts' low levels of schooling. Fully a third in 1931 and a quarter a decade later were children and, concurrently, 41

---

[28] In 1931 11.7 percent of the 21,927 Vancouver working women were in trade, another 24.1 percent in office work, the figures rising in 1941 to 14.5 and 24.2 percent. *Census of Canada*, 1931, v. 7, pp. 238-49; and 1941, v. 7, pp. 218-23. On female employment possibilities during the interwar years, see Veronica Strong-Boag, "The Girl of the New Day: Canadian Working Women in the 1920s," *Labour/Le Travailleur* 4 (1979), pp. 137-46.

TABLE 3

Birthplace of Vancouver Residents, by Percentage,
Sex and Geographical Area, 1931

	West End	Business District	East End	Hastings	Cedar Cottage	Mount Pleasant	Fairview	Kitsilano	West Point Grey	Total
MALES										
Canada	45.1	32.0	28.0	53.0	53.6	53.3	58.5	59.2	59.2	48.6
Maritimes	3.9	3.4	2.0	3.1	2.7	3.1	4.2	4.2	3.6	3.3
Quebec	2.2	1.9	1.1	1.0	1.3	1.1	1.8	1.6	1.8	1.5
Ontario	11.7	10.1	5.1	6.9	7.6	7.8	13.1	12.6	12.0	9.3
Prairies	9.0	5.2	2.6	8.2	9.4	9.6	8.0	10.0	10.1	7.7
B.C.	18.1	10.9	17.1	33.7	32.4	31.5	31.2	30.7	31.7	26.7
Britain and possessions	41.0	28.3	12.6	35.2	36.8	36.6	27.3	33.4	33.5	30.1
Britain	38.8	27.2	12.0	33.9	35.4	35.5	25.6	31.9	31.9	28.8
Possessions	2.2	1.1	0.6	1.3	1.4	1.1	1.7	1.5	1.6	1.3
Europe	6.6	15.2	14.7	6.9	5.2	4.9	4.1	2.2	2.3	7.1
Northwest	4.7	11.1	7.6	4.6	3.4	3.0	2.2	1.4	1.3	4.4
Southeast	1.7	3.9	6.9	2.1	1.8	1.9	1.8	0.8	0.8	2.7
United States	5.6	4.3	1.7	3.3	3.6	3.2	4.6	4.1	4.0	3.6
Asia	1.5	20.1	42.9	1.5	0.8	1.9	5.4	1.1	0.9	10.4
China	1.1	19.1	36.5	0.7	0.5	1.7	2.0	0.5	0.5	8.5
Japan	0.4	0.9	6.4	0.7	0.3	0.2	3.3	0.5	0.4	1.9
FEMALES										
Canada	50.1	47.7	54.1	54.0	53.7	54.7	61.1	59.4	59.6	56.0
Maritimes	4.5	3.0	1.7	2.6	2.4	2.7	4.3	4.2	3.4	3.3
Quebec	2.3	2.1	0.9	0.8	1.1	1.1	1.9	1.9	1.6	1.5
Ontario	13.0	9.1	4.2	6.6	6.8	8.3	13.4	13.1	12.9	10.1
Prairies	11.1	10.7	5.9	9.0	10.2	10.0	10.6	11.4	10.9	10.1
B.C.	18.9	22.5	40.6	35.0	33.2	32.5	30.7	28.6	30.7	30.9
Britain and possessions	38.1	32.4	15.5	35.4	37.5	36.8	26.3	31.5	32.0	32.0
Britain	36.2	31.2	14.7	34.4	36.4	35.7	25.0	29.9	30.6	30.8
Possessions	1.9	1.2	0.8	1.0	1.1	1.1	1.3	1.6	1.4	1.2
Europe	3.9	9.3	12.6	5.6	4.1	4.0	4.1	2.7	2.5	4.7
Northwest	2.9	6.1	4.3	3.9	2.6	2.4	2.6	1.7	1.7	2.8
Southeast	0.9	3.0	8.0	1.7	1.3	1.6	1.4	0.9	0.8	1.8
United States	7.4	8.5	4.2	4.3	4.3	4.1	6.1	5.6	5.4	5.3
Asia	0.4	2.0	13.6	0.7	0.4	0.4	2.3	0.7	0.4	1.8
China	0.1	0.6	2.8	0.1	0.1	0.1	0.2	0.1	0.1	0.3
Japan	0.2	1.4	10.6	0.6	0.3	0.2	2.1	0.5	0.3	1.5

TABLE 3 *(Continued)*

Birthplace of Vancouver Residents, by Percentage,
Sex and Geographical Area, 1931

	West End	Business District	East End	Hastings	Cedar Cottage	Mount Pleasant	Fairview	Kitsilano	West Point Grey	Total
BOTH SEXES										
Canada	47.8	36.7	35.3	53.5	53.6	54.0	59.8	59.3	59.4	52.1
Maritimes	4.2	3.3	1.9	2.8	2.6	2.9	4.3	4.2	3.5	3.3
Quebec	2.3	1.9	1.1	0.9	1.2	1.1	1.8	1.8	1.7	1.5
Ontario	12.4	9.8	4.8	6.7	7.2	8.0	13.3	12.9	12.5	9.7
Prairies	10.1	6.9	3.5	8.6	9.8	9.8	9.3	10.7	10.5	8.8
B.C.	18.5	14.4	23.7	34.3	32.8	32.0	30.9	29.6	31.2	28.7
Britain and										
possessions	39.3	29.5	13.4	35.3	37.1	36.7	26.8	32.4	32.7	31.0
Britain	37.3	28.4	12.8	34.1	35.9	35.6	25.3	30.8	31.2	29.7
Possessions	2.0	1.1	0.6	1.2	1.2	1.1	1.5	1.6	1.5	1.3
Europe	5.2	13.4	14.1	6.3	4.6	4.5	4.1	2.5	2.4	6.0
Northwest	3.8	9.6	6.7	4.3	3.0	2.7	2.4	1.6	1.5	3.6
Southeast	1.3	3.7	7.2	1.9	1.5	1.8	1.6	0.8	0.8	2.3
United States	6.5	5.5	2.4	3.8	3.9	3.6	5.4	4.9	4.7	4.4
Asia	0.9	14.7	34.8	1.1	0.6	1.2	3.8	0.9	0.7	6.4
China	0.6	13.6	27.2	0.4	0.3	0.9	1.1	0.3	0.3	4.7
Japan	0.3	1.1	7.6	0.7	0.3	0.2	2.7	0.5	0.3	1.7

NB: Totals include individuals not specified by province or country.

and 45 percent respectively were natives of the province compared with a third across the city. Just half of the females born in an English-speaking country — Canada, Britain or the United States — were British by ethnic origin, indicating that many of the area's female children, like their male counterparts, were the offspring of "foreign" immigrants. More specifically, whereas 11 percent of females in 1931 and 8 percent in 1941 had been born in Japan, 23 and 21 percent were Japanese by ethnic origin, many of them very possibly the offspring of prewar male immigrants who had subsequently brought "picture brides."[29]

Contemporary observations by school officials confirm the extent to which East End children shared in, and were affected by, the distinctive

[29] Of 1,670 Japanese-born females resident in Vancouver in 1931, fully 42.7 percent had arrived within the past decade, probably before 1928, when immigration restrictions effectively halted the practice. *Census of Canada*, 1931, v. 4, pp. 466-69.

TABLE 4

Birthplace of Vancouver Residents, by Percentage,
Sex and Geographical Area, 1941

	West End	Business District	East End	Hastings	Cedar Cottage	Mount Pleasant	Fairview	Kitsilano	West Point Grey	Total
MALES										
Canada	55.5	39.9	43.6	60.0	60.8	61.8	62.0	65.4	64.7	58.1
Maritimes	3.3	3.8	2.0	2.3	2.2	2.4	2.9	3.1	3.0	2.7
Quebec	2.0	2.2	1.3	1.0	1.0	1.0	1.5	1.7	1.5	1.4
Ontario	11.0	9.3	4.7	5.5	6.3	6.9	8.9	11.1	10.4	8.2
Prairies	18.9	11.3	6.9	11.6	14.2	13.7	14.1	13.9	12.4	12.9
B.C.	20.1	13.2	28.8	39.6	37.0	37.7	34.6	35.5	37.3	32.7
Britain	32.3	23.0	14.4	28.0	28.8	27.8	24.6	24.0	27.2	25.6
Europe	5.7	14.8	15.6	7.0	5.7	5.2	5.6	2.9	2.6	6.9
United States	4.0	3.8	2.4	2.9	2.8	2.9	3.5	3.6	3.4	3.3
China	0.6	16.3	16.3	0.4	0.6	0.8	1.3	1.1	0.4	3.6
Japan	0.3	1.3	6.8	0.6	0.2	0.3	1.6	1.4	0.3	1.4
FEMALES										
Canada	59.3	60.8	62.4	61.7	60.8	62.4	65.7	66.1	66.0	63.4
Maritimes	3.1	2.6	1.3	1.9	1.9	2.2	2.9	3.6	3.0	2.6
Quebec	1.9	1.3	1.0	0.8	0.8	0.9	1.5	1.8	1.6	1.3
Ontario	11.1	7.5	3.4	5.4	5.7	6.6	10.1	11.1	10.6	8.5
Prairies	22.6	24.3	11.4	13.6	14.8	14.5	16.9	16.6	14.9	16.2
B.C.	20.5	25.0	45.3	39.9	37.5	38.1	34.1	33.0	35.8	34.7
Britain	29.1	20.1	12.0	27.6	29.9	28.3	23.2	22.9	25.3	25.0
Europe	3.6	8.2	12.1	5.7	4.7	4.2	4.4	2.8	2.3	4.6
United States	6.0	7.3	3.6	3.8	3.6	4.1	6.1	5.6	4.8	4.6
China	0.2	1.1	1.5	0.1	0.1	0.1	0.2	0.2	0.2	0.3
Japan	0.3	1.7	7.6	0.5	0.1	0.3	1.1	1.0	0.2	1.0
BOTH SEXES										
Canada	57.6	46.5	50.8	60.8	60.8	62.1	63.9	65.8	65.3	60.7
Maritimes	3.2	3.4	1.7	2.1	2.1	2.3	2.9	3.4	3.0	2.7
Quebec	2.0	1.9	1.2	0.9	0.9	0.9	1.5	1.7	1.6	1.4
Ontario	11.0	8.7	4.2	5.4	6.0	6.7	9.5	11.1	10.5	8.3
Prairies	21.0	15.4	8.6	12.6	14.5	14.1	15.5	15.3	13.7	14.5
B.C.	20.3	16.9	35.1	39.8	37.3	37.9	34.3	34.2	36.5	33.7
Britain	30.5	22.1	13.5	27.8	29.3	28.0	23.8	23.4	26.2	25.3
Europe	4.5	12.7	14.3	6.4	5.2	4.7	5.0	2.8	2.5	5.8
United States	5.1	4.9	2.9	3.3	3.2	3.6	4.0	4.7	4.1	3.9
China	0.4	11.5	10.6	0.2	0.3	0.5	0.7	0.6	0.3	2.0
Japan	0.3	1.4	7.1	0.6	0.2	0.3	1.4	1.2	0.3	1.2

NB: Totals include individuals not specified by province or country.

TABLE 5

Ethnic Origin of Vancouver Residents, by Percentage,
Sex and Geographical Area, 1931

	West End	Business District	East End	Hastings	Cedar Cottage	Mount Pleasant	Fairview	Kitsilano	West Point Grey	Total
MALES										
British	85.5	57.3	26.9	81.3	85.2	84.9	78.8	90.0	91.0	72.8
Europeans	12.8	21.2	20.9	15.7	12.9	12.3	11.3	8.3	7.7	14.0
Northwest	9.4	15.4	10.6	11.1	8.9	8.6	7.4	6.2	5.6	9.9
Southeast	1.9	5.0	8.9	4.1	3.7	3.1	1.7	1.1	1.2	3.8
Jews	1.4	0.7	1.3	0.3	0.2	0.5	2.0	1.0	0.9	1.0
Chinese	1.0	19.4	39.6	0.9	0.6	1.9	2.2	0.5	0.5	9.1
Japanese	0.6	1.6	11.7	1.6	0.7	0.4	6.3	1.1	0.7	3.5
Blacks	nil	0.3	0.4	0.1	neg	0.1	neg	nil	nil	0.1
FEMALES										
British	87.0	72.3	38.4	83.0	86.0	86.2	82.1	89.4	90.7	82.0
Europeans	12.1	22.5	27.8	14.6	12.6	12.5	12.1	9.3	8.5	13.3
Northwest	9.3	15.9	10.7	10.5	9.0	8.7	8.7	7.2	6.6	9.0
Southeast	1.5	5.7	13.9	3.6	3.3	3.2	1.5	1.2	1.1	3.2
Jews	1.1	0.8	2.9	0.4	0.1	0.5	1.8	0.7	0.8	1.0
Chinese	0.1	1.2	9.0	0.2	0.2	0.4	0.4	0.1	0.1	0.9
Japanese	0.5	3.1	23.3	1.7	0.7	0.5	4.6	1.2	0.6	3.2
Blacks	nil	0.5	0.6	0.1	neg	neg	neg	nil	neg	0.1
BOTH SEXES										
British	86.3	61.8	30.1	82.1	85.6	85.6	80.5	89.7	90.8	77.1
Europeans	12.4	21.6	22.8	15.2	12.7	12.4	11.7	8.8	8.1	13.7
Northwest	9.3	15.5	10.6	10.8	9.0	8.6	8.1	6.7	6.1	9.5
Southeast	1.7	5.2	10.3	3.9	3.5	3.1	1.6	1.1	1.2	3.5
Jews	1.3	0.7	1.7	0.4	0.2	0.5	1.9	0.8	0.8	1.0
Chinese	0.5	14.0	31.1	0.6	0.4	1.2	1.3	0.3	0.2	5.3
Japanese	0.6	2.0	15.0	1.6	0.7	0.4	5.4	1.2	0.7	3.8
Blacks	nil	0.3	0.5	0.1	neg	0.1	neg	nil	nil	0.1

attributes of the older generation. A 1920 survey of underweight primary pupils found that at one Strathcona school 48 percent were sleeping three or more to a room, 24 percent four or more, fully 14 percent five or more, proportions far higher than anywhere else in the city.[30] Four years later came the statement that the school's "pupils are chiefly Orientals and foreigners": "many of them cannot speak English when they enter

[30] At the second Strathcona school they were lower at 28, 12 and 4 percent, and in Grandview somewhat less but still above the city mean. Vancouver Board of School Trustees, *Annual Report*, 1920, pp. 40-43.

TABLE 6

Ethnic Origin of Vancouver Residents, by Percentage,
Sex and Geographical Area, 1941

	West End	*Business District*	*East End*	*Hastings*	*Cedar Cottage*	*Mount Pleasant*	*Fairview*	*Kitsilano*	*West Point Grey*	*Total*
MALES										
British	83.8	53.5	35.9	78.9	81.3	81.9	77.4	83.9	89.3	75.2
Chinese	0.6	17.9	20.7	0.4	0.8	0.1	1.3	1.1	0.4	4.3
Japanese	0.7	2.5	15.1	1.6	0.4	0.9	3.9	3.9	0.6	3.2
FEMALES										
British	83.3	60.5	38.6	79.5	82.3	83.0	79.9	84.4	88.8	79.4
Chinese	neg	4.0	8.2	0.1	0.3	0.4	0.5	0.1	0.1	0.9
Japanese	0.5	4.4	21.0	1.5	0.4	0.7	3.1	3.0	0.6	2.9
BOTH SEXES										
British	83.5	55.7	36.9	79.2	81.8	82.4	78.7	84.2	89.0	77.3
Chinese	0.3	13.5	15.9	0.3	0.5	0.3	0.9	0.6	0.2	2.6
Japanese	0.6	3.1	17.3	1.5	0.4	0.8	3.5	3.4	0.6	3.1

NB: Information not given for other major ethnic groups.

school." A comment at the end of the decade attributed the very high failure rate in grade 1 at a second Strathcona school to "foreign parentage, undernourishment, low mentality and an environment which fails to provide experiences essential to mental growth."[31] Whereas under normal conditions between 12 and 13 percent of primary pupils would be enrolled in grade 8, just 8 percent of Strathcona children and 9 percent of their contemporaries in Grandview achieved that milestone.[32]

The demographic attributes of East End and Business District residents contrasted sharply with the rest of the interwar city, where lived 80 percent of the population in 1931, over 85 percent a decade later. There the elements of communality that distinguished Vancouver as a whole were

[31] *Ibid.*, 1924, p. 73, and 1929, p. 98.
[32] British Columbia, Department of Education, *Annual Report*, 1923/24, pp. T32-49; 1924/25, pp. M32-51; 1925/26, pp. R34-53; and 1926/27, pp. M24-37. Data is unavailable for other years. Similarly, although citywide 7.2 percent of primary pupils annually gained admission into high school, just over 4 percent of East End children did so. Vancouver Board of School Trustees, *Annual Report*, 1924, p. 31; 1925, p. 24; and 1926, p. 26. Data is unavailable for other years. Pupil absentee rates in the East End were among the highest in the city, averaging 0.9 instances annually at the two Strathcona schools and 0.5 at the Grandview school compared with 0.3 across Vancouver primary schools. *Ibid.*, 1919, p. 76; 1920, p. 84; 1921, p. 78; and 1922, p. 88, with no later data available.

TABLE 7

Principal Religious Affiliation of Vancouver Residents,
by Percentage, Sex and Geographical Area, 1931

	West End	Business District	East End	Hastings	Cedar Cottage	Mount Pleasant	Fairview	Kitsilano	West Point Grey	Total
MALES										
Anglican	41.6	19.8	9.5	30.8	32.3	27.8	28.4	35.5	36.2	27.5
United	17.7	10.0	9.2	25.4	23.4	27.0	29.4	32.7	31.4	22.7
Presbyterian	15.5	14.8	6.7	17.5	19.0	18.9	13.5	11.1	13.1	14.1
Baptist	2.9	2.3	1.3	4.4	4.8	5.5	4.5	5.0	4.4	3.8
Lutheran	3.6	10.7	7.4	5.1	3.6	3.4	1.7	1.2	1.0	4.2
Catholic	9.7	13.7	12.6	10.1	9.1	8.2	8.0	7.6	6.6	9.5
Jewish	1.3	0.7	1.2	0.3	0.2	0.5	2.0	1.0	0.9	0.9
Confucist and Buddhist	0.9	21.2	37.2	1.5	0.7	2.0	6.3	0.8	0.8	9.5
FEMALES										
Anglican	41.9	25.1	14.7	32.0	32.8	28.1	28.9	34.1	35.6	31.0
United	20.0	15.8	16.0	26.3	24.1	29.0	32.3	33.6	31.8	27.3
Presbyterian	14.9	17.7	9.6	16.8	18.6	18.0	12.5	10.3	12.8	14.6
Baptist	3.5	4.1	2.9	4.6	5.3	6.0	5.1	5.5	4.5	4.8
Lutheran	2.5	7.7	4.8	4.4	3.3	2.9	2.3	1.8	1.2	3.0
Catholic	9.8	19.5	18.3	10.1	8.7	8.4	7.9	7.9	7.2	9.6
Jewish	1.1	0.9	2.9	0.4	0.1	0.5	1.8	0.7	0.8	1.0
Confucist and Buddhist	0.3	4.5	23.5	0.9	0.3	0.4	3.5	0.6	0.5	2.8
BOTH SEXES										
Anglican	41.8	21.4	10.9	31.4	32.6	27.9	28.6	34.8	35.9	29.1
United	18.9	11.7	11.1	25.8	23.7	28.0	30.9	33.2	31.6	24.8
Presbyterian	15.2	15.7	7.5	17.1	18.8	18.4	12.9	10.7	12.9	14.3
Baptist	3.2	2.8	1.7	4.5	5.0	5.8	4.8	5.2	4.5	4.3
Lutheran	3.0	9.8	6.7	4.8	3.4	3.2	2.0	1.5	1.1	3.6
Catholic	9.8	15.5	14.2	10.1	8.9	8.3	7.9	7.8	6.9	9.6
Jewish	1.2	0.7	1.7	0.3	0.2	0.5	1.9	0.8	0.8	1.0
Confucist and Buddhist	0.6	16.2	33.4	1.2	0.5	1.2	4.9	0.7	0.7	6.4

manifest. At least nine out of every ten residents had been born in an English-speaking country. Between eight and nine were British by ethnic origin. Moreover, everywhere excepting Fairview, where about 5 percent were Japanese, the majority of residents of "foreign" origin were north-western European, many of them Scandinavian, and so not visibly distinguishable from their counterparts of British background. Proportions

TABLE 8

Principal Religious Affiliation of Vancouver Residents,
by Percentage, Sex and Geographical Area, 1941

	West End	Business District	East End	Hastings	Cedar Cottage	Mount Pleasant	Fairview	Kitsilano	West Point Grey	Total
MALES										
Anglican	40.7	21.3	15.5	31.7	31.4	30.1	28.4	36.0	35.8	30.4
United	19.6	10.2	10.3	24.1	25.0	26.4	27.0	29.3	30.8	23.4
Presbyterian	15.8	16.3	11.5	16.9	17.1	17.5	14.7	11.6	13.2	14.9
Baptist	2.7	2.2	2.7	4.9	5.7	5.4	4.9	4.0	4.8	4.3
Lutheran	4.0	9.2	6.0	5.3	4.5	3.9	3.3	1.5	1.2	4.1
Catholic	10.9	16.8	20.2	11.1	8.8	8.7	9.2	7.9	7.7	10.9
Jewish	1.2	0.7	0.9	0.3	0.3	0.5	2.0	1.5	1.3	1.0
Confucist and Buddhist	0.9	18.5	27.0	0.9	0.7	1.3	4.2	4.4	0.4	5.7
FEMALES										
Anglican	40.2	24.3	17.5	31.5	30.8	29.2	27.7	34.9	34.8	31.3
United	21.9	16.0	14.6	25.9	26.4	28.0	29.7	30.9	32.4	26.9
Presbyterian	13.7	15.7	12.1	16.1	16.4	16.8	13.8	10.5	12.3	13.9
Baptist	3.0	3.5	4.2	5.5	6.3	6.1	5.4	4.4	4.7	4.9
Lutheran	3.4	6.6	4.7	4.7	4.3	3.6	2.9	1.8	1.3	3.2
Catholic	12.4	22.5	23.0	10.9	8.4	8.3	9.4	8.8	8.3	10.9
Jewish	0.9	0.6	1.4	0.3	0.3	0.5	1.8	1.3	1.2	1.0
Confucist and Buddhist	0.3	5.4	16.6	0.4	0.3	0.5	2.3	1.9	0.2	2.1
BOTH SEXES										
Anglican	40.4	22.2	16.2	31.6	31.1	29.7	28.1	35.4	35.3	30.9
United	20.8	12.0	11.9	25.0	25.7	27.2	28.4	30.1	31.6	25.1
Presbyterian	14.6	16.1	11.7	16.5	16.7	17.1	14.2	11.0	12.7	14.4
Baptist	2.8	2.7	3.3	5.2	6.0	5.8	5.2	4.2	4.7	4.6
Lutheran	3.7	8.4	5.5	5.0	4.4	3.7	3.1	1.7	1.2	3.7
Catholic	11.7	18.6	21.3	11.0	8.6	8.5	9.3	8.4	8.0	10.9
Jewish	1.1	0.6	1.1	0.3	0.3	0.5	1.9	1.4	1.2	1.0
Confucist and Buddhist	0.6	14.3	23.0	0.6	0.5	0.9	3.2	3.1	0.3	3.9

British by ethnic origin did fall slightly during the 1930s, the greatest decline being six percentage points in Kitsilano, partly accounted for by growth among the Japanese who appear to have been spreading westward along False Creek. Thus, to the extent that minorities escaped residence in the two core areas, it was, apart from small pockets of Japanese, primarily "invisible" immigrants, often in family groupings, who accomplished the feat. For instance, of the 1,857 Scandinavians by birth living in the East End and Business District in 1931, 87 percent, all ages included, were male, whereas the additional 5,830 who had spread out across the rest of the city were almost evenly divided by sex.[33]

Ethnic homogeneity did not signify any diminution in residential differentiation by socio-economic status. Such pre-existing structural conditions as differing average lot sizes between Point Grey and South Vancouver largely predetermined that, for instance, the mean value of building permits issued in the former, 1922-26, was $3,134, compared with just $996 in the latter.[34] A South Vancouver resident writing in 1920 had termed his municipality "the rendezvous of the artisan, the working classes generally," "the home of the industrial classes."[35] Nine years later a city planner considered South Vancouver, along with Hastings Townsite, the most suitable areas of residence for "those who have to earn their livelihood by manual labor," "a place where they can build modest homes which should differ only in size from that of the more opulent employers."[36] Conversely, Point Grey continued to exercise appeal among the wealthy and socially pretentious: of 1,200 entries with a Vancouver, South Vancouver or Point Grey address in a 1927 social register, fully half lived in Point Grey, just over a quarter in the West End, the remainder primarily in Fairview or Kitsilano.[37] A 1928 social survey of the three

[33] The same phenomenon was evident with the Finns: the 880 in the East End and Business District were 78 percent male, while the 653 scattered elsewhere across the city were just 43 percent male. On the other hand, the 513 Yugoslavs living in these two areas were 77 percent male, the 163 elsewhere 75 percent male. Comparably minor differences were evident in the case of racial minorities. The 10,307 Chinese born in the East End and Business District were 97 percent male, as were 81 percent of the 1,351 resident elsewhere. The 2,448 Japanese born in the two areas were 61 percent male, compared with 58 percent of the 1,685 living elsewhere. And 56 percent of the 257 blacks in the two areas were male compared with 46 percent of the 65 resident elsewhere. Unfortunately, similar data is unavailable for 1941. However, the breakdown of that census into smaller social areas does provide the additional piece of information that the Japanese resident in Fairview and Kitsilano were primarily concentrated along False Creek.

[34] Harland Bartholomew, *A Plan for the City of Vancouver, British Columbia* (Vancouver, 1928), p. 32. Also see Holdsworth, p. 189, and Roy, *Vancouver*, pp. 106 and 117. Over the first nine months of 1928, the average house constructed in Point Grey cost $4,120 as opposed to $2,524 in South Vancouver and $2,686 in Vancouver. See Vancouver YMCA, "Vancouver Survey — October 1928," 2, series A-1, v. 21, file 9, in Vancouver City Archives.

[35] A. H. Lewis, *South Vancouver, Past and Present* (Vancouver: Western Publishing, 1920), p, 18.

[36] Bartholomew, *Vancouver, including Point Grey and South Vancouver*, p. 26.

[37] Just 4 percent resided elsewhere, comprising 32 living in Mount Pleasant, 6 in the Business District, 1 in South Vancouver, 1 in Hastings Townsite, and 1 in the East End, who was the local Anglican rector. Margaret Wharf Russell, comp., *Greater Vancouver Social and Club Register* (Vancouver: Clark & Stuart, 1927).

civic jurisdictions by the Vancouver YMCA predicted that, while "the Oriental section [of the population] and unskilled laborers" might choose residence in the East End, "those engaged in commercial pursuits with growing incomes and cultures" would increasingly opt for the district west of Cambie, "artisans and skilled workers" for the area to the east.[38]

The 1931 and 1941 census data suggest that for individuals with the financial means to reside anywhere in the city the choice may have been age-related, families of high status already established in the West End being less liable to move to the West Side than were their younger married counterparts choosing between the two areas. In 1931 West End males averaged 36 years of age, females 35, being in each case half a dozen years older than their West Side contemporaries. Concurrently, in both 1931 and 1941 twice as many residents of Fairview, Kitsilano and West Point Grey, about one in five, were children than in the West End. One in twenty West End males and virtually one in five females had been widowed, again proportions larger than on the West Side. The West End population had become skewed toward females, who comprised 52 percent of adults in 1931, 56 percent a decade later, both proportions the highest in any city area.[39] While this phenomenon was in part an inevitable concomitant of the ageing process, it was also due to an influx of young women, possibly employed in the nearby Business District or as domestics in the mansions that still dotted the area amidst a growing number of apartments.[40] Fully a third of female adults living in the West End during the interwar years were unmarried and, compared to the total aged 10 to 14, the number 15 to 19 was double and that 20 to 24 fully three to four times larger. Among the two older age groups the sex ratio was particularly skewed toward females at well over 60 percent. An

[38] Vancouver YMCA, "Survey," p. 3.

[39] The division of the 1941 census into social areas by sex and age reveals the areas of concentrated female residence. Young women aged 20 to 24 made up 62 percent of the adult population in the vicinity of Vancouver General Hospital, possibly explained by their employment as nurses or nurses in training. Women between 20 and 24 comprised 60 percent of Shaughnessy residents, a consequence perhaps of the availability of domestic employment. The same logic may explain 56 percent of residents of West Point Grey aged 25 to 44 being female. As well, 54 percent of residents aged 45 to 54 in Mount Pleasant near False Creek were women. Given that one in six adult females in that neighbourhood were widows, perhaps the area had special appeal to mature women on their own in need of modest accommodation.

[40] In 1931 3,199 Vancouver women, or 14.6 percent of the total number employed, worked as domestics; in 1941 3,350 or 12.3 percent. Exactly half of Vancouver's female domestics in each of these census years were aged 16 to 24.

increasing number, as in the Business District, were recent arrivals from the prairies.

Even though the population of the West End, male and female, was both ageing and being supplemented by younger newcomers, many of them prairie-born, the area's overall socio-economic orientation appears to have changed remarkably little from its prewar origins. Compared with every other area, residents were peculiarly British in orientation, as measured both by birth and by affiliation with the establishment Church of England, or Anglican church, membership in which still provided for many visible affirmation of declared middle-class status by British standards. Virtually 40 percent of residents were British-born in 1931, as were 31 percent a decade later. Fully 42 percent were Anglican in 1931, over 40 percent in 1941, totals most closely approached in Kitsilano and West Point Grey with 36 percent in each of the two census years. As late as 1941 84 percent of West End residents were British by ethnic origin, a proportion surpassed only by West Point Grey's 89 percent. Educational levels were among the highest in the city, exceeded only by the proportions of West Side residents with thirteen or more years of schooling, probably a reflection of residential proximity to both the University of British Columbia and Vancouver General Hospital. Although it is, of course, impossible to determine from census data how many of the same individuals who had lived in the West End in its earlier period of socio-economic dominance still resided there, it does at the least appear that the area continued to attract individuals of comparable ethnic and socio-economic attributes. Indeed, in the 1927 social directory noted above, even though Point Grey, or West Side, addresses were more numerous, the number residing in the West End was actually slightly higher — at 5.7 versus 5.4 percent — when calculated as a proportion of each area's total population.

If the West Side was much more family oriented than the West End, the East Side was even more so. In 1931 well over a quarter of Hastings, Cedar Cottage and Mount Pleasant residents were children. Between seven and eight of every ten adults were married. Not surprisingly, given contemporary observations concerning the modest character of South Vancouver, under 6 percent had 13 or more years of schooling. The East Side contained greater proportions of British-born than did the West Side, in 1931 35 to 37 percent compared with 27 to 33 percent. Conversely, just over half of East Side residents in 1931 had been born in Canada compared to almost 60 percent on the West Side; by 1941 the proportion had reached 60 percent on the East Side but was virtually two-thirds further west. However, membership in the Anglican church was greater in the two West Side areas of Kitsilano and West Point Grey at 35 and 36 percent than on the East Side, where it ranged between 28 and 33 percent, providing yet additional confirmation that East Side residents, in this case primarily British-born, were of generally lower socio-economic status than those on the West Side, so more prone to be Non-Conformist in orientation.

III

Residential differentiation received its conscious, outward expression each time Vancouver residents went to the polls. The most useful level at which to explore voting behaviour is, for a number of reasons, the annual civic elections for the Vancouver school board.[41] Elections for aldermen were fought at the ward level, the force of personality thereby making difficult citywide comparison of voting preferences.[42] While both the parks and school boards were chosen at large, the utility of the former is limited by the relative sparsity of candidates and generally low-keyed, uneventful nature of campaigns.[43] In contrast, elections for school trustees regularly attracted a variety of aspirants, whose characteristics visible to contemporaries can be correlated with voting behaviour by geographical areas.

Civic electoral behaviour during the interwar years perforce divides into two time periods, with two necessary points of division: the amalgamation of South Vancouver and Point Grey in January 1929 and the onset of depression by 1930. The metropolis which obtained permanent geographical shape through amalgamation contained up to that date not one but three civic governments, each with its own school board. However, South Vancouver had an elected board only after 1923, when self-government was restored following a half decade of provincial supervision due to fin-

---

[41] Details on elections, including ballots and results by ward or district, are available in "Nominations and Elections," v. 1, 1886-1924, and v. 2, 1924-49, MCR4, Vancouver City Archives. Additional information can be found in city newspapers including the *Province, Sun, World, British Columbia Federationist* and *Labor Statesman*, particularly during the week before and after each election. On Vancouver politics prior to 1914, see McDonald, "Elite." Also useful are Paul Tennant, "From Democracy to Oligarchy: the Vancouver Civic Political Elite, 1886-1980" (paper presented to Canadian Political Science Association, 1981); Tennant, "Vancouver Civic Politics, 1929-1980," *BC Studies* 46 (Summer 1980): 3-27; and Gibson, pp. 157-58.

[42] The exception was the years 1920-22, when proportional representation held.

[43] See press coverage of campaigns in *Sun* and *Province*, William Carey McKee, "The History of the Vancouver Park System, 1886-1929" (M.A. thesis, Department of History, University of Victoria, 1976), esp. pp. 85-87 and 134; and Gibson, p. 158.

ancial difficulties, and Point Grey's board was chosen by acclamation in six out of nine elections over the decade.[44] The two boards did, nonetheless, reflect the municipalities' dominant socio-economic orientations. Of the eight South Vancouver trustees, half held such modest, working-class occupations as carpenter, plasterer, electrician and streetcar conductor, two of them running with the endorsement of a left-wing political organization.[45] The remainder comprised two women, a businessman and a retiree. In sharp contrast, just two members of Point Grey's boards were modest men — one a newspaper proofreader, the other a carpenter — whereas eight were professionals, another six businessmen, and two women.

As a consequence, it is the twenty-one Vancouver civic elections held between 1920, the first postwar year when school board positions were contested, and 1939 that provide the most systematic base for analysis. There eligibility to vote was limited to male and female British subjects, property owners and tenants, who were not Chinese, Japanese, East Indian or native Indian, racial groups denied the vote until after the Second World War. Neither was any "lodger, boarder or temporary occupant of rooms" accorded the franchise.[46] The January 1921 election was the last in which property owners could vote in as many city wards as they held property; thereafter each individual had one vote to be exercised in one of the areas in which property was owned.[47] While visual examination of

[44] South Vancouver Council Minutes, I-B-2 to I-B-7, and Point Grey Municipal Council Minutes, 5-A-7 to 5-B-7, Vancouver City Archives, which unfortunately only contain partial electoral data. Also see Vancouver Board of School Trustees, *Annual Report*, 1928, pp. 170 and 194; and Roy, *Vancouver*, pp. 116-17. Occupations taken from Vancouver city directories.

[45] See *British Columbia Federationist*, 11 January and 12 December 1924, and *Labor Statesman*, 26 November 1926 and 12 October 1928.

[46] The voting age was 21. Property under tenancy had to have an assessed value of $300. Where property was leased, rented or occupied by two or more persons, each could vote if the assessment divided between them was sufficient; "otherwise, no one shall be entitled to vote in respect of such property." However, a married man could not vote as a tenant where the property was owned by his wife. As well, corporations on the assessment roll could vote through an authorized agent. "An Act to revise and consolidate the 'Vancouver Incorporation Act,'" 1921, section 8, in British Columbia, *Statutes*, 1921, pp. 310-11. The provisions of the 1921 act were extended to Point Grey and South Vancouver in "An Act to include the Inhabitants of The Incorporation of South Vancouver and the Corporation of Point Grey, and the Respective Areas thereof, within the City of Vancouver," 1928, in British Columbia, *Statutes*, 1928. Racial minorities were accorded the vote in 1949; see "An Act to amend the 'Vancouver Incorporation Act, 1921,'" section 4, in British Columbia, *Statutes*, 1949, pp. 269-70.

[47] "An Act to Revise and Consolidate the Vancouver Incorporation Act," 1900, section 5, in British Columbia, *Statutes*, 1900, p. 282.

the civic voters' lists makes clear that a large variety of ethnic names were included, no check is possible as to who actually cast their ballots.[48]

The proportion going to the polls varied widely across the city. That the lowest level should have been in the East End, where about 5 percent of adults resident in the area voted in school board elections, 1928-33, is hardly surprising, given that many residents were disenfranchised by race, others by seasonal transiency or living arrangements. Next came the Business District and West End with 7 percent each, to some extent a reflection of similar factors but also possibly of the two areas' relatively small proportions of children and thereby interest in school matters. During this half decade participation was noticeably higher on the East than West Sides. Fully 19 percent of adults voted in Hastings, as did 18 percent in Cedar Cottage and 16 percent in Mount Pleasant. The only comparable West Side area was West Point Grey with 17 percent, followed by Kitsilano with 14 and Fairview with 12.[49]

While the basis upon which the minority of residents who went to the polls actually chose between candidates can never be fully determined, certain elements of information were generally available and, it might be theorized, at the least affected individuals' decision-making process, especially since the filing deadline for candidates and thereby the beginning of active campaigning was just a week before election.[50] Half the positions on the school board, which totalled seven prior to amalgamation, nine thereafter, were contested annually. Once names were known, the daily newspapers usually devoted a front-page story to the upcoming election, noting who were the incumbents. As well as having opportunities to hear

[48] Official voters' lists are available in Vancouver City Archives.

[49] Total number of votes cast for school board candidates in each area in the three elections before and after the 1931 census was divided by the number of vacancies to be filled, and then by total adult population aged 20 and above, as given in the 1931 census, which used the same geographical divisions as did these six elections. In the 1932 election, the votes cast for the single one-year position on the board were preferred as more accurately representing the number of voters, and these figures suggest that many voters did not make choices to fill all the vacancies. If such were the case generally — and indeed it is also indicated by the greater number of individuals who voted for mayor — then all these percentages are low. They are also skewed downward by virtue of the census data including individuals aged 20 and above whereas the minimum voting age was 21.

[50] The principal qualification for candidates, in addition to being able to vote, was to have $500 in clear title of real property for six months prior to nomination. See statutes and *British Columbia Federationist*, 15 December 1922, and *Province*, 7 December 1938. Elections were at first held in January, from 1922 on the second Wednesday of December, except for 1928, when the first election for the amalgamated Vancouver, South Vancouver and Point Grey occurred in October. *Vancouver Municipal Yearbook*, esp. 1929, p. 4.

contestants in person, prospective voters could learn more about many of them from newspaper ads appearing a day or two before election. Information on the ballot, provided by the candidates, contained name and an occupational designation.[51]

As well, some aspirants were ideologically identified by virtue of endorsement by organized labour or a left-wing political party.[52] At first such endorsements appeared only in the city's labour press, although stories in mainstream dailies sometimes referred to specific individuals as "labour candidates."[53] Beginning with the election held immediately prior to amalgamation, endorsements by left-wing groups were also inserted in daily papers.[54] From 1933 the newly founded Co-operative Common-

[51] The 1921 and January 1922 ballots also included candidates' addresses; the 1920 and 1923 ballots only names.

[52] The principal sources of information checked for such endorsements were the mainstream and labour press on the assumption that, if not publicized there, endorsement was, even if it did occur, of little real significance in determining electoral behaviour. Candidates were endorsed by the Federated Labor Party in 1921 (Angus MacInnes), 1922 (MacInnes), 1923 (W. J. Downie); the Vancouver and District Labor Representation committee in 1923 (Downie); the Canadian Labor Party in 1924 (Downie, A. V. Lofting and Robert Skinner), 1925 (Lofting), 1926 (Lofting); the Independent Labor Party in 1927 (Fred Knowles), 1928 (W. W. Lefeaux, R. F. Rigby, S. T. Wybourn), 1929 (Isabella Steenbekkers, Rigby, Wybourn), 1930 (Susie Lane Clark, R. H. Neelands, Rigby), 1931 (Clark, H. W. Oakes, Wybourn); the Trades and Labour Council in 1923 (Downie), 1928 (Rigby, Lofting, Ed Rogers, Wybourn), 1931 (James Blackwood, who was not, however, considered as a labour candidate since he had already been elected six times without left endorsement); the Socialist Party in 1931 (Wybourn), 1932 (Clark, Alfred Hurry, Oakes, Wybourn); the CCF in 1933 (Frank Buck, Hurry, Oakes), 1935 (Ronald Macaulay, Mildred Osterhout), 1936 (Buck, Clark, William Offer, William N. Wallace), 1937 (Osterhout), 1938 (James Bawn, John Evans, Wybourn); Labor-Progressive Party in 1938 (Effie Jones). Individuals were considered still to be labour candidates even when not endorsed in a subsequent election on the assumption that they would still possess such an orientation in the public mind (Lofting in 1929, Neelands in 1932, 1934, 1936, 1938). *British Columbia Federationist*, 15 April 1921, 23 November and 7 December 1923; *B.C. Workers News*, 13 December 1935 and 11 December 1936; *Labor Statesman*, 5 December 1924, 4 December 1925, 26 November 1926, 9 December 1927, 12 October 1928, 6 December 1929, 21 November 1930, 3 and 11 December 1931, December 1932; *Province*, 10 December 1935; 8 December 1936, 1 December 1937, 7 December 1938; *Sun*, 11 December 1923, 13 December 1932; 14 December 1933; and Richard Grey Stuart, "The Early Political Career of Angus MacInnes" (M.A. thesis, Department of History, UBC, 1970), pp. 15-16. For detail on the endorsement process, see Paul A. Phillips, *No Power Greater: A Century of Labor in British Columbia* (Vancouver: British Columbia Federation of Labour, 1967).

[53] For instance, *Province*, 9 January 1920 and 13 December 1923; and *Sun*, 5 January 1922.

[54] This election also saw the appearance of a " 'Citizen's League' of Greater Vancouver," which endorsed a number of candidates of different political orientations but subsequently disappeared from public view as a political force. *Province*, 16 October 1928.

wealth Federation endorsed candidates, and it was largely in order to counter the success of this left-oriented political party, which elected three aldermen in the December 1936 civic election, that the Non-Partisan Association was formed a year later by a coalition of Liberal and Conservative political interests with the explicit goal of endorsing acceptable candidates.[55] By 1938 the NPA had gained control of civic government, in large part through its co-optation by endorsement of virtually all incumbents, including in the case of the school board trustees of modest occupation and left orientation.[56]

Thus, three principal factors probably distinguished school board candidates to contemporaries: (1) ballot designation as supplemented by the immediate campaign rhetoric; (2) possible left-wing endorsement; and (3) incumbency or non-incumbency. Each of these variables is usefully correlated with voter preferences in the nine geographical areas. Since all eighty-one candidates possessed apparent Anglo-Saxon surnames, that element of the ballot has less utility than do occupation designations, which divide into four principal categories. Seventeen of the eighty-one candidates were women, generally identified on the ballot as "housewife" and focusing their campaign on previous experience with parent-teacher and child welfare groups.[57] Overall, the thirty-nine candidacies by these

---

[55] R. P. Pettipiece, A. M. Anderson and Alfred Hurry, all CCF-endorsed, were elected aldermen in December 1936. Anderson resigned shortly thereafter. In a second by-election, in early 1937, Helena Gutteridge, CCF-endorsed, was elected, with her re-election in December 1937 being the last CCF victory before the complete domination of the city council by NPA-endorsed candidates. *Province*, 12 and 14 December 1936 and 9 December 1937; Andrea Smith, "The CCF, NPA, and Civic Change: Provincial Forces Behind Vancouver Politics, 1930-1940," *BC Studies* 53 (Spring 1982): 45-65; and Roy, *Vancouver*, pp. 119 and 179, fn65.

[56] James Blackwood and R. H. Neelands. *Province*, 1 December 1937 and 7 December 1938. It should be noted, however, that while Neelands focused on his trades union credentials at each election (see *Province*, 10 December 1934, and *Sun*, 7 December 1936), he had not been endorsed by the left since 1930. The NPA adopted a similar policy at the aldermanic level in 1937 by endorsing the incumbent R. P. Pettipiece, previously a CCF candidate, who, however, then lost the election. As well, the labour connections of other candidates were emphasized by the NPA in the press, as in the case of a prominent lawyer: "he is consul for various labor unions and is familiar with the labor man's point of view." *Province*, 6 December 1937. The sole school board incumbent who retained a leftist affiliation in the 1937 campaign was Mildred Osterhout, who was soundly defeated by an NPA slate, whose lowest member garnered 3,476 votes against her 2,323. Through the war years, except for the re-election in 1944 of a highly successful female incumbent previously endorsed by the NPA but this time running as an "Independent," only NPA candidates would be elected to the school board. See *Province*, 14 December 1939, 12 December 1940, 11 December 1941, 10 December 1942, 9 December 1943 and 14 December 1944.

[57] Thirteen designated themselves as "housewife," the other four as "widow," "teacher retired" and "social worker." One candidate ran only in 1920, an election without

seventeen women were the best received, garnering on average, as table 9 details, 57 percent of votes cast with two-thirds resulting in election. Twenty-six of the sixty-four candidates were, like 5 percent of Vancouver employed male adults, professionals, primarily lawyers or engineers.[58] Their forty-four candidacies received 54 percent of votes cast and, again, two-thirds were successful. Another nineteen candidates held occupations in business and finance, such as merchant, contractor or insurance agent, shared by about 12 percent of employed male adults.[59] In general the forty-four business candidacies were less well received, garnering overall just 44 percent of votes cast, as a consequence of which only a third resulted in election. The remaining nineteen male candidates were members of what might be termed Vancouver's modest majority, employed, as were about 80 percent of their contemporaries, in such dominantly wage-labour positions as clerk, artisan and manual worker.[60] Overall, these fifty-six modest candidacies obtained 46 percent of the vote and were successful about 40 percent of the time. Unlike professional and business candidates, whose campaign rhetoric most often centred, to quote a West End physician, on "an Economical and Businesslike administration of school matters," modest candidates generally argued, as did a decorator running for the first time in 1920, for the "education of the masses and not for the classes."[61]

---

association on the ballot. See, for instance, *Province*, 8 December 1925 and 19 December 1935; and *Western Woman's Weekly* 5, no. 5 (7 January 1922).

[58] Ten were lawyers, 7 engineers, 4 accountants, 2 physicians and 1 each a professor, writer and architect. The exact proportions of professionals in the employed adult male population were 6.2 percent in Vancouver city in 1921, no data being available for South Vancouver and Point Grey, 5.6 percent in 1931 and 5.3 percent in 1941. *Census of Canada*, 1921, v. 4, pp. 554-75; 1931, v. 7, pp. 238-49; and 1941, v. 7, pp. 212-23.

[59] Nine were merchants, business or shop proprietors, 4 builders or contractors, 2 manufacturers, 2 real estate or insurance agents, 1 a lumberman and 1 a broker. The exact proportions so employed in Vancouver were 15.6 in 1921, 12.1 in 1931 and 11.9 percent in 1941.

[60] Three were carpenters, 3 conductors and 1 each a civic employee, clerk, decorator, depot master, electrician, mail carrier, motorman, plasterer, secretary of a union, sheet metal worker, sign writer, telephone employee and warehouseman. The exact proportions so employed in Vancouver were 77.5, 81.9 and 81.9 percent. In addition, 0.6, 0.4 and 0.8 percent of employed Vancouver males were farmers. An alternative division of occupations would be to separate out "clerks" into a separate group and label the remaining occupations "working-class" rather than the more general "modest." The division used here seems more consistent with contemporary perceptions concerning occupational groupings in Vancouver. On its validity, also see McCririck, pp. 7 and 12fn1.

[61] *Province*, 12 January 1921, and *British Columbia Federationist*, 2 January 1920. Also see *Sun*, 8 and 9 January 1922, and *Province*, 11 January 1922.

TABLE 9

*Mean Percentage of Votes Received by Vancouver School Board Candidates,
by Occupation and Geographical Area, 1920-1939*

	West End	Business District	East End	Hastings	Cedar Cottage	Mount Pleasant	Fairview	Kitsilano	West Point Grey	Total
1920-27										
Professional (n=19)	67.4	66.8	56.6	52.5	55.6	54.0	59.0	63.6	64.5	59.7
Business (19)	41.8	44.4	42.2	34.0	37.4	37.6	41.6	42.5	38.0	40.1
Modest (12)	42.9	47.3	61.3	73.1	64.0	69.8	52.6	46.1	45.8	56.2
Female (9)	70.2	63.8	68.8	77.5	76.1	73.0	73.9	72.0	73.7	72.1
1928-39										
Professional (25)	58.2	59.3	48.6	43.6	42.5	43.1	53.1	55.5	54.7	50.1
Business (25)	52.0	54.3	44.8	42.1	42.8	45.2	50.9	50.8	49.0	47.6
Modest (44)	37.1	37.2	43.7	47.9	49.1	48.9	38.8	38.6	38.3	42.9
Female (30)	51.9	47.4	53.8	54.9	53.2	50.3	54.1	50.9	52.9	52.2
1920-29										
Professional (30)	60.6	60.6	51.0	45.4	48.1	46.7	53.6	57.5	58.4	53.0
Business (25)	38.2	40.9	38.6	32.0	35.3	35.6	39.9	39.1	35.1	37.3
Modest (24)	33.7	35.9	46.9	55.5	51.0	54.8	39.6	36.1	35.8	43.9
Female (17)	54.0	49.9	53.6	58.4	57.2	54.6	55.7	55.9	57.5	55.7
1930-39										
Professional (14)	65.6	66.7	54.4	51.9	48.2	50.1	60.0	62.2	60.1	56.9
Business (19)	60.0	62.0	50.3	47.3	47.2	50.2	57.4	57.9	56.3	53.7
Modest (32)	41.9	42.0	47.9	51.6	53.3	52.3	43.4	43.3	43.0	47.1
Female (22)	58.0	52.2	60.2	61.4	59.4	56.3	61.0	68.8	57.9	57.6
Total										
Professional (44)	62.2	62.5	52.1	47.4	48.2	47.8	55.6	59.0	58.9	54.2
Business (44)	47.6	50.0	43.7	38.6	40.5	41.9	46.9	47.2	44.3	44.4
Modest (56)	38.3	39.5	47.5	53.3	52.3	53.4	41.8	40.2	39.9	45.8
Female (39)	56.1	51.2	57.3	60.1	58.5	55.5	58.7	63.2	57.7	56.8

The explanation for the differing appeal exercised by women, professionals, businessmen and modest men must be sought at the level of neighbourhood, or geographical area. Whatever the time period, whether the division be amalgamation or the onset of depression, women consistently received the highest level of support across areas, with half or more of voters in each area generally casting a ballot in their favour. The sole exception was the Business District, where the vote accorded female candidacies averaged 5 or more percentage points less. Indeed, in fully half the thirty-nine candidacies over the two decades, the smallest proportion of votes came in the Business District, whose relatively few voters were probably a combination of business people owning property there and residents locally employed. Both groups were largely male and in the latter case very likely childless, thereby perhaps less sympathetic to women's credentials.[62]

Both professionals and businessmen found their most receptive audience in the Business District and adjoining West End. The highest proportion of votes accorded the forty-four professional candidacies came three-quarters of the time in one of the two areas, for the forty-four business candidacies almost two-thirds of the time.[63] Conversely, professionals and businessmen generated little enthusiasm on the East Side, where the lowest level of support for professional candidacies came more than 80 percent of the time, for business candidacies about 70 percent.[64] Prior to amal-

---

[62] Overall, 19 of the 39 female candidates received their lowest level of support, calculated as the lowest proportion of votes cast in an area for any candidate, in the Business District. This occurred in 7 of 9 cases 1920-27, 12 of 30 1929-39, 11 of 17 1920-29 and 8 of 22 1930-39. There is some suggestion that women received a significant proportion of their support from female voters. Under proportional representation, voters were to mark their ballots in order of preference rather than merely placing an "x" before favoured candidates. In December 1922 one Mount Pleasant poll recorded "no fewer than ninety-two spoiled ballots in the count for school trustees," many of them "marked with an 'X' for Mrs. Hopkins and evidently cast by women." This account noted further how female poll clerks, employed for the first time, persisted despite "stern glances from male workers" in cheering whenever votes were called out for the sole woman running for trustee. *Province*, 14 December 1922.

[63] Overall, 15 of the 44 professional candidates received their highest level of support in the Business District, an additional 17 in the West End. The phenomenon occurred 5 and 8 times respectively out of 19 candidacies 1920-27, 10 and 9 of 25 1929-39, 8 and 12 of 30 1920-29 and 7 and 5 of 14 1930-39. Overall, 16 of the 44 business candidates received their highest level of support in the Business District, an additional 11 in the West End. The phenomenon occurred 8 and 5 out of 19 candidacies 1920-28, 8 and 6 of 25 1929-39, 10 and 6 of 25 1920-29, and 6 and 5 of 19 1930-39.

[64] Overall, 14 of the 44 professional candidacies received their lowest level of support in Hastings, 10 in Cedar Cottage and 12 in Mount Pleasant. The phenomenon occurred 8, 0 and 6 times respectively out of 19 candidacies 1920-27, 6, 10 and 6

128 BC STUDIES

gamation and the depression, least interest was expressed in Hastings and Mount Pleasant, thereafter in Cedar Cottage. The appeal of professional candidacies regularly surpassed those by businessmen, as evidenced by their higher mean vote and success rate in securing election. During the 1920s, a professional candidacy received, whatever the geographical area, half again as many votes on average as did a business candidacy; thereafter, 5 to 10 percent more votes, the narrower differential possibly attributable to vastly different economic conditions and thereby changing perceptions of the expertise demanded on the board. As a consequence, the proportion of successful business candidacies rose dramatically from four out of twenty-five during the 1920s to eleven of nineteen over the next decade, whereas the success rate of professional candidacies remained fairly constant at two out of three over the two decades.

The allegiance accorded men of modest occupation was greatest on the East Side. Virtually half of their fifty-six candidacies prior to amalgamation received their highest proportion of votes in Hastings, most of the remainder in Mount Pleasant. In the later period the two areas vied with Cedar Cottage for the honour.[65] Whatever the time period, modest candidacies did least well in the West End — if not there, then in the Business District or West Point Grey.[66] The relative lack of success of modest men in securing election lay primarily in the large differential in voter support between geographical areas: prior to amalgamation modest candidacies received on average over half again as many votes on the East Side as in the Business District, West End, Kitsilano or West Point Grey. Thereafter, although the differential moderated, modest candidacies still garnered about a quarter more votes on the East Side than in any other geographical area excepting the East End, where their vote, whatever the time period, lay about half way between the extremes.

---

of 25 1929-39, 9, 2 and 12 of 30 1920-29, and 5, 8 and 0 of 14 1930-39. Overall, 16 of the 44 business candidacies received their lowest level of support in Hastings, 9 in Cedar Cottage and 5 in Mount Pleasant. The phenomenon occurred 10, 2 and 1 times respectively out of 19 candidacies 1920-27, 6, 7 and 4 of 25 1929-39, 12, 2 and 2 of 25 1920-29 and 4, 7 and 3 of 19 1930-39.

[65] Overall, 16 of the 56 modest candidacies received their highest level of support in Hastings, 11 in Cedar Cottage and 13 in Mount Pleasant. The phenomenon occurred 6, 0 and 5 times respectively out of 12 candidacies 1920-27, 10, 11 and 8 of 44 1929-30, 10, 2 and 9 of 24 1920-29, and 6, 9 and 4 of 32 1930-39.

[66] Overall, 18 out of 56 modest candidacies received their lowest level of support in the West End, 12 in the Business District and 7 in West Point Grey. The phenomenon occurred 7, 2 and 2 times out of 12 candidacies 1920-27, 11, 10 and 5 of 44 1929-30, 9, 8 and 2 of 24 1920-29, and 9, 4 and 5 of 32 1930-39.

A quarter — twenty-one — of the eighty-one interwar school board candidates were left-endorsed. The policy objectives to which such individuals were meant to adhere resembled those of modest aspirants, not surprising given that twelve of the twenty-one were modest men. As expressed in a labour newspaper, "absolutely free and equal educational opportunities, from the primary school to the university" were essential "if the working class children are to be properly taken care of" and not "placed on the labour market at the age of fifteen years and so with only a partial education." The emphasis was on expansion rather than on economy of operation, a dichotomy which became more apparent once the depression took hold. As early as December 1929 a West Side lawyer, formerly a Point Grey trustee, was arguing that "schools are being built in a too expensive manner," whereas the next year a Mount Pleasant depot master urged "economy by spending wisely."[67]

As table 10 details, the forty-seven left-endorsed candidacies obtained 41 percent of the vote overall and achieved election about a quarter of the time.[68] Here, even more so than with modest men as an occupational group, residential differentiation played the critical role: in the years prior to amalgamation, left-endorsed candidacies averaged 63 percent of the vote in Hastings and 60 percent in Mount Pleasant compared with just 25 percent in the West End and about 30 percent in West Point Grey, Kitsilano and the Business District. In other words, left-endorsed candidacies garnered well over twice as large a proportion of votes cast on the East Side as elsewhere in Vancouver. Again the partial exception was the East End, where the vote lay between the two extremes, although generally closer to East Side levels. In this earlier period, almost 80 percent of candidacies received their highest proportion of votes in Hastings, two-thirds their lowest proportion in the West End, otherwise either in West Point Grey or the Business District.[69]

[67] *Labor Statesman*, 5 December 1924, 4 December 1925, 3 December 1926 and December 1932; *Sun*, 19 December 1929; and *Province*, 7 December 1930.

[68] McInnes in January 1922, Lofting in 1926, Knowles in 1927, Neelands in 1930, 1932, 1934, 1936 and 1938, Hurry in 1932 for a one-year term, Buck in 1933 and 1936, and Osterhout in 1935.

[69] Overall, 24 out of 47 left-endorsed candidacies received their highest level of support in Hastings, 7 in Cedar Cottage and 12 in Mount Pleasant. The phenomenon held in 7, 1 and 1 instances respectively out of 9 candidacies 1920-27, in 17, 6 and 11 of 38 1929-30, in 0, 1 and 18 1920-29 and in 15, 6 and 4 of 20 1930-39. Overall, 16 received their lowest level of support in the West End, 15 in the Business District and 9 in West Point Grey. The phenomenon held in 6, 1 and 3 instances respectively 1920-28, in 10, 14 and 7 1929-39, in 8, 7 and 2 1920-29, and in 8, 8 and 7 1930-39.

TABLE 10

Mean Percentage of Votes Received by Left-endorsed Vancouver School Board Candidates, by Occupation and Geographical Area, 1920-1939

	West End	Business District	East End	Hastings	Cedar Cottage	Mount Pleasant	Fairview	Kitsilano	West Point Grey	Total
1920-27										
Professional (n=2)	25.1	29.8	43.1	48.1	44.1	42.1	31.1	28.1	28.1	35.7
Modest (7)	25.3	32.4	51.4	67.1	53.1	65.3	37.2	31.7	31.7	44.5
Total (9)	25.3	31.9	49.6	62.9	51.1	60.3	35.9	31.0	30.4	42.6
1928-39										
Professional (3)	47.2	46.6	45.7	46.5	46.4	51.4	45.1	46.6	50.3	48.6
Modest (26)	30.3	30.1	40.1	46.9	48.9	47.2	32.5	34.6	32.7	39.0
Female (9)	33.8	31.1	49.3	55.9	54.0	51.0	33.3	34.0	35.3	43.0
Total (38)	32.7	31.7	42.8	49.0	49.3	48.5	34.3	34.0	34.3	40.8
1920-29										
Professional (3)	25.1	27.6	37.2	40.1	36.3	36.9	26.6	25.3	25.8	31.3
Modest (14)	21.3	25.1	40.1	52.2	45.1	52.8	29.8	27.1	26.9	36.8
Total (18)[1]	21.3	24.6	38.1	48.1	42.1	48.4	28.1	27.1	25.8	34.5
1930-39										
Professional (2)	58.3	58.3	55.8	57.7	59.3	63.8	58.8	60.1	64.8	61.7
Modest (19)	35.1	34.6	44.3	50.4	53.2	49.7	36.2	39.0	36.6	42.7
Female (8)	36.8	34.0	53.8	61.0	58.7	54.8	36.3	36.9	38.4	46.7
Total (29)	35.5	36.1	47.7	53.8	55.2	52.1	37.8	39.9	39.0	45.1
Total										
Professional (5)	38.3	39.9	44.1	47.1	45.5	47.7	39.5	39.2	41.4	43.4
Modest (33)	29.2	30.6	42.5	51.1	49.8	51.0	33.5	34.0	32.5	40.2
Female (9)	33.8	31.1	49.3	55.9	54.0	51.0	33.3	34.0	35.3	43.0
Total (47)	31.3	31.7	44.1	51.7	49.6	50.8	34.6	33.4	33.6	41.1

[1] Also includes one left-endorsed female candidacy.

Some moderation in support for left-endorsed candidacies occurred after amalgamation, probably due more to a far greater number of candidacies than to any major shift in voter orientation within the six geographical areas following their enlargement through the addition of South Vancouver and Point Grey. The basic voting pattern remained unchanged, with candidacies still garnering over half again as many votes on the East Side as everywhere else in the city excepting the East End, which during the depression years moved closer to East Side levels. Following amalgamation, half the left-endorsed candidacies received their highest level of support in Hastings, the remainder almost always in Mount Pleasant or Cedar Cottage. In 80 percent of the cases, the lowest proportion of votes came in the Business District, West End or West Point Grey.[70]

The occupation of left-endorsed candidates affected their voter appeal across the city. Just as was the case generally, the five professional and nine female candidacies did best, each garnering on average 43 percent of the vote compared with 40 percent for the thirty-three modest candidacies. Despite being left-endorsed, professional candidacies still obtained 38 to 41 percent of the vote in the West End, Business District and West Side compared with the 29 to 34 percent accorded modest candidacies and 31 to 35 percent given female candidacies. Thus, in the case of professionals occupational identification and the status implied therein may have overridden political orientation in some voters' minds, whereas females, by virtue of being left-endorsed, jeopardized part of their humanitarian appeal. On the other hand, candidacies by left-endorsed professionals did less well on the East Side, receiving just 45 to 48 percent of the vote, than did those by left-endorsed modest men with 50 to 51 percent and women with 51 to 56 percent. The same relative preferences held during the different time periods, except that two pre-amalgamation candidacies by a naturopathic physician were relatively unsuccessful city-wide.

The most general effect of incumbency was to ensure re-election, and such was the case over these two decades fully fifty-two of sixty times, due most often to a growing consensus of support across the city. Three of the eight exceptions occurred in cases where the incumbent was left-endorsed

---

[70] The location of support for left-endorsed candidacies for the school board paralleled aldermanic preferences during the time period when the ward comprised the electoral unit. In January 1920 James Reid, "representing labour," gained election in ward 7, essentially Hastings Townsite. In the next election, a "labour candidate," R. P. Pettipiece, received most first-choice votes city wide for alderman. Buoyed by his feat, he ran next year for mayor and was resoundingly defeated. In December 1925 Angus MacInnes, an incumbent "labour" school trustee, was elected alderman in ward 8, centring on eastern Mount Pleasant and District Lot 301 and in this essay termed "Mount Pleasant." MacInnes was returned a year later when aldermanic terms were extended to two years and again after amalgamation in ward 7, an area geographically similar to the older ward 8 excepting for its extension southward to include a slice of South Vancouver. By the 1930 civic election MacInnes had been elected a member of parliament. A perennial "labour" candidate, Walter Deptford, ran successfully in ward 7 both that year and in 1932. In 1934 Deptford ran as a "labour candidate" after the CCF endorsed Alfred Hurry in the ward; the two together garnered 850 more votes than the winner in the three-man race. *Province*, 9 January 1920, 16 December 1922, 13 December 1923, 10 December 1925, 9 December 1926, 18 October 1928, 11 December 1930, 15 December 1932 and 13 December 1934.

TABLE 11

Mean Percentage of Votes Received by First-time Vancouver School Board Candidates Identified Primarily by Occupation, 1920-1939[1]

	West End	Business District	East End	Hastings	Cedar Cottage	Mount Pleasant	Fairview	Kitsilano	West Point Grey	Total
1920-27[2]										
Professional (n=11)	66.3	64.8	52.5	47.9	51.8	50.0	56.1	61.5	62.5	56.7
Business (5)	34.2	35.8	33.1	32.6	30.2	34.3	36.6	35.6	37.8	33.9
Female (4)	54.5	48.9	53.5	69.5	69.6	65.1	59.3	56.4	56.8	59.8
1928-39										
Professional (10)	57.0	58.0	45.6	40.0	38.3	38.2	52.3	56.2	54.1	47.2
Business (8)	53.1	55.1	41.3	37.4	36.3	37.6	50.8	50.5	48.3	44.7
Modest (2)	22.4	23.2	32.3	30.7	31.7	33.7	26.5	22.5	22.0	27.4
Female (6)	46.4	41.7	42.9	44.2	37.9	38.2	45.4	44.0	47.8	43.4
1920-29										
Professional (16)	59.3	58.5	48.2	43.0	46.0	44.0	50.5	53.5	55.8	50.5
Business (6)	30.1	32.8	29.6	29.0	27.7	30.7	32.7	31.7	33.3	30.4
Modest (3)	35.0	37.9	48.0	49.3	47.3	48.6	40.2	37.6	37.2	42.5
Female (7)	51.5	46.6	46.7	57.0	55.6	51.9	54.5	52.2	54.5	52.9
1930-39										
Professional (5)	70.2	71.5	52.5	47.7	43.3	45.7	66.6	76.4	67.1	57.4
Business (7)	64.2	65.1	48.1	43.2	41.2	42.9	60.1	59.9	57.1	52.4
Female (3)	35.0	37.9	48.0	49.3	47.3	48.6	40.2	37.6	37.2	42.5
Total										
Professional (21)	61.9	61.6	49.2	44.1	45.8	44.4	54.3	59.0	58.5	52.1
Business (13)	45.9	47.7	38.1	35.6	33.9	35.3	45.4	44.6	44.3	40.5
Modest (3)	35.0	37.9	48.0	49.3	47.3	48.6	40.2	37.6	37.2	42.5
Female (10)	47.0	44.2	47.1	54.9	53.3	51.0	50.6	48.2	49.8	50.1

[1] Also excludes incumbents from South Vancouver and Point Grey running in Vancouver after amalgamation.

[2] Excludes one modest candidacy.

and, probably as a consequence, unable to achieve credibility in the West End, Business District and West Side. However, trustees once defeated at the polls usually fared poorly when they chose, as occurred several times, to run repeatedly in the hope of eventually securing re-election.

Given the almost predictive effect of left-endorsement and of incumbency, it becomes useful to re-examine the effect of ballot designation by separating out only non-left-endorsed first-time candidacies, as in table 11. The same general pattern held as with all candidacies: overall, the twenty-one professional and eleven female candidacies did better with 50 and 52 percent of the vote than did the twelve business and three modest candidacies with 41 and 43 percent respectively. The geography of support remained unchanged. Once again, professionals appear to have possessed the greatest inherent occupational prestige: the proportion of the vote accorded non-left-endorsed first-time professional candidacies was just 2 to 3 percentage points lower across the different geographical areas than the proportion accorded all professional candidacies, incumbent or not. The decline in support for first-time non-left-endorsed female candidacies was, by comparison, several times greater at 5 to 10 percentage points, suggesting that while their sex, and the humanitarianism of their campaign rhetoric, was inherently appealing, its attraction increased even further with incumbency and, presumably, evidence of performance during that incumbency. A similar differential existed with business candidacies, especially on the East Side and in the East End, where support for newcomers was upwards to 7 percentage points lower, signifying they too had to prove themselves.

Graphs 1-5 turn the equation on its head, so to speak, by focusing not on the three principal variables distinguishing candidacies to contemporaries but rather on the geographical areas themselves. The graphs depict what would have been the composition of school boards had each area been able to select its own board from among all the candidates. Not surprisingly, while women would have formed a roughly equal proportion of every area board, the remaining members would have differed markedly, with the East Side selecting a high proportion of modest candidates, the West End, Business District and West Side choosing primarily professionals and businessmen. Left-endorsed candidates would have formed almost four times greater a proportion of East Side boards than in the West End, Business District and West Side. The reality of residential differentiation became manifest each time Vancouver voters went to the polls.

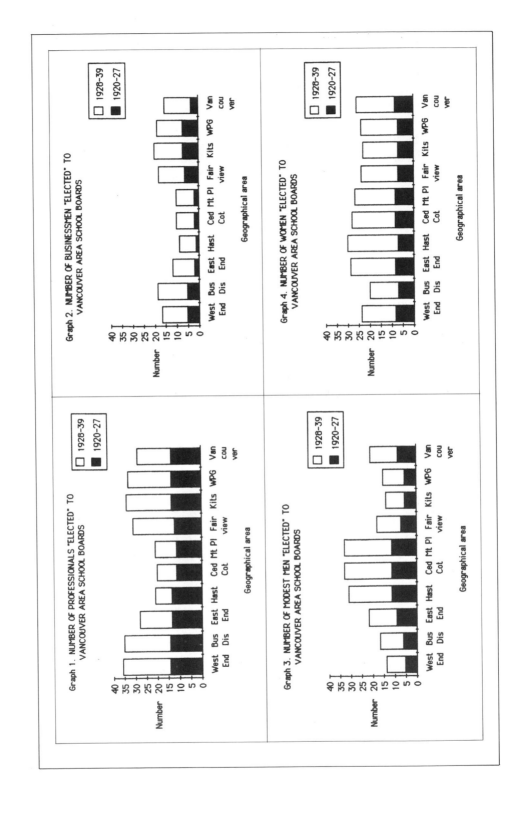

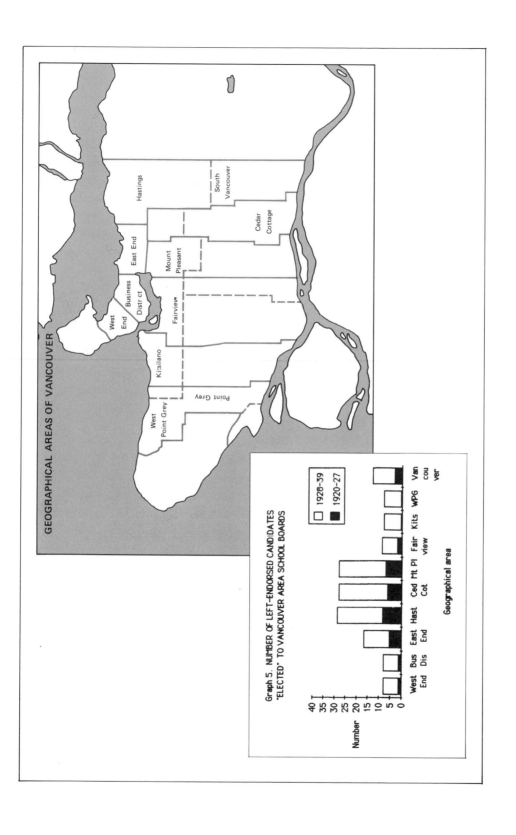

GEOGRAPHICAL AREAS OF VANCOUVER

West End
Business District
East End
Hastings
West Point Grey
Kitsilano
Point Grey
Fairview
Mount Pleasant
Cedar Cottage
South Vancouver

Graph 5. NUMBER OF LEFT-ENDORSED CANDIDATES "ELECTED" TO VANCOUVER AREA SCHOOL BOARDS

1928-39
1920-27

Number

40
35
30
25
20
15
10
5
0

West End
Bus Dis
East End
Hast
Ced Cot
Mt Pl
Fair view
Kits
WPG
Van cou ver

Geographical area

IV

Despite the consistency which existed in voting behaviour within and between geographical areas of interwar Vancouver, it would be a mistake to conclude that residential differentiation, or the force of neighbourhood, dominated decision-making to the exclusion of community. Numerous times over the two decades, voters spoke with a common voice, preferring what might be termed consensus candidates, that is, the same individuals were either most voted in every one of the nine geographical areas in a particular election or at the least secured election in every area. On four occasions an incumbent topped the polls in every geographical area: neighbourhood and community became one. In 1923 and 1925 it was Mrs. Dora Macaulay, an incumbent "housewife" who ran on her record and then did not seek re-election in 1927. Her campaign combined the rhetoric associated with female candidacies with what was probably considerable general appeal by promising at one and the same time a "woman's viewpoint on all educational matters for the betterment of the child" and "Economy, Efficiency and Co-operation." The same electoral feat was achieved in 1930 by Thomas Brooks, a South Vancouver "merchant" who was formerly reeve and trustee in that municipality. Brooks' campaign stressed his "courage to vote for what he deems advisable in the best interests of the educational system," including in that first year of depression a city bylaw to improve school grounds. Over his next decade of board membership Brooks at least once again was the preferred candidate in every geographical area. Consensus was also inspired by James Blackwood, the decorator who had joined the board in 1920 with the "education of the masses" slogan. Blackwood had already been the preferred choice one or more times in every area except Cedar Cottage prior to 1939, when he swept the poll even there. Like Macaulay and Brooks, Blackwood was clearly able to unite Vancouver voters, in 1931 even securing the endorsement of the left. Both men were, not surprisingly, co-opted by the NPA with Brooks continuing as trustee to 1951, Blackwood to 1945.[71]

Over the two decades a diversity of individuals secured election in every geographical area. Out of a total of thirty-two successful candidacies prior to amalgamation, fully eighteen occurred citywide. Five of these were by women, including Macaulay also in her first attempt at re-election in 1921. Nine were by professionals, one by a businessman and three by

[71] *Province*, 11 December 1923, 8 December 1925, 7 December 1930, and *Labor Statesman*, 11 December 1931.

modest men.[72] Of the six consensus candidacies by non-incumbents, five were by professionals, the other by a woman, again individuals whose attributes had the greatest inherent appeal to voters. Of fifty-nine successful candidacies after amalgamation, over half, or thirty-one, were elected by consensus. Of these, twelve were by women, six by professionals and eight by businessmen, including five by Brooks. The remaining five were by modest men, in four instances Blackwood but in the fifth R. H. Neelands, a printer and veteran trades union organizer and politician from South Vancouver. Like Brooks and Blackwood, Neelands clearly demonstrated sufficient capacity as incumbent to overcome occupation and, in his case, also left-wing political orientation.[73]

The most difficult candidacies around which to secure consensus were, not unexpectedly, those that had been left-endorsed. Nonetheless, such occurred twice during the post-amalgamation depression years. In 1934 all four incumbents, including Neelands, were returned in a situation where the alternatives were three relative unknowns. Two years later, Dr. Frank Buck, a UBC academic prominent in the CCF who had previously served one term on the board, was elected by consensus, due in part certainly to his professional reputation.

Thus, beyond the demographic and socio-economic differences which divided Vancouver residents lay a considerable degree of consensus. Despite a consistent commitment to the left, voters on the East Side did not hesitate to prefer candidates of other backgrounds and political orientations: the school boards that Hastings, Cedar Cottage and Mount Pleasant would have selected, had they voted as separate entities, contained only some of the left-endorsed and modest candidates who ran for the board together with a sizeable proportion of professionals and even businessmen. While the West End, Business District and West Side were far less amenable to boards containing modest and particularly left-endorsed candidates than was the East Side willing to accept professionals and businessmen, the former did make such selections from time to time, particularly when an individual had through incumbency disarmed their fears. Even when candidates were elected to the city's school board primarily on the basis of their receiving a very high proportion of votes in just one part of the city, which occurred most often in the case of modest

[72] Due to a paucity of non-professional candidates in the December 1923 election, at least one professional had to be selected.

[73] Due to a paucity of non-female candidates in the December 1937 election, of non-business candidates in the December 1934 election, and of non-modest candidates in the December 1939 election, at least one individual of such occupation had to be selected.

men, they nonetheless did receive some votes from across the city. Only in
the case of left-endorsed candidacies was the mean differential more than
double between geographical areas, but even then at least one in five
voters in each area so cast their ballot. As well, all nine geographical
areas of the city, with the partial exception of the Business District,
shared a common preference for female candidates, possibly because
such individuals were seen as most suitable to deal with matters concerning children or perhaps because they did not have a ballot designation
signifying socio-economic status, as did males defined by occupation. The
consequence was that Vancouver school boards elected during the interwar years contained not only representatives from both sexes and the three
major occupational groupings, but also from the left. More importantly,
had city areas chosen their own boards, all would have had in common a
sizeable number of professionals and women along with some business and
modest men, many of them elected by consensus. After amalgamation
even left-endorsed candidates would, for at least one term, have been a
part of every area board.

The contemporary evidence suggests, further, that the sole ideological
force active in civic politics during most of these two decades, the left,
was not so much intent on complete control as it was on fair representation of its perceived interests, which were geographically aligned with the
East Side. The number of candidates endorsed in a single election never
exceeded three prior to amalgamation, four thereafter. As one left-endorsed aspirant phrased it: "The Labour party is out to raise the living
and cultural standard of the working class." Commenting on a left-
endorsed candidate resident in the Hastings area, Vancouver's labour
newspaper observed in 1926: "This is a working-class district, that is one
reason why the working class should have direct representation on the
school board." Two years later the paper acknowledged that even if
forces on the left did obtain control, the consequence would not be radical change, since "the curriculum and agenda of the schools" were essentially in place. Moreover, the representatives of working-class interests
accepted that they had to earn respect at the ballot box. A 1927 candidate complained that up to that time representation on the school board
had been "confined almost exclusively to the so-called businessmen," but

better educational opportunities have shown the workers that the employing
class have no monopoly on the brains of the community, and they have also
seen that when a representative of their own class was elected he compared
very favourably with the representatives of the other classes.[74]

[74] *Labor Statesman*, 9 December 1927, 3 December 1926 and 10 December 1928.

By the interwar years Vancouver had, then, developed a considerable sense of community, whose parameters had essentially been put in place during Vancouver's first quarter century: the fortuitous became the permanent. Within that community lay distinctive geographical areas and neighbourhoods, exercising their own decision-making power at the polls but nonetheless bound together, with the probable exception of the East End, by shared demographic attributes and electoral priorities. Only in the East End and possibly some parts of the Business District were ethnic and racial minorities congregated together in such large numbers as to become their own enclave apart from the rest of the city and so act in a distinctive fashion at the polls. Such was, however, not the case. The small proportions who did, or possibly could, cast their ballot in the East End fluctuated widely in their loyalties, perhaps because no candidate during the interwar years resided in the area or, indeed, publicly referred during a campaign to its unique educational situation rooted in residents' ethnic diversity. Choices made at the polls may have been arbitrary, highly personalistic, or simply varied greatly between Strathcona and Grandview.

Elsewhere in the city, including the Business District, the dominant ethos was British, either directly by virtue of birth or by ethnic background. And the British-born did not act politically as a group, as evidenced by the wide differences in voting preferences between their two principal areas of settlement, the West End and East Side. Clusters of "foreigners" existed across the city and, while they may have felt some unity by virtue of their numbers, they were probably not generally perceived as separate in the same sense as in the East End. Moreover, where ethnicity was European, a period of residence or birth in Canada, very possibly the prairies, had increasingly intervened to distance individuals from their origins. Most adults, apart from the West End, Business District and East End, were also joined together by their common stage in the life cycle, being generally married, often with children, and thus personally committed, as manifest in voting behaviour for the school board, to the city's overall well-being.

The two major events of the interwar years which might have fundamentally altered voting patterns within and between geographical areas — the amalgamation of South Vancouver and Point Grey in 1929 and the onset of depression a year later — effected little change. That the shifts were only a matter of degree confirms, in the first case, that the character of settlement in South Vancouver had paralleled that in the eastern half of Vancouver's periphery extending from Hastings Townsite

through District Lot 301 to Mount Pleasant just as that in Point Grey
had been similar to Fairview and Kitsilano. The basic division was between the East Side and the West Side. And that division was, as evidenced by contemporary observations and corroborated by elements of
the census data, socio-economic rather than ethnic in nature. Thereby
lies, so it would seem, the explanation for the importance attached by
voters to ballot designation and to ideological orientation. The limited
effect of the depression on electoral behaviour suggests, for its part, that
changes in economic conditions were not of themselves sufficient cause to
alter voters' socio-economic, or class, orientations, buttressed as they were
by the force of neighbourhood, albeit complemented by commitment to
the community as a whole.

*   *   *

In the final analysis, however, the examination here pursued of census
and electoral data is no more than speculative, tantalizing more than it
defines in any overall sense the parameters existing in interwar Vancouver between community and neighbourhood. Analysis only of school
board elections, and then only by nine geographical areas, is at best sug-
gestive. The extent to which preferences extended to the parks board and
city council must be pursued, with analysis of the latter tailored to the
existence of wards. In cases where civic electoral returns were officially
broken down not only by wards but also by polls, as sometimes occurred
during these two decades, such analysis would determine more precisely
the boundaries of neighbourhood as expressed through the ballot. The
tentative thesis offered here that candidates' occupations affected electoral
behaviour could, at the poll level, be adequately tested by, for instance,
correlating preferences with dominant occupations in a polling area as
revealed in city directories. Attention also needs to be given to elections
at the provincial and federal levels, where voter turnout was higher and
choices made thereby more representative of the population at large.

Until then many questions remain unanswered — for instance, the basis
of women's appeal and the expressed preference for professionals over
modest men or businessmen, both occupational groupings more numeri-
cally dominant in the city. Also perplexing is the apparently limited role
of the depression in altering voting patterns, apart from somewhat increasing businessmen's appeal. Perhaps, as was suggested here, the critical
variable determining behaviour at the polls was not the state of the
economy. Neither was it ballot designation or occupation as such but
rather class — more specifically, the relationship which had grown up

in Vancouver between the owners and managers of capital and the sellers of labour. And, unfortunately, the role of labour and the left in Vancouver also remains largely unexplored.[75]

The census data defines a separate, if complementary, research agenda. The continued presence well past the years of mass immigration of a geographically concentrated population of ageing, largely single, possibly transient males begs examination, as do the emerging clusters of both younger and older females, who may or may not have grouped together due to proximity of employment. Far too little is known about the settlement patterns of Vancouver's ethnic and racial minorities. Correlation of religious denominations with ethnicity, as introduced here, makes church records a priority for analysis. Prairie migration both to Vancouver and to British Columbia as a whole remains largely unexplored. Only when at least some of these threads are unravelled will the relationship existing in interwar Vancouver between neighbourhood and community begin to be understood.

[75] Important new exceptions are *Working Lives: Vancouver 1886-1986* (Vancouver: New Star, 1985), and the essay by R. A. J. McDonald in this volume. On another potentially valuable approach to analyzing civic politics, looking both at candidates' less visible qualities and at their behaviour subsequent to election, see J. E. Rea, "The Politics of Class: Winnipeg City Council, 1919-45," pp. 232-49 in Carl Berger and Ramsay Cook, ed., *The West and the Nation: Essays in Honour of W. L. Morton* (Toronto: McClelland & Stewart, 1976).

The Confinement of Women:
Childbirth and Hospitalization in Vancouver, 1919-1939[*]

VERONICA STRONG-BOAG AND KATHRYN McPHERSON

Only relatively recently have large numbers of women been confined to institutions for the delivery of their children. The institutionalization of childbirth has radically transformed a major human experience, and the impact of this transformation has been a subject of debate among mothers, childbirth reformers, medical professionals and social scientists.[1] For its defenders, the hospital has served as an important vehicle for wider distribution of obstetrical supervision and treatment with a concomitant reduction of maternal morbidity and mortality. Critics have responded that delivering these services within the confines of a hierarchical, bureaucratized institution has contributed to the medicalization of childbirth, depriving women of control over their bodies and creating new psychological and physiological disorders.

As this contemporary debate rages, historians have begun to examine the historical process whereby doctors appropriated, and to some degree women relinquished, control over childbirth.[2] This study contributes to

[*] We would like to thank Lynn Bueckert, Anita Clair Fellman, Robin Fisher, Linda Hale, Andrée Levesque, Indiana Matters, Angus McLaren, Arlene Tigar McLaren and the anonymous referee from *BC Studies* for their comments on earlier drafts of this article. We would also like to acknowledge the support of the S.S.H.R.C. Strategic Grant 498-83-0014.

[1] See Ann Oakley, *Women Confined: Towards a Sociology of Childbirth* (London: Billing & Sons Ltd., 1980); Shelly Romalis, ed., *Childbirth: Alternatives to Medical Control* (Austin: University of Texas Press, 1981); and Tim Chard and Martin Richards, eds., *Benefits and Hazards of the New Obstetrics* (Philadelphia: J. B. Lippincott Co., 1977). See in particular Oakley's "Cross-cultural Practices," pp. 18-33, in which she distinguishes between the medical treatment women received and the broader issue of the "medicalization" of pregnancy and childbirth, that is "people's dependence on medicine and ... the control of health and sickness by the medical profession," p. 19.

[2] See Barbara Ehrenreich and Deirdre English, *For Her Own Good: 150 Years of the Experts' Advice to Women* (London: Pluto Press, 1979); E. Shorter, *A History of Women's Bodies* (New York: Basic Books, Inc., 1982); and Nancy

that ongoing investigation by examining the medicalization of childbirth in Vancouver during the 1920s and 1930s. It begins with a discussion of the general trends in maternal care and then turns to the specific obstetrical treatment provided by the Vancouver General Hospital (VGH). Within this institutional setting medical professionals found new opportunities to set the terms on which the city's women experienced childbirth.

Although the issue of maternity has attracted recent attention from historians of British Columbia and Canada as a whole, the focus of their work has been on pre-natal and post-natal care of reproductive women.[3] Few works concern themselves more directly with issues related to the delivery process. One article on the effect of abortion deaths on maternal mortality in B.C. makes some useful mention of the treatment by medical practitioners of unwillingly pregnant women, but their care is not of concern to the authors' argument.[4] Of greater relevance are two works dealing with the shift from home to hospital deliveries in twentieth-century Ontario. That transition is closely identified with fears about levels of maternal and infant mortality and the campaign of the medical profession to control health care. Both authors conclude that hospitalization itself did little to improve women's chances for survival before World War II. What was improved in the hospital was doctors' opportunity to monopolize the provision of services during confinement.[5] A less critical view is presented in an article examining attempts to reduce maternal mortality in British Columbia. That author sees hospitalization as a substantial advance which parturient women recognized and utilized.

Schrom Dye, "History of Childbirth in America," *Signs: Journal of Women in Culture and Society* 6, 11 (1980): 97-108.

[3] See, for example, Norah Lewis, "Advising the Parents: Child Rearing in British Columbia During the Inter-War Years" (Ph.D. thesis, U.B.C., 1980); Suzann Buckley, "Ladies or Midwives? Efforts to Reduce Infant and Maternal Mortality," in Linda Kealey, ed., *A Not Unreasonable Claim: Women and Reform in Canada 1880s-1920s* (Toronto: Women's Press, 1979); and Strong-Boag, "Intruders in the Nursery: Childcare Professionals Reshape the Years One to Five, 1920-1940," in J. Parr, ed., *Childhood and Family in Canadian History* (Toronto: McClelland & Stewart, 1982).

[4] Angus and Arlene Tigar McLaren, "Discoveries and Dissimulations: The Impact of Abortion Deaths on Maternal Mortality in British Columbia," *BC Studies* 64 (Winter 1984-85): 3-26.

[5] Jo Oppenheimer, "Childbirth in Ontario: The Transition from Home to Hospital in the Early Twentieth Century," *Ontario History* 75, 1 (March 1983): 36-60, and Catherine Lesley Biggs, "The Response to Maternal Mortality in Ontario, 1920-1940" (M.A. thesis, University of Toronto, 1982). Biggs argues that only the introduction of sulpha drugs in 1937 made hospital birthing as safe as home delivery.

However, the author's conclusion that institutionalization of the delivery process was the logical follow-up to good pre-natal care and just as essential to the reduction of maternal mortality stops short of considering either the nature of hospital obstetrical therapy itself or possible alternative methods and facilities for distributing obstetrical services.[6]

Improved maternal care was desperately needed in post-World War I Vancouver. During the 1920s, B.C., with the lowest birth rate of the provinces, also had one of the highest rates of maternal mortality. As table 1 indicates,[7] maternal mortality rates per 1,000 births in B.C. ranged from 4.7 to 6.7 between 1926 and 1935, then dropped permanently below the 5.0 mark in 1936 and slid steadily to 3.1 in 1940. While in 1926 B.C. had been significantly above the Canadian average of 5.7

TABLE 1

Maternal Mortality Rates per 1,000 Live Births in Canada,
by Provinces, 1926-1940

Year	Canada	P.E.I.	N.S.	N.B.	Que.	Ont.	Man.	Sask.	Alta.	B.C.
1926	5.7	4.6	4.6	6.4	5.2	5.6	5.9	7.1	5.9	6.5
1927	5.6	2.4	6.8	6.2	4.9	6.0	5.1	5.4	6.4	6.7
1928	5.6	6.1	5.2	5.8	5.3	5.8	5.1	5.8	6.8	5.9
1929	5.7	7.8	4.2	7.3	5.3	5.4	6.8	6.2	7.3	5.6
1930	5.8	2.9	6.7	5.4	5.5	6.2	5.2	5.1	6.5	5.8
1931	5.1	6.9	4.7	5.6	4.8	5.4	4.8	4.4	5.0	6.3
1932	5.0	6.4	4.6	5.8	5.1	5.1	4.8	4.9	3.8	5.3
1933	5.0	4.1	4.7	6.0	5.0	5.4	4.1	4.6	4.5	4.7
1934	5.3	5.1	6.2	5.1	5.5	5.6	3.8	4.4	5.0	5.1
1935	4.9	4.0	5.3	4.6	5.4	5.0	4.2	4.1	4.3	5.2
1936	5.6	5.6	4.3	6.6	6.0	5.7	5.4	4.5	5.8	4.7
1937	4.9	5.7	3.0	3.7	5.2	5.2	4.3	4.6	4.8	4.5
1938	4.2	2.5	4.2	4.5	5.2	3.8	2.9	2.5	4.3	3.8
1939	4.2	7.5	4.1	4.8	4.6	4.3	3.5	3.3	3.6	3.1
1940	4.0	2.9	4.2	4.8	4.5	3.7	3.9	3.2	4.0	3.1

[6] N. Lewis, "Reducing Maternal Mortality in British Columbia: An Educational Process," in B. K. Latham and R. J. Pazdro, eds., *Not Just Pin Money* (Victoria: Camosun College, 1984), pp. 337-55.

[7] Canada. House of Commons, Special Committee on Social Security, *Health Insurance*, Report of the Advisory Committee on Health Insurance Appointed by Order-in-Council, P.C. 836, 5 February 1942, p. 266.

maternal deaths, it had improved substantially upon the national figure of 4.0 fourteen years later. In comparison to rural areas of the province, Vancouver was a slightly more dangerous place for mothers, but the discrepancy in favour of the countryside remained about the same as it was nationally and much less striking than it was in Ontario and Nova Scotia.[8] Figures from a 1942 report cite 26 deaths or 6.9 per 1,000 live births in the city for the 1926-30 period, 15 deaths or 4.5 per 1,000 live births between 1931 and 1935 (a decrease of 34.8 percent), and 14 maternal deaths or 3.5 per 1,000 live births for the 1936-40 years (a decrease of 22.2 percent). While the precise pattern of this downward trend is not discernible, it is clear that a major decrease in Vancouver's maternal mortality occurred in the 1930s.

Meanwhile, B.C. led the nation in the institutionalization of its parturient women. In 1942 the House of Commons' Special Committee on Social Security discovered that B.C. had dramatically increased its rate of hospitalization from 48.3 percent to 84.4 percent of live births between 1926 and 1940. These figures were extremely high when compared with the lowest figures in the country, reported for P.E.I. and Quebec, which ranged respectively from 2.7 percent to 26.2 percent and from 4.8 percent to 15.6 percent over the same years. Even Ontario, with its shift from 24.9 percent to 62.1 percent, far from matched the west coast. The only province to come at all close to B.C.'s rates was Alberta, but even in 1940 it reported only 72.9 percent of live births in its hospitals.[9] As the most highly urbanized of all the provinces, B.C.'s figures are not surprising, particularly in light of Vancouver's preference for hospital births, which began early in the century[10] and continued almost unabated during the 1930s (table 2).[11]

8 *Ibid.*, pp. 257-58, "from 1926 to 1930 [Vancouver] had an annual average of 26 deaths or a rate of 6.9 per 1,000 live births, but by 1936 to 1940 the average annual rate had dropped to 3.5 or 14 deaths." In 1939, 17 rural women died in childbirth compared to 21 urban women. Dr. Helen MacMurchy, *Maternal Mortality in Canada* (Ottawa, 1927) cites mortality figures for the early 1920s, but they are based on a survey of physicians' cases rather than on the more complete statistics of the 1942 *Health Insurance* report.

9 *Health Insurance*, p. 309.

10 See L. O. Stone, *Urban Development in Canada* (Ottawa: DBS, 1967), p. 39, for statistics on rates of urbanization. See Margaret Andrews, "Medical Attendance in Vancouver: 1886-1920," in S. E. D. Shortt, ed., *Medicine in Canadian Society. Historical Perspectives* (Montreal: McGill-Queen's, 1981), pp. 431-34, for an assessment of one doctor's obstetrical patients who, beginning in the 1890s, turned slowly to hospital deliveries.

11 Compiled from *B.C. Sessional Papers*, Reports of the Provincial Board of Health, 1929-1941/2. These figures are for registered births. Neil Sutherland claims that in the early 1930s unregistered births in B.C. were over 5 percent of the total regis-

TABLE 2

*Percentage and Number of Live Births in
Vancouver Institutions, 1928-1939*

1928	67.9%	2,589
1929	70.6%	2,731
1930	76.8%	3,076
1931	77.8%	2,902
1932	78.5%	2,708
1933	79.8%	2,543
1934	75.7%	2,407
1935	77.9%	2,529
1936	80.2%	2,733
1937	83.8%	3,166
1938	86.0%	3,522
1939	89.0%	3,657

Overall, these trends indicate a percentage drop in maternal mortality substantially greater than the percentage increase in hospital births in the late 1920s and the 1930s. In addition, relatively high levels of hospitalization appear to have preceded any substantial reduction in maternal mortality. This lack of correlation suggests that there was no necessary causal relationship between increased hospitalization and mothers' survival rates in Vancouver.[12] But if pregnant women were not obviously spared death by hospital confinement, another group reaped evident benefits. For the medical profession, struggling to maintain its dominant position in health care, institutions in which it could regulate medical practice, eliminate non-medical competition and in time develop an effective therapy were promising indeed.[13] The spread of hospital care

---

tered births. Neil Sutherland, "Social Policy, 'Deviant' Children, and the Public Health Apparatus in British Columbia Between the Wars," *Journal of Educational Thought* 14, 2 (August 1980): 80-91.

[12] In "Cross-cultural Practices" Oakley places the "home-hospital" debate in an international framework. Comparing Britain, with high rates of hospitalization, to the Netherlands, which supports mid-wife assisted home-confinements, Oakley concludes that the "correlation between the rise in hospital delivery and falling maternal and perinatal mortality rates cannot be taken as cause-and-effect" (p. 25), and that home birth has been a central feature of improved maternal health in many societies.

[13] For an instructive analysis of the role institutions played in the development of the Maritime medical profession see Colin Howell, "Reform and the Monopolistic Impulse: The Professionalization of Medicine in the Maritimes," *Acadiensis* X, 1 (1981): 3-22.

correlates very positively with doctors' drive for professional dominance in the health care delivery field. Vancouver's expectant mothers, like other patients, were the presumed beneficiaries of doctors' enhanced authority. The nature of that advantage is examined below.

It was an overwhelmingly male profession which in the 1920s and 1930s presided over women in their experience of childbirth. Not only were there very few female doctors in the city, but obstetrics as a field was, ironically enough, especially difficult for women to enter. In 1939 VGH typically allowed only one female interne and St. Paul's Hospital none.[14] In contrast to this exclusion from the profession, women supplied a critical part of the patient load. Targeted for special attention by local and national health agencies, pregnant women readily became consumers of medical advice which promised relief from the threat of disaster. For general practitioners such patients were essential in establishing a clientele.[15]

Yet, for all its significance in persuading Canadians of the value of medical superintendence and in providing doctors with entrée to the treatment of entire families, obstetrics was very late emerging as a specialty and remained a lowly cousin of more glamorous fields such as surgery. Just as inauspicious was its special affinity for surgical and later chemical and endocrinological solutions to labour problems.[16] For students, inadequate training in obstetrics remained a continuing problem. VGH, for example, only offered its internes two months on the maternity wards; if any individual wanted more experience, he had to arrange to trade assignments with a colleague.[17] In his address to the Toronto convention in 1928, the president of the American Association of Obstetricians, Gynaecologists and Abdominal Surgeons damned existing medical programs in his field in both Canada and the United States. He pointed out that McGill and Toronto, among many other schools, allocated surgery much more time, despite the fact that obstetrics was the backbone of most general practices.[18]

[14] See "Hospitals Approved for Interneships," *Canadian Medical Association Journal* (henceforth *CMAJ*) (September 1939): 304-05.

[15] Lewis, "Reducing Infant Mortality," p. 342.

[16] On these associations see R. W. Wertz and D. C. Wertz, *Lying In: A History of Childbirth in America* (N.Y. and London: The Free Press and Collier MacMillan, 1977).

[17] Provincial Archives of British Columbia (PABC), Sound and Moving Image Division, West Coast Medical History Collection, Interview with Dr. Emile Therrien, 2,370: tape 1, track 1.

[18] Dr. Palmer Findley, "The Teaching of Obstetrics," *American Journal of Obstetrics and Gynaecology* (henceforth *AJOG*) (November 1928): 611-24. For more details on the training of Canadian GPs and its shortcomings, see S. E. D. Shortt, " 'Be-

Owing in large part to the absence of a medical school, Vancouver was later than Montreal, Toronto and London, Ontario, in developing a body of recognized and certified obstetrical experts. By 1940 the American College of Surgeons had approved only Toronto General Hospital and Royal Victoria in Montreal for graduate training in obstetrics and gynaecology. Canadians, usually associated with the university medical faculties of McGill, Toronto or Western Ontario, were regular contributors to the premier publication, the *American Journal of Obstetrics and Gynaecology (AJOG)*, from its inception, but between 1920 and 1945 no B.C.-based doctor published so much as a research note. In contrast, Alberta with its medical school in Edmonton produced several submissions. The pages of the *Canadian Medical Association Journal (CMAJ)* were equally dominated by eastern contributors, with only the very occasional appearance by a B.C. writer.

There were attempts to remedy this situation. Although it did not establish a Committee on Maternal Welfare until October 1938, the Vancouver Medical Association (VMA) was an eager proponent of a more educated and specialized body of doctors in the province.[19] Its sponsorship of summer schools brought leading specialists from all across North America to lecture to B.C.'s doctors on the newest developments in their areas, and obstetrics was a regular part of these programs.[20] The inauguration in 1924 of a monthly publication, the *VMA Bulletin*, spread further news of changes in medical practice and procedure. The *Bulletin* produced a number of obstetrical articles from 1924 through to 1945, but most appear to have echoed, often by some years, concerns voiced by the more prestigious journals.

Such limited publishing credentials were accompanied by relatively little interest in acquiring specialist certification. The American Board of Obstetricians and Gynecologists, organized in 1930, for example, held regular exams after March 1931, but the first Vancouverite was not successful until 1938; the second until 1939. No others were certified before 1945.[21] While some Vancouver practitioners undoubtedly oriented

---

fore the Age of Miracles': The Rise, Fall, and Rebirth of General Practice in Canada, 1890-1940," in Ch. G. Roland, ed., *Health, Disease and Medicine* (Toronto: Hannah Institute for the History of Medicine, 1982).

[19] C. T. Hilton, "Maternal Welfare," *Vancouver Medical Association Bulletin* (henceforth *VMAB*) (September 1939): 352-53.

[20] See, for example, Dr. B. P. Watson, "Antepartum Haemorrhage," *YMAB* (August 1927): 339. Dr. Watson was a professor of medicine at Columbia University.

[21] The first was A. C. Frost, the second Edward M. Blair. See first biannual and then annual examination reports, *AJOG*, 1931-45.

Vancouver General Hospital, ca. 1925

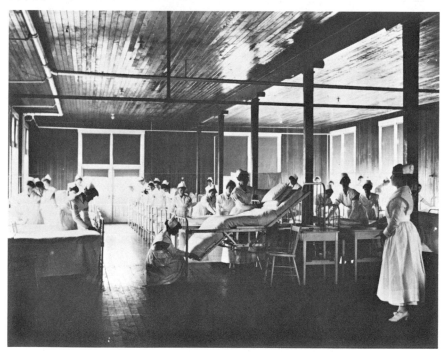

Vancouver General Hospital, ward interior, ca. 1919

more toward professional developments in Britain and Europe,[22] their training seemed to be overwhelmingly North American in origin. The near-absence of specialist credentials from the American Board further confirms relatively low levels of obstetrical training on the part of the city's doctors.

This was the case, for example, with the first two heads of obstetrics and gynaecology at VGH, Doctors William B. Burnett and Walter Turnbull, who received their early medical education in Canada. Burnett, chief throughout the 1920s and much of the 1930s, was an 1899 McGill graduate who never took any specialized obstetrical training. He was, however, a member of the Pacific North West Obstetrical and Gynaecological Association and the American Gynaecological Association. Turnbull graduated from Toronto in 1903 and some twenty years later took post-graduate studies in "obs & gyn" in Europe, New York, Boston and Buffalo.[23] Both men published in their chosen field in the *VMA Bulletin* but in neither the *AJOG* nor the *CMAJ*. On balance, Vancouver then does not appear to have been a centre of obstetrical expertise in anything but a regional sense.

Although the city lacked an elite corps of obstetricians, doctors' training, reinforced regularly by that of immigrant professionals, combined with the directives of the medical press and powerful health institutions such as Vancouver General Hospital to ensure that the great majority of physicians and their treatments differed little from those found in Canadian or American cities of a similar size. Given the shortcomings in training and licensing, there is no reason to believe that Vancouver was exempt from the "meddlesome midwifery" on the part of obstetrician and GP alike of which medical literature regularly complained.[24] "Meddling" could take many forms, from the use of x-rays, to administration

[22] The *Register* of the B.C. Medical Association during these years suggests that doctors with European or British training remained a minority of Vancouver practitioners. In 1920, 40 of 275 doctors (14.55 percent) living in Vancouver had trained or been licensed in England, Scotland or Ireland. By 1930 this figure had declined to 12.94 percent (44 of 340). In 1939, 12.71 percent (53 of 409) of Vancouver's doctors had credentials from Great Britain. BCMA *Register* 1920, 1930, 1939.

[23] See Vancouver Academy of Medicine, BCMA Biographical Files.

[24] See, for example, M. R. Bow, "Maternal Mortality as a Public Health Problem," *CMAJ* (August 1930): 169-73; Robert Ferguson, "A Plea for Better Obstetrics," *CMAJ* (October 1920): 901-04; J. R. Goodall, "Maternal Mortality," *CMAJ* (October 1929): 447-50; E. D. Plass, "The Relation of Forceps and Caesarian Section to Maternal and Infant Morbidity and Mortality," *AJOG* (August 1931): 176-99, and E. Johns, "The Practice of Midwifery," *Canadian Nurse* (January 1925): 11.

of anesthetics and substances such as pituitrin to produce more rapid contractions, to artificial induction of labour, to versions (turning the child manually in the womb), to episiotomies (cutting several inches through skin and muscles of the perineum, the area between the vagina and anus), to the use of low, mid and high forceps, to Caesarian sections and the use of manual or chemical means to extract the placenta. Such substances and techniques all presented problems even to the relatively skilled practitioner. And yet, for a number of reasons, they were tempting and their use tended to increase throughout these decades. On the one hand, they promised to save time for the "busy practitioner"[25] and to assert his authority over the timing and experience of delivery. On the other hand, as doctors pointed out, they often responded "to the pleadings of the patient and the relatives to 'do something.' "[26] Mortality and morbidity rates associated with intervention worried contemporaries, some of whom, like those in Montreal at Royal Victoria Maternity Hospital, became eager to label themselves "conservatives."[27] Unfortunately, it is impossible to tell how much such intervention contributed to rates of maternal death and disability. Many procedures, for example, added to the possibility of haemorrhage, but this in turn might be countered by new blood transfusion techniques. The actual human cost of medical intervention, like that of abortion, remains a matter of speculation.[28]

[25] *CMAJ* (July 1920): 678.

[26] Ross Mitchell, "The Prevention of Maternal Mortality in Manitoba," *CMAJ* (September 1928): 293. See also D. Bjornson, "An Obstetrical Retrospect," *CMAJ* (December 1925): 1236-39, and W. K. Burwell, "Report from Staff (Gynaecological Division) of Vancouver General Hospital," *VMAB* (June 1937): 192-97. In 1919 the Ontario Medical Society was addressed by a representative of the Labour Party of Toronto, "who declared that, more particularly in obstetrics, labour felt itself at the disadvantage of being unable to secure for the wives of their class, those advantages that wealth could command." It is not, however, clear what those advantages were — whether mechanical, manual or chemical intervention or social and economic benefits of supervision and assistance during and after pregnancy. *CMAJ* (April 1920): 305.

[27] Wesley Bourne, M.D., "Anaesthesia in Obstetrics," *CMAJ* (August 1924): 702-03, concerning obstetrical anaesthesia at the Montreal Maternity Hospital. Bourne claims "it may be seen at once that we are conservative; we think advisedly so." W. W. Chipman makes similar claims for conservativism at the Montreal Maternity Hospital. *CMAJ* (June 1926): 681-82. Others proclaimed themselves "moderates"; see, for example, J. W. Duncan, "The 'Radical' in Obstetrics," *AJOG* (August 1930): 225.

[28] In the years 1931-40, for example, puerperal haemorrhage was "the third largest contributing factor to maternal mortality in Canada ... the percentage of deaths from haemorrhage to the total maternal deaths has ranged from 11.3 in 1931 to 16.5 in 1939." *Health Insurance*, p. 260. See also M. Blair, "The Role of Haemorrhage in Mortality Rates in Pregnancy and Childbirth," *CMAJ* (February 1945): 168.

This question of excessive obstetrical intervention unsettled collegial relations within the medical profession. Lacking authority over the actions of doctors in private practice, hospital administrators and specialists across the continent sought to influence medical practice through their control over hospitals. As part of its certification standards which identified a modern North American institution, the American College of Surgeons informally set up in 1928, and soon required for approved hospitals, a "Minimum Standard for Obstetric Departments in Hospitals." This included a "properly organized and equipped department of obstetrics, providing exclusive and adequate accommodation for mothers and the newborn," "segregation or isolation of infected mothers," "adequate clinical laboratory, x-ray and other facilities, under competent supervision," the administration of a "competent, registered nurse, who has executive ability and assistance," adequate supervision by a chief or head of service or department, adequate and complete records, major obstetrical procedures to be performed only after consultations, the adoption of a standard for morbidity, minimum monthly review/analysis of obstetrics, and the opportunity for theoretical instruction and practical experience for student nurses.[29] Such external directives for standardized care were powerful inducements to change, and Vancouver's major hospitals — St. Paul's, Grace and VGH — all struggled to maintain certification standards.[30]

Crucial to the effort to standardize procedures was the formation in 1918 of the B.C. Hospitals' Association, which annually brought together the senior medical and administrative personnel of the province's health institutions. Repeated constantly was the message that the application of more "scientific" and bureaucratic methods would save the mothers of the province and guarantee the authority of medically trained professionals. VGH's decision in the late 1920s to restrict its public wards to staff physicians typified efforts to assert control over the delivery of health care and indicate by example the standards which private practitioners were expected to imitate. Yet, ironically, in spite of complaints that unsupervised GPs attempted dangerous procedures in private practice, by promoting hospitalized care administrators and specialists brought women into an environment where the staff and the equipment, and thus the opportunity and temptation, for greater intervention were more readily available. For example, elaborate preparation procedures, such as shav-

29 M. T. MacEachern, "The Program of the American College of Surgeons for Maternal Care in General Hospitals," *AJOG* (March 1938) : 535-40.

30 *American College of Surgeons Bulletin* 3A (October 1935) : 80.

ing, enemas and lysol washes, and the insistence on stirrups, arm straps and a lithotomy position in which a woman lay on her back with her legs in the air were taken for granted as part of the normal environment of the modern hospital.[31]

The advantages for general practitioners and hospital medical staff of institutionalized confinement are clear. Women's motives for utilizing hospital services are less amenable to study, in part because few women recorded their thoughts or feelings on their experiences in childbirth and in part because they were rarely consulted by those who claimed to serve them. There is little doubt, however, that fear of childbirth loomed large in many women's lives.[32] One city social worker acknowledged this in observing that "women are very, very frightened of this coming child and their health is undermined on account of that."[33] The prospect of death or lifelong disability[34] undermined pleasure taken in intercourse, encouraged a certain fatalism or denial, as with mothers' resistance to telling daughters the "whole" story,[35] and, more positively, inspired the search for better birth control and obstetrical assistance.[36] Finally, women's acquiescence to medical directives was ensured by repeated assurances from public health authorities and the popular media that experts know best and that doctors alone could guarantee the happy termination of pregnancy.[37] In general, while the safety of mother and child was presented as a legitimate concern, a woman's right to some say over the course of childbirth was not. As the Chairman of the Maternal Welfare Committee of the Canadian Medical Association concluded, "cooperation is more to be desired than self-reliance" in the nation's mothers.[38]

[31] See M. MacEachern, *Hospital Organization and Management* (Chicago: Physicians' Record Co., 1935).

[32] For a sensitive discussion of women's anxieties see Judith Walzer-Leavitt, " 'Science' Enters the Birthing Room: Obstetrics in America since the Eighteenth Century," *Journal of American History* 70, 2 (September 1983): 281-304.

[33] PABC, GR707, B.C. Royal Commission on State Health Insurance and Maternity Benefits, 1929-32, Transcript, Mrs. Fischer, p. 318.

[34] See Robert E. McKechnie II, *Strong Medicine: History of Healing on the Northwest Coast* (Vancouver: J. J. Douglas Ltd., 1972), pp. 155-56, for his description of physical damage to women.

[35] See, for example, the reticence of the mother in the account by "Violet Teti Benedetti," *Opening Doors: Vancouver's East End*, Daphne Marlatt and Carole Itter, eds., Sound Heritage Series, VIII, no. 1 & 2 (Victoria, 1979).

[36] See Angus McLaren, "Birth Control and Abortion in Canada, 1870-1920," *Canadian Historical Review* LIX (1978): 318-40.

[37] See Strong-Boag, "Intruders in the Nursery" for its discussion of the authority of medical professionals.

[38] W. B. Hendry, "Maternal Welfare," *CMAJ* (November 1934): 520.

Yet traditionally, women had often looked to collective solutions to the rigours of childbirth. Female relatives, neighbours and friends regularly pooled resources and knowledge in efforts at mutual aid.[39] This familiar female culture was undermined by the transiency which was so much a feature of expanding cities like Vancouver, but perhaps still more by concerted attacks from modern health and childcare professionals. Women's would-be advisors shored up their own claims to authority by ridiculing customary exchanges of information as "old wives' " tales.[40] As consumers in a society where scientific and technical knowledge was increasingly the property of professionals, prospective mothers were far from being the sole arbiters of their own destiny. The economics of a class and patriarchal society, in which material resources were distributed unevenly in general and within the family in particular, also placed major restraints on real choice in labour.[41]

To be sure, midwives or nurses were possible alternatives to male domination, although the unsupervised work of both was rigorously opposed by doctors. Just as forceps had been monopolized by male practitioners earlier,[42] their twentieth-century successors were no more eager to share the results of obstetrical advances. The determination to maintain control over the use of anesthetics was typical.[43] The result was often, as a former nursing superintendent at VGH knew when she cited a senior VON authority, that "nurses are given a very inadequate maternity training so far as the technique of delivery is concerned. We are warned on no account to take a case without a doctor, and with our training we are not likely to do so. We make an attractive setting for a good obstetrician and an unwilling and critical collaborator with a poor one." She bluntly concluded, "The medical profession is responsible for this condition. They

---

[39] Hilda Murray's "The Traditional Role of Women in a Newfoundland Fishing Community" (M.A. thesis, Memorial University of Newfoundland, 1978) describes a female culture which survived well into the twentieth century in a stable Newfoundland community.

[40] See, for example, Jane Lewis, *The Politics of Motherhood: Child and Maternal Welfare in England, 1900-1939* (London: Croom-Helm, 1980) and Strong-Boag, "Intruders in the Nursery."

[41] See the discussion of the unequal distribution of family income in Marjorie Griffin Cohen, "The Decline of Women in Canadian Dairying," *Histoire sociale/Social History* 18 (November 1984): 307-34, and V. Strong-Boag, "Pulling in Double Harness or Hauling a Double Load: Women, Work and Feminism on the Canadian Prairie," forthcoming in *Journal of Canadian Studies.*

[42] See Wertz and Wertz, *Lying In*, pp. 34-35.

[43] See, for example, Dr. Wesley Bourne of McGill, "The Administration of Chloroform in Obstetrics by Nurses," *Canadian Nurse* (November 1930): 585-87.

do not fear the competition of the nurse in any other department of medicine."[44]

Meanwhile, the medical establishment remained as opposed to midwives as it had been in previous decades.[45] True, the persistent lack of care and assistance for Canada's mothers and mothers-to-be, and the knowledge of low maternal mortality rates achieved by northern European countries which promoted midwife-assisted childbirth, led some medical commentators to support the reintroduction of midwives or obstetrical nurses.[46] Charlotte Hanington, superintendent of the Victorian Order of Nurses (VON) for Canada from 1917-23, placed her career on the line over her unsuccessful attempts to import midwives to Canada.[47] However, the disruption during urbanization of community and neighbourhood networks in which midwives traditionally had worked, combined with the absence of provision for their training or licensing, meant that creating a corps of skilled midwives would have required a major reallocation of resources and priorities. Most members of the medical establishment were unable or unwilling to envision such a move and held fast to the belief that "we have committed ourselves for generations to the policy of physician-accouchers. We cannot turn back now even if we should wish to."[48]

Policy aside, there did occur for many years a significant, albeit declining number of non-institutional births in the city, and not all were

---

[44] C. Hannington, cited in Ethel Johns, "The Practice of Midwifery in Canada."

[45] Buckley, "Ladies or Midwives?"; Kathy Kuusisto, "Midwives, Medical Men and Obstetrical Care in Nineteenth Century Nova Scotia" (M.A. thesis, University of Essex, 1980) argues that by 1900 midwives in Nova Scotia had been marginalized, and eliminated as serious competition to doctors. In "Traditions and Neighbourhoods: The Folklife of a Newfoundland Fishing Outpost" (M.A. thesis, Memorial University of Newfoundland, 1971), G. J. Casey states that, in the community he studied, at least one midwife practised. She "had received no formal training except advice and the experience from some older midwife, and occasionally the advice of a medical person" (p. 119). Nancy Schrom Dye in "History of Childbirth in America" argues that the modern period in the history of childbirth in America began in the 1920s when physicians emerged as the unchallenged birth attendants. Authors such as Buckley and Kuusish suggest that in Canada this periodization is applicable, though Casey's work is an important reminder of the different pace of developments in some rural areas.

[46] See H. M. Little, "What's the Matter With Obstetrics," *CMAJ* (May 1929): 647, who concluded "there is crying need for specially trained obstetric nurses, call them midwives if you will."

[47] Buckley, "Ladies or Midwives?", pp. 144-47.

[48] J. R. Goodall, "Maternal Mortality," p. 449. For a discussion of community disruption which accompanied Vancouver's rapid rate of urban growth, see D. L. Matters, "A Report on Health Insurance: 1919," *BC Studies* 21 (Spring 1974): 28-32.

under medical supervision. Between 1925 and 1929, for instance, Vancouver recorded at least 1,743 deliveries by midwives out of a total of
19,730.[49] Such lay help persisted despite critics. One of the latter, more
sympathetic than most, described such competitors as "women, good-
hearted souls and all that sort of thing, practising maternity work and
calling themselves maternity nurses, and they have absolutely no such
qualifications; they know absolutely nothing about the work. They don't
know about sterilizing; they don't know the first rules of procedure. . . .
They happen to drop in at a neighbour's house when a case is coming
off." The critic conceded that "when it is an easy birth, they get through
all right, but when there are complications it works out different."[50]
Lacking legal status, these attendants must have hesitated to call in
medical authorities when complications did arise, but so long as the pregnancy was normal and hospitals remained centres of infection and intervention, domestic surroundings and experienced, if unlicensed, care might
be a very sensible solution.[51] Whatever their professional qualifications,
such women were cheap, potentially extremely helpful with domestic
duties and reassuringly familiar when compared with their more scientific
and impersonal rivals. Complaints regarding women's difficulty in finding
unlicensed attendants indicate the role non-medical care continued to
play for some expectant mothers in these years.[52]

For less affluent women wishing institutional services, the options actually available in Vancouver in the 1920s and 1930s were very much
limited by class and ethnicity. Oriental and native patients found that
segregated facilities and/or different standards awaited them whenever

[49] W. N. Kemp, "The Stillbirth Problem in Relation to Iodine Insufficiency," *VMAB*
(December 1933): 58.

[50] PABC, GR707, B.C. Royal Commission on State Health Insurance and Maternity
Benefits, 1929-32, Transcript, Mrs. Sadie Moore, p. 314.

[51] A May 1929 *CMAJ* editorial by H. M. Little of the Montreal Maternity Hospital
criticized the contemporary obstetrical surgical procedures and claimed, "Obstetrics
is still in the large majority of cases a matter for the home," "What's the Matter
With Obstetrics?", p. 646. This opinion was supported by the international statistics for midwife deliveries often reported in the journal. For example, McGill professor of obstetrics and gynaecology J. R. Goodall's article, "Maternal Mortality,"
cites an Aberdeen, Scotland, inquiry into maternal mortality which discovered the
maternal mortality rate of institutions to be five times greater and doctors' rate two
times greater than that of midwives. *CMAJ* (October 1929): 447-50.

[52] Mrs. McLachlan's testimony before the 1929-32 Commission on State Health
Insurance and Maternity Benefits, "You can pick up all kinds of help to do housework when you cannot pick up a trained nurse," is representative of such complaints. PABC, GR707, Royal Commission, Transcript, p. 324.

they applied to hospitals.[53] Even when race was no barrier to access, poverty, which growing numbers faced throughout these decades, meant reliance on the VON, hospital out-patient services and public wards. The pre-natal clinic established at VGH in 1932 saw women lining up along 12th Avenue. As the Women's Auxiliary noted, many outpatients "had a scanty breakfast — or, if coming for a blood test, none at all — leaky shoes on and no rubbers, the one cotton housedress a year issued by Central Clothing, and a raincoat." After walking or waiting for a street-car, they then waited for an hour or two "on a hard wooden bench" for a doctor to see them.[54] Costs of confinement itself, reckoned in 1921 as $35 for a normal delivery, $50 with haemorrhage, $45 with instrumental labour and $35 if a miscarriage occurred, were far beyond the budgets of many families.[55] Not unexpectedly, the first thing a woman often asked herself when she failed to menstruate was "How am I going to foot the bill?"[56] It is hard to be surprised that abortion tempted many.[57] Others resigned themselves to charity, and such cases made up a majority of VGH's public wards.[58] In fact, the pressure on VGH facilities became so serious in the early years of the depression that no normal obstetrical cases were admitted to public wards without the consent of the medical super-intendent.[59] It was arranged with the City Relief Office to provide $10 to the VON and $20 to a doctor to provide for charity patients at home.[60]

During these years some unmarried mothers, especially younger ones, turned to a variety of rescue homes operated by the city's churches. Some

[53] For instance, for some years, oriental maternity patients were regularly released some days sooner after childbirth than their sisters of European origin. See PABC, GR749, B.C. Provincial Secretary, Health Insurance Research, "Report on Information Collected and Compiled in Reference to Certain Phases of Hospital Work in British Columbia," 1934, p. 17.

[54] "Report of the Social Service Committee of the Women's Auxiliary," *Annual Report* of VGH, 1935, p. 37.

[55] PABC, GR706, B.C. Royal Commission on Health Insurance and Maternity Benefits 1919-21, File 2/5, "Report on Health Insurance, 1921," p. 55.

[56] PABC, GR707, B.C. Royal Commission on State Health Insurance and Maternity Benefits 1929-32, "Transcript of Evidence," Appendix H, V. II, testimony of Mrs. Manifold of the Women's Navy League, p. 317.

[57] See McLaren and McLaren, "Discoveries and Dissimulations."

[58] See for example PABC, GR706, Royal Commission on Health Insurance and Maternity Benefits 1919-21, File 4/5, "Proceedings," testimony of Dr. MacEachern, p. 668.

[59] In 1933, 772 of 1,773 or 43.5 percent of deliveries at VGH were in the public wards. While the number of deliveries in the VGH Maternity Building increased between 1934 and 1940 from 1,605 to 2,490, the percentage of public ward deliveries decreased from 31.2 percent to 20.9 percent.

[60] "Report of the Out-Patients' Department," *Annual Report* of VGH, 1933, p. 61.

of these, as with the homes maintained by the Catholic Church and the Salvation Army, were associated with hospitals where girls often became patients in the public wards before returning to religious chaperonage.[61] Their special anxieties about the future of themselves and their babies must have only too often made the birthing process itself all the more intimidating and alienating.

Middle- and upper-class women, with greater financial resources, might choose to deliver at home, but for them the most specialized and certified of assistance was available. They might elect a licensed private maternity hospital or home, although these almost disappeared over the twenty years.[62] Probably more important were the services of the small group of specialists appearing in the city who increasingly limited private practice to obstetrics and sometimes to obstetrics and gynecology.[63] Such privileged treatment continued into VGH, where home-like private rooms with meals on a silver service promised the best of results. Here too the perennial servant problem of the middle class was solved, at least in the short term, and prospective mothers could benefit from the compulsive standards of cleanliness which advertising's hard-sell told them should also characterize their own homes.[64] By 1920 the days were over when "no self-respecting woman, however much she dreaded the coming ordeal or the upsetting of her household, resultant upon its advent, would entertain for a moment the suggestion of going to the hospital. The hospital was only for the outcast and the unfortunate."[65] The belated passage in December 1926 of a municipal money bylaw to finance a new maternity

---

[61] See Andrée Levesque, "Deviant Anonymous: Single Mothers at the Hôpital de la Miséricorde in Montreal, 1929-1939," *Historical Papers*, Canadian Historical Association, 1984, for her useful discussion of the distinctive treatment received by women bearing children out-of-wedlock. Unfortunately, it is not clear whether this extended to differences on the obstetrical table itself, although one suspects this may indeed be the case.

[62] See listings under "Hospitals" in *Wrigley's B.C. Directory* for Vancouver 1919-1939. See also Margaret W. Andrews, "St. Luke's Home, Vancouver, 1888-1936," *Journal of the Canadian Church Historical Society* 24, 2 (1982): 90-98, for an example of an Anglican initiative in this area which succumbed to the superior obstetrical resources of the large hospitals.

[63] Vancouver physicians such as Harold Caple and Isabel Day travelled east in the 1930s for six to twelve months' post-graduate work in obstetrics and gynaecology, though according to the Vancouver Medical Association records the number of doctors specializing in this way were few. Vancouver Academy of Medicine, VMA Biographical Files.

[64] For a very useful discussion of middle-class responsiveness see Wertz and Wertz, *Lying In*, ch. 5.

[65] Dr. A. S. Munro, "The Hospital — Past, Present and Future," *Proceedings* of the First Convention of the Hospitals of B.C., 1918, p. 11.

building, eventually completed in 1929, made VGH all the more attractive a choice for those who could afford $5 and more a day, plus physicians' fees, for privacy.

For all the differences which distinguished female experience, the fact or the possibility of childbirth encouraged bonds of sympathy between races and classes. The creation, for instance, of such national institutions as the federal Division of Child Welfare and the VON, which were instrumental in developing effective pre- and post-natal maternal and child care, owed a great deal to first-wave feminism's proclivity for women helping women.[66] Provincially, the campaigns of women's organizations for maternity insurance benefits and mothers' allowances, like the activities of the VGH Women's Auxiliary and the auxiliaries to the other hospitals, were very much predicated on a sympathetic appreciation of the difficulties of motherhood shared by all women.[67]

Submissions by the city's women's groups to the provincial Royal Commissions on Health Insurance and Maternity Benefits of 1919-21 and then of 1929-32 reflect both the consensus within the women's community over the problems of inadequate maternity assistance and the changing beliefs as to how these problems could be solved. The 1919-21 Commission recommended that a maternity benefit be paid to women, or wives of men, who earned less than $1,200 per year. These women would be given $35 per child and $25 per additional child born within twenty-four hours, if proof was presented that the mother was attended by a qualified doctor or, if no doctor was available, a qualified nurse.[68] Although there was some difference of opinion as to how and to whom benefits would be administered, the concept of a cash benefit was approved by the sixty-nine women's groups represented. There was also the strong sense that women, whatever their situation, should be insured as a group. A speaker for women in the Vancouver Trades and Labor Council endorsed universal coverage, arguing "all mothers should be covered because there are a number of people who would look upon it

---

[66] See Lewis, "Advising the Parents" and "Reducing Infant Mortality," and Strong-Boag, "Intruders in the Nursery."

[67] See Linda Hale, "The British Columbia Woman Suffrage Movement, 1890-1917" (M.A. thesis, U.B.C., 1977); Gillian Weiss, "As Women and as Citizens: Club-women in Vancouver, 1910-1928" (Ph.D. thesis, U.B.C., 1984) and Susan Walsh, "Equality, Emancipation and a More Just World: Leading Women in the B.C. CCF" (M.A. thesis, S.F.U., 1984).

[68] PABC, GR706, B.C. Royal Commission on Health Insurance and Maternity Benefits 1919-1921, Box 1, File 1, "Report on Maternity Insurance, 1921," p. 9.

otherwise as a charity." A representative from the Women's Forum also advocated the inclusion of married and unmarried mothers, urging women "let us stick together."[69]

Three points are especially significant in these hearings: first is the unanimous support for benefits by women of different classes; second is the support for a cash payment directly to pregnant women, which would increase women's consumer power in the obstetrical care market; and third is the discussion of maternity benefits as distinct from other types of health insurance. It is noteworthy that the general superintendent of VGH reserved his opinion on maternity benefits until advantages to the province's institutions could be demonstrated. In his mind, evidently, concern for the hospital outweighed the need to provide women with choice in the health care market.[70]

By the time of the 1929-32 Commission, the degree of concern over maternal health had heightened, but with new solutions that VGH's general superintendent would have found very congenial. As J. H. Mc-Vety of the B.C. Hospital Association advised, "have the maternity benefit part of the general scheme, recognizing it just as though it were a sickness" paid directly to the institution or individual providing the service so the money will be spent as intended, not "diverted."[71] Women's testimony now also advocated direct financing of institutions and organizations. Unlike hospital representatives, however, women appeared less defenders of the institutions than cognizant of the shortcomings of the private health care market. As one woman concluded, "It is impossible for the majority of families today to pay $35 a week for a trained nurse. And so few families can afford to put down $25 before the mother can go to a hospital."[72]

This social concern over high levels of maternal mortality, pressure within their profession for doctors to perform obstetrical interventions within an approved hospital and the limited choice of assistance for home deliveries combined to promote the growth of institutional births in post-World War I Vancouver. By 1940 safer confinements meant utilizing professional staff and enhanced equipment within updated specialty wards and out-patients' services such as provided by VGH, the publicly

[69] *Ibid.*, File 4, "Proceedings," pp. 522-28.

[70] *Ibid.*, p. 698.

[71] PABC, GR707, Royal Commission on State Health Insurance and Maternity Benefits 1929-32, "Transcript of Evidence," Appendix H, V II, p. 357.

[72] *Ibid.*, p. 316.

funded institution which accommodated more than one-half the city's hospital deliveries during these two decades.[73]

Conditions in the province's largest hospital were, however, far from satisfactory during these years. Major investigations of VGH in 1912, 1930 and 1936 all described concerns with overcrowding, underfinancing, questionable procedures and limited facilities.[74] Maternity patients suffered along with others. In 1920 VGH's maternity wards, not untypically, experienced "a very pressing lack of accommodation, and such a large number of cases had to be handled constantly that at times . . . facilities were not capable of coping with the work."[75] Not unexpectedly, the maintenance of isolation and the restriction of infection were very difficult to guarantee. Although the need for a separate maternity facility was evident from the first study, the 1920 defeat in every ward in the city of a money bylaw requesting $500,000 to build a new maternity building and a new nurses' residence retarded improvements until the end of the decade. Even with its construction in 1929 there were problems, as one head maternity nurse remembered: "That maternity building . . . my goodness, you ran your feet off. It was a headache! It was very cheaply built, you know. The plumbing was dreadful. You could hear every sound. You could be in a private room and hear every cough and sneeze above you and below you. . . . The plumbing made so much noise and the hot water pipes cracked in the night . . . but the doctors thought it was alright . . . "[76]

Nor was accommodation the only cause for discomfort. The 1930 Commission, which included as chairman Dr. A. K. Haywood, VGH's future general superintendent, and Dr. Malcolm MacEachern, former

---

[73] At present the available documentation on the major alternatives to confinement within VGH — St. Paul's Hospital, run by the Sisters of Providence since 1892; Grace Hospital, managed by the Salvation Army beginning in 1927; and St. Vincent's, run by the Sisters of Charity from 1939 — is scanty. Still less is known about the operations of such small, privately owned, licensed and unlicensed institutions as Tolmie Maternity Home and Impey Maternity Hospital, both operating in the 1920s. VGH remained the largest maternity facility throughout the period. In 1935, for instance, VGH reported 1,585 births while St. Paul's reported only 683 and Grace another 370. See *Vancouver Sun*, 31 December 1935.

[74] B.C. Royal Commission on Vancouver General Hospital, *Report*, 1912; Vancouver Hospital Survey Commission, *Report upon the Hospital Situation of Greater Vancouver*, 1930; W. H. Welsh, M.D., with comments by A. K. Haywood, M.D., *A Study of the Vancouver General Hospital*, March 1936.

[75] "Report of the Medical Departments of the Hospital," *Annual Report* of VGH, 1920, pp. 44-45.

[76] PABC. Sound and Moving Image Division, Vancouver General Hospital Collection, Interview with Helen King, 520, tape 2, track 2, transcription, p. 2.

general superintendent, condemned routine examinations of maternity patients "which are not in accord with the teachings of the leading obstetricians who warn against certain practices in normal cases."[77] This critical assessment flew in the face of the earlier assertion by VGH's head of obstetrics that "every doctor . . . is a good maternity doctor because of the practical training he received in this department as a student, and by dint of the two cases he handled all by himself while 'Interne' in the surgical ward afterwards."[78] The Commission's further complaints about record-keeping and the refusal of some physicians to accept the discipline of up-to-date procedures suggested how far VGH and at least some of its medical chiefs had strayed from MacEachern's earlier standards.

As general superintendent of VGH between 1913 and 1923 and founder of the B.C. Hospitals' Association, MacEachern was instrumental in establishing standards which won VGH accreditation by the American College of Surgeons soon after the war. An energetic administrator, his talents soon took him far from Vancouver, eventually to become Associate Director of the American College of Surgeons and its Director of Hospital Activities. His *Hospital Organization and Management*, originally published in 1935 and reprinted many times, became a classic in the field. MacEachern himself donated a first edition to VGH's Internes' Library. The inclusion of a substantial section on obstetrical care was close to the heart of an author who was also the inventor of the MacEachern Obstetrical Table and former Surgeon and Medical Superintendent of the Montreal Maternity Hospital. MacEachern's influence in Vancouver was reaffirmed throughout the 1920s and 1930s by regular visits back to his former home and such official duties as membership on the Vancouver Hospital Survey Commission in 1930.[79]

The appointment of the Commission's chairman as general superintendent that same year was an obvious attempt to bring about reform. Dr. Haywood, M.B. (Tor.), M.R.C.S., L.R.C.P., who took the superintendency over from 1930 to 1947,[80] shared MacEachern's enthusiasm for

[77] Vancouver Hospital Survey Commission, *Report*, 1930, p. 88.

[78] Burnett, "Maternity Work in the Small Hospital," *Report* of the Proceedings of the Convention of the Hospitals of B.C., 1918, p. 81.

[79] On these visits see the B.C. News section of the *CMAJ*. On MacEachern himself see *The Canadian Who's Who*, vol. VI, 1952-4, pp. 648-49. See also Margaret Andrews, "Medical Services in Vancouver, 1886-1920; A Study in the Interplay of Attitudes, Medical Knowledge, and Administrative Structures" (Ph.D. thesis, U.B.C., 1979), especially chapter 3.

[80] *Who's Who Among Physicians and Surgeons*, vol. 1, 1938, ed. J. C. Schwartz (N.Y., 1938), p. 747. Also Anne S. Cavers, *Our School of Nursing, 1899-1949* (School of Nursing, Vancouver General Hospital, n.d.), p. 87.

raising hospital standards, but his dedication to making VGH a fully up-to-date and efficient operation ran full tilt into the municipal and provincial cutbacks to hospital funding in the depression.[81] Wards W and X, for example, had to remain in the basement of the old main building. Despite being badly ventilated, without proper conditions for segregating patients, and containing inadequate provision for nursing and food service, they supplied the only accommodation "for a decent woman patient who might have become septic during childbirth or abortion."[82] There, because the Maternity Building itself lacked provision for isolating infected patients, she would join prostitutes and others needing treatment for VD. On the other hand, Haywood's era did see the revival of the Women's Auxiliary, which had collapsed in 1926 under the weight of its responsibilities for managing much of the Out-Patient Department and supplying the hospital with many of its regular supplies. Renewal of the Auxiliary's assistance with layettes, food and practical advice to maternity patients entering the public wards was a significant benefit, for all the accompanying assumptions of superiority and authority.[83]

Such sympathetic support was especially important when, as one Vancouver practitioner acknowledged, it was too easy for doctors to be insensitive when dealing with obstetrical patients. Noting that pregnancy bordered "on the pathological," a growing belief within the profession, he urged his colleagues to postpone internal examinations during the first consultation with nervous patients and to make every effort to be helpful and supportive.[84] Such admonitions may well have been taken to heart, but after 1929, when public ward patients were denied the services of private practitioners and assigned routinely to the staff service, the reassurance of whatever prior contacts had been made with a sympathetic doctor disappeared, at least for the poor. The barring of family members from delivery rooms, in contrast to the likelihood of their presence at home births, still further depersonalized an institutional environment which might promise safety but also readily imposed alienation. It would be hard for an already overworked nursing staff — predominantly student nurses being taught the gospel of cleanliness, neatness and routine

---

[81] For a useful discussion of these funding problems see Harry M. Cassidy, *Public Health and Welfare Organization* (Toronto: Ryerson Press, 1945).

[82] Haywood in Walsh, *A Study of the VGH*, n.p.

[83] See the work and reports of the Women's Auxiliary in the *Annual Reports* of VGH.

[84] Dr. C. F. Covernton, "Problems of Primipara," *VMAB* (May 1931): 179-83.

procedure — to compensate for the emotional and personal deficiencies of such a system.[85]

The procedures recommended upon the onset of labour continued the objectification of the patient. Her hair was arranged in "two tight braids"; the area around the vagina was shaved and bathed with soap, water and lysol. She was given only a liquid diet, "even though she does not ask for it" and was to excrete every hour. In the meantime, the prospective mother was checked regularly for her own and the baby's pulse rate.[86] In the delivery room itself she was surrounded by doctors, nurses and students, commonly strangers, hidden in gowns, caps and masks. She herself was similarly disguised with elaborate draping. At this point the woman and her physician faced a number of options which varied not only with her condition but with shifting fashions in obstetrics and the relative skill and knowledge of those in attendance.

Unfortunately, given available records, dating the introduction at VGH of particular drugs and techniques is difficult. Between 1922 and 1929 the hospital's annual reports did include appendices citing statistics for the various areas of medical and surgical treatment. However, few surgical or manual and no chemical procedures are specified for obstetrical cases, and while the type, frequency, outcome and average stay of obstetrical cases are indicated, no information regarding the relationship between particular therapies and patient health is offered. It is nearly impossible to gain insights from these reports into the efficacy of hospital obstetrical practices. Individual practitioners may have recorded this information, and hospital medical staff may have included it on record cards for public patients, but if so only a relatively small number of doctors benefited. The city's medical profession and the public in general were left largely in the dark about the success of various obstetrical practices.

New kinds of records were created by VGH from at least 1933. These records emphasized the type and frequency of medical procedures employed by the hospital on maternity patients and provided staff and practitioners generally with empirical evidence with which to evaluate scientifically current obstetrical practices. The appearance of articles in the *Vancouver Medical Association Bulletin* and the *Canadian Medical Association Journal* which presented statistical analyses of VGH's obstet-

---

[85] Like other Canadian hospitals, the VGH staffed its wards with student nurses enrolled in the VGH School of Nursing. For a discussion of the content of nursing training see Kathryn McPherson, "Nurses and Nursing in Early Twentieth Century Halifax" (M.A. thesis, Dalhousie University, 1982), chap. 2.

[86] MacEachern, *Hospital Organization*, pp. 866-75.

rical interventions indicated the wider dissemination of this evidence within the medical profession in the 1930s.[87] This shift in the nature of published statistics reflected the mounting preoccupation with the promise of intervention and the desire to confirm the "scientific" basis of medical action.

Just as with the statistical record, chemical treatments appear to have been in a state of some flux during these years. Chloroform and ether, old stand-bys from the 1840s, continued to be used into the 1920s. Their use was, however, more restricted since the possibility of damage to liver and kidneys was now recognized.[88] Twilight sleep, a combination of morphine to deaden the pain and various amnesiac drugs, notably scopalomine, had been used in Canada since its development in Germany in the early twentieth century, but its potential for causing vertigo and delirium in the mother and narcoticizing the baby limited its popularity severely.[89] Also available to doctors were rectal anaesthesia, although this

---

[87] W. K. Burwell, "Report from Staff (Gynaecological Division) of Vancouver General Hospital," *VMAB* 13 (1937): 193-97, and F. Sidney Hobbs, "Maternity Statistics," *CMAJ* (January 1943): 48-51. Obstetrical statistics for the 1920s can be found in VGH *Annual Reports*. According to Frederick J. Fish, VGH's director of medical records, the VGH changed its record-keeping system in 1932. This "effort at standardization which, although purely local, will have, it is hoped, an effect for good," included adopting the Massachusetts General Hospital interpretation of disease nomenclature and discarding "the classification books, in which all diagnoses were recorded heretofore, . . . in favor of the more handy and efficient 'Kardex' cabinet." See F. J. Fish, "The Medical Records System of the Vancouver General Hospital, Vancouver, B.C.," *Bulletin of the American College of Surgeons* 18, 2 (June 1933): 52-58.

[88] Dr. G. M. Feldert, "Alleviating the Pains of Childbirth," *Canadian Nurse* (August 1920): 470.

[89] For more negative views see U. E. Bateson, "Twilight Sleep in Obstetrical Practice in Reports of Cases," *CMAJ* (June 1925): 639-40; W. Bourne, "Anesthesia in Obstetrics," *CMAJ* (August 1924): 702-03. For a more positive assessment see Ross Mitchell, "The Use of Pituitary Extract and Scopalomine-Morphine in Obstetrics," *CMAJ* (May 1921): 351-55. See also the critical editorial which follows Mitchell's article. This condemned the "tendency in certain countries and localities" to make use of drugs recommended by Mitchell "as an incentive to the patient to choose certain centres as her temporary place of abode. To promise a patient the application particularly of the latter [i.e., twilight sleep] . . . has led without question to its abuse, and in large extent its discredit." *CMAJ* (May 1921): 366. In another article D. Bjornson, "An Obstetrical Retrospect," *CMAJ* (December 1925): 1236-39, asserts that modern women knew about, and demanded, twilight sleep, ether, etc., leaving young practitioners in a quandary. A later editorial claimed that one of the causes of maternal mortality in Canada was "the insistence of mothers and their relatives and friends on the speedy termination of labour"; see "Maternal Mortality and the Practice of Obstetrics," *CMAJ* (February 1929): 180-81. There is some non-medical evidence that individual women did actively seek out chemical assistance in labour; for example, see Laura Salverson, *Confessions of an Immigrant Daughter* (Toronto: University of Toronto Press, 1981). However, Canadian women did not collectively demand greater

demanded considerable control by the patient,[90] and a combination of nitrous oxide and oxygen.[91] The latter seems to have become especially popular. It did, for all the usefulness and success noted by a prominent Vancouver doctor, however, definitely require the presence of an anaesthetist.[92] This added not only to the numbers of strange attendants surrounding the patient but also to her final bill at VGH as elsewhere.[93] Only with the introduction of spinal anaesthetics in the 1940s would choices change substantially, and even then the additional expense remained.

The extent of medical intervention also varied from private to public wards. There is some indication that staff doctors were rather more conservative than private practitioners. One report, examining VGH records for 1934, 1935 and 1936, made this point about induction, arguing that "when one is dealing with a private patient ... there is a real urge to make it truly successful, to get it over with. Patients are not much impressed with the idea of going home and coming back and, as a result, the doctor gets the blame; it is rather poor advertising." This staff doctor believed that patients should not in fact be induced solely because they were at term, but he noted that VGH's chief of obstetrics disagreed with him.[94] This self-proclaimed conservatism changed markedly once it came to a discussion of the use of low forceps, admittedly much less serious than the mid or high variations. Usually done "for the benefit of the interne on the service," their employment was supervised by a resident or staff member. The author thought that more patients might be delivered this way since "it wouldn't hurt ... and it would be a great help to the interne who is soon to embark in private practice." With his own primipara cases he preferred "prophylactic low forceps and median episiotomy" as a matter of course.[95] Despite this predilection, he observed that

availability of twilight sleep to the same extent as their American sisters, who publicly campaigned for such intervention to ease the lot of their sex. For the U.S., see Wertz and Wertz, *Lying In*, pp. 150-54, and Judith Walzer-Leavitt, "Birthing and Anesthesia: The Debate Over Twilight Sleep," *Signs* 6, 1 (1980): 147-64.

[90] See R. N. Ritchie, "Rectal Anaesthesia in Obstetrics," *Canadian Nurse* (July 1924): 352-54, and J. D. Graham, "Rectal Anesthesia in Obstetrics," *CMAJ* (September 1925): 935-39.

[91] W. Bourne, "Nitrous Oxide-Oxygen Analgesia and Anaesthesia in Obstetrics," *CMAJ* (November 1921): 818-22.

[92] Bergland, "The Relief of Pain in Labour," pp. 57-59. See also MacEachern, *Hospital Organization*, p. 282.

[93] See Haywood, *Hospital Survey Commission* 1930, pp. 89-90.

[94] Burwell, "Report from Staff," p. 193.

[95] *Ibid.*, p. 195.

instrumental deliveries are far more common on the private than on the staff side." Even then they made up a small part of the caseload in these years since 1,253 of 1,519 confinements, or 82.49 percent, were assessed as normal, with 129 cases of low forceps, 27 of midforceps, 20 of version, 45 of caesarian section and 45 breech deliveries.[96]

This staff doctor's preference for instrumental intervention, however "moderate," helped change the percentage of so-called "normal" deliveries over the longer period 1933-1941, when only 13,359 of 18,539 or 72.2 percent were so identified at Vancouver General.[97] This trend occurred despite the retirement in 1937 of Dr. Burnett, head of obstetrics, who had been a devotee of elective versions and whose patients made up a majority of these interventions.[98] Table 3[99] reveals some significant trends.

What stands out here is the difference, not always large but almost always present, between private and public patients. The fact that 44 percent of false labours over the 1933-41 period occurred in the public ward, which accounted for only 26 percent of VGH's deliveries in those years, indicates a willingness on the part of staff doctors and their charity patients to wait for natural labour rather than attempt induction.[100] In almost every case the degree of medical intervention, including all types of forceps and the very dangerous, if "glamorous," C-section,[101] was greater on private wards. Explanations for this phenomenon vary. Patients anticipating difficulty may have made additional efforts to raise funds to pay for confinement and doctors' fees. Certainly more and more women were turning to private or semi-private accommodation over these years. What cannot be ignored, however, is the fact that interventions such as versions or C-sections added to medical fees and incomes while simultaneously asserting the supremacy of the professional. They also commonly shortened the length of the delivery, a boon perhaps to a weary mother but always to a busy practitioner. Nor is the fact that the majority of cases were delivered by GPs without significance.[102] Obstetricians regu-

---

96 *Ibid.*, p. 196.

97 F. Sidney Hobbs, "Maternity Statistics," *CMAJ* (January 1943): 49.

98 *Ibid.* See also Burnett, "Versions," *VMAB* (November 1928): 42; "It is essential for every obstetrician to be able to do a version."

99 Calculated from Hobbs, "Maternity Statistics," table 1, p. 49.

100 *Ibid.* Burwell states that in public wards "one may not hesitate to let the patient return home after one or two unsuccessful inductions of labour where no obstetrical abnormality is present," "Report from Staff," p. 193.

101 Burwell, "Report from Staff," p. 196.

102 Hobbs, "Maternity Statistics," p. 48.

TABLE 3

Maternity Statistics, VGH, 1933-1941

		1933	1934	1935	1936	1937	1938	1939	1940	1941	Total
Deliveries	To*	1773	1605	1647	1728	1991	2191	2343	2490	2771	18,539
	Pr	1001	1104	1171	1231	1463	1592	1748	1970	2426	13,706
	Pu	772	501	476	497	528	599	595	520	345	4,833
False	To	117	63	55	57	54	59	80	76	62	623
labour	Pr	44	37	29	16	37	33	45	55	51	347
	Pu	73	26	26	41	17	26	35	21	11	276
Normal	To	1363	1111	1245	1265	1447	1547	1684	1763	1934	13,359
deliveries	Pr	680	704	830	834	969	1042	1168	1306	1634	9,167
	Pu	683	407	415	431	478	505	516	457	300	4,192
Caesarians	To	45	48	69	48	61	70	74	87	110	612
	Pr	29	38	49	33	52	58	68	82	101	510
	Pu	16	10	20	15	9	12	6	5	9	102
% of	To	2.5	2.3	4.1	2.7	3.0	3.1	3.1	3.4	3.9	3.3
Caesarians	Pr	2.9	3.4	4.2	3.6	3.6	3.6	3.9	4.2	4.2	3.7
	Pu	2.1	2.0	4.2	1.7	1.7	2.0	1.0	.96	2.6	2.1
Versions	To	52	63	26	31	22	13	11	8	3	229
	Pr	49	51	22	27	17	9	11	5	3	194
	Pu	3	12	4	4	5	4	—	3	—	35
High	To	3	2	—	—	2	5	2	7	5	26
forceps	Pr	3	2	—	—	1	2	2	7	5	22
	Pu	—	—	—	—	1	3	—	—	—	4
Mid	To	61	69	67	59	62	102	121	121	149	811
forceps	Pr	38	59	58	51	59	85	102	111	146	709
	Pu	23	10	9	8	3	17	19	10	3	102
Low	To	249	312	240	325	397	454	451	504	570	3,502
forceps	Pr	202	250	212	286	265	395	397	459	537	3,103
	Pu	47	62	28	39	32	59	54	45	33	399

*To=Total; Pr=Private; Pu=Public

larly condemned this group for attempting treatments beyond their experience or understanding. Their interventions were characterized as frequently providing later employment for gynaecologists.[103]

[103] Robert Ferguson, "A Plea for Better Obstetrics," *CMAJ* (October 1920): 901-04. Ferguson claimed that 30 percent of the work of gynaecologists was created by bad obstetrics. John Osborn Polak of Brooklyn, N.Y., claimed that 60 percent of gynaecological cases were direct results of poor obstetrical practice, "Effect of Popular Gynaecological Procedures on the Future Child-Bearing Women," *CMAJ* (September 1924): 797-803.

TABLE 4

Percentage of Maternal Morbidity, VGH, 1933-1941

	Total	Private	Public
1933	4.6%	3.5%	6.1%
1934	5.4%	3.6%	9.5%
1935	4.4%	3.0%	7.6%
1936	6.1%	4.1%	11.9%
1937	5.4%	3.5%	10.0%
1938	7.5%	7.5%	7.5%
1939	7.4%	9.7%	5.2%
1940	6.8%	7.3%	5.0%
1941	5.3%	5.4%	4.9%

TABLE 5

Percentage of Maternal Mortality, VGH, 1933-1941

	Total	Private	Public
1933	0.5%	.8%	.3%
1934	0.5%	.5%	.6%
1935	0.3%	.3%	.2%
1936	0.3%	.4%	.2%
1937	0.05%	.05%	—
1938	0.1%	.1%	—
1939	0.04%	.04%	—
1940	0.2%	.2%	—
1941	0.03%	.03%	—

The trends in maternal morbidity and mortality, as evident in tables 4[104] and 5,[105] also reveal differences between private and public wards but are somewhat inconclusive about the exact effect of differential treatment over the nine years surveyed.

At the very least, however, it is fair to say that the benefits of private care in terms of these two major variables are uncertain. The erratic

[104] Calculated from Hobbs, "Maternity Statistics," table II, p. 50.
[105] *Ibid.*

pattern of morbidity over the years 1933-41 also suggests that the hospital experienced considerable difficulty in controlling infection. The introduction of sulfonamide drugs in the late 1930s, as acknowledged by one 1943 observer, appeared to have been critical in lowering pregnancy's dreaded costs.[106]

In keeping with its effort to maintain institutional standards, Vancouver General made some attempt to regulate doctors' regimes. The increase in the incidence of C-sections, for example, prompted a rule requiring the prior consent of the general superintendent or one of his assistants.[107] In other developments the institution concurred. The steady increase in episiotomies revealed in table 6[108] reflects a trend which was becoming normative in North American hospitals.[109]

TABLE 6

Percentage of Episiotomies, VGH, 1933-1941

	Total	Private	Public
1933	8.7%	14.4%	1.7%
1934	13.2%	17.7%	3.6%
1935	13.5%	17.2%	6.5%
1936	17.6%	22.2%	9.9%
1937	23.3%	27.1%	13.1%
1938	28.4%	31.3%	20.7%
1939	32.3%	34.2%	27.1%
1940	35.3%	35.1%	35.8%
1941	36.6%	38.3%	25.2%

Again there is a significant difference between private and public wards. In every year but one the patient under the care of her own physician faced a substantially higher chance of experiencing this form of intervention. It is also quite clear, however, that episiotomies were being "democratized" over this period as well.

106 *Ibid.*, p. 51. See also Biggs, "The Response to Maternal Mortality in Ontario," for a discussion of the role sulfanomide drugs played in that province's maternal health.

107 See G. McKee, "A Review of Caesarian Sections in the Vancouver General Hospital, 1941," *VMAB* (April 1943): 206-10.

108 Calculated from Hobbs, "Maternal Statistics," table II, p. 50.

109 Wertz and Wertz, *Lying In*, pp. 141-43.

Once the baby arrived, and if the hospital was not overcrowded, the woman might rest in the delivery room under observation for an hour. Should there be bleeding, pituitrin and ergometrine would be given; haemorrhage, with its threat of shock, brought the administration of intravenous fluids by a specialist.[110] After her pulse returned to safe levels and there were no signs of distress, the woman would be returned to her room, where the extent of comfort and nursing care depended on a private or public location. The increasing employment of registered nurses, still assisted by students, in these decades, especially the 1930s, also brought changes to patient care.[111] That transformation, with its promise of more knowledgeable staff, undoubtedly helped convince expectant mothers to choose hospitals for their confinements. What it actually meant in terms of real contact is more difficult to say.

In her own bed the patient could not expect unregulated access to her new baby. The modern hospital of VGH's ambition imposed a strict regimen based on the most up-to-date strictures about successful child care. Breast-feeding was a central dictum, but some procedures, such as MacEachern's recommendation that it was "most important" not to nurse the baby for at least six to eight hours after delivery,[112] very likely made it more difficult. The attempt to inculcate regular habits right from the onset may have had the same effect, as with the "Standing Orders" for

[110] M. Blair, "The Role of Haemorrhage," pp. 166-69.

[111] 1931 B.C. Hospital statistics report a 1:2 nurse-patient ratio, with 455 nurses (181 graduate nurses and 274 students) responsible for up to 1,153 patients. PABC, GR707, Box 5, Appendix D "Hospital Statistics, B.C. 1931." However, these figures do not reflect the fact that nurses worked in shifts and were not all on the wards at one time. Nor was their distribution in the hospital even. Some wards and wings required higher levels of staffing, while the staffs of private wings were augmented by graduate nurses hired by individual patients. As staff requirements grew, so too did the number of students accepted into the school, but by the mid-1920s shortage in student residence space began limiting enrolment. Staff shortages and unhealthy working and living conditions for students became so acute in the 1930s that the hospital was forced to hire Graduate or Registered Nurses on its staff, a move which most Canadian hospitals did not have to resort to until the 1940s and 1950s. These graduate nurses faced the same long hours and heavy work load as student nurses, and in 1940 the superintendent of nursing was still claiming that "in our desperate effort to keep expenses down to what we think the city 'will stand for,' we have been placing an all too great burden on our staff, which has necessitated the unpleasant closing of our eyes to continuous long overtime." *Annual Report* of VGH, 1940, p. 22. Thus the employment of graduate nurses did not necessarily improve the availability of nurses to patients, though graduate nurses could be relied on for swifter, calmer responses in emergencies and more experienced execution of therapeutic techniques. For a comparison of VGH nursing staff size to those across the country see J. M. Gibbon and Mary S. Mathewson, *Three Centuries of Canadian Nursing* (Toronto: Macmillan Company of Canada Limited, 1947), pp. 489-91.

[112] MacEachern, *Hospital Organization*, p. 283.

an efficient obstetrical department which recommended feedings at precise four-hour intervals for three days and "only fifteen minutes" at a
time with the mother. Later, twenty minutes would be allowed on the
same schedule.[113] The baby herself or himself was carefully tagged and
distinctively stenciled with the family surname by exposure to a sun-
lamp.[114]

Mothers' activities were also closely regulated. They were to recline in
bed until the fifth or sixth day, only then to sit up if all went well. Not
until five or so days passed were they allowed out of bed for limited
periods. They were not to leave the hospital for twelve to fourteen days.[115]
VGH seems to have observed this rule throughout these years, despite
the circulation problems it might have caused for the patient, the added
risk of infection and the contribution such stays made to the hospital's
chronic problem with overcrowding.[116] On the other hand, it may be
that mothers without urgent domestic responsibilities awaiting their
arrival looked forward to such respites from labour.[117]

Throughout this course of treatment women and their relatives undoubtedly demanded the full range of up-to-date procedures which might
in any way ease childbirth's pains and dangers. For them, like the professionals they consulted, there were trends and fads. Nevertheless, however much they might "shop around," prospective mothers were finally
expected to deliver themselves into the hands of their doctors. Joint
decision-making was not encouraged. MacEachern's influential recommendation that "No information regarding baby other than 'favorable'
is to be given mother by the nurse"[118] represented a common enough
attempt to control the flow of information and thus to determine the
process.

---

[113] *Ibid.*, pp. 870-71.

[114] Vancouver City Archives, *Sun* and *Province* Clipping File, "VGH," "General
Hospital is Mother to 27,395 Babies," 2 November 1935.

[115] MacEachern, *Hospital Organization*, p. 283.

[116] In the early 1930s white maternity patients between the ages of 16 and 45 in the
VGH, St. Paul's and Grace were hospitalized on average between 12.32 and 12.70
days each. *PABC* GR749, "Report on Information Collected and Compiled in
Reference to Certain Phases of Hospital Work in British Columbia," 1934. Given
the shortage of space at the VGH in these years, it is not surprising that "The
gynaecological and obstetrical section of the staff keeps constant watch upon the
efficacy of their treatment and their efforts towards reducing the length of stay in
hospital." Frederick J. Fish, "The Medical Records System of the Vancouver
General Hospital, Vancouver, B.C.," *American College of Surgeons Bulletin* (June
1933) : 56.

[117] Wertz and Wertz, *Lying In*, chap. 5.

[118] MacEachern, *Hospital Organization*, p. 869.

Once home, the model patient was to continue consultations with her doctor and public health nurse. The reality for many women, however, was an immediate return to postponed duties and tasks.[119] Domestic labour and family budgets made medical visits a low priority for many families in the days before medicare. The highly centralized services of the hospital did not easily follow the patient upon release, and it was only too likely that poverty in the case of the clients of the public wards would undo whatever good had been achieved.[120] The conditions of poor nutrition and abysmal housing which undermined women's health in the city at large remained for the most part untouched.[121]

Within the confines of the hospital women encountered a highly bureaucratized set of procedures presided over by male medical professionals. In this setting, where pregnancy was so readily defined as an illness, doctors found ample opportunity to assert their overriding authority and an equal temptation to employ techniques of intervention which dramatically influenced the pace and quality of childbirth. As a group women found themselves more highly regulated. Patients' status in the world beyond the walls of the institution was also reaffirmed by individual assignment to private rooms or public wards. Differences in treatment appear to have continued into the delivery room itself, where private patients were more likely to encounter intrusive procedures such as C-sections and forcep delivery. Over time, however, the common denominator of sex was powerful and the experience of public patients came to match that of the more fortunate.

Just as it is hard to credit hospitalization with responsibility for a significant reduction in maternal mortality in these years, it is difficult to judge the effectiveness of new medical regimes in improving women's experience of confinement. Given an allocation of public resources which favoured institutions and doctors rather than home care and domestic assistants, choices for pregnant women were limited. The absence of real

[119] See Strong-Boag, "Keeping House in God's Country," in R. Storey and C. Heron, eds., *On the Job* (Toronto: McGill-Queen's, 1986) for its discussion of the extent of home based work.

[120] In 1920 Dr. MacEachern acknowledged this problem, stating that many poor women, whose health had improved during their stay at VGH, return home and "drift back into poverty condition." His solution, "more care of the financial condition," was beyond the mandate or resources of the hospital. PABC, GR706, B.C. Royal Commission on State Health Care and Maternity Benefits 1919-21, Proceedings, Letter from Dr. MacEachern, p. 7.

[121] See W. Peter Ward and Patricia C. Ward, "Infant Birth Weight and Nutrition in Industrializing Montreal," *American Historical Review* 89 (February 1984): 324-45, for an insightful discussion of the effects of maternal malnutrition on infant health.

alternatives and the medical profession's ability to campaign for its own interpretations of the road to good health directed women to the relief that hospitals could provide. Some patients benefited from advances in medical procedure such as blood transfusions and anaesthetics which were most safely performed in a hospital setting. Relief, however, did not include provision for allowing women to make an informed choice about their experience of confinement nor address factors in the community which made pregnancy and illness in general the special burden of the poor. The overall result in these two decades was to leave decision-making firmly in the hands of professionals, who alone were deemed capable of understanding the physiology of women and the relative benefits of intervention. In time, however, disillusionment would set in. This would provide fertile ground for women's rebellion against the tyranny of the medical expert and their demand for informed choice and effective therapy in childbirth.

The Triumph of "Formalism":
Elementary Schooling in Vancouver from the 1920s to the 1960s*

NEIL SUTHERLAND

In *Survey of the School System*, published in 1925, J. H. Putman and
G. M. Weir blamed the "state of intellectual torpor" that they found
"markedly evident" in British Columbia education on the "formal discipline theory of studies current almost everywhere throughout the Province." Advocates of this theory believed that education consisted of training such "faculties" of the mind as memory and reasoning because such
training generalized itself. Through studying algebra and formal grammar, for example, one trained the reasoning faculty and came to be able
to apply this talent to actual situations throughout life. Putman and Weir
also discovered that lay people in British Columbia "who regard education chiefly as learning out of a book" shared the formal doctrine with
professionals. If a teacher, so parents believed, "drills incessantly on the
formal parts of grammar and arithmetic or the facts of history and geography, he is ... a good teacher."[1]

A major strain in the history of Canadian education during the first
half of the twentieth century was the effort made by educational theorists
and school officials to overcome the popularity of formalism. Hilda
Neatby examined the results of these efforts as they manifested themselves
in the curricula of the 1950s. Her survey of these materials indicated
that the reformers had apparently triumphed and that the new fare, in
contrast to the old, provided "so little for the mind."[2] However, when

* This paper is a much revised version of one first presented to the Canadian History
of Education Association Conference, Toronto, 1982. It is built out of the memories
of about forty anonymous interviewees. Readers will soon discover my enormous
debt to them, which I gratefully acknowledge. I am also indebted to John Calam,
George Tomkins and John Murray for their comments and suggestions and to
Denise Newton for her research assistance. The final form of the paper is also a
product of the work of the Canadian Childhood History Project, to which both the
Social Sciences and Humanities Research Council and the University of British
Columbia have given generous support.

1 British Columbia, Department of Education, *Survey of the School System*, by J. H.
Putman and G. M. Weir (Victoria: King's Printer, 1925), pp. 118-21.

2 Hilda Neatby, *So Little for the Mind* (Toronto: Clarke, Irwin, 1953).

175

one looks behind the curricula at what actually went on in classrooms, one finds that formalism in anglophone Canadian education was as strong in the 1950s as it had been in the 1920s. In fact, most of the improvements of the Froebelians, the "new" educators, and the Canadian "progressives" — a transformed curriculum, improved teacher education, more thorough inspection and supervision, and the like — had worked to refine and strengthen traditional modes of teaching and learning. Nevertheless, Professor Neatby accurately characterized Canadian education not only as it was in the 1950s, but as it had been over the whole of the twentieth century: it did not and had never done much to train the minds it served.

To substantiate this argument I will employ elementary schooling in Vancouver — including South Vancouver and Point Grey — as a case study.[3] I will begin by looking carefully at schooling as it appeared to the pupils. To do so I will describe an elementary school that I have assembled mostly out of the memories of some who attended school in Vancouver between the end of the First World War and the end of the 1950s.[4] There I will follow the pupils through their day, their week and their school year, describing what they learned and how their teachers taught it. Next, I will explain how the school ensured its "peace, order and good government." Finally, I will survey certain structural features of this school and its social context that, in my view, made formalism inevitable.

I

To children just starting out, schooling was only one segment of lives that were already engaged in a round of activities associated with families, friends and congregations, and with playmates of yard, street and playground. While this new segment of the circle loomed large in the minds

[3] In 1929 the municipalities of Vancouver, South Vancouver and Point Grey were amalgamated. In 1923 British Columbia extended the regular elementary school program from seven years to eight. In the late 1920s school districts began to introduce junior high schools for grades 7, 8 and 9. The depression, however, severely retarded their growth. On the other hand, declining secondary enrolment provided more space for them after 1938. In 1945-46, 54 percent of grade 7 and 8 pupils in Vancouver attended elementary schools, 30 percent junior high schools and 16 percent junior-senior high schools. Vancouver School Board, *Annual Report*, 1948, p. 93; British Columbia, Department of Education, *Report*, 1945-46, pp. MM 173-75.

[4] The methodology that I am employing in my ongoing study of childhood in anglophone Canada from the end of the First War to the 1960s is described in "The Role of Memory in the History of Childhood," an unpublished paper presented to the Canadian Historical Association, June 1985. This paper will appear in a publication of the Canadian Childhood History Project.

of all children, it was only one part of it, a fact which must be kept in mind as one notes their recollections of schooling. For families who centred their lives around a religious or ethnic organization, then the congregation, or a congregation-like association, impinged on the school as well; pupils tended to find their first school friends and playmates among those already well known to them through those activities, such as Sunday school. While very few have forgotten the very first day of school — "I could *smell* how clean my clothes were that day" — many of those interviewed had much sharper recollections of events that happened outside school than they do of early days or even of any days inside school. One person's only memory of his first two years of school, for example, is of the big bully of the grade 1 class: "I was petrified of him." (The strength of this particular recollection is testified to by the fact that the bully's name was the only one that he could recall from among his classmates of those early years.)

Most children starting school had been initiated into its ways long before they arrived for their first day. Parents, brothers and sisters, playmates and older children all helped to craft in the pre-school child expectations of a traditional sort of schooling. The characteristics of the teaching staff, the rituals of discipline and the content of the curriculum were part of the lore of childhood. On a bright summer day a brother, sister or an older playmate had taken the prospective beginner to the schoolyard. Together they had climbed the fire escape to peer into the shadowed classrooms; the neophyte heard exaggerated tales of "rubber nose," or "weasel mouth," or "Dynamite D," or "the strap," or "Mr. X," who cast so all-pervasive an aura over the school of which he was the principal that in the minds of some pupils he and his school almost merged together as one being.

Some children — the less sceptical, the less realistic, the more gullible, perhaps — were afraid to start school and often remained intermittently frightened by it throughout the whole of their school careers. They knew about events which gave a grim touch of reality to the apocryphal lore: of W from down the lane being strapped for throwing a spitball, of X's rash brought on by fear of physical education classes, of Y's stomach cramps before each weekly spelling test, of Z's outburst of tears when a page of her exercise book had been ripped out by her teacher. They expected such things to happen to them too. Some feared other children. Those whose families moved occasionally or frequently had to go through the ritual of "starting to school" a number of times. Some children recall feeling "inferior" and "insecure" or even frightened after each move. Others felt only lightly touched by changing schools. One boy remembers a moment of concern at recess on the first day at a new school — his third — when one big boy said to another, about him, "Do you think you can take him?" but it was all talk that quickly faded away.

Most beginners were only partly taken in by ritual tales of "horrors" ahead; they recalled the carefree departures of friends and neighbours to school as recently as the previous June and themselves set off in the same way; typically, children were "very excited about school." Most departed for their first day with their mothers. Some insisted that their mothers accompany them for the first few days and, very occasionally, the first few weeks. Some, even among those who were really keen to go to school, cried when their mothers left them on the first day. Most quickly overcame their initial shyness. And, however they came and whatever their expectations of how the school would be ordered, most beginners shared one very clear idea of what they would do in school. They were going to learn to read. After a half century many can recall stories such as "Chicken Little," and even phrases and sentences such as "pretty pink ice cream from a pretty pink glass," "Cut, cut, said the King," and "I am a boy. My name is Jerry," which were among the first that they decoded.[5]

Despite problems posed by periods of rapid growth, Vancouver generally provided substantial concrete and brick schools for its pupils. Well maintained, most stood out as the most impressive buildings in their neighbourhoods. The front of each school presented its best side to the community; the building was set back behind low fences which protected lawns and shrubs. At about eight o'clock each morning the janitor or monitor raised the flag in front of the school. Since most had above-ground basements, those using the main entrance of the school — forbidden to pupils — climbed a set of wide granite steps and entered on one side of a double door. Most schools had a boys' entrance and a girls' entrance, generally at ground level. Behind the school lay the main play-

---

5 "Chicken Little" appeared in *The Canadian Readers: Book One A Primer and First Reader* (Toronto: Macmillan, 1922), pp. 74-80. I have not been able to find out from which books the first two sentences came, but the person who recollected the third is obviously recalling an early story in the reader by Henrietta Roy, Elsie Roy, P. H. Sheffield and Grace Bollert, *Highroads to Reading: Jerry and Jane: The Primer* (Toronto: Ryerson and Macmillan, 1932). On page 3 appears a story entitled "Jerry," and beneath it "I am a boy. My name is Jerry. I am in the toy store." British Columbia began replacing the "Canadian Readers" with the "Highroads Readers" in the mid-1930s. British Columbia, Department of Education, *Report*, 1934-35, pp. S64-65.

ing field. Since intensive use made grass impossible, this part of the playground was usually covered with packed earth and gravel, which meant that those who fell on the playing field often tore their skin or pitted their knees.

Most children arrived at school well before the bell. On all but the worst days they played outside. On very wet or very cold days they would gather in the basement play areas of those schools which had such facilities. Since basements were usually dark, noisy and unventilated, children tended to avoid them if they could. Unless they were one of those privileged pupils who had minor housekeeping or administrative tasks to perform before school, they were not admitted to the corridors or classrooms before the bell. If the school was a large one, the children would play in sharply segregated areas of the playground; the older boys monopolized the largest field, the older girls and the primary children played in their smaller areas. The duty teacher circulated from field to field, sometimes carrying the brass bell by its clapper. If she taught one of the primary grades she might have a small chain of girls attached to each hand.

Although the children were socially more or less integrated in their play, even on the playground they displayed characteristics that showed some of the sharp differences between them. To eyes accustomed to the present rich range of pupil garb, hairstyles, and so on, all pupils in this earlier era would appear very drab indeed. Even in the middling levels of society, children bathed less frequently than they do today. More children then than now did not bathe at all. Children had fewer clothes and changed them far less frequently. Some boys wore heavy boots, often with metal plates around the toes and with "blakeys" on toes and heels. Despite the admonitions of teachers and nurses, many wore only cheap "runners" in the summer and when it was dry, and "gumboots" when it was wet or snowy. A few wore runners whatever the weather. Some were unkempt and even dirty, while others wore clean but threadbare clothes. One of the latter recalls always having "hand-me-down clothes" and boots that at first were too big, for a time just right, and then, "for another interminable while, they were too small." Unlike the children of the employed working class or middle classes, such children "had nothing new . . . after Woodward's 95-cent day." Nor did they wear "Lindbergh" helmets, with their plastic goggles and straps that did up under the chin.

At about five to nine, those schools equipped with bell towers or electric bells sounded a warning ring. In other schools a senior pupil or a teacher circulated through the corridors and on the grounds ringing the brass hand bell. At the bell, monitors collected the sports equipment. The children moved rapidly to the inside or outside assembly point for their classes. There they lined up in pairs; girls in front, boys behind. The younger children held hands with their partners. Many of the girls moved to an already-reserved place in the line. Since the front was a much-coveted position, those who wanted it reserved it by placing coats, lunch bags or other possessions there, or even lined up well ahead of the bell to ensure their prime positions. At the bell, the boys raced up and tussled either for first position behind the girls or for the very last position in the lines. The principal, vice-principal or the duty teacher appeared and stared — or even roared — the children into silence. He or she then signalled the classes one by one to march into their classrooms. The classes passed more or less silently down corridors, some of which had a line painted down the middle. Teachers stood vigilantly by the doors of their rooms. After the children entered their rooms they placed their coats and lunches in the right place — some classes had dark, high-ceilinged cloakrooms which were often the scene of semi-silent scuffling, shin-hacking, and the like — and then moved to their desks. Those with problems in hearing or seeing — again more then than now — sat at the very front of the room. In the 1920s some teachers arranged their pupils according to their academic rank in the class, a practice which had disappeared by the 1950s.

The children entered classrooms that were, by today's standards, somewhat dark and gloomy. Incandescent bulbs, usually encased in milky glass globes, hung from the ceilings. In a context of "constant watchfulness," these were only turned on when teachers or sometimes even principals made the important decision that artificial light was really necessary.[6] The left-hand side of the room was covered by windows which could be opened and closed. In all but the new schools of the 1950s, freshly washed black slate blackboards — on which white chalk was used — covered two or even three of the other sides of the room. On one panel of the blackboards the teacher or some favoured pupils had gently tapped chalk brushes on onionskin stencils to etch out a ghostly scene appropriate to the season — autumn leaves, or Santa Claus, or valentines — and coloured it with soft coloured chalk. Another panel displayed the

---

[6] See the comment on the cost of school lighting by R. H. Neelands, chairman of the Vancouver School Trustees Finance Committee for 1940; in Vancouver School Board, *Reports*, 1939 and 1940, p. 68.

list of classroom monitors, whose tasks included cleaning blackboards and chalk brushes (*never* on the side of the school), operating the pencil sharpener, filling ink wells from copper containers or glass bottles with delicate glass stems, watering plants, and so on. Beneath the monitors came the "detention" list which, first thing in the morning, held only the names of those miscreants who had collected more of these punishments than they had yet been able to serve. Other lists showed those receiving milk, those who had bought war savings stamps, or other unofficial records.

The morning's seat work covered much of the rest of the blackboard. In the upper grades this was sometimes concealed by a rolled-down map or maps; sometimes one of the world, British Empire in red, or Canada surrounded by Neilson's chocolate bars. Above the front blackboard hung a portrait of King George V and Queen Mary or, later, King George VI and Queen Elizabeth. From 1927 onward children gazed at a sepia reproduction of Rex Wood's lifeless copy of Robert Harris' "Fathers of Confederation," which the Canadian Club had presented to schools in celebration of the fiftieth anniversary of Confederation. In 1940 it was joined, courtesy of the Kiwanis Club, by a coloured picture of the Union Jack, beneath which appeared the words:

> "One Life One Fleet
> One Flag One Throne
> Tennyson"[7]

In some classrooms these pictures were flanked by such scenes of British prowess as the capture of Quebec, the Battle of Trafalgar and the signing of the Magna Carta. Above the other boards hung model alphabets, health posters, or murals created by the pupils. Some open shelves holding atlases and class-set textbooks sat under the windows or in a corner beside the teacher's desk.

The floors were either oiled wood or brown "battleship" linoleum. Individual desks were generally screwed onto wooden runners. The seat in front of the front desks held texts and marked and unmarked exercise books. A metal ink well or glass ink bottle sat in a hole that had been bored into the top of the right hand corner of the slightly sloping desk. A pencil trough crossed the top of it. Below lay a shelf for storing pencil boxes, crayons, textbooks and scribblers. On the days when the windows could not be opened the characteristic classroom odour was particularly

---

[7] The wording is taken from a copy now in the possession of Jean Barman. See also Vancouver School Board, *Report*, 1940, p. 55.

strong: on the one hand, plasticine, sour paste, pencil shavings, orange peels in the waste baskets, chalk dust, oiled floors and dust bane; on the other stale bodies and sweaty feet, occasionally enriched by "fluffs." The air in the cloakrooms, which were rarely ventilated, often caught the breath of those entering them. Characteristic sounds complemented these smells: steam radiators clanked, "blakeyed" toes and heels clattered down the aisles, chalk screeched on the blackboard, and bells divided the day into its segments.

Each teacher began the day by calling the roll and marking the class register. The children responded, "Present, Miss X," or "Here, Mr. Y." In the 1920s and 1930s some teachers preceded roll call with a scriptural reading or Biblical story and, more often, a prayer. From 1944 onward, teachers read, without introduction or comment, a prescribed selection from the King James version of the Bible. After the reading the teacher said, "Class stand," paused for quiet, and the children recited "The Lord's Prayer" in unison.[8] Next, teachers conducted the daily health inspection; they looked for nits, clean hands, clean nails, clean faces, combed hair and possession of a handkerchief. Once a week they collected the milk money and, during the war, quarters for war savings stamps. They gave iodine tablets to those who had paid a dime for a year's supply.[9] Pupils who aspired to be nurses "would count out the tablets with a tongue depressor onto a tray and then carry them around the room, pushing out each kid's with the depressor." Monitors gave out new pen nibs to those who needed them, from which children had to suck the thin coating of wax off before they would hold ink. As these routines came to an end, the children took out their scribblers and texts for the first lesson. The timetable, in later years by law posted in a prominent position in the classroom, dictated the regular pattern of the events of the day and of the week.

Whether pupils attended elementary school cheerfully, apprehensively or in a state of fear, the curriculum, the teaching methods and the pattern of school discipline combined to press them into a single mode of learning. Even those who then enjoyed it now recall a system that put its rigour into rote learning of the times tables, the spelling words, the "Lady of the Lake," the capes and bays, "the twelve adverbial modifiers (of

[8] See British Columbia, Department of Education, *Report*, 1943-44, p. B30; British Columbia, *Statutes*, 1944, c. 45.

[9] In 1930, 3.9 percent of Vancouver pupils had goiter. By 1936 this had declined to 1.1 percent. Vancouver School Board, *Report*, 1937, pp. 31-32.

place, or reason, of time ...)" and the Kings and Queens. It was a system based on teachers talking and pupils listening, a system that discouraged independent thought, a system that provided no opportunity to be creative, a system that blamed rather than praised, a system that made no direct or purposeful effort to build a sense of self-worth.

Teachers taught groups of children rather than individual youngsters. Except for classes in which there was more than one grade and for the teaching of reading in the lower grades, the whole class usually constituted a single group. Primary reading groups went, in turn, to the front of the room where they sat on little chairs or on the floor in a semicircle in front of their teacher. After the teacher conducted a "phonics" drill, she introduced and drilled the new words. Then, in what was often the highlight of the day, the children each read a short segment of the day's story. "I enjoyed it when it was my turn to read," recalls one; another explains that the dull repetition didn't matter at all because "learning to read was such a fabulous thing." While one reading group was at the front with the teacher, the other two or three did seat work at their desks. (One page of an unlined scribbler, completed in 1933, shows, in its owner's printing, "the cat sits on the rug," "the rug is by the fire," "the fire is warm," followed by a coloured drawing of a cat, a fire and a rug.) Some primary classes had library corners or "interest centres" or sand tables to which the children who had finished their seat work could go. Others had a dress-up box or store where children quietly practised using money made from cardboard circles or milk bottle tops.

Although the tone varied a great deal from room to room, the methods of teaching the whole class were remarkably consistent from teacher to teacher and subject to subject. Teachers began each lesson by reviewing what they had taught in the previous one. Often they worked — or had a pupil come up and work — an example on the blackboard. Then they went over, item by item, the exercise that was to have given practice in what had been taught. In arithmetic, language, spelling and grammar classes a number of boys and girls would move up to the blackboard to work a question from the exercise or spell one or more words from the week's list. The rest of the class was supposed to watch for mistakes. Teachers would move along the board, releasing those who had the correct answer or taking those in error through the question again. In reading lessons teachers reviewed by correcting questions, *always* answered in sentences ("that were never to start with 'Because', or 'And', or 'But' "), that tested pupils' comprehension of the story, or had pupils read aloud dictionary definitions of the "new" words that they had copied into their exercise books. In arithmetic, teachers conducted individual or group drills of the number facts or the times tables ("What a proud thing it was" to come first in an arithmetic race.) In history, geography and home economics classes pupils raised their hands to answer questions based on yesterday's "notes," or identified the places pointed to on a wall map, or passed exercise books forward or back for classmates for marking to ensure that the correct word had been placed in a "blank" in a paragraph, copied from the blackboard, that had summarized a section of the textbook.

When teachers decided that most of the class were ready for the next segment of the subject, they instructed the pupils to put down their pens, pencils and rulers, place their hands on their desks or behind their backs and "sit up straight and face the front." With all eyes thus on the blackboard, teachers then demonstrated, sometimes through question-and-answer, the letter for handwriting, the syllables in, or the pronunciation of, the new spelling words, or took the pupils a further step in the language, arithmetic or grammar sequence. Again, some pupils would move eagerly and more would move reluctantly to work examples on the blackboard, or teachers would lead the class in chanting a "drill" of the spelling, or the times tables, or the number facts, or the capitals of the provinces. In reading, history, geography and science lessons, the pupils often read, in sequence, from textbooks. Some teachers conducted this reading in a regular and predictable pattern, up one row and down the next. Others, to keep the pupils alert, "called out our names at random and we would respond immediately." In some classes, children were allowed to volunteer to read. Those who read well read long bits and those who read badly short ones. ("I could read with 'expression,' — but sometimes would say the wrong word, and would be embarrassed.") Some teachers passed over the really poor readers altogether or had them read while the class did seat work. Some teachers or schools required pupils to stand by their desks or even at the front as they read or when they answered questions — a requirement that produced a certain clatter as they raised and lowered the seats of their desks and occasionally knocked pencils and books off their desks as they moved into the aisle. Teachers broke into the sequence to read themselves, to thrust a question at wandering minds or to explicate some point in the text. Most pupils found these sessions boring. Wool-gathering was common. Those who read well had long since read ahead and mastered the content. Those who did not worried only about getting through their own portion. Some doubted that the period would ever come to an end.

Teachers occasionally varied this routine in science classes by performing experiments for their pupils. As they did so, they laid out what they were doing step by step on the blackboard according to a precisely prescribed form that called for tackling a "problem" through a sequence that led from a "plan" through "apparatus and materials," "method," "observations," to a "conclusion" sometimes written out even before the experiment was begun.[10] Similar presentations characterized the introduction of something new in manual arts, manual training and home economics.

Teachers closed the oral part of lessons with an explanation of the seat work which was to follow. In the upper grades, teachers often assigned exercises laid out in the prescribed texts to be completed in lined exercise books. Most "scribblers," as they were called, had solid-coloured covers made of heavier, shiny paper. In most classrooms pupils were expected to provide a scribbler for each subject. In some primary classes pupils used exercise books made of newsprint on which the children could only use pencils, which tore easily and which were hard to erase. Admonished to "keep between the lines," pupils wrote a couple of rows of "ovals," and other practice elements in writing, some rows of the letter in capital and then lower case form, and a list of words in which the letter appeared. In the rooms of teachers who were writing "purists," pupils had to use H. B. MacLean's "whole arm" or "muscular movement" method of handwriting.[11] They wrote a sentence to illustrate each of the spelling words or "syllabicated" the list. They worked many arithmetic questions that employed the new skill or wrote out and "diagrammed" sentences in ways that showed understanding of the newest wrinkle in usage or parsing form. They wrote out dictated drills in arithmetic and spelling. They wrote friendly letters, business letters and thank you notes. They wrote short essays ("Study pages 94, 95, 96, 97, 98 and the first paragraph on page 99 and write . . . a full account of Edward the III's reign . . . ").

[10] See George H. Limpus and John W. B. Shore, *Elementary General Science* (Toronto: Macmillan, 1935), pp. 11-12.

[11] H. B. MacLean, *The MacLean Method of Writing: Teachers' Complete Manual: A Complete Course of Instruction in the Technique and Pedagogy of the MacLean Method of Writing for Teachers of Elementary Schools, Junior and Senior High Schools, Commercial Schools, and Normal Schools* (Vancouver: Clarke & Stuart, 1921). The note at the foot of the title page of the 31st edition says that it is authorized for use in British Columbia, Quebec, Nova Scotia, Prince Edward Island, New Brunswick and Newfoundland.

Much seat work in science, history, geography, health and even home economics consisted of copying notes from the blackboard. In the upper grades these notes were characterized by systems of headings, sub-headings, sub-sub-headings and the like. Those whose older brothers or sisters had preceded them in the classroom soon discovered that some teachers used the same notes year after year. Often these notes were so copious — "reams and reams" of them covering board after board — that pupils groaned inwardly and sometimes outwardly at the sight of them, and even the recollection of them can still create a sinking feeling in some stomachs. One teacher "covered the blackboard with notes and that's how we learned English." Teachers often left blanks in the notes that pupils were to fill in by referring to the textbook. The straight pens with steel nibs that had to be dipped frequently in the ink well and which often blotted added a further arduous dimension to the task, especially for those whose motor co-ordination was not very good, who were left-handed, or whose teachers insisted on "muscular movement."

Pupils freed themselves from the bonds of this routine as best as they could. Some learned to talk to neighbours in such a way that they were rarely seen or heard or to throw balls or wads of paper when the teacher was not looking. Some "mastered the skill of copying ... without ever needing to comprehend" and were thus able "to dream outdoor matters while rarely missing a word." Others travelled to the pencil sharpener as frequently as they felt they could get away with the practice. This activity was especially popular in classrooms where the sharpener was on the bookcase under a window; then one "could have a look out of the window."

Pupils also welcomed such changes in routine as those which came in health classes when they were asked to copy diagrams and in geography when they sketched or traced maps (sometimes against the classroom window), recorded the names of mountains, rivers and cities from a black-board list, and then coloured these maps. Occasionally pupils did history or geography "projects" on such topics as British Columbia, or totem poles, or logging, or "our new allies, the Russians." Some recall that they occasionally made models, such as a fort in history class, using plasticine and card paper. Most recall that they made butter in grade 1 or 2. ("We each took a turn shaking.")

While the pupils worked, some teachers moved about the room correcting questions, checking on the neatness of the work and adding to explanations. In primary classes they awarded gold, blue and red stars or coloured stickers to those whose work reached a high standard. Other teachers increased the store of notes on the blackboard, erasing and adding new material to one panel after the other — sometimes more quickly than some pupils could copy — in what in many rooms became an endless sequence. Still others sat at or on their desks or watched the children from a favourite standing place by the window. All regularly surveyed the class to ensure that heads were down, that no whispered conversations took place and that no notes were passed. They acknowledged the hands that were raised, answered questions or permitted pupils to go to the pencil sharpener or the lavatory, one child at a time. As the period drew to a close, some teachers summarized the main points that they had tried to make in the lesson. They reminded the pupils of what was to be finished before the next period, they assigned even more material for homework or they dispatched monitors to collect exercise books for marking. Over the course of the day, and especially in the lower grades, teachers collected many piles of scribblers.

Music, art, industrial arts, home economics and physical education had welcome or unwelcome characteristics that made them somewhat different from the other subjects. First, children generally found their classes in these subjects somewhat livelier than the others. Second, they often brought their competence to the classroom rather than learning it there. Finally, their competence, or lack of it, often made the children look upon them as either high or low points in the weekly routine. Aside from a small amount of what was called "music appreciation" — that is, listening to a classical piece played by teacher or pupils or on a recording or school broadcast — most school music consisted of singing. Classes began with vocal exercises using the tonic sol fah scale, often displayed on such commercially produced cards as "Curwen's Modulator." Taking their cue from the piano or tuning fork, the children moved first up the scale — "doh, ray, me, fah, soh, lah, te, doh" — and then down it again. Next the teacher took the pupils through parts of it: "doh, ray, me, ray, doh." Sometimes the teacher would have the children run through their songs in this form first, before teaching the words. In many classrooms pupils then sang such "ridiculous songs" as "Hearts of Oak" and "Early One Morning" from Sir Ernest MacMillan's inaccurately titled *A Canadian Song Book*.[12] Some teachers could make this bill-of-fare enjoyable. "We had a good music program, with lots of British songs," one person recalls.

[12] Sir Ernest MacMillan, ed., *A Canadian Song Book* (Toronto: Dent, 1937). The first edition of this text appeared in 1928.

Another remembers that her music teacher made it "so enjoyable we really wanted to sing for him." In many schools teachers sorted out the best singers to prepare, some thought endlessly, for the annual music festival. Many who took part in the festival remember it as one of the really great days in the school year; we "got at a minimum a complete day off!" Others, especially self-styled "crows," did not enjoy music very much but only really disliked it when they were asked to sing alone. One or two teachers apparently punished misbehaviour in the music classroom by requiring the guilty to sing solos to their classmates.

In physical education teachers concentrated on those who already could perform well. They paid less attention to basic skills than they did in reading and arithmetic. If the facilities were available and their parents had provided the strip, pupils changed into white shirts, blue shorts for boys, tunics and bloomers for girls, and running shoes. If the class was conducted on a hardwood floor in a gymnasium or school auditorium the school would insist on rubber-soled shoes as the minimum acceptable strip. The class would line up in rows or teams and the teacher would take them through such exercises as touching toes or astride jumping of the sort originally laid out in the Strathcona Trust *Syllabus*.[13] Next the teacher would take the class through some activities that practised skills related to whatever sport was emphasized at the moment. In softball season, for example, pupils tossed balls back and forth and practised batting and bunting, and teachers batted "grounders" out to be retrieved. The period then culminated in the playing of one or more games of softball. In some classes teams would be picked to last over the season; in others the best players were picked as captains each day and, as captains selected their teams, the children received a finely honed demonstration of exactly how their peers evaluated their compe-

[13] Strathcona Trust, *Syllabus of Physical Exercises for Schools* (Toronto: Executive Council, Strathcona Trust, 1911). This was the first edition of the Canadian version of this British manual. In the 1960s Lorne Brown recalled that he had been taught at the Vancouver Normal School in the 1920s to take his pupils through a calisthenics sequence which he had memorized as IT AB LAB:

I — for introductory activity
T — for trunk exercise
A — for arm exercises
B — for balance activity
L — for lateral trunk exercise
A — for activity; usually a form of relay
B — for breathing

Lorne E. Brown, "Personal Reflections — Physical Education in B.C. . . . 1927 to 1967," unpublished paper, n.d. (1967?).

tence. Those who were picked towards the end still recall the self-contempt this system engendered. Sometimes, however, even the incompetent were lucky. One less-than-athletic student still has a "vivid recollection of when I was on third base and just reached out and caught the ball; what a fabulous feeling it was, just to catch a ball."

Since the subject had neither a text nor a festival to ensure consistency, art programs in these years differed more than most subjects from teacher to teacher and from school to school. Recollections of art in the primary grades, often supported by artifacts, focus on craft activities, especially those involving making such things as woven place mats, book marks and pen wipers out of burlap. Intermediate grade pupils also sewed burlap, measured, folded and pasted cardboard and sometimes made things out of soft wood. In art, as contrasted to "manual arts" classes, pupils sketched still lifes, copied drawings illustrating perspective, made designs that "always involved a ruler" and did a variety of paintings. Tasks tended to be specific; there was "no free-lancing at all." In painting many recall a misordered sequence that began with water colours — in their "little Reeves tins" — in the early grades and only permitted the most senior and capable to work with the easier-to-use poster paints. Some had art teachers who made the subject really exciting for the pupils; we did "all kinds of sketching, water colours, poster paints; we put up big displays at one end of the school ground on sports day for our parents to see the work."

Most former pupils recall their home economics and manual training classes with pleasure. While they may not always have enjoyed these subjects, only really nasty teachers could make them actively dislike them. Those who had some practical bent often looked on them as the high point of the week and remain grateful for what they were taught. ("She was fussy, and taught me to be fussy.") Girls who had already learned some cooking or sewing at home sometimes became impatient at the slow pace of their classes, but they also enjoyed the annual tea or "parade of fashion" at which they showed off their skills to their mothers. In industrial arts, one less-than-handy lad remembers that "you got to make the occasional simple object that had a use. . . . So we did pencil boxes, simple stands for mom's flower pots, some sort of wall bracket, etc. I remember spending five or six months alone remaking the lid to my pencil box until I managed one that fit snugly. Meanwhile more adept pupils finished small end tables in time for Mother's Day."

Beginning in the mid-1920s, Vancouver made traditional practices more efficient by "platooning" some of its schools.[14] In platooned, or "departmentalized," schools pupils moved from room to room, some of which had special equipment, to visit specialist teachers, many of whom had some extra training leading to a provincial "specialist" certificate. Others seem to have "specialized" in what they were good at doing or teaching, what they enjoyed teaching or what the principal assigned to them. Platooning also had its special set of routines. On the bell, or in those rooms in which the teacher regularly said, "The bell is for me, not for you," on his or her signal, the pupils would gather up their materials. The children then lined up in pairs to move from room to room. Although officially forbidden to talk in the corridors, most pupils looked upon moves as pleasant breaks in the day. However, those moving to the rooms of the vicious fretted at what was ahead and those leaving them were sometimes giddy with relief at having survived another day in their presence.

Friday brought some variation in school routines. Pupils did the final draft of the week's writing exercise in their "compendiums." In spelling and other subjects the teacher dictated the weekly test, which the children wrote out on thin strips of foolscap. Some teachers then "read out the results of these weekly and other tests so all would know who came first and last." The tests might be followed by spelling bees or games such as arithmetic baseball. For some children Friday afternoon brought a relaxation in the rigidity of the week's work. Teachers read stories or perhaps a chapter from a novel by Walter Scott or Charles Dickens — sessions recalled with special warmth. In many schools pupil officers conducted the weekly meeting of the Junior Red Cross.[15] In others older pupils dispersed to a range of "clubs" for the last period of the day.

Many schools also marked the end of the week with a school assembly. After the pupils had filed, class by class, to their appropriate place in the school hallway, on the gymnasium floor, or into auditorium chairs, the principal or music teacher led the school in "O Canada." (For many

[14] Lord Tennyson School pioneered platooning in 1924. By 1938 all elementary schools employed some form of specialist teaching. Vancouver School Board, *Report*, 1925, pp. 11-12; *ibid.*, 1937-38, pp. 64-65. The origins of platooning are described in Raymond E. Callahan, *Education and the Cult of Efficiency: A Study of the Social Forces That Have Shaped the Administration of the Public Schools* (Chicago: University of Chicago Press, 1962), pp. 128-36.

[15] A "demonstration" Junior Red Cross meeting conducted by a class at Tecumseh School in May 1936 is described in "Practical Citizenship," *B.C. Teacher* (June 1936), pp. 17-19. By 1945-46, 253 Vancouver elementary classes had Junior Red Cross branches. British Columbia, Department of Education, *Report*, 1945-46, p. MM 77.

years Vancouver schools used the Laurence Buchan version, in which they pledged to be "At Britain's side whate'er betide.")[16] Two or three classes then presented items that they had prepared: a song that they would later sing in the music festival, a play taken from a reader or some acrobatics learned in physical education. Sometimes assembly programs drew attention to talented individuals who would play or sing a classical piece or perform a dance. Classes which had had the best turnout or parents at the last Parent-Teacher Association received a banner. During the Second World War the principal or a visitor would honour the classes which had bought the most war savings stamps or collected the most metal or paper for the regular salvage drives. Sometimes Henry Mac-Lean himself would demonstrate fine handwriting, do some magical tricks and present MacLean's writing certificates to those whose writing came up to standard. ("Getting a MacLean's . . . certificate was a big deal!") In some schools the pupils would all join together to sing a hymn, a patriotic song, a Christmas carol or a round such as "Row, row, row. . . . " In nearly every school the penultimate item on the program was the principal's message: he — or, in a very few high schools, she — usually addressed some problem of school or community governance.[17] The principal explained that some pupils were "hanging around" too long after school, or that there was too much talking in the halls, or that there was too much fighting to and from schools, or that the police were about to crack down on those who rode their bicycles on the sidewalk or who had not renewed their bicycle licences.[18] Finally the children all stood to sing "God Save the King" and then marched back to their classrooms.

Some events broke irregularly into class and school routines. Pupils enjoyed those occasions when the teacher wandered or was drawn from the subject into discussion. "The room hushed" because pupils did not want to break the thread. Some teachers told war stories or recounted

[16] In some schools the Buchan version was pasted onto the inside cover of the Mac-Millan *Song Book*.

[17] In the 1920s one woman in Vancouver, one woman in Point Grey and nine women in South Vancouver held school principalships for one or more years. By the school year 1930-31 only one woman — a former South Vancouver principal — still held the role. After Miss E. M. Dickson retired in 1934, all forty-nine Vancouver elementary schools had male principals. British Columbia, Department of Education, *Report*, 1935-36, pp. H165-H182.

[18] A junior high school annual of the era, however, notes that at the school assembly the student chairman always called on the principal, P. N. Whitley, "for some of his brief remarks. These may be in the nature of admonition, commendation, but rarely condemnation." Vancouver, Point Grey Junior High School, *The Explorer*, 1942, n.p.

Lord Tennyson School, Division 3, ca. 1923

Cecil Rhodes School, 1949, Grade 1

personal adventures. Others talked about their families; one told "about all the people in her family who had t.b., and how terrible it was." All pupils spent part of a day early in September carefully covering their textbooks with covers provided by the Royal Bank, on the back of one edition being the verse: "Lay this to heart among your rules: — / Wisely I'll save and wisely spend; / Make pennies, dimes and nickels tools / That fashion fortune in the end." Especially deft and well-behaved girls in the upper grades finished their own covers and moved on to a primary classroom to help out the children there.

During outbreaks of such infectious diseases as measles, chicken pox, mumps and scarlet fever, or during the seasonal visit of lice, the school nurse would inspect each of the pupils. Sometimes the teacher, principal or nurse would warn children about men hanging around the school grounds, admonishing them to go directly home after school and not talk to any strangers on the way. At other times individual children would be called out of class to visit the nurse, the school doctor or the school dentist or to attend a toxoid or vaccination clinic. Pupils particularly welcomed fire drills. They enjoyed not only the events themselves but also preparing for the music festival, for the Christmas concert, for maypole dancing on May Day, for a tea or fashion show in home economics, for a production of a play or operetta and for sports day. Those who attended one elementary school in the 1930s remember the delight they took in their production of "The Mikado."

Occasionally events outside of the school impinged on what went on in it. Influenza closed the schools for some weeks in 1918, and a fuel shortage did so in 1943. One interviewee recalls forming up to see the Prince of Wales in 1919 and giving him a cheer when he gave them the day off.[19] Another remembers being urged to listen to the coronation of George VI on the radio and making in class a little crown to wear while doing so.[20] More remember the royal visit of 1939. Some made scrapbooks of it in their classes or learned to sing "Land of Hope and Glory." All classes went out to watch, with great excitement, "as they whisked by" on their drives about the city.[21] During the Second World War pupils

[19] See Vancouver *Province*, 22 September 1919, for the role children played in this visit.

[20] "On May 11th, 1937, every school in the city entered wholeheartedly into the observance of the crowning of H.M. King George VI and H.M. Queen Elizabeth, and many fine programs were given." Vancouver School Board, *Report*, 1937, p. 11.

[21] The routes, with each school's place along them, are laid out in *Vancouver Sun*, 25 May 1939, p. 3.

knitted for the Red Cross and bought war savings stamps. In some
schools that early casualty among the elements of the "new" education,
the school garden, reappeared for a time as the "victory garden." "We
planted things that grew quickly"; pupils were supposed to persuade
their parents to plant such gardens at home. Some school gardens had
short-term and long-term effects. "I persuaded my parents to plant
potatoes in our yard; to this day my hobby is vegetable gardening." On
a more serious and more frightening note, pupils practised what they
would do in an air raid; in one school they went to the school basement,
in another they filed out into the playground, where "the principal blew
a whistle and we would all fall down." In another the principal gave a
vivid description of just how bombers would destroy Vancouver in air
raids. In a fourth the janitor added to the fear occasioned by a Japanese
submarine shelling the lighthouse at Estevan Point, in June 1942, by
telling the children it was "the beginning of the end."[22]

II

The ways in which pupils and teachers behaved toward each other were
what bound them and the curriculum together to make a school. Thus
recollections of what was taught, how it was taught and who taught it
lead naturally into an elaboration of what is implicit therein about how
elementary schools controlled their pupils and how the pupils responded
to that control. First, an overall observation. Discussions of "fair" and
"unfair," usually initiated by interviewees, often burn through with an
intensity that belies the fact that the events discussed took place not the
day before but sometimes four or more decades ago. One teacher "was
very annoyed and took four of us into the cloakroom where she used the
ruler on our knuckles. It was grossly unfair: she had watched a note go
through the four people before she intervened." Another marked a set of
tests without noting anything on the papers, returned them to the children to mark their own, asked the youngsters to call out their marks and
then excoriated those who had yielded to the temptation to pad. Another,
who believes that corporal punishment is a "beneficial" device and that
schools would be better places if strapping were restored, "to this very
day feels wrongly punished" on two out of the three occasions he was

[22] The minutes of a staff meeting held at Charles Dickens School on 5 October 1942,
note "Re Air Raids (1st) If there is time — Send class home. (2nd) If there is
only a little time, send pupils to the basement. (3rd) If there is no time, pupils
and teachers under their desks. N.B. If you hear any anti-air craft fire, there is no
time to go home."

strapped. In this context one must note that children of these years seem to have been predisposed to accept the consequences of just about any code of conduct so long as the school administered it fairly.

People's recollections of their teachers divide into four rough categories. Many children could classify some teachers even before they went to school; the rest quickly learned the process. They gave — and as adults generally continue to give — their highest rating to those teachers who emphasized the fundamentals, who drilled frequently and tested often, who concentrated on having their pupils learn those things that both community and educational tradition told them were the "core" curriculum. These teachers knew their business and they taught this curriculum thoroughly and systematically. "Good" teachers also taught this curriculum in a particular way. They had dominant, overpowering personalities. They conveyed a sense that what they did, and what they wanted their pupils to do, was of immense importance. They were sometimes harsh, severe, humourless and frightening. They sometimes yelled at their pupils. They ran "no nonsense" classrooms in which routines were all-pervasive and cast in a code that itemized many "thou shalt nots." Some pupils also knew that these were good teachers because "you KNEW you'd learned a thing. The evidence was there because you could REPEAT the learning accurately — even years later." Good teachers, however, were also fair teachers. They dispensed their rebukes, their detentions, even their whacks with a ruler or more severe forms of corporal punishment rarely, in an even-handed way and in strict accordance with the rules. It was appropriate, it was fair, for these teachers to give special attention to the best pupils — to those who learned the rote packages, obeyed the rules meticulously and did everything neatly — so long as these children did not receive blatant favouritism. Good teachers did not pick on children unfairly. In this regard, pupils believed it was "fair" for teachers to ride herd on those who did not do their homework or who were often unruly, and even on those who were not very bright, so long as the teachers did so without malice and so long as the breach in the rules was evident to all.

A much larger group of teachers were "nice." Such teachers are remembered less sharply, less vividly than the others; recollections of them tend to be enveloped in a pleasant haze. One was "always warm and friendly"; another was a "lovely person, an excellent teacher"; a third was "a very quiet man; we kids thought he was really nice"; a fourth was "a very kind man, the first one who really challenged us; he made you think about things." A principal of the 1930s is remembered as "not at all a fearsome man; he was very gentle, and had the children's respect." Such people apparently taught well and easily; they mothered or fathered their charges without all the elaborate apparatus that characterized the classroom of the "best" teachers. They did, however, use a paedagogy almost identical to that of their more overbearing colleagues. Although few people remember them in this way, I hypothesize that they were probably as effective in carrying out the bread-and-butter tasks of teaching as were their more famous and martinet-like colleagues. (One former pupil, however, argues that, in contrast to the efforts of the "good" teacher, what the "nice" teacher taught didn't seem to have the same mental precision or self-evident value and worthiness as the product of the "good" teacher's teaching.)

If the above are memory's satisfactory elementary teachers, two other sorts also stand out. One was made up of teachers and principals who were mean, nasty, sarcastic, cruel or even vicious. They constantly put their pupils down. One recalls a teacher who called her, alternatively, "Dummy" and "Fatty"; and another who described her classmate as a "filthy little pig" because she ate garlic. There was also Miss W, who "smiled when you stumbled, and then waited for the moment to pin the truth on you," Miss X who announced that she was "sick and tired of calling out 'foreign' names," Miss Y who mocked those who stuttered until they cried, and Mr. Z, a principal who "ruled by fear . . . ; the whole place cringed while he was around." On the really dark side there were, as well, the principal who fondled girls and the school physician who sexually assaulted some of the boys. Such teachers usually employed a paedagogy that was not very different from other teachers. They differed from their colleagues mostly in that, instead of being respected or liked by their pupils, they were feared and hated. Only in retrospect did these people achieve a dubious sort of merit; some former pupils gradually came to look upon the fact that they had "survived" these teachers as evidence that they had in their classes taken a major step towards adulthood.

Finally, pupils looked on a few teachers with contempt. These unfortunates displayed their ineffectiveness or their incompetence in a variety of ways. They could not explain things clearly. The oral parts of their lessons rambled, their notes were incoherent. They could not keep order; they sometimes broke down and wept. Some tried to bribe the children to behave with candy or even money. While most disappeared in a year or less, a few persisted to become almost legendary objects to be scorned by class after class of pupils. Whether they stayed or left, they received no compassion or mercy from either pupils or parents.

Two main themes characterized overall school discipline in this era. The first and dominant mode was that imposed by the school. It displayed itself in a continuum that at one end had the presence, the personality, the aura of the teachers and the principal and at the other, the strap and expulsion. School staffs held back the latent barbarism they perceived in the children with an increasingly severe range of sanctions that began with displeasure and ended with corporal punishment. Teachers and parents justified this range of measures by appealing to a very long-standing tradition; to the proverbial "Spare the rod and spoil the child." The second mode saw some schools introducing a range of practices through which the children were to learn what was sometimes called democratic self-control. Through a system of door, stair, hall, playground and other monitors, the older and abler in fact enlisted with teachers and principals in the task of teaching and maintaining appropriate standards, especially among the younger children.[23] Thus democratic self-control was tightly circumscribed by traditional disciplinary means which were brought in these years to a peak of effective performance.

The presence of the seasoned teacher was clearly the first line of defence against barbarism. Teachers had presence; pupils and their parents expected them to possess it. Teachers with this quality said, "Do this," and the children did it. All but ineffectual teachers exerted their personalities with more or less intensity on their pupils and expected, and received, a reasonably automatic compliance with their directions. Even those who created a loving atmosphere in their classrooms did so in this broader context. The woman who now recalls, "I knew who the teacher was and did as I was told," speaks for her classmates as well as herself. Presence surely came with experience, but neophytes set out, self-con-

[23] A student at Point Grey Junior High School put the case for student government in the school annual very well: "Citizens of Canada should practise the principles of democracy. It is wise to start early. Is the Student Government of our school of value to us? Yes! It is a great help. It teaches us the laws of democracy easily and thoroughly. Everyone has the opportunity to express his opinions freely. What more can a student ask! As the years go by, this practice of democracy learned in school becomes more valuable to the citizen. There may be a student here who will become a member of parliament. There are others who will fill important public offices. As citizens we will help to elect the members of parliament. Each student should be thankful for the opportunities given him at school, and should make use of these opportunities to improve his school and later his country." Vancouver, Point Grey Junior High School, *The Explorer*, 1940, p. 38.

sciously, to acquire it. Eighteen- and nineteen-year-olds stare at us from Normal School annuals of these years with an intensity that makes them look older, more severe, and altogether more formidable than the twenty-two or twenty-three-year-old beginning teachers of the 1980s.[24]

Teachers backed up their demands that pupils meet certain standards of behaviour and work habits with an armoury of sanctions. They gave children "the ray." They gave them the cutting edge of their tongues; they spoke sharply, they made nasty and sometimes sarcastic remarks, they spoke more and more softly, coldly, ominously; they shouted and even raged against their charges. ("She really lambasted us; she had a short fuse"; "I recall his scarlet face and his ferocious temper.") Many maintained full control solely through verbal means. Others made children sit or stand in a corner, or even on the floor under the sand-table; they kept children in at recess, at lunch hour and after school. One person recalls being kept in after school, asking to leave the room, being refused, and then wetting his pants. "I stayed away for three days." Teachers made pupils sit up straight, motionless, with hands behind their backs, for periods of time up to half an hour. They forced chewers to put their gum on the ends of their noses or behind their ears. They gave extra work of an excruciatingly boring and valueless sort, such as eight or nine digit long division questions and their proofs, the writing of lines — some wrote such things as "I will not chew gum," or "Silence is golden," five hundred to a thousand times —, the copying of pages out of textbooks or dictionaries, and the memorization of poems ("Mr. X gave me two weeks to memorize all . . . of Poe's 'The Raven' or be strapped by the principal") and assigned those classroom and school chores not popular with "monitors" such as picking up paper and other garbage in the school and on its grounds. They sent miscreants to school detention halls, where the duty teacher or vice-principal imposed sanctions, often with great severity of tone. Some teachers and schools kept elaborate systems of "demerit" records, through which offending pupils progressed through an increasingly severe range of sanctions. Fewer schools and teachers employed the opposite of this system by giving out merit points for good behaviour and providing minor rewards — such as being dismissed first — to those pupils or rows of pupils which collected the most points.

[24] John Calam drew my attention to what old annuals and class photographs tell us about the determined maturity of beginning teachers of earlier eras. Perhaps this characteristic reinforced the view of pupils that all their teachers "were as old as the hills." One, recalling a teacher of the 1930s who "wore her hair in a bun and had dark clothes," was really surprised when she read that this teacher had just retired.

Teachers and principals kept corporal punishment as their ultimate sanction short of expulsion. Classroom teachers often employed less formal — and unlawful — sorts of physical punishment. Former pupils recall teachers who spanked youngsters on the bottom or slapped them on the hands or about the shoulders and, occasionally, on the face. Other teachers pinched the upper arm or the earlobe or hit victims on the top of the head with tightened knuckles. Still others used pointers, rulers, chalk brushes, gym shoes or other bits of school equipment to hit children on their bottoms, hands, knuckles, shoulders, elbows — especially on the "funnybone" — and, rarely, heads. A somewhat fondly remembered grade 1 teacher, who enrolled forty-six pupils in the year recalled, "stepped on their toes as she hit them with a ruler." A few, carried by temper almost beyond control, sometimes dragged children from their desks to shake them, to bang them against walls or even to manhandle them out of the classroom. Unlike the cold formality that so often characterized corporal punishment by a principal, classroom teachers sometimes struck out in a high pitch of unleashed emotion. A few teachers tried to be light-hearted, even affectionate, in their physical punishment. On these occasions the ritualized rules of the "game," especially as it was played between boys and men teachers and in such all-boy classes as those in physical education or industrial arts, required that the victim enter, however reluctantly, into the game-like spirit with which they tried to characterize these events. In the same jocular way, some teachers threw chalk, chalk brushes and even textbooks at their charges.

For really serious violations of class or school codes, children were sent to or summoned by the school principal. Pupils found these interviews with the principal to be extremely stressful occasions; some were tongue-tied into silence. Being strapped was not an inevitable product of a trip to the "office," but it happened often enough for youngsters to be extremely wary of visiting there. Once a principal decided to strap a boy or, more rarely, a girl, he followed a routine — almost a ritual — laid down by the department of education.[25] The principal summoned a witness, explained the crime and punishment to the latter, positioned the subject carefully, administered the strokes and counted them out in a firm voice, and then recorded the event in a special book. Some princi-

---

[25] Corporal punishment was rooted in the Canadian Criminal Code. Statutes, precedents and reported cases are discussed in Peter Frank Bargen, *The Legal Status of the Canadian Public School Pupil* (Toronto: Macmillan, 1961), pp. 125-33; see also *Manual of the School Law and School Regulations of the Province of British Columbia* (Victoria: King's Printer, 1944), pp. 127-28.

pals removed their jackets and hung them up on a coat hanger. Others emphasized the formality of the occasion by buttoning their jackets. If there was more than one victim, those waiting their turn either watched or listened from just outside the door. The worst thing was when friends were there "because then you couldn't cry." One person, recalling his first four on each hand, says, "I couldn't understand the pain, it was so intense." Since principals used these events as much to deter as to punish, they often permitted the sounds to carry their warning through the school; the appearance back in the classroom of a red-eyed and red-handed victim quickly reinforced the message. A few even prolonged the misery by administering punishment over more than one session or by announcing it and then postponing its administration to noon hour or after school, or even to another day.

Although girls sometimes received corporal punishment of the informal classroom sort, they rarely took part in the ritual in the office. However, all were aware of its place in the school. Some of the older girls were perhaps thrilled by its happening to the boys. When one looks at this difference between the sexes more systematically, however, one sees that it appears to be the product of two sorts of influences. On the one hand, teachers seem to have demanded more docile conduct from girls than they did from boys. On the other, children themselves structured much of the different ways that boys and girls behaved. Most beginners of both sexes probably came to school disposed to conduct themselves appropriately. However, as they got to know other children, as they formed same-sex friendships, groups and gangs, as they integrated themselves into the playground pecking order, the sexes came to have different norms as to how they should behave toward each other and toward the school. These norms seem to have almost completely governed what happened to children between their homes and their classrooms. Further, they seem to have had more influence even inside classrooms than many teachers were aware.[26]

If parents and teachers often justified stern discipline and corporal punishment by appealing to proverbial wisdom, their approach was also deeply rooted in fear. On the one hand, they feared that without severe sanctions, family, classroom, school and society would quickly descend into disorder and even barbarism; on the other hand they feared for the

[26] In another phase of the work of the Canadian Childhood History Project I am looking at the "culture of childhood" and how it structured much of the lives of children.

future of the unchastened. Many still believed that the "old Adam" was very close to the surface in boys and especially in early adolescence. In the eight-grade elementary school some teachers in the upper couple of grades seem to have seen a barely suppressed violence in some of the boys; in responding to it savagely they perhaps transformed their own fears into realities. In turn, these violent episodes communicated such beliefs and fears to the younger pupils and gave them notions of a sort of behaviour that one day they might well perform. The school's informal communication system passed down and exaggerated stories of epic disciplinary events in the upper grades. These tales seem to have kept certain youngsters in a state of anticipatory tension over much of their school days "feeling that the certainty of it occurring to you was not only high, but pre-ordained." Many now recall the paradox in this system; it terrified the good children who only very occasionally got caught up in its machinery but gave those who were often punished and who "could take it" an heroic status among their peers. X, for example, was one of those boys "who was strapped two or three times a year." One day he kicked a football at a school window; "it took him three kicks to get it through the window. He just stayed there until the teacher came and took him away" for the usual punishment.

By the 1920s nearly all school-aged children in Vancouver spent at least a few years in school. Despite the general belief that they all would benefit from the experience, a few may actually have been worse off than their counterparts in earlier times. In the era before attendance laws were vigorously enforced, fractious boys — and, occasionally, girls — who fell behind because of large classes, poor teaching, irregular or poor attendance, or little or no disposition or perhaps ability to learn, dropped out of school and disappeared into the community. Now their parents or economic conditions or truant officers forced them to stay in school. Some may have benefited from the extended experience; others, no better taught or able to learn than their predecessors, were oppressed by it. Some withdrew entirely into themselves; they became those ciphers in class photographs whose names no one can now recall. Others, such as X above, found their outlet in being "tough." They moved along the very edge of forbidden practices and behaviours, they dominated the cloak-room and the boys' playground, they used bad language just at the edge of earshot of the teacher, they fought each other and they carried "roll-ings" or cigarettes in their pockets which they smoked just out of sight of the school. They quit school as soon as they were old enough to do so or when they received the school's ultimate sanction and were expelled.

Learning to survive was thus an important part of the hidden curriculum of the school. Its pupils had first of all to learn how to deal with their fears: their fear of the other children in their own class, their fear of the bigger children who might harass them to and from school or on the playground, their special fear of "tough" boys and girls, their fear of teachers and the principal, their fear of the strap. Most children obviously learned to manage, or at least to live with, their fears. It is important to note that those whom I interviewed reported that, overall, they enjoyed much of their school experience. ("I sure enjoyed my days at school, even if I wasn't good at it.") A few were less fortunate. What was school really like for those who decline to talk about it because they still do not want to conjure with memories they say are really unpleasant?

III

According to Putman and Weir, the alternative to formal discipline was "the project method." They pointed out that it was paedagogically sound to select "big projects of study as cores of interest, from which the child's investigations radiate in [as] many directions as the spokes from a wheel." Thus older youngsters might investigate "the various factors that have built up the Okanagan fruit industry and describe the industry as it is now carried on" or younger children "might spend a whole term on a study of what the people of Vancouver eat and wear and where their food and clothing came from."[27]

Since Putman and Weir's recommendations were very much in the mainstream of then-current educational theory, British Columbia gradually put many of them into effect. In a series of what were really administrative reforms, the province standardized the curriculum and the time allotments for each subject, adopted the notion of the junior high school, eliminated high school entrance examinations, tightened standards for admission to the Normal schools and promoted school consolidations. After the Liberals won the provincial election of 1933, Weir became Minister of Education. In 1935 he embarked on a major revision of the curriculum. By 1937 his department produced a new course of study which was over 1,600 pages long. In the words of one of its chief architects, H. B. King, the philosophy characterizing this new curriculum "may be briefly expressed as the promotion of individual growth and

[27] *Survey of the School System*, pp. 118-21.

social adjustment through purposeful activity."[28] The philosophy of the new education — now generally called progressive education — thus lay at the heart of the new program. Nonetheless, if my interviewees are to be believed, then all of the changes that took place in education outside of the classroom had very little effect on what went on behind its doors. The "good" teacher who "drills incessantly" kept Vancouver elementary schools in a torpid formal state for at least three decades after Putman and Weir made their report.

Why Canadian education had become formal lies outside of the scope of this paper.[29] What is of interest here is why formalism persisted and even extended its sway in Vancouver — and elsewhere in Canada — despite the fact that most theorists attacked it so vigorously and, indeed, its opponents had come to dominate the provincial department of education and the upper levels of the Vancouver school system.[30] A good part of the answer to this question lies within the school system itself. To introduce integrated learning of the sort and on the scale envisioned by Putman, Weir and King, schools must have appropriately educated and trained teachers and appropriately sized classes. In these years Vancouver met neither condition.

To organize "big projects of study" in such a way that the children's "investigations" led to intellectual growth placed two demands on teachers. First, they themselves must have received the sort of education that showed them the connections between the different branches of knowledge; and second, they must have had the sort of professional training that taught them to structure activities through which children could come to see the connections. In fact, however, and as table 1 demonstrates, the vast majority of Vancouver's elementary teachers had only high school level academic training. From the early 1920s onward, those with second-class certificates had their junior matriculation, and those

[28] British Columbia, Department of Education, *Report*, 1939-40, p. B32. For the Putman-Weir report and its results, see F. Henry Johnson, *A History of Public Education in British Columbia* (Vancouver: University of British Columbia, 1964), ch. 7, 8 and 12 and Jean Mann, "G. M. Weir and H. B. King: Progressive Education or Education for the Progressive State?", in J. Donald Wilson and David C. Jones, eds., *Schooling and Society in Twentieth Century British Columbia* (Calgary: Detselig, 1980), ch. 4.

[29] For a comprehensive analysis of this question, see George S. Tomkins, *A Common Countenance: Stability and Change in the Canadian Curriculum* (Toronto: Prentice-Hall, 1986).

[30] Robert Patterson clearly shows that the Vancouver experience was representative of the situation in other parts of Canada. See his unpublished paper, "Progressive Education: The Experience of English-Speaking Canadians, 1930-1945."

TABLE 1

Qualifications of Elementary School Teachers and Principals in
Vancouver, South Vancouver and Point Grey in
1924-25, 1934-35, 1944-45 and 1957-58

Qualifications	1924-25	1934-35	1944-45	1957-58[1]
Academic Certificate	106	99	138	
First Class Certificate	260	377	424	
Second Class Certificate	370	219	103	Over 60 percent
Third Class Certificate	21	13	6	
Others Enrolling Classes	6	6	10	
TOTAL	763	714	681	

[1] Changes in the way that the data was reported make it impossible to make exact comparisons of the 1950s with earlier years. However, of the 2,606 elementary school teachers and principals in school districts of over 100,000 people — thus including Vancouver — about 60 percent, or 1,551, had either one or two years of education and training past grade 12. Since many of those with higher qualifications were principals, one can still say that the substantial majority of elementary teachers had an education and training very similar to their earlier counterparts. British Columbia, *Report of the Royal Commission*, p. 192.

Compiled from data in British Columbia, Department of Education, *Report*, 1924-25, pp. M32-M48, M68-M70, M76-M83; *ibid.*, 1934-35, pp. S43-S59; *ibid.*, 1944-45, pp. Y-210-Y227.

with first-class certificates their senior matriculation. Although the latter had taken what purported to be the equivalent of a first year of Arts, most had done so in a high school, with their high school teachers merely extending on the sort of knowledge they had taught them in the years up to junior matriculation. Few if any Vancouver or other Canadian high schools, whose classroom life Robert Stamp has characterized as "circumscribed by a prescribed curriculum of traditional subjects, authorized textbooks, deductive reading, and external examinations," taught even their best students a modicum of the sort of independent thought that is a prime product of a liberal education.[31] At best, students came to "love" one or more of their subjects. That love, however, did not include any independent or systematic way of extending their competence in these subjects. Nor, to use modern jargon, did it give them any sense of their disciplinary "structures." "I didn't think a thought in the whole of school," recalls one student with an excellent academic record; "I just regurgitated."

In addition to their junior or senior "Matric," elementary teachers had one year of Normal school which they may have taken in two or three segments spread over a number of years or, after 1922, in a single nine-month term.[32] The first task of the Normal school was to ensure that its students knew what they were going to teach; that their spelling, hand-writing, grammar, arithmetic skills, and so on, were up to the grade 8 level. Its next task was to initiate its students in practices that would enable them to teach these subjects first in a multi-graded rural classroom and then in a graded consolidated or urban school. Thus training for much of the new as well as the traditional education was limited and perfunctory. Nonetheless, the time spent in an environment in which a discussion of teaching dominated both formal and informal discourse probably helped well-disposed young people to make the transition from one role to another in the highly structured system.[33]

In their practice teaching and in their early years in the profession these young people naturally modelled themselves on the best practitioners who had taught them and on the best they saw in their schools; they became proficient at their craft by doing it in the way it had been done to them. Most modelled themselves on those teachers, described above, who emphasized the fundamentals and rigorous discipline in equal measure. Most forged themselves in the crucible of the one-roomed rural school. Hard work, dedication and concern for their pupils clearly characterized most of the products of such training and early experience. Although many undoubtedly had the ability, very few had the training to

[31] Robert M. Stamp, "Canadian High Schools in the 1920's and 1930's: The Social Challenge to the Academic Tradition," Canadian Historical Association, *Historical Papers*, 1978, p. 92.

[32] Johnson, *Public Education in British Columbia*, pp. 86, 210; for an analysis and an evaluation of the Normal schools, see John Calam, "Teaching the Teachers: Establishment and Early Years of the B.C. Provincial Normal Schools," *BC Studies* 61 (Spring 1984): 30-63.

[33] See Irene Howard, "First Memories of Vancouver," Vancouver Historical Society *Newsletter*, v. 13 (October 1973), for a brief account of Normal schooling from a student's perspective.

introduce their pupils to the joys of intellectual activity of any sort, let
alone those which were supposed to emerge from projects. Indeed, as the
traditional system became more efficient, more systematic and more
effective, it simply co-opted the elements of the new education as it
ignored its goals.[34] Further, most teachers — even the growing corps of
"specialists" — conveyed to children, to colleagues and to parents the
sense that there was in each subject only one right way of doing things.

Even if those with academic certificates or other forms of advanced
education had somehow acquired a theoretically sound and practical
approach to progressive or other new ways of organizing classroom learning, they would have found enormous difficulty in putting it into practice. In addition to the almost insuperable problems posed by trying to
function independently in a system that pressed pupils, teachers and principals into the formal mode, the very size of classes made other forms of
teaching and learning virtually impossible. In classes that averaged for
most of these years about forty pupils — see table 2 — teachers could not
get to know their charges as individuals. Class size forced them to teach
to the whole class, to let the good look after themselves and to let the
weakest fall by the wayside. Their responsibility for so many children
probably also forced all but the ablest teachers to take a stance in their
classrooms that emphasized children's weaknesses and propensity to err,
to capitalize on their vulnerability, and to keep an extremely wary lookout
for bad behaviour. In these circumstances, when some teachers introduced "projects" or "activity units" into their classrooms they did so
merely as an occasional change of pace in such subjects as social studies,
science or art. Like their other colleagues, they continued to teach, to
apply again modern jargon to what they did, factual material from the
lower levels of the taxonomy. They tested their pupils' memories and
evaluated their work habits; what they did is best epitomized in their
answer to a question common in classroom discourse until relatively
recently: "Yes, neatness *does* count."

And neatness also "counted" in the community as a whole. Pupils,
parents and employers in Vancouver continued to believe that education
was "learning out of a book." While I have learned from interviews less
on this point than I have on others, such evidence as I have suggests that
parents of all social classes shared in this common viewpoint as to the
nature and value of elementary schooling. They knew what children

---

[34] See Timothy A. Dunn, "The Rise of Mass Public Schooling in British Columbia,
1900-1929," in Wilson and Jones, *Schooling and Society*, ch. 1.

TABLE 2

*Class Size in Vancouver, South Vancouver and Point Grey in
1924-25, 1934-35, 1944-45 and 1957-58*

Number of Pupils Per Class	Number of Classes			
	1924-25	*1934-35*	*1944-45*	*1957-58*[1]
Over 60	0	1	0	
55 - 59	4	0	0	
50 - 54	27	7	3	
45 - 49	120	67	14	
40 - 44	249	287	82	Average size about 34
35 - 39	213	239	178	
30 - 34	93	78	241	
25 - 29	29	13	115	
20 - 24	6	9	22	
15 - 19	17	9	21	
10 - 14	2	3	2	
Under 10	2	0	3	
TOTAL NUMBER OF CLASSES	762	713	681	

[1] In Vancouver, 35,918 elementary pupils were divided into 1,064 divisions, making an average class size of 33.78. British Columbia, Department of Education, *Report*, 1957-58, p. W18.

Compiled from data in British Columbia, Department of Education, *Report*, 1924-25, pp. M32-M48, M68-M70, M76-M83; *ibid.*, 1934-35, pp. S43-S59; *ibid.*, 1944-45, pp. Y210-Y227.

Closure of classes in 1924-25 and 1935-36 accounts for the different totals in tables 1 and 2.

should learn, they knew how teachers should teach it, and they knew how principals and teachers should maintain order. Indeed, because parents and employers lacked the daily empirical testing of their expectations against the real world of the classroom, they often held — and over these years continued to hold — the most rigid of formalistic expectations of what school should be like.

That working-class parents apparently held the same views on elementary education as did their middle-class counterparts may, at least initially, seem somewhat surprising. As such contemporary analysts as Henry Giroux and Michael Apple have argued, both the "objectified" knowledge of the provincial curriculum and its concomitant paedagogy represent a middle-class view of the world.[35] If their analysis is correct, then the Vancouver school system presented middle-class elementary schooling in a way that did not differ quantitatively or qualitatively from one part of the city to another. While my interviews revealed considerable differences among aspects of the non-school lives of Vancouver children from one neighbourhood to another, recollections of schooling were surprisingly similar. Thus Vancouver schools sorted children within schools rather than between schools.[36] As we have seen, they continually told those who were not as able as their peers that they were not going to climb very far up the educational ladder. Nonetheless, formal schooling of the sort offered in Vancouver schools met, in a rough and ready way, somewhat different class needs. At the political level, organized labour in the city supported free public education, and working-class people ran for, and were elected to, the school boards.[37] At the personal level, in a city composed of people born elsewhere, or their children, parents took particularly seriously their role as educational strategists for their children. In this role most parents insisted that their children at least get their "entrance" — still in common parlance long after the actual examinations had been abolished — as their basic educational credential. For those who left school at the end of grade 8 or over the next couple of years, "entrance" certified that they had well and truly mastered the three "R's."[38] For those who aspired to the wide range of occupations and other

[35] Henry A. Giroux, *Ideology, Culture & the Process of Schooling* (Philadelphia: Temple University Press, 1981); Michael W. Apple, *Ideology and Curriculum* (London: Routledge P. Kegan Paul, 1979.)

[36] This statement is supported both by my interviews and by an examination of such data as class size and teacher qualification for selected schools from different neighbourhoods in the city.

[37] Jean Barman, "Neighbourhood and Community in Interwar Vancouver" in this volume.

[38] Between the 1920s and the 1950s Vancouver children significantly increased the number of years they spent in school. While exact retention rates are extremely difficult to compute, enrolment and related data provide a clear indication of trends. Of the cohort born in 1918, about one-third stayed in school to enrol in grade 11; of the cohort born in 1928, over 40 percent did so; and of the cohort born in 1938, over 60 percent did so. These percentages are provincial ones, but other compilations suggest that Vancouver youngsters stayed in school for slightly

levels of training for which matriculation was necessary, entrance admitted them to the high school.

*   *   *

On 5 September 1934 the teachers of Charles Dickens School assembled for their first staff meeting of the school year. The principal, J. Dunbar, introduced the exchange teacher from Ontario, outlined the procedure for getting new sand for sand tables, discussed how a teachers' badminton club could function and explained how to get boots, shoes and school supplies for desperately needy children. He also reminded the teachers about such policies as those regarding substitutes, posting their names on the doors of their classrooms, keeping their class registers and turning in their previews to him every week. A quarter of a century later the staff of Queen Elizabeth School gathered, on 6 September 1960, for their first staff meeting. The principal, I. D. Boyd, introduced the five new teachers and the new nurse, explained that French would be taught to grades 5 and 6, and asked that all teachers attend the first meeting of the Parent-Teachers Association. He also reminded the teachers about such policies as those regarding substitutes, signing in in the morning, keeping their daybooks and seating plans up-to-date and preparing previews for each two-and-one-half monthly period in the school year. These staff meeting minutes both clearly display a similar administrative underpinning for formal learning. Visits to classrooms in both schools would have revealed that nearly all teachers believed in, and followed, traditional practices. Further, their stance received strong support from the provincial Royal Commission on Education, the Chant Commission, that in its 1960 *Report* endorsed a traditional view of education.[39] Over the 1960s, however, pupils, parents, teachers and employers abandoned the long-lived consensus on elementary education. Some began to take seriously the child-centred rhetoric of contemporary child-rearing and educational literature and to insist that it be employed in the schools. Elementary teachers gradually became well enough educated that they could structure the learning in their classrooms in the context of new theories about learning and teaching. Some families came to believe that the school has so downplayed formal learning that transfer training was no longer taking

---

longer periods of time than did those for the province as a whole. British Columbia, *Report of the Royal Commission on Education* (Victoria: n.pub., 1960), pp. 43-49.

[39] *Ibid.*, passim.

place, and they lamented its passage. A decade of changes in curricula and teaching practices would transform elementary schooling in Vancouver. If formalism did not entirely disappear over these years, by the early 1970s one could no longer use the term to characterize elementary schooling in the city.

The Incidence of Crime in Vancouver During the Great Depression*

JAMES P. HUZEL

"*Crime Wave Sweeps Vancouver*" ran the headline in the *Vancouver Sun* on 7 January 1930.[1] Two days later an editorial followed that claimed most offences were not the work of professional criminals but rather of "men whom hunger and poverty had made desperate."[2] On 1 November 1930 another editorial linked crime conditions to unemployment and suggested solving both problems by hiring a large squad of extra policemen.[3] A more violent crime wave was referred to in March 1932, when it was claimed that 575 major crimes in which revolvers had figured[4] had occurred in Vancouver since the beginning of that year. Concern was again voiced on 21 July 1932, the headline in the *Sun* proposing another possible solution: "*City May Operate Jobless Shelters to Restrict Crime.*"[5] Even the Victoria *Colonist*, in the same year, noticed the "*Reign of Crime*" in Vancouver, claiming that the B.C. police were intent on coming to the aid of the local force to "*Clean Up*" crime in the city.[6]

The press was not alone in linking the sudden onslaught of Vancouver's depression in October 1929 to increased criminal activity. The

* I would like to thank the H.S.S. Grants Committee of U.B.C. for providing funding which aided, in part, the research on which this article is based. I would also like to thank Elaine Fairey and Logan Hovis for their valuable research assistance, and especially Virginia Green of the Arts Computing Centre, who performed the computer programming without which this study could not have come to fruition. My thanks, as well, to the staff of the Vancouver City Archives for their valuable assistance, and to Staff Sergeant Swan of the Vancouver Police Department for providing important information. I would also like to thank Murray Greenwood and DeLloyd Guth for reading an earlier draft of this paper. Some of the latter's suggestions must await elaboration in forthcoming work. I owe a special debt of gratitude to my wife Gail for her painstaking research over the years.

[1] *Vancouver Sun*, 7 January 1930, p. 1.

[2] *Ibid.*, 9 January 1930, p. 6.

[3] *Ibid.*, 1 November 1930, p. 6.

[4] *Ibid.*, 23 March 1932, p. 6.

[5] *Ibid.*, 21 July 1932, p. 1.

[6] Cited in *ibid.*, 6 May 1932, p. 1.

211

police themselves were certain of the connection. As early as 7 November 1929, the Vancouver Police Commission noted a rise in petty thieving and housebreaking.[7] Although Police Chief W. J. Bingham had initially denied that a crime wave was upon the city, he nevertheless claimed in his *Annual Report* for 1929 that the "unemployment situation results in many destitute men falling into petty crime" and that "clearing camps in the interior would rid the City of a menace difficult to handle...."[8] In February 1930 Bingham reported to the Vancouver Police Commission that "many of the large numbers of unemployed men in the city were becoming desperate and were committing crimes" and noted an increase in hold-ups and shopbreakings.[9] On 3 December a special meeting of the Police Commission was convened to discuss the "epidemic of holdups and burglaries."[10] In his *Annual Report* of that year Bingham explained that the increase in stolen property could "be accounted for in part by the state of general depression and mass unemployment."[11] Police Chief C. E. Edgett elaborated on this theme in 1932:

> With few exceptions, those arrested for Robbery with Violence were found to be local youths and residents of Vancouver, who had been before the Courts for minor offences as Juveniles and otherwise. The present economic situation and its attendant unemployment is no doubt in a large measure contributory to this condition.[12]

The demands of community and business associations likewise provide evidence of a growing concern about rising crime. The Vancouver Central Ratepayers Association passed a resolution early in 1930 suggesting that assistance be requested from the RCMP and, if necessary, the Pro-

---

[7] See *City of Vancouver: Board of Police Commission Minutes*, 7 November 1929, p. 178. Vancouver City Archives, 75(A)5. Hereinafter these documents will be referred to as *Van. Police Minutes*. The Vancouver City Archives will be referred to as V.C.A.

[8] See *Annual Report of the Chief Constable of the City of Vancouver 1929*, p. 31. V.C.A., S.25. Hereinafter these documents will be referred to as *Van. Police Annual Report* with the year cited. For Bingham's denial see the *Vancouver Sun*, 10 January 1930, p. 1 and 1 February 1930, p. 1.

[9] *Van. Police Minutes*, 4 February 1930, p. 219 and 12 February 1930, p. 222. V.C.A., 75(A)5.

[10] *Ibid.*, 3 December 1930, p. 52.

[11] *Van. Police Annual Report*, 1930, p. 3. V.C.A. S.25.

[12] *Van. Police Annual Report 1932*, p. 2. V.C.A., S.25. Edgett also speculated on another cause of this condition: "The craving for excitement and amusement by present-day youth, and the glorification of crime as exemplified by the modern 'Movies' may possibly have a bearing on it also."

vincial Police to cope with the rise in unlawful activity.[13] In January 1932 the Grandview Ratepayers Association urged city council to press for an amendment to the Criminal Code forbidding the manufacture, importation and sale of revolvers and other lethal weapons. The preamble to their resolution — unanimously endorsed by city council and adopted in principle by the Vancouver Police Commission — read:

And Whereas the present economic distress is accentuating unemployment and either directly or indirectly driving many of our young men into the ranks of the criminal class, and because of the ease with which such lethal weapons may be procured, rendering such men a serious menace to law-abiding citizens, Be It Resolved. . . . [14]

In addition, groups such as the Merchant Tailors Exchange and the Vancouver Real Estate Exchange directed specific complaints to the Vancouver Police Commission. In March 1931 the former wrote to the Commission referring to the recent numerous robberies of tailor shops in town, resulting in "severe losses" to their members, and urged "a special effort on the part of the Police Force."[15] The latter, in December 1933, complained about the theft of plumbing, lighting and other fixtures from vacant houses and urged a special investigation to cope with this widespread "evil."[16]

Abundant contemporary commentary, then, suggests an association between depressed economic conditions and rising trends in crime. What contemporaries thought, however, and what actually occurred might be two very different things. Did crime, in fact, increase during Vancouver's Depression? If so, can one specify which types of criminal activity were most sensitive to the downswing in the economy? How do crime levels in the 1930s compare with those prevailing in Vancouver's earlier history? One of the major aims of this paper is to address these specific questions.

Beyond that, my intentions are wider-ranging. Although in recent years Canadian historians have expressed a burgeoning interest in varying aspects of the law, crime and society, this field has not received nearly the attention that it has in Europe and the United States. In particular, Canadian cities still await the long-term historical consideration of crime,

[13] This resolution was brought before the Vancouver Police Commission. See *Van. Police Minutes*, 12 February 1930, p. 224. V.C.A., 75(A)5.

[14] See *ibid.*, 20 January 1932, pp. 178-79. V.C.A., 75(A)6; see also *Police General Files*, 75(C)6, fol. 5.

[15] *Van. Police Minutes*, 16 March 1931, p. 96. V.C.A., 75(A)6.

[16] *Ibid.*, 28 December 1933, p. 71. See also *Police General Files*, V.C.A., 75(D)2, fol. 7.

police and community accorded to urban centres such as London, New York and Boston.[17] The present article — the basis of a larger study — attempts a beginning.

Finally, Vancouver will be utilized as a test case within the extensive debate on the impact of economic conditions on crime. The literature, both historical and criminological, on this theme is at once voluminous and contradictory, although surprisingly few studies have concentrated specifically on the Depression of the 1930s. Once again, most of the historical work has focused on Europe and the U.S.A. In both earlier and more recent writings two clear categories emerge: those authors who posit, albeit with varying degrees of qualification, a direct relationship between increasing destitution and crime, and those who strongly deny such an association. Classic works by Thomas on nineteenth-century England and Radzinowicz on Poland between 1927 and 1934, for example, found positive correlations between certain types of property crimes and deteriorating economic conditions.[18] These pioneering conclusions are confirmed in more recent works by Short on the 1930s depression in the U.S.A.,[19] Beattie on seventeenth- and eighteenth-century

[17] For recent historical work on Canada see D. J. Bercuson and L. A. Knafla, eds., *Law and Society in Canada in Historical Perspective* (University of Calgary, Studies in History, No. 2, 1979) and L. A. Knafla, ed., *Law and Justice in a New Land: Essays in Western Canadian Legal History* (Agincourt, Ontario: Carswell, 1986). Both these collections of articles contain excellent biographies. Unfortunately the latter publication appeared too late to be incorporated in this study. For England see J. S. Cockburn, ed., *Crime in England, 1550-1800* (London: Methuen and Co. Ltd., 1977), and in particular the comprehensive bibliography by L. A. Knafla contained therein. For France and Germany see Howard Zehr, *Crime and the Development of Modern Society: Patterns of Criminality in Nineteenth-Century Germany and France* (London: Croom Helm Ltd., 1976). For the U.S.A. see Eric H. Monkkonen, *Police in Urban America 1860-1920* (Cambridge: Cambridge University Press, 1981); Robert M. Fogelson, *Big City Police* (Cambridge, Massachusetts: Harvard University Press, 1977); David R. Johnson, *Policing the Urban Underworld: The Impact of Crime on the Development of the American Police 1800-1887* (Philadelphia: Temple University Press, 1979); and Sidney L. Harring, *Policing a Class Society: The Experience of American Cities 1865-1915* (New Brunswick, New Jersey: Rutgers University Press, 1983). For studies specific to major cities see Wilbur R. Miller, *Cops and Bobbies: Police Authority in New York and London 1830-1870* (Chicago: The University of Chicago Press, 1977); Roger Lane, *Policing the City: Boston 1822-1885* (Cambridge, Massachusetts: Harvard University Press, 1967).

[18] D. S. Thomas, *Social Aspects of the Business Cycle* (New York: A. Knopf and Co., 1927). L. Radzinowicz, "The Influence of Economic Conditions on Crime," *Sociological Review* XLVIII (September 1942): 188-201. See also Sam Bass Warner, *Crime and Criminal Statistics in Boston*, repr. ed. (New York: Arno Press, 1974), pp. 30-34. Originally published 1934.

[19] See J. F. Short, "An Investigation of the Relationship between Crime and the Business Cycle" (unpublished Ph.D. dissertation, University of Chicago, 1951).

England,[20] Zehr for nineteenth-century France and Germany[21] and Monkkonen for the late nineteenth- and early twentieth-century U.S.A.[22] The views of these historians, moreover, are echoed by contemporary criminologists such as Chester, Silberman[23] and R. W. Gillespie, who, for example, concludes that "results of studies relating unemployment to crime show general, if not uniform, support for a positive correlation between these two variables."[24]

Numerous authors, however, have remained highly suspicious of these suppositions. Sellin's classic study of the Great Depression in the U.S.A. found no direct link between Depression and crime.[25] A. M. Carr-Sanders earlier had reached similar conclusions for England.[26] More recently, G. B. Vold summed up his comprehensive review of research linking unemployment to crime thus: "The obvious inference is that the general relations of economic conditions and criminality are so indefinite that no clear or definite conclusions can be drawn."[27] Ivan Jankovic is even more sceptical:

There is little evidence that poverty, as such, is positively correlated with crime, and no evidence at all that changes in unemployment rates are positively correlated with changes in crime rates.[28]

The above, of course, is but a brief sampling of the range of conclu-

[20] J. M. Beattie, "The Pattern of Crime in England 1660-1800," *Past and Present* 62 (February 1974): 47-95.

[21] Zehr, *Crime and Modern Society*.

[22] Monkkonen, *Police in Urban America*.

[23] Ronald C. Chester, "Perceived Relative Deprivation as a Cause of Property Crime," *Crime and Delinquency* 22 (1) (1976): 17-30. Charles F. Silberman, *Criminal Violence, Criminal Justice* (New York: Random House, 1978).

[24] R. W. Gillespie, *Economic Factors in Crime and Delinquency: A Critical Review of the Empirical Evidence* (Washington, D.C.: National Institute of Law Enforcement and Criminal Justice, 1975), p. 4. See also E. H. Sutherland and D. R. Cressey, *Criminology*, 10th ed. (Philadelphia: Lippincott, 1978), pp. 235-36.

[25] T. Sellin, *Research Memorandum on Crime in the Depression*, repr. ed. (New York: Arno Press, 1972). Originally published in 1937. Sellin does note, however, the correlation between bad economic conditions and rising burglary in England and Massachusetts (pp. 62 and 63).

[26] A. M. Carr-Sanders, "Crime and Unemployment," *Political Quarterly* V (July-September 1934): 395-99.

[27] G. B. Vold, *Theoretical Criminology* (New York: Oxford University Press, 1958), pp. 181-82.

[28] Ivan Jankovic, *Punishment and the Post-Industrial Society: A Study of Employment, Crime and Imprisonment in the United States* (Ann Arbor: University Microfilms International, 1978), p. 117.

sions in the research literature pertaining to Europe and the U.S.A. Work
on Canada in the depression is much sparser but likewise suggests somewhat contradictory results. Tepperman's national study, although primarily interested in the punitiveness of the courts, does suggest that
criminal activity increased during the Depression and posits a close correspondence between conviction rates and unemployment.[29] He cites as
well the numerous references in Broadfoot's *Ten Lost Years 1929-1939*
to argue for an increase in petty acquisitive crime caused by impoverish-
ment.[30] Gallacher, using Supreme Court of B.C. indictments, argues that
offences against property increased significantly in Greater Victoria with
the advent of the Depression.[31] A recent study by Watson which explores
crime in Calgary between 1924 and 1934, however, argues that "except
for a brief increase in property related offences early in the Depression,
the city's crime rate was remarkably stable; indeed, in some cases, it
declined from pre-Depression levels."[32] The following discussion, although
specific to Vancouver, will attempt, where possible, a broader comparative perspective and will argue that rising property crime was connected
closely to increasing destitution in the Great Depression.

If one goes beyond the literary evidence provided by contemporaries,
rich as these materials are, it is necessary to construct a series of crime
statistics for Vancouver both during and before the Great Depression.
The City of Vancouver possesses an excellent series of Police Court
Monthly Reports which span, with surprisingly few gaps, the years 1907

[29] Lorne Tepperman, *Crime Control: The Urge Toward Authority* (Toronto: Mc-
Graw-Hill Ryerson Ltd., 1977), p. 178.

[30] *Ibid.*, p. 179. Tepperman is correct in stressing Broadfoot's evidence linking poverty
and crime. At times, however, Broadfoot's interviewees seem to indicate that so
prevalent was economic distress it was futile to steal: "... who would you shoot
and take his [sic] money, nobody had any money, nothing to make it worth your
while." See Barry Broadfoot, *Ten Lost Years 1929-1939: Memories of Canadians
Who Survived the Depression* (Toronto: Doubleday Canada Ltd., 1973), p. 358.
See also James H. Gray, *The Winter Years* (Toronto: Macmillan, 1966), p. 30,
where he suggests that unemployment led to property theft.

[31] D. T. Gallacher, "City in Depression — The Impact of the Years 1929-1939 on
Greater Victoria, B.C." (unpublished M.A. thesis, University of British Columbia,
1970), p. 151. The figures upon which he bases this conclusion, however, are very
small. Only five indictments for property crime occurred between 1927 and 1929
compared to fifty-three in the period 1930-33 (p. 210). Supreme Court indictments, moreover, represent only a tiny minority of all cases heard in Greater
Victoria, and do not provide sufficient support for Gallacher's conclusions.

[32] Neil B. Watson, "Calgary: A Study of Crime, Offenders and the Police Court,
1924-1934" (unpublished M.A. thesis, University of Calgary, 1978), p. 131. This
is the only treatment to date of crime in a Canadian city during the Depression.
His study mainly concentrates on the period 1929-1934.

to 1937.[33] These reports are accurate summaries taken from the voluminous Police Court Calendars[34] and provide for each month and for each specific crime the total number of adults prosecuted before the Police Court magistrates, with a further breakdown of total convictions, total cases dismissed or withdrawn, and total cases committed for trial in higher courts. This information was supplemented where relevant with printed criminal statistics provided by the Dominion Bureau of Statistics.[35] Computerization of the data generated yearly totals of all prosecutions and convictions for the years 1906-40 occurring in the Vancouver Police Court. Since only a tiny minority of total cases were sent to higher court (at most 2.7 percent), these totals clearly capture the vast majority of criminals convicted.

For the purposes of analysis, particular categories and sub-categories of prosecutions and convictions were selected out from the overall totals.

[33] These reports were headed "STATEMENT OF CASES DISPOSED OF IN THE POLICE COURT FOR THE MONTH ENDING. . . . " with the particular month and year specified. They are in possession of the V.C.A., in the *Police General Files* numbered 75(A)12 through 75(D)4. Reports are missing for April through December 1920, for all of 1921, for January through April 1922, and for May through November 1934. It is estimated that the Police Court tried perhaps nine out of every ten people accused of breaking the law. More serious cases were referred to trial in the County Court after appearing in the Vancouver Police Court. The most serious cases were dealt with in the Supreme Court. Thus, trends revealed through the use of Police Court statistics, especially with respect to prosecutions, clearly will reflect overall patterns of crime in Vancouver. For a brief discussion of the early justice structure in British Columbia see Vincent Moore, *Angelo Branca: "Gladiator of the Courts"* (Vancouver: Douglas and McIntyre, 1981), p. 19. For a detailed treatment of the structure, jurisdiction and procedures of adult courts in Canada and the provinces see Stuart Ryan, "The Adult Court," in *Crime and Its Treatment in Canada*, ed. W. T. McGrath (Toronto: Macmillan of Canada, 1965), pp. 136-208.

[34] The Police Court Calendars comprise 103 volumes spanning the years 1895 to 1961. See V.C.A. 37(C)5 through 42(B)29. They contain the following information for each individual case appearing before the court: date of appearance, name of presiding magistrate, name, and sex (after 1919) of offender, date of offence, charge, name of complainant, name of prosecuting attorney, plea, name(s) of witness(es), how disposed of, and general observations. It is hoped eventually to obtain the substantial funding that would be necessary to exploit this vast resource. The present study utilizes the summaries contained in the Police Court Monthly Reports. The Court Calendars were utilized briefly, however, for two purposes: (1) certain sample months were used to confirm the accuracy of the Police Court Monthly Reports and (2) vagrancy cases for the years 1907-15 were tabulated to provide data on the specific types of vagrancy not given in the Monthly Reports.

[35] These statistics commenced in 1920 and were used mainly to provide total yearly prosecutions and convictions for the years 1920, 1921, 1934, 1938, 1939 and 1940, where data was either incomplete or missing in the Police Court Monthly Reports. See Canada, Dominion Bureau of Statistics, Judicial Statistics Branch, *Annual Reports of Criminal Statistics* (Ottawa: King's Printer, 1921-41). Data for individual cities are given in the "Police Statistics" section.

This was possible for the years 1907 through 1937, with the exception of
1921, for which no data could be found. The Police Court Monthly
Reports, of course, contain a vast array of criminal offences, many of
which are not directly relevant to the discussion at hand. These would
include a host of municipal By-Law offences (often referred to as "bark-
ing dog" violations), as well as traffic infractions, which increased to the
point where in 1936 they constituted 28 percent of all cases before the
Vancouver Police Court. All prosecutions under the Criminal Code as
well as a number of the more serious breaches of federal and provincial
acts were chosen for inclusion in this analysis.[36] These crimes were further
subdivided into three broad categories — crimes against the person,
crimes against property and crimes against the peace, the latter including
"morality" offences. In addition, the general groupings were broken down
into fifteen subcategories.[37]

The use of judicial material in the form of prosecutions and convictions to determine levels of criminality, of course, is fraught with difficulties long familiar to students of criminal statistics. Such data will
obviously not include the "dark figure" of crime — the huge number of
violations that go unreported or undetected. Prosecutions and convictions,
moreover, depend on a chain of circumstances commencing with the willingness of individuals to report criminal violations, the arrest of the
suspect, the laying of the charges, the decision to prosecute and final
resolution of the case. All these stages, in addition, are clearly influenced
by social attitudes especially in the realm of police activity where various
political and community groups often could bring pressure to bear on the
propensity to arrest and prosecute. J. M. Beattie conveniently sums up
this problem when he states that "modern opinion inclines to the view

[36] Thus all traffic offences except those included in the Criminal Code were excluded
as well as all municipal bylaws. Breaches of federal and provincial acts included
mostly pertain to various Drug and Liquor Acts. Prosecutions under the Indian Act
were also included. Fortunately no major revision to the Criminal Code was made
during the period under study. For the new code of 1953-54 see J. C. Martin, the
Criminal Code of Canada (Toronto: Cartwright and Sons, 1955).

[37] The categories were as follows: (A) CRIMES AGAINST THE PERSON — (i)
physical violence causing death (2) physical violence causing bodily injury (3) no
physical violence (4) sexual crimes; (B) CRIMES AGAINST PROPERTY —
(1) violent crimes against property (2) general theft (3) non-violent crimes
against property (4) malicious offences against property; (C) CRIMES AGAINST
THE PEACE — (1) offences against the administration of law and justice (2)
offences against public order (3) vagrancy (4) liquor related offences (5) gambling (6) drugs (7) prostitution. These categories were adapted from those generally employed by Statistics Canada.

that the most reliable sample of actual crime is that obtained as early in the process as is possible" — i.e., crime "known to the authorities."[38]

Fortunately, Vancouver does possess this kind of information for years and types of crime crucial to this study. The Police Department in their *Annual Reports* for 1938, 1939 and 1940 presented statistics spanning the years 1929 to 1940 tabulating crimes reported to them, broken down into a number of categories pertaining to property theft.[39] Such data, which come closest to measuring the actual incidence of crime, do not exist, however, prior to 1929. Any assessment, therefore, of long-term patterns of crime in Vancouver must rely on the aforementioned court statistics. To be sure, such sources have been used to good effect by a number of historians.[40] Extreme caution, however, is warranted. One must be sensitive to changes in police efficiency as well as to shifts in policy stimulated by political and public pressure.

The following analysis will focus mainly on the relationship between property crime and poverty with particular emphasis on the 1930s. Ideally, one would like to explore this relationship by relating individual offenders and their social characteristics to shifts in specific types of property crime over time. Vancouver unfortunately lacks the type of source material for such individual-level study. The voluminous Police Court Calendars, which list by name and type of offence every individual appearing before the police magistrates, provide information pertaining to gender but do not specify occupation, age, ethnicity, civil status or residency. Arrest and charge books which often provide such data do not survive. Individual police case files would provide similar material but are not accessible to the researcher. One must rely, therefore, on aggregate-level analysis which explores the relationship between temporal changes in rates of various property crimes and various indicators which represent changing levels of poverty.

Such a methodology, of course, is subject to the "ecological fallacy"; that is, attributing criminal actions to particular subgroups of the popu-

---

[38] Beattie, "Pattern of Crime in England," p. 54. For an excellent discussion of this issue as well as the use of criminal statistics in general see Thorsten Sellin and Marvin E. Wolfgang, *The Measurement of Delinquency* (New York: John Wiley and Sons, 1964), pp. 19, 36-40.

[39] *Van. Police Annual Reports 1938, 1939 and 1940*, pp. 19, 20 and 18 respectively. V.C.A. S.25.

[40] Some recent works are Lane, *Policing the City: Boston*; Roger Lane, "Urbanization and Criminal Violence in the Nineteenth Century," *The Journal of Social History* II (December 1968): 156-63; Beattie, *"Pattern of Crime in England,"* and Zehr, *Crime and Modern Society*. For western Canada see Thomas Thorner, "The Incidence of Crime in Southern Alberta," in *Law and Society in Canada*, eds. Bercuson and Knafla, pp. 53-88.

lation — namely the destitute — without direct biographical evidence linking particular groups to particular crimes. Nevertheless, this aggregative method, although far from ideal, has been employed judiciously by numerous historians.[41] It will allow one to determine whether the severe economic dislocation of the Depression years witnessed a rise in property crimes when compared to Vancouver's previous history as well as to assess whether, within the 1930s, property crime was correlated with short-term fluctuations in the economy.

It is necessary, then, to construct indices which reflect the changing economic and social conditions of Vancouver's population. Bartlett has provided us with an excellent real wage index covering the period 1901 to 1929 as well as yearly series pertaining to percentage unemployment in trade unions and the value of building permits issued.[42] The latter two series were carried forward to 1940.[43] A yearly average index of employment, moreover, was compiled for the years 1922 to 1938.[44] In addition, a series was created comprising the yearly amount of municipal relief expenditure provided to Vancouver's poor spanning the entire period from 1906 to 1940.[45] This series should approximate most closely to changing levels of poverty within the city. Population estimates were taken from *Annual Reports* of the City of Vancouver.[46] Since Van-

[41] In addition to the works by Beattie and Zehr cited in footnote 40 see Monkkonen, *Police in Urban America*, pp. 65-85. See also Ted Robert Gurr, Peter N. Grabosky and Richard C. Hula, *The Politics of Crime and Conflict: A Comparative History of Four Cities* (Beverley Hills, Sage Publications Inc., 1977).

[42] Eleanor A. Bartlett, "Real Wages and the Standard of Living in Vancouver, 1901-1929," *BC Studies* 51 (Autumn 1981): 3-62. The revised Bertram and Percy Index, yearly average prices, was utilized in this study. See table 10, p. 53.

[43] Percentage unemployment in trade unions was taken from *The Labour Gazette*, 1930-1940. The value of building permits was gleaned from the Dominion Bureau of Statistics, *Canada Yearbooks*, 1930-1940.

[44] Data for Vancouver were based on tables entitled "INDEX NUMBERS OF EMPLOYMENT BY PRINCIPAL CITIES," in *The Labour Gazette*, 1922-1938. The index takes 1926 = 100.

[45] These figures were compiled from the City of Vancouver Social Services *Annual Reports*, V.C.A., S.I. Unfortunately no gross figures are available for the yearly expenditure of charities.

[46] See in particular City of Vancouver, *Annual Report*, 1941, p. 63 V.C.A. The method of arriving at the annual population estimates is not spelled out. Base Census Years were utilized and yearly intercensal changes were more than likely based on multipliers applied to City Directory totals. These figures clearly separate out Vancouver from its surrounding suburbs and (since they span the years 1886-1940 and originate from a single source) possess a degree of internal consistency. Bartlett makes brief use of these statistics. See Bartlett, "Standard of Living in Vancouver," p. 7n. See also Norbert Macdonald, "Population Growth and Change in Seattle and Vancouver, 1880-1960," in *Historical Essays on British Columbia*, eds. J. Friesen and H. K. Ralston (Toronto: McClelland & Stewart Ltd., 1976).

couver's fortunes were linked to the wider economy of British Columbia, relevant material pertaining to cyclical fluctuations in the province during the inter-war period was consulted.[47]

Crime data obviously must be analyzed in conjunction with shifts in the total population and usually are expressed as per 100,000 people. This will be the format utilized here. One must remember, however, that the city of Vancouver was amalgamated with the suburbs of Point Grey and South Vancouver on 1 January 1929, thus adding well over 80,000 to the new expanded municapility. Vancouver's population thus increased from 149,262 in 1928 to 240,421 in 1929. Unfortunately crime statistics for Point Grey and South Vancouver have not survived. Since it is likely that general crime rates were lower in these suburbs than in the city proper, the amalgamation would probably tend to artificially deflate crime rates in the 1930s. To be sure, this does not pose a problem in assessing the short-term changes in crime rates between 1929 and 1940 or between 1906 and 1928, but it does mean that the validity of long-term comparisons might be affected.[48]

Although the following discussion will concentrate mainly on crimes against property in the 1930s, one should begin perhaps with an examination of overall patterns of crime throughout our entire period. Graph 1 gives annual rates of prosecutions and convictions per 100,000 for all cases appearing in the Vancouver Police Court through the years 1906 to 1940. It would appear that the general crime rate dropped in the 1930s and that the 1920s experienced the highest rates over the long term. Table 1 represents mean rates for select periods prior to 1940 and indeed bears this out. Both prosecution and conviction rates for the period 1930-

---

[47] See L. Blain, D. G. Paterson and J. D. Rae, "The Regional Impact of Economic Fluctuation During the Inter-War Period: The case of British Columbia," *Canadian Journal of Economics* 7 (August 1974): 381-401; and Larry A. Blain, "Regional Cyclical Behaviour and Sensitivity in Canada 1919-1973" (unpublished Ph.D. thesis, University of British Columbia, 1977).

[48] Difficulties in this regard can be overcome to some extent by paying close attention to the absolute totals of prosecutions and convictions. Where such totals actually fall in the 1930s below levels observed in earlier periods, this clearly would reflect real declines in the crime rate since one would expect the addition of Point Grey and South Vancouver to increase the actual number of cases now brought before the Vancouver Police Court. Where crime rates per 100,000 increase in the 1930s, this will generally reflect real increases which are cancelling out the artificial deflation produced by adding so much additional population. It is possible, of course, that the wealthier area of Point Grey might have higher levels of breaking and entering than Vancouver in the pre-1929 period, thus perhaps inflating rates for this type of crime in the 1930s. High levels in Point Grey, however, may have been cancelled out by lower levels in the less affluent South Vancouver suburb. In the absence of relevant statistics, such reflections are pure speculation. In any case trends between 1929 and 1940 are not affected by such considerations.

39 were considerably lower than in the 1920s and lower still than in the period 1914-21. It is likely that the overall rates for the 1930s were somewhat artificially deflated by the amalgamation of 1929. Nevertheless, the fact that the absolute totals of prosecutions and convictions in the 1930s were often lower than in the late 1920s would suggest a real decrease in the general crime rate.[49] Rates did move noticeably upward in 1930, the first year of the Great Depression, as well as in the years 1913 and 1920, when earlier downswings in the economy had occurred.[50] The most prominent feature, however, is the marked peak in both prosecution and conviction rates in the years 1925 to 1928 and their subsequent fall in the 1930s. Such a pattern is perhaps not surprising. In most cities studied thus far in Europe, the United States and Canada — London, Stockholm, Chicago, Boston, Buffalo and Calgary — the 1930s witnessed declining rates for general crime, signalling an overall long-term improvement in public order. Although the reasons for this decline are extremely complex, Gurr is right to suggest that the long-run improvement in the effectiveness of social control — the technique of legal criminalization, uniformed policing and incarceration — as well as declining levels of interpersonal aggression played important roles in this regard.[51]

All students of criminal statistics are agreed, however, that general crime rates — which comprise such a vast array of different offences —

[49] See graph 1(A) in Appendix for absolute totals of prosecutions and convictions 1906-1940.

[50] Bartlett cites three major depression periods in Vancouver prior to the Great Depression — the years 1907-08, 1913-15 and 1920-22. See Bartlett, "Standard of Living in Vancouver," p. 32. The worst year of the 1920-22 Depression was 1921, and unfortunately an exhaustive search failed to produce any data for this year. By 1922 economic conditions had improved considerably. The percentage of unemployment in trade unions fell from 23.5 percent in 1921 to 12.4 percent in 1922. The real wage index moved upwards from a level of 104.8 in 1921 to 108.0 in 1922. The value of building permits more than doubled between 1921 and 1922, rising from $3,045,132 to $8,661,695. There are grounds then for arguing that 1922 was not a severe Depression year. Table I and subsequent tables therefore include 1922, with the years 1923 to 1928 as years of relative prosperity.

[51] See Ted Robert Gurr, "Development and Decay: Their Impact on Public Order in Western History," in James A. Inciardi and Charles E. Faupel, eds., *History and Crime: Implications for Criminal Justice Policy* (Beverley Hills: Sage Publications Inc., 1980), pp. 35, 36, 43 and 44. For London and Stockholm see Gurr, Grabosky and Hula, *The Politics of Crime and Conflict*, pp. 112, 160 and 281-320. For Chicago see Ted Robert Gurr, *Rogues, Rebels and Reformers: A Political History of Urban Crime and Conflict* (Beverley Hills: Sage Publications Inc., 1976), p. 63. For Boston see Theodore N. Ferdinand, "The Criminal Patterns of Boston," *American Journal of Sociology* 73 (July 1967): 87. For Buffalo see Elwin H. Powell, *The Design of Discord: Studies of Anomie* (New York: Oxford University Press, 1970), p. 125. Data on Calgary is in Watson, "Calgary: A Study of Crime," M.A. thesis, p. 16.

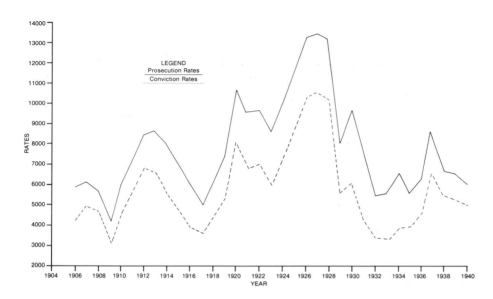

GRAPH 1

Total Prosecution and Conviction Rates per 100,000:
Vancouver, 1906-1940

TABLE 1

Mean Prosecution and Conviction Rates per 100,000,
for Select Periods — Vancouver, 1906-1939*

Period	Prosecution Rates	Conviction Rates
1906-1913	6491	5071
1914-1921	7511	5294
1922-1928	11440	8641
1930-1939	6820	4719

* These periods comprise roughly equal time periods spanning important phases in Vancouver's history. The period 1906-13 covers the pre-WWI period. The years 1914-21 cover WWI and its aftermath. The years 1922-28 span the relatively prosperous years of the twenties. The period 1930-39 covers the Great Depression. The year 1929 was omitted since amalgamation occurred in this year. The deflation in rates here would unduly bias the 1920s values in a downward direction. (No conclusions presented here were affected by excluding 1929.) Mean rates presented here and in following tables were calculated by averaging the yearly rates within each period.

can tell us little of significance about the inter-relationships between criminal activity and socio-economic change. Clearly one must probe further and observe patterns occurring within certain crucial categories of crime. Graphs 2, 3 and 4 examine longitudinal trends from 1907 to 1937 in prosecution and conviction rates in three broad categories: crimes against the person, crimes against property, and crimes against the peace.[52] Table 2 provides mean rates for these three groupings in select periods.

The long-term shifts revealed in these data suggest a number of conclusions. If the general crime rate fell in the 1930s, this appears to be due to a precipitous decline in the large volume of crimes against the peace which began in the late 1920s and reached a trough in 1933 and 1934 (graph 4). Table 2 clearly reveals that the period 1930-37 witnessed the lowest levels in Vancouver's history. The declines here were most marked with respect to morality offences; namely, liquor-related infractions, gambling, drugs and prostitution. Prosecution rates for prostitution, for example, dropped 70 percent in the period 1930-37 when compared with 1922 to 1928. Rates of prosecution for gambling, liquor and drug offences fell 59, 61 and 89 percent respectively.[53] Lesser declines are observed for prosecution and conviction rates relating to crimes against the person (graph 2). These rates dropped in the 1930s and remained relatively stable. Table 2 shows a pronounced long-term decline from the high rates observed in the 1907-13 period.

The only category of crime experiencing increased rates for prosecutions and convictions in the 1930s was crime against property, which generally rose in the early 1930s, reaching an all-time peak in 1934, and then tapered off between 1935 and 1937 (graph 3). In terms of absolute volume such crime reached unprecedented heights in the 1930s.[54] It is significant as well that the earlier depression years of 1907-08, 1913 and 1920 also revealed peak rates within their respective decades. This certainly suggests some connection between increasing property crime and depressed economic conditions. Over the long term, however, the pattern

[52] For the subcategories contained within these groupings see footnote 37 above. Crimes against property in the following graph and tables exclude malicious offences against property such as arson and vagrancy (h), since the analysis is focused on property theft. Estimates for 1920, 1922 and 1934 were made on the basis of partial data for these years using seasonal trends in proximate years. No data were available for 1921. For absolute totals of prosecutions and convictions see graphs 2(A), 3(A) in Appendix A.

[53] See table 1(B). Appendix B.

[54] See graph 2(A). Appendix A.

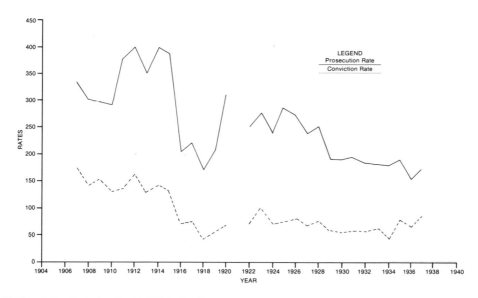

GRAPH 2

Prosecution and Conviction Rates per 100,000:
Crimes Against the Person — Vancouver, 1907-1937

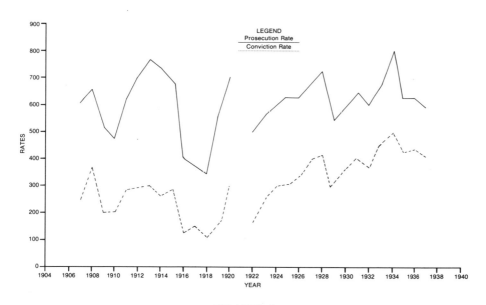

GRAPH 3

Prosecution and Conviction Rates per 100,000:
Crimes Against Property — Vancouver, 1907-1937

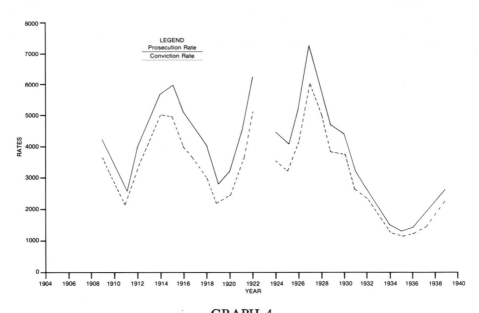

GRAPH 4

Prosecution and Conviction Rates per 100,000:
Crimes Against the Peace — Vancouver, 1907-1937

TABLE 2

Mean Prosecution and Conviction Rates per 100,000,
by Category of Crime — Vancouver, 1907-1937*

Period	Crimes vs. Persons		Crimes vs. Property		Crimes vs. Peace	
	Pros.	Conv.	Pros.	Conv.	Pros.	Conv.
1907-1913	339	149	626	272	4331	3839
1914-1920	278	88	545	206	4409	3448
1922-1928	262	87	608	311	5221	4304
1930-1937	183	66	639	417	2064	1745

* No data are available for 1921, 1938, 1939.

is complicated by the fact that both prosecution and conviction rates rose
steadily in the relatively prosperous years between 1922 and 1928. It is
nevertheless the case that both prosecution and conviction rates for crimes
against property in the 1930s display the highest average levels ever
recorded in Vancouver's history prior to 1938 (table 2).

These long-term patterns raise a host of fascinating questions. An analysis of crimes against the person and morality offences will be left to further investigation since, on the surface at least, they appear least responsive to the economic effects of the Great Depression. Forthcoming work will suggest that the long-term decline in crimes against the person throughout the period under review is clearly a reflection of the steady decline in assaults against individuals which comprise the majority of offences in this category. Interpersonal violence perhaps was becoming subject to much stronger internal and external controls, and its fall from high levels prior to 1914 also may indicate a move away from the more turbulent "frontier" nature of early Vancouver society. Such hypotheses at this stage, however, must remain highly tentative. The drastic decline in the rates for morality offences in the late 1920s and 1930s, it will be suggested, does not indicate an actual decline in such offences, but rather reflects the unwillingness or inability of the police to arrest. It is perhaps not entirely coincidental that three major investigations into police corruption were initiated over the very period (1928-36) when prosecutions and convictions for morality crimes dropped to the lowest levels ever recorded in Vancouver's history prior to World War II.[55]

The discussion that follows will focus on the relationship between property crimes and the economy, both over the long term and within the years of the Great Depression. The general category of crimes against property was further broken down into three more specific areas: violent crimes against property, general theft and non-violent crimes against property. Violent crimes against property include more serious and violent cases of theft such as robbery, robbery with violence, hold-ups, burglary and breaking and entering. General theft contains a wide range of petty theft such as shoplifting as well as the theft of automobiles and bicycles. Non-violent crimes against property comprise various types of fraud, embezzlement, forgery, counterfeiting and false pretences.[56] Graphs 5, 6 and 7 present long-term trends in prosecution and conviction rates

[55] The whole issue of violence in Vancouver as well as the relationship between the police, vice and politics will be explored in a book being researched entitled "Crime, Community and the Police: Vancouver 1886-1940." For the investigations into conditions in the Vancouver Police Department see *Vancouver Police Inquiry 1928*, V.C.A. 37(D)12 - 37(D)22. For the January 1935 investigation see Police Chief W. W. Foster's report to the Chairman and members of the Vancouver Police Commission in *Mayor's Correspondence* 33-B-5, vol. 12, V.C.A. For 1936 see the *Macdonald Inquiry* and the *Tucker Report* 75(F)3 and 75(F)4 respectively in the V.C.A.

[56] Once again malicious offences against property such as arson and vagrancy (h) are excluded from analysis.

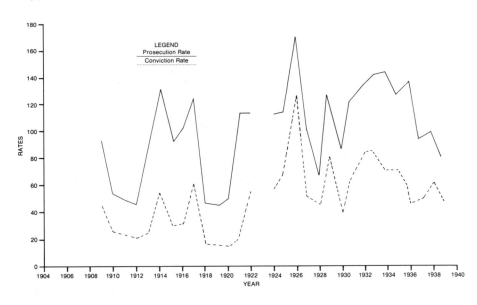

GRAPH 5

Prosecution and Conviction Rates per 100,000:
Violent Crimes Against Property — Vancouver, 1907-1937

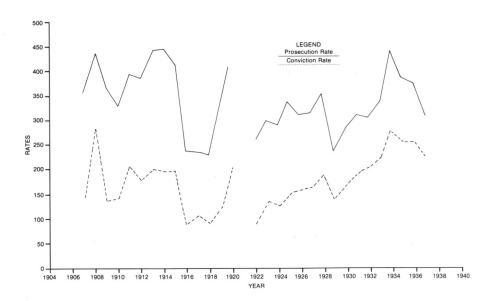

GRAPH 6

Prosecution and Conviction Rates per 100,000:
General Theft — Vancouver, 1907-1937

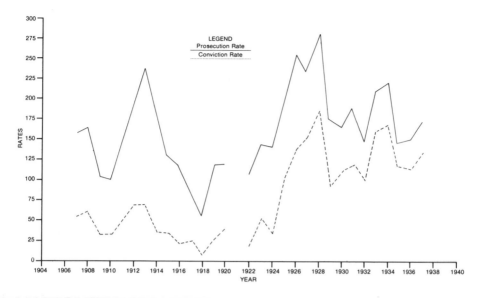

GRAPH 7

Prosecution and Conviction Rates per 100,000:
Non-violent Property Crimes — Vancouver, 1907-1937

TABLE 3

Mean Prosecution and Conviction Rates per 100,000,
Property Crimes — Vancouver, 1907-1937*

Period	Violent Crimes vs. Property		General Theft		Non-Violent Crimes vs. Property	
	Pros.	*Conv.*	*Pros.*	*Conv.*	*Pros.*	*Conv.*
1907-1913	79	33	389	185	158	54
1914-1920	86	30	342	145	116	30
1922-1928	111	66	312	147	194	98
1930-1937	119	65	345	225	174	126

* No data are available for 1921, 1938, 1939.

for these categories, and table 3 provides mean rates for select periods to 1937.

The most observable patterns occur with respect to general theft and violent property crime. The former (graph 6), which constitutes the majority of property violations appearing in the Vancouver Police Court, reveals a steady rise in the worst years of the Great Depression between 1929 and 1934, and then a decline through 1937. These general theft rates, as well, reveal an extremely close correspondence with earlier depression years, rising in 1908, 1913-15 and 1920. Mean rates for the period 1930-37 were clearly higher than in the 1920s (table 3). In absolute terms the volume of such prosecutions and convictions reached uniquely high levels in the 1930s.[57] It should be pointed out that the period 1907-13 reveals a higher mean prosecution rate than the 1930s, although there might be factors applicable to this earlier period, such as the substantially higher proportion of males in the population, tending to inflate rates unduly when compared to the 1930s.[58]

In terms of violent property crimes rising rates are observed only in the very early 1930s (graph 5). On the whole, there is less correspondence with earlier Depression years. Particularly noticeable are the peaks occurring in the relatively prosperous years of 1912 and especially 1924. Nevertheless, the 1930s as a whole reveal the highest mean rate for prosecutions in the pre-1938 period (table 3). The sheer volume of such prosecutions in this period was unprecedented. Conviction rates, however, remain stable between 1930 and 1937 when compared with the 1920s.[59]

The data thus far indicate that with regard to general theft and violent property crime the early years of the Great Depression, particularly prior to 1934, experienced increases, and that for the period 1930-37 as a whole rates were generally higher than in Vancouver's previous history.

[57] See graph 6(A). Appendix A.

[58] The population of Vancouver, of course, was much lower in this period than in the 1930s. The population stood at 60,100 compared to a 1937 population of 259,987. Thus a smaller number of prosecutions would carry greater weight between 1907 and 1913. There might have been, as well, a greater visibility of crime in a smaller population. More importantly, however, it is clear that Vancouver had a highly distorted sex-ratio in 1911 with roughly 150 males for every 100 females, a much higher ratio than the 114 males for every 100 females in 1931. (See *Census of Canada 1951*, vol. I, table 17). Such a preponderance of males — a higher risk group for crime than females — might unduly inflate rates for general theft in the earlier period when compared to the 1930s. Forthcoming work which will treat the pre-1930s period in more detail will argue also that the police were cracking down on crime in this period, especially when compared to the period 1929-34.

[59] The fact that the conviction rate in the 1930s does not rise in conjunction with the prosecution rate is due to a higher percentage of violent crimes against property being referred to higher courts during this period. Between 1930 and 1937 almost 19 percent of all cases initiated in the Vancouver Police Court on charges of violent property crime were sent to higher court, compared to 14 percent in the period 1922-28. In the 1930s only 3 percent of cases for general theft were so referred. Thus conviction rates for violent property cases are not as reliable an indicator of overall convictions when compared to similar rates for general theft. For total prosecutions relating to violent property crime see graph 5(A), Appendix A.

Non-violent property crimes reveal a less clear-cut trend in the 1930s (graph 7). Prosecution rates reached all-time peaks in the later 1920s and declined on average in the period 1930-37 when compared with 1922 to 1928 (table 3).[60] Within the lower levels of the 1930s, peaks occurred in 1931 and 1934. Since non-violent property crime clearly reflects levels of fraud and embezzlement, it appears that this type of crime flourished in the boom years of the late 1920s where opportunities for such criminal activity no doubt expanded rapidly, and then fell in the 1930s when such opportunities declined. It may well be, too, that greater vigilance during the Depression by those with money to lose played a role. The pattern here with respect to the 1920s and 1930s is very similar to Gurr's findings for London and Stockholm in terms of white-collar crime.[61]

The preceding observations, of course, have been based largely on direct visual observations of trends in various types of prosecution and conviction rates. Might correlations between annual indicators of Vancouver's economy and such rates reveal associations between levels of property crime and destitution in the Great Depression? Table 4 presents yearly time series correlation coefficients between different categories of property crime and crucial social and economic indices for the years 1929-37 where crime data is available.

With regard to correlations involving rates for property crimes as a whole between 1929 and 1937, all coefficients score high in the direction of an association between downswings in the economy and increased property prosecutions and convictions (table 4). Increases in the average yearly percentage of persons unemployed in trade unions, for example, are positively correlated with overall increases in property crime. As the average employment index (an index reflecting the number of persons employed) rose, overall property crime declined. The strongest and most

[60] The rise in the mean conviction rate for non-violent crimes against property in the period 1930-37 (table 3) is due to a marked decrease in the percentage of cases dismissed or withdrawn. In the period 1922-28, 47 percent of such cases were so disposed compared to only 22 percent in the 1930s. This would suggest that the courts in the latter period were coming down harder on this type of offence.

[61] See Gurr, Grabosky and Hula, *The Politics of Crime and Conflict*, pp. 632-37. It must be remembered, as well, that there is probably more of a time lag between the committing of white-collar crime and eventual prosecution than of other types of property theft. Thus the peak in 1931 may reflect crimes committed as early as 1928 or 1929. Forthcoming work will test this hypothesis by employing the Police Court Calendars. It should be noted, in addition, that the peak in 1934 was well below levels in the late 1920s and below the peak in 1913. This latter peak again might reflect the time lag hypothesis and pertain to white-collar crimes committed in the boom years of 1911 and 1912.

232 BC STUDIES

significant correlations, however, pertain to fluctuations in the value of building permits and per capita relief expenditure. The former, which is considered a good indicator of cyclical trends,[62] reveals a very high negative correlation with total property crime; that is, as construction activity increased, indicating general economic improvement, property crime as a whole declined. Per capita relief expenditure, most closely approximating poverty levels, displays, on the whole, the most positive association with increases in property crime. As the amount per head rose, reflecting increased levels of indigence, so did rates for overall property crime.

A glance again at table 4 clearly reveals that within the broad category of overall property crime general theft rates are most closely associated

TABLE 4

Pearson Correlation Coefficients: Property Prosecutions and Convictions with Economic Indicators for the Same Year — Vancouver, 1929-1937

		Average % trade union un- employ- ment	Average employ- ment index	Value of building permits	Per capita relief expen- diture
Prosecution Rate	All Property Crimes	+.58 (.10)	—.62 (.08)	—.54 (.13)	+.61 (.08)
Conviction Rate	" " "	+.64* (.05)	—.63 (.07)	—.84* (.01)	+.86* (.01)
Prosecution Rate	Violent Property Crimes	+.48 (.19)	—.38 (.30)	+.09 (.82)	—.12 (.76)
Conviction Rate	" " "	—.01 (.97)	+.21 (.59)	+.47 (.20)	—.53 (.14)
Prosecution Rate	General Theft	+.55 (.13)	—.56 (.12)	—.79* (.01)	+.85* (.01)
Conviction Rate	" "	+.52 (.15)	—.53 (.14)	—.88* (.01)	+.88* (.01)

* Significant at the 5% level. Significance levels in brackets. No difference to the conclusions drawn occurred when crime was lagged one year behind the economic indicators. These correlation coefficients are generally higher than observed elsewhere. See Vold, *Theoretical Criminology*, pp. 174-78; Gurr, Grabosky and Hula, *The Politics of Crime and Conflict*, pp. 208, 210-11, and 310-11; and Zehr, *Crime and Modern Society*, pp. 45, 51 and 59.

[62] See Bartlett, "Standard of Living in Vancouver," p. 8.

with the economic indicators. In particular very strong significant positive correlations can be observed between per capita relief expenditure and general theft rates (+.85 and +.88). As the value of building permits rose, general theft rates declined. Coefficients pertaining to average percentage unemployment and the employment index are clearly in directions supporting the hypothesis linking economic downswing with increased levels of general theft.

Correlations with respect to violent property crime rates given in table 4 reveal, on the whole, much weaker coefficients than general theft. Not much reliance, however, can be placed on conviction rates since almost one-fifth of all cases pertaining to this type of crime appearing in the Vancouver Police Courts were sent to higher courts.[63] Even with respect to prosecution rates, coefficients are negligible when violent property crime rates are related to the value of building permits or per capita relief expenditure. Some association does emerge, however, between rising average yearly unemployment and increasing prosecution rates for violent property theft.

The foregoing discussion of crime pattern based on prosecution and conviction rates and their correlation with various economic indices suggests that the onset of the Great Depression contributed to an increase in both the rate and volume of total property crime mainly as a result of increases in general theft, which comprised the bulk of such crimes. Both overall property crime and general theft rates rose in the early severe years of the Depression (graphs 3 and 6), reaching peaks in 1934 and then tapering off in 1935, 1936 and 1937. The high coefficients that these types of crime reveal when correlated with economic indicators clearly reflect such a pattern (table 4). Violent crime rates against property display, on the whole, less obvious trends, rising between 1929 and 1932 and then fluctuating through 1937 (graph 5). The lower coefficient values observed with respect to this type of crime again confirm these variations.

As stated at the outset, however, one must remember that increasing prosecution and conviction rates do not necessarily reflect real increases in crime levels. Higher prosecution rates, for example, may be due to a growth in police efficiency, leading to a greater ability or propensity to arrest. Evidence for the early 1930s, though, suggests that the efficiency of the police was in fact declining. The strength of the force, for example, dropped from 357 men in 1930 to 336 in 1935, and then steadily in-

[63] See note 59, above.

creased to a high of 384 in 1939.[64] The *Vancouver Police Annual Report* for 1930, moreover, stated that the "necessity of withdrawing men from regular duties to assist in the controlling of parades of the unemployed, as well as the lack of efficient motor equipment, had done much to hamper the Department during the year."[65] These sentiments were echoed in the 1931 *Annual Report*, which claimed that "much valuable time which would otherwise be devoted to investigation and suppression of crime was taken up in curbing street demonstrations and maintaining 'the Peace'."[66] Wage cuts were introduced in March 1932 and further reductions made in February of the following year.[67] Thus, at the very time that prosecution rates for property crimes were rising, police effectiveness was more than likely on the decline. These rates of prosecution, then, probably reflect real increases in such criminal activity.

Furthermore, the early 1930s gave no indication of an effective campaign to clean up crime in the city. It was not until his landslide mayoralty victory in December 1934 that Gerry McGeer, in concert with his newly appointed Police Chief and Board of Police Commissioners, attempted a serious drive against criminality. McGeer had introduced his campaign in November 1934 with the slogan: "Are you for me or the underworld?"[68] Incumbent Mayor Taylor replied by echoing a retort he had given in his earlier 1928 campaign: "I don't believe in running Sunday School City."[69] The effectiveness of McGeer's attempts to rid Vancouver of crime in 1935 and 1936 is yet to be determined. A glance back at graphs 3, 5, 6 and 7 certainly indicates that his clean-up campaign in these years did not lead to increasing prosecution rates for property crimes — rates, in fact, decreased. In any case, the point to be made is that such policies emerged too late in the 1930s to have been a factor influencing rising rates prior to 1935.[70]

[64] See the Dominion Bureau of Statistics, *Annual Criminal Statistics* for the 1930s. The totals given here correspond exactly with those provided in the *Van. Police Annual Reports* that survive.

[65] *Van. Police Annual Report 1930*, p. 4. By 1932 the Vancouver Police equipped twenty-one of its thirty-two cars with radios. The overall impression, however, is one of declining efficiency. See *Van. Police Annual Report 1932*, p. 4.

[66] *Ibid., 1931*, p. 2.

[67] See *Van. Police Minutes*, 10 March 1932 and 21 February 1933. V.C.A. 85(A)6 and 75(A)7. Wages were reduced by up to 20 percent depending on the salary level.

[68] *Vancouver Sun*, 14 November 1934, p. 1.

[69] *Vancouver Sun*, 27 November 1934, p. 1.

[70] The situation in the early 1930s was in marked contrast to the mid and late 1920s. The number of police, for example, increased steadily from 223 in 1922 to 263 in

The evidence, then, indicates that rising prosecution rates for property crime were not unduly influenced by levels of police efficiency or political pressure in the early thirties. It nevertheless clearly remains the case that the most reliable, if still imperfect, indicators of the real volume of crime are offences known to the police. To be sure, there will be variations in levels of reporting, but over the short term these will not pose great problems. Clearly, this type of information should provide for a better assessment of actual crime trends in the 1930s.

The data presented in the following graphs span the years 1929 to 1940 and are based on police statistics pertaining to property offences known as well as on the annual value of stolen property presented in their annual reports.[71] This material, since it covers the years 1938, 1939 and 1940, provides the added advantage of observing trends at the tail end of the Depression. Graph 8 presents annual figures on the value of all known stolen property in Vancouver between 1929 and 1940 expressed in dollars per 1,000 population. Graph 9 gives annual rates per 100,000 population for breaking-and-entering offences known to the police, while graph 10 provides similar information with respect to robbery with violence. Breaking and entering offences are combined with those for robbery with violence in graph 11 to reveal trends for violent theft as a whole. Graph 12 displays rates for all thefts known to the police. These rates include, in addition to the aforementioned violent thefts, all petty theft, as well as automobiles and bicycles known to have been stolen

1928, just prior, that is, to amalgamation. The police, moreover, claimed in 1925 that crime "has not materially increased during 1925 despite a noticeable increase in the number of arrests." See *Vancouver Sun*, 31 December 1930, p. 1. The Police Commission Minutes and the newspapers are replete, in addition, with references to clean-up campaigns, crackdowns on all types of crimes, and especially raids on liquor and gambling establishments as well as on bawdy houses. In December 1927 the Attorney General promised to aid in prosecuting criminals. See *Van. Police Minutes*, 13 December 1927 (75)(A)5, pp. 31-32, V.C.A. For evidence of raids and a tightening up of law enforcement see especially *ibid.*, 7 May 1925, 12 August 1925, 18 September 1925, 28 November 1927 and 15 November 1928. See also the *Vancouver Sun* and in particular 3 January 1925, 9 January 1925, 11 August 1925, 27 May 1926, 30 December 1926. It is likely that such raids, moreover, turned up more property offences. Increased police efficiency, then, might partly explain rising property prosecution and conviction rates in the 1920s.

71 Vancouver Police Department *Annual Reports* for the years 1929, 1930, 1931, 1932, 1938, 1939 and 1940 were consulted. All of these are in the V.C.A. except for 1931, which is held in the North West History Room of the Vancouver Public Library. Additional data for the years 1934 through 1937 were kindly provided by Staff Sergeant Joe Swan of the Vancouver Police Force. Unfortunately no *Annual Reports* could be found for the years 1921-28. It is likely that none were published in these years. Earlier reports between 1906 and 1917 and for 1920 do survive in various locations but do not provide statistics on offences known to the police.

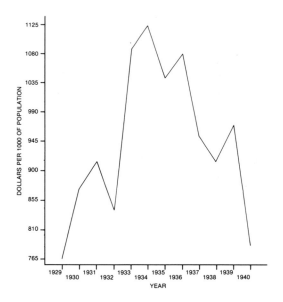

GRAPH 8

Stolen Property Rate per 1,000 — Vancouver, 1929-1940

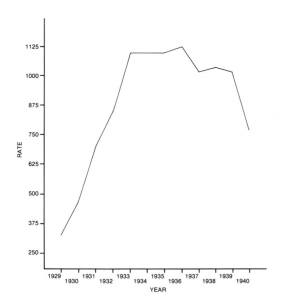

GRAPH 9

Breaking and Entering Rate per 100,000 — Vancouver, 1929-1940

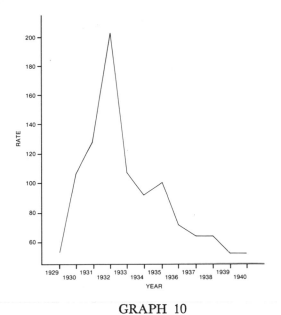

GRAPH 10

Robbery with Violence Rate per 100,000 — Vancouver, 1929-1940

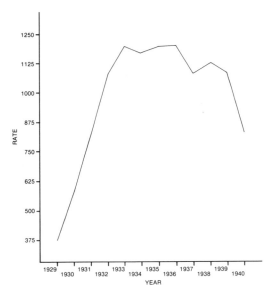

GRAPH 11

Violent Theft Rate per 100,000 — Vancouver, 1929-1940

between 1929 and 1940. Typically, the annual reports give no indication of offences relating to fraud or embezzlement, and thus one cannot examine white-collar crime in this context.

The patterns revealed in these graphs certainly confirm and, indeed, enhance the conclusions respecting prosecution and conviction rates. The value of stolen property, for example, rises markedly in the early thirties, peaking in 1934, and generally declines thereafter (graph 8).[72] Rates for breaking and entering reveal even steeper increases in the early years of the Depression, reaching high levels in 1933 which were maintained through 1939 (graph 9). Robbery with violence displays equally steep increases, peaking in 1932 and falling thereafter (graph 10). Graph 11, which provides rates for all violent property offences, suggests that this type of crime remained more persistent during the Depression than earlier evidence with respect to prosecution and conviction rates indicates (see graph 5 above). The overall pattern observed here is clearly a reflection of the high rates for breaking-and-entering offences. A perusal of graph 12, which pertains to the total volume of property theft offences in the Great Depression, leads to a similar conclusion. It was claimed earlier that crimes against property as a whole, based on prosecution and conviction rates, peaked in 1934 and then declined through 1937 (see graph 3 above). The data at hand pertaining to offences reveal a sharp decline in 1932,[73] but indicate a return to high levels which persisted as late as 1936.

By 1940 all indicators of property crime offences had fallen below peaks reached during the Depression, in some cases to levels comparable to or below those prevailing in 1929. The years 1938 and 1939, which suffered late but less severe downswings in the economy,[74] experienced slight rises in crime rates, particularly with respect to violent property offences. On the whole, this analysis of offences known to the police suggests that the Depression's impact on property crime extended well beyond the early thirties and was, in general, more persistent than indicated by reference to prosecution and conviction rates.

Correlation coefficients were run for the various categories of property offences known between 1929 and 1940 against the major economic

---

[72] The pattern here conforms closely to that observed with respect to prosecution and conviction rates for crimes against property in graph 3 presented earlier.

[73] The decline in 1932 is most likely due to the steep decline in stolen automobile offences, which numbered 3,162 in 1931 and fell to 1,912 in 1932. This might also partly explain the fall in the value of stolen property in 1932 (graph 8).

[74] My economic indicators show rising per capita relief expenditure and unemployment in 1938 and a decline in the value of building permits in 1939.

indicators utilized earlier. Table 5 clearly supports the hypothesis that depressed economic conditions were conducive to rising rates of crime against property. As in the similar analysis previously, the strongest correlations emerge with respect to per capita relief expenditure and the value of building permits. The values of stolen property, breaking-and-entering offences, violent theft and total theft rise markedly with increases in relief expenditure and decline with increasing values of building permits. All property crime rates, moreover, tend to increase as unemployment rises and fall as the employment index moves upwards, although the coefficients here are not as strong. The weakest coefficients are with violent robbery as against the value of building permits and per capita relief expenditure. This, while somewhat puzzling, may reflect the probability that these crimes were the work of professional criminals who earned their living from burglary and therefore were less likely to commit crimes in response to changing economic conditions.[75]

TABLE 5

Pearson Correlation Coefficients: Property Offences Known with Economic Indicators — Vancouver, 1929-1940

	Average % trade union unemployment	Average employment index	Value of building permits	Per capita relief expenditure
Value of Stolen Property Rate	+.55 (.07)	—.53 (.12)	—.70* (.01)	+.80* (.01)
Breaking and Entering Rate	+.48 (.11)	—.47 (.17)	—.90* (.00)	+.86* (.00)
Robbery with Violence Rate	+.75* (.01)	—.54 (.10)	—.33 (.29)	+.29 (.35)
Violent Theft Rate	+.60* (.04)	—.54 (.10)	—.94* (.00)	+.90* (.00)
Total Theft Rate	+.55 (.07)	—.58 (.08)	—.68 (.09)	+.81* (.01)

* Significant at the 5 percent level. Significance levels in brackets. No difference to the conclusions drawn occurred when crime was lagged one year behind the economic indicators. These correlation coefficients generally are higher than observed elsewhere.

[75] This still would not explain the relatively strong positive correlation of robbery with violence as against unemployment. More work on this specific crime is clearly needed. For a discussion of the professional burglar see Johnson, *Policing the Urban Underworld*, pp. 44-45.

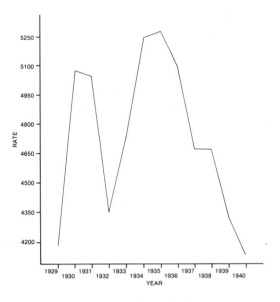

GRAPH 12

Total Theft Rate per 100,000 — Vancouver, 1929-1940

What general conclusions can one draw from the preceding analysis in terms of crime during the Great Depression in Vancouver? Looking at prosecution and conviction rates from a long-term perspective, it is clear that general crime rates dropped markedly in the 1930s. This, in itself, is not surprising since other cities, including Calgary, experienced declines in such rates. What does stand out, however, is the magnitude of the fall, especially with respect to morality offences. Although Calgary experienced declines in the latter category between 1929 and 1934, these apparently were not nearly of Vancouver's magnitude.[76] As stated earlier, a full exposition of this important phase in the history of Vancouver crime patterns must await further research.

Within the overall pattern of general crime, it was observed that the only types of crime to rise in the 1930s were those against property, and specifically violent offences of this kind as well as general theft. With regard to these categories, it was pointed out that in terms certainly of

[76] Watson uses arrest figures to show that prostitution and gambling arrests declined from fifty-six and seventy-two respectively in 1929 to twenty-three and fifty-five respectively in 1934. These represent declines of 58 percent in prostitution and 19 percent for gambling. The figures here are too small, however, to draw valid comparisons, especially in percentage terms, with Vancouver. See Watson, "Calgary: A Study of Crime," M.A. thesis, table 6, p. 68.

sheer volume but also of rates of prosecutions and convictions, the levels attained on average in the 1930s were higher, in most cases, than ever seen in Vancouver's previous history. Given the strong possibility, moreover, that amalgamation more than likely artificially deflated such rates in the 1930s, the figures presented for the Great Depression, if anything, underestimate the extent of such criminal activity. It should be noted, as well, that every indicator of Vancouver property crime — prosecution rates, conviction rates and offences known to the police — rose between 1929 and 1931 with the exception of the non-violent category. This indicates that many of the contemporaries quoted at the outset of this study were not far off the mark in their observations. No doubt they were acutely conscious of the rapid and unprecedented increases in the sheer volume of property crime.

Vancouver in the early years of the Depression conformed closely to the experience of a wide range of cities in the United States and Europe. Boston, New York and Chicago, for example, all witnessed increasing rates of breaking and entering, robbery and larceny between 1929 and 1931.[77] London and Stockholm reveal similar patterns in relation to known indictable thefts and reported thefts respectively.[78] In Calgary, the only Canadian city for which a comparable study exists, arrests for general theft rose between 1929 and 1931, while robbery with violence and housebreaking increased only in the year 1930.[79]

Although Vancouver's very early Depression years were typical of urban property crime patterns elsewhere, the trends observed later in the 1930s diverge from the experience of cities like London and Stockholm, which witnessed declines, or at least a levelling off, of rates for property offences in the mid-years of the Depression.[80] Calgary experienced sharp

---

[77] See Warner, *Criminal Statistics in Boston*, tables 7 and 8, pp. 144-45. See also Theodore N. Ferdinand, "The Criminal Patterns of Boston," pp. 93, 94 and 96. Unfortunately no study of crime in Seattle has been carried out. This city would be the most logical choice for a comparison with Vancouver.

[78] See Gurr, Grabosky and Hula, *The Politics of Crime and Conflict*, pp. 628-29 for London and p. 282 for Stockholm. The other cities included in this work are Sydney and Calcutta.

[79] Watson, "Calgary: A Study of Crime," M.A. thesis, pp. 40, 44, 45 and 47.

[80] Rates for London generally fell through the mid-1930s and experienced slight rises after 1936. Stockholm's rates remained stable throughout the 1930s, rising only in 1939. See Gurr, Grabosky and Hula, *The Politics of Crime and Conflict*, pp. 628-29 and p. 282. Buffalo, New York, however, exhibits a pattern similar to Vancouver's with rising property crime in the mid-years of the Depression. See Elwin H. Powell, *The Design of Discord*, p. 121. Boston reveals a steady increase in burglaries in the 1930s and much smaller increases in larcenies in the late Depression. See Ferdinand, "Criminal Patterns of Boston," pp. 94 and 96.

declines in all categories of property theft between 1931 and 1934.[81] In Vancouver, however, property crime levels peaked in most cases either in 1934 or as late as 1936, suggesting that the Depression had a more persistent effect on property crime than elsewhere.

It would be unwise, at this stage, to push such comparisons too far. What they do suggest, aside from some interesting questions for comparative analysis, is that Vancouver provides yet another case study illustrating the impact of the Great Depression on rising property crime. Furthermore, the relatively high degree of correlation observed between such crime and indices reflecting poverty and unemployment must cast serious doubt on the arguments of those who categorically deny any positive correlation between rising indigence and theft.[82] The fact that the strongest positive correlations that emerged were between per capita relief expenditure and most offences against property suggests that during the 1930s, at least, a denial of such a relationship would run contrary to historical experience.

There are further implications here with respect to municipal relief expenditure. Watson has argued that increasing amounts of such expenditure was a key factor in bringing down property crime in Calgary between 1931 and 1934, under the assumption that such provision reduced the necessity to steal.[83] Short had earlier posited a similar thesis with respect to the depression in the U.S.A.[84] Such clearly was not the case in Vancouver, where rates for property crimes rose almost in unison with increases in relief. Was relief more generous in Calgary? Since Watson gives no per capita figures on such public expenditure, one would have to undertake a comparative analysis of municipal relief systems in both cities to answer this question fully. What one can say is that in Vancouver, at least, provisions were far from adequate and very grudgingly bestowed. Lane, in fact, has argued that even single men in relief camps were well sustained compared to city families on municipal relief. One individual summed up being on relief as a situation where "you practically get down on your knees every week or so, and beg for your handout of dole tickets."[85]

[81] Watson, "Calgary: A Study of Crime," M.A. thesis, pp. 40, 44, 45 and 47.

[82] See above, pp. 214-16.

[83] Watson, "Calgary: A Study of Crime," M.A. thesis, pp. 40, 44, 45 and 47.

[84] Cited in *ibid.*, pp. 12-13.

[85] Marion Lane, "Unemployment During the Depression: The Problem of the Single Unemployed Transient in British Columbia, 1930-1938" (unpublished Honours Essay, University of British Columbia, 1966), pp. 66-67. The quotation she gives is from the Vancouver *Province*, 3 August 1935, p. 7.

This study, of course, has utilized aggregate rates of property crime in conjunction with very broad social and economic indicators in order to test for associations between the two. Although the evidence suggests that the Great Depression was closely related to rising rates of property crime, the specific mechanisms by which this happened are far from clear. As Tepperman points out, there is clearly more involved here than economic need:

> More important, Radzinowicz argues that the crime rate increases not so much when the level of prosperity is low as when it drops precipitously. Crimes committed under these circumstances are not crimes of want but result from anomie, a loss of social and normative constraints, and other psychological and psychiatric factors. Because of the subtle relationship between economic deterioration and criminal behavior, time may pass between changes in the one and changes in the other, and the two changes may differ in intensity, but moving in the same direction at about the same time. Finally ... prosperity is less effective in reducing the incidence of crime than is a depression in raising the incidence.[86]

Clearly, in order to examine such fine distinctions one would like to move from aggregate-level analysis to individual-level analysis. As emphasized earlier, this study is subject to the "ecological fallacy." But given the paucity of data on individual offenders it is impossible, at this stage, to link particular subgroups of individuals to particular crimes. Future research will attempt to merge information provided in the detailed Police Court Calendars with City Directories, although it is unlikely that this will provide sufficiently representative samples for analysis since the latter type of evidence is skewed toward the more stable and prosperous groups in Vancouver's population. Indeed, individual-level methodology often runs the risk of committing the "individualistic fallacy" whereby results from subgroups are inappropriately generalized to entire populations.

Historians, of course, rarely have the luxury of ideal sources at their disposal. Criminal statistics, moreover, are the most difficult of all social statistics to compile and interpret. If the preceding pages are full of "perhaps" and "suggests," the author makes no apologies, but rather is reminded of G. R. Elton's recent remarks in his introduction to a collection of historical writings on crime: "As the frequent signals of doubt, uncertainty and cautious reserve indicate, the essays here assembled are

---

[86] Tepperman, *Crime Control*, p. 182.

the work of scholars pioneering in something like a wilderness."[87] Part of
this important terrain in Vancouver's history has been charted here, and
one hopes that the results, though necessarily tentative, will stimulate
further exploration by social historians.

[87] G. R. Elton, "Introduction: Crime and the Historian," in Cockburn, ed., *Crime
in England*, p. 1.

APPENDIX A

*Total Prosecutions and Convictions for Various Types of Crime:
Vancouver, 1906-1940*

The following graphs 1(A) through 7(A) provide yearly totals of prosecutions and convictions for different categories of crime in Vancouver between
1906 and 1940. The most significant patterns are the fall in the overall
volume of general crime between the years 1930-36 [graph 1(A)] and especially the very steep decline between 1928 and 1934 in crimes against the
peace [graph 4(A)]. Note, in contrast, the rise to unprecedented levels in
crimes against property [graph 3(A)], violent crimes against property [graph
5(A)] and general theft [6(A)].

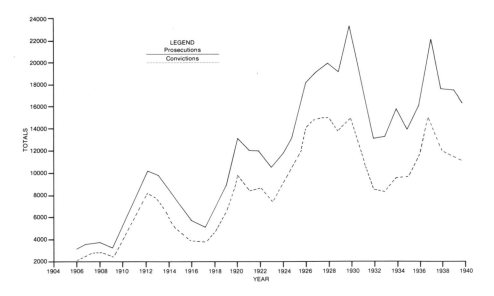

GRAPH 1(A)

Total Prosecutions and Convictions — Vancouver, 1906-1940

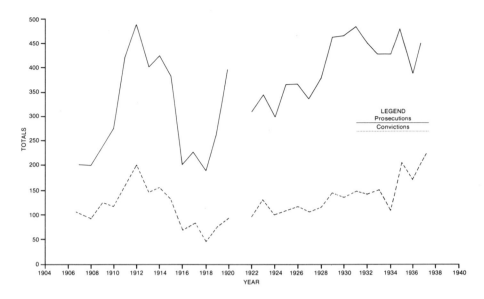

GRAPH 2(A)

Total Prosecutions and Convictions:
Crimes Against the Person — Vancouver, 1907-1937

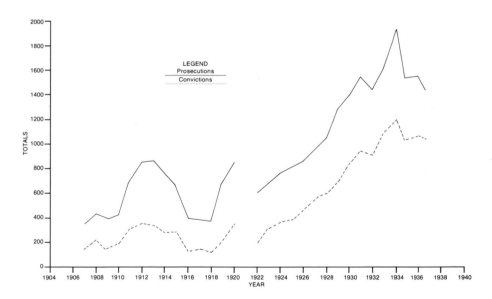

GRAPH 3(A)

Total Prosecutions and Convictions:
Crimes Against Property — Vancouver, 1907-1937

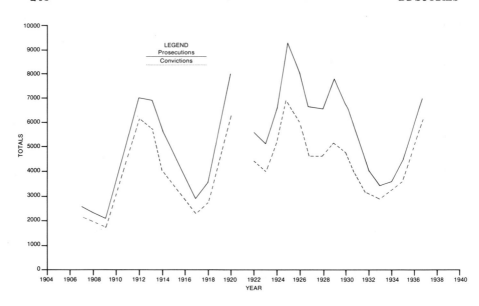

GRAPH 4(A)

Total Prosecutions and Convictions:
Crimes Against the Peace — Vancouver, 1907-1937

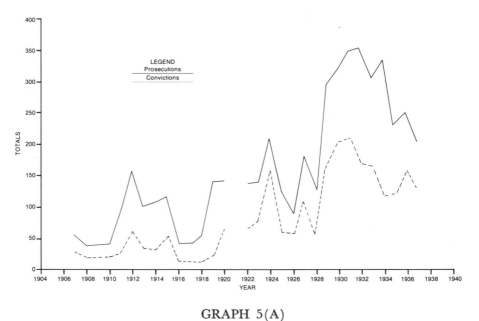

GRAPH 5(A)

Total Prosecutions and Convictions:
Violent Crimes Against Property — Vancouver, 1907-1937

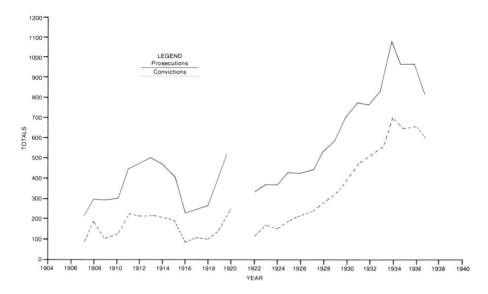

GRAPH 6(A)

Total Prosecutions and Convictions:
General Theft — Vancouver, 1907-1937

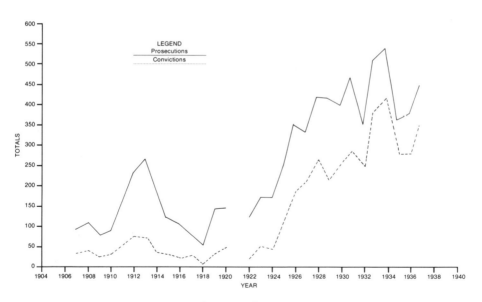

GRAPH 7(A)

Total Prosecutions and Convictions:
Non-Violent Property Crimes — Vancouver, 1907-1937

APPENDIX B

Decline in Morality Prosecutions and Convictions, 1922-1937

TABLE 1(B)

Decline in Prosecution and Conviction Rates for Morality Crimes:
Vancouver — 1922-1937

Period	Liquor		Gambling		Drugs		Prostitution	
	Pros.	*Conv.*	*Pros.*	*Conv.*	*Pros.*	*Conv.*	*Pros.*	*Conv.*
1922-1928	1839	1338	1654	1563	232	171	962	903
1930-1937	712	611	673	609	25	16	293	269
% Decline	61.2%	54.3%	59.3%	61.0%	89.2%	90.6%	69.5%	70.2%

The Mothers' Council of Vancouver:
Holding the Fort for the Unemployed, 1935-1938

IRENE HOWARD

In April 1935 the single unemployed men in the National Defence Camps in British Columbia, under the leadership of the Relief Camp Workers' Union, walked out en masse and gathered in Vancouver to confront the authorities with their demand for work and wages. The response of Mayor Gerald Grattan McGeer was to read the Riot Act in Victory Square. The date is well remembered, for 23 April 1935 brought to a head the smouldering unrest of the unemployed. For the next three years, the economy still in crisis, they continued to petition, demonstrate and organize. In May 1938 the relief camp workers precipitated a second major confrontation — the Post Office sit-down strike. During these three years the Mothers' Council of Vancouver supported the unemployed, especially throughout the two major strikes, providing food, clothing and shelter for those who did not qualify for relief, joining wholeheartedly in demonstrations and rallies, and initiating their own forms of protest. Although a superficial account of the Mothers' Council might suggest that it was a traditional women's organization acting in an auxiliary capacity to the Relief Camp Workers' Union, close study reveals that the Council took a pre-eminently political direction, independently attempting to influence governments and contributing substantially to the public debate on what turned out to be an insoluble problem.

"Remember the women of Paris marching on Versailles for bread," remarked an anonymous onlooker as ten mothers from Vancouver led a contingent of the unemployed up Government Street in Victoria in one of the last episodes of the Post Office sit-down strike. The remark was intended to be facetious; in fact it was historically perceptive. For although the women of Vancouver did not get caught up in violence like the women of Paris in 1789 (and of the Commune in 1871), they had a good deal in common with their revolutionary sisters: a grand impatience with the authorities in charge and the will to engage in militant action to solve an economic problem. In England during the Chartist period of the 1830s, women joined with men in demonstrations, according to one

249

BC STUDIES, nos. 69-70, Spring-Summer 1986

historian even acting "almost as shock troops." In the textile workers' strike of 1912 in Massachusetts, immigrant women "picketed in freezing weather, pregnant women and others with babies in their arms marching with their placards for 'Bread and Roses.' "

British Columbia women have also been militant participants in labour struggles. Vancouver Island miners' wives confronted Premier McBride in Victoria with his responsibilities in the coal miners' strike of 1912-14. In 1935 at Corbin in the Kootenays, miners' wives were on the picket line; some were injured in the fight with police. In 1946 loggers' wives from the Lake Cowichan Women's Auxiliary led the International Wood-workers of America strike trek to the provincial legislature. The women of the Greenham Common peace camp in England, the women of Iceland halting the country's business by a one-day strike — all belong to a long tradition of political protest among women. The Mothers' Council of Vancouver finds an appropriate place in that tradition.[1]

The Mothers' Council must be seen in another context as well, that of socialist women for whom the fight for women's rights has been only part of the workers' struggle for full human rights. Indeed some feminists, like Sylvia Pankhurst, eventually moved to the socialist arena and gave precedence to the larger cause of working-class revolution. Not all radical women subsumed their feminist aspirations in this way. Many followed the lead of German Socialist Clara Zetkin (1857-1933), who assigned a paramount role to women's organizations outside the formal structure of the Party. Such groups, she believed, fostered personal growth, creating independent, thinking women with strong, socialist wills. Separate

[1] Anonymous onlooker: *Vancouver Sun*, 21 June 1938, p. 1. Women of Paris: Darline Gay Levy et al., trans. and ed., *Women in Revolutionary Paris, 1789-1795* (Chicago: University of Illinois Press, 1979), pp. 36-42. Chartists: Dorothy Thompson, "Women and Nineteenth Century Radical Politics," in *The Rights and Wrongs of Women*, ed. Juliet Mitchell and Ann Oakley (Harmondsworth, Eng.: Penguin, 1976), p. 119. Textile workers: Sheila Rowbotham, *Women, Resistance and Revolution* (Harmondsworth, Eng.: Penguin, 1974), pp. 110-11. Miners' wives: Dorothy G. Steeves, *The Compassionate Rebel: Ernest Winch and the Growth of Socialism in Western Canada* (Vancouver, B.C.: J. J. Douglas Ltd., paperbound edition, 1977), pp. 20-22: "They [the Cumberland women] got some accordion-players and a procession led by the musicians and sometimes by women dancing the highland fling would play the strike-breakers to the mine entrance and await them to play them back again." Stuart Jamieson, *Times of Trouble: Labour Unrest and Industrial Conflict in Canada, 1900-1966*, Task Force on Labour Relations, Study No. 22 (Ottawa: Information Canada, 1968), p. 221. Women's Auxiliary: Sara Diamond, "A Union Man's Wife: The Ladies' Auxiliary Movement in the IWA, the Lake Cowichan Experience," in *Not Just Pin Money: Selected Essays on the History of Women's Work in British Columbia*, ed. Barbara K. Latham and Roberta J. Pazdro (Victoria, B.C.: Camosun College, 1984), p. 295.

women's organizations could also reach out to non-political women and gather them into the socialist fold, a more sensitive kind of proselytizing than that which characterized the usual public political meeting. The wisdom of creating separate organizations for women was questioned by some socialists; Lenin, after all, maintained that women should not form a special group within the Party. But he also distinguished between feminist autonomy and "practical revolutionary expediency" as applied to unpoliticized women.[2] In the Vancouver of the thirties, left-wing women,[3] many with a history of feminist activism, adopted this pragmatic approach: their Mothers' Council was one of those women's groups formed, in part at least, for the practical purpose of giving women a voice and encouraging them to use it.

No historical accounts exist of the Mothers' Council or the other left-wing women's groups associated with it, for both women generally and left-wing movements have until recently been omitted from "official" history. It is only in the last twenty years that scholars have turned their attention to these two fields of study and that archivists have actively sought to acquire the necessary documents. Even so, biographies of left-wing women and accounts of their organizations are only now beginning to be written, and standard histories of the Co-operative Commonwealth Federation (CCF) continue to emphasize "the male perspective, even though, especially in the provincial B.C. party, women played key roles."[4] Supplying the need for a history of left-wing women from a feminine perspective, Joan Sangster breaks new ground and opens the way for

---

[2] Jane Slaughter and Robert Kern, "Introduction," *European Women on the Left: Socialism, Feminism and the Problems Faced by Political Women, 1880 to the Present*, ed. Slaughter and Kern (Westport, Conn.: Greenwood Press, 1981), pp. 6-7. Karen Honeycut, "Clara Zetkin: A Socialist Approach to the Problem of Women's Oppression," in Slaughter and Kern, p. 38.

[3] In this essay the phrase "left-wing women" will denote women in the Co-operative Commonwealth Federation (CCF) and the Communist Party of Canada (CPC) along with their sympathizers.

[4] Susan Walsh, "Equality, Emancipation and a More Just World: Leading Women in the British Columbia Cooperative Commonwealth Federation" (M.A. dissertation, Simon Fraser University, 1983), p. 10. The political careers of Helena Gutteridge, Laura Jamieson, Dorothy Steeves and Grace MacInnis are studied in relation to their "dual roles" as feminists and as socialists.
Women are all but completely missing from the CPC History Commission's *Canada's Party of Socialism: History of the Communist Party of Canada, 1921-1976* (Toronto: Progress Books, 1982). Brief accounts of the Women's Labour League and the Congress of Canadian Women and of CPC views on the WLL and the Women's Lib movement of the sixties are given in Ivan Avakumovic, *The Communist Party in Canada: a History* (Toronto: McClelland & Stewart, 1975), pp. 74 and 247-49.

further detailed work in this field with her recent comprehensive study, "Canadian Women in Radical Politics and Labour, 1920-1950."[5]

However, the task of writing left-wing women into the history of Canada will not be an easy one, for in many cases their records (and this is true of the Mothers' Council) are not to be found. There is no problem finding archival materials for large women's organizations which have become institutions — the National Council of Women, for example, or the Women's Institute. The leading women in such organizations had a strong feeling of belonging to an important and continuing tradition whose history obviously had to be preserved. But women in less permanent regional and local organizations, no matter what their politics, have not had sufficient sense of their own importance to preserve their records. Given their almost complete exclusion from the pages of history and the pre-eminence there of the male experience, it is little wonder that when it came time to deal with their accumulated papers, they destroyed them. Even the ebullient Effie Jones (1889-1985), well-known as a communist contender in Vancouver politics for two decades, was no proof against the prevailing indifference to women's history.[6] She had preserved the records of the Housewives' League of Vancouver (1938-43) through the repressive political climate of the thirties and early forties, when, chairing meetings of the League, she felt impelled to warn members that undercover agents were present at the back of the room. Finally, in her old age

[5] Ph.D. dissertation, McMaster University, 1984 (publication forthcoming). See also Joan Sangster, "The Communist Party and the Woman Question, 1922-1929," *Labour/Le Travail* 15 (Spring 1985): 25-56, and "Women of the 'New Era': Women in the Early CCF," in *Building the Cooperative Commonwealth*, ed. W. Brennan (Regina: University of Regina, Canadian Plains Research Centre, 1985).

[6] Some of the more cautious among British Columbia socialists and communists burned their papers or buried them, along with their Marxist books, for fear of being caught in a police raid with incriminating evidence (interviews with Emil Bjarnason, 9 October 1985, and Ruth Bullock, 4 October 1985). Grace MacInnis, former CCF MLA, recalls that her own political involvement began during the Winnipeg General Strike of 1919 during which her father, J. S. Woodsworth, was arrested. At her mother's bidding, Grace packed her father's books and papers in a box and hid them in the woods. Her mother further instructed Grace not to tell her where they were, for if the RCMP came to search the house, Mrs. Woodsworth wanted to plead ignorance (interview with Grace MacInnis by Anne Scotton, SP 164:1, University of British Columbia Library, Special Collections Division (UBCL)).
    During the McCarthy era of the fifties, the peace movement was particularly vulnerable to the "guilt by association" tactic of anti-communists. The fear and distrust of the times was such that splits occurred in the peace movement. In the much respected Women's International League for Peace and Freedom, which has consultative status with the United Nations Economic and Social Council, a division occurred among members, as a result of which, it was discovered some years later, their records from the beginning (1921) to the mid-fifties had been destroyed by a former member (interview with Sheila Young, Vancouver, 22 October 1985).

in the 1970s she concluded that her papers were "of no interest to any-one." "I destroyed them all," she said.[7]

There is a certain irony in the fact that the left-wing historian, in the absence of membership lists and minute books, may find lists of members, accounts of meetings, correspondence and all manner of newsletters and other printed ephemera in police records. It is evident from the Van-couver Police Department files that the meetings and other activities of the CCF Women's Central Group, the Mothers' Council and the Women's Labour League were all under surveillance during the relief camp workers' strike of 1935 and the Post Office sit-down strike of 1938. Yet even here women have received short shrift, for it appears that the undercover agent was no more able than any other male observer of the time to view the participation of women in politics with anything but condescension. In his report on left-wing response to the reading of the Riot Act, one Vancouver agent commented with benevolent contempt, "I have never seen so many women running around, one would think it was election night."[8]

Dependent as it is on such limited sources as the left-wing and daily press and interviews, the history of the Mothers' Council must necessarily be incomplete, at least in terms of the requirements of traditional male-oriented history.[9] This does not mean that the Council must be excluded

[7] Interview with Effie Jones, tape 3588-1, Women's Labour History Collection (WLHC), Provincial Archives of British Columbia (PABC). The B.C. Federation of Labour and SFU Library have copies. When storage space was a problem a woman might find room for her husband's "more important" papers and destroy her own. Conversation with Ruth Bullock, North Vancouver, 4 October 1985. On censorship in Canada during the thirties, with particular reference to Section 98 of the Criminal Code, see F. R. Scott, "Freedom of Speech in Canada," *Proceedings of the Canadian Political Science Association*, 5, May 1933, 169-89.

[8] Unaddressed and unsigned memorandum, 27 April 1935, in Vancouver City Police Department (VCPD) files. Cited in "Documents Related to the Vancouver Strike and the On to Ottawa Trek," in Ronald Liversedge, *Recollections of the On to Ottawa Trek*, ed. Victor Hoar (Toronto: McClelland & Stewart, 1973), p. 155. In addition to their obvious political bias, such reports are often inaccurate as to names and so poorly written as to be obscure. Police files on the single unemployed for 1935 and 1938 are in Vancouver City Archives (VCA). See esp. Loc. 75 (F)2 and 75 (E)7.

[9] The Attorney-General's papers, PABC, provided a few letters from the Mothers' Council. Their correspondence with Vancouver City Council was noted in city council minutes, but the letters themselves were not deposited with Vancouver City Archives.

Left-wing newspapers consulted: the CCF *Commonwealth*, superseded by the *Federationist*; the communist *B.C. Workers' News*, superseded by the *People's Advocate*.

Of the women interviewed, the two who remembered most about the Mothers' Council telescoped the Council with another organization in the process of creating

from serious study. It does mean that certain kinds of research — for example, a quantitative study of the composition of the rank and file membership — cannot be undertaken. Instead, new ways of perceiving and handling the already available material have to be employed.[10] In this essay, re-reading the daily press from a woman's point of view provided factual information which had heretofore been ignored. Newspapers also yielded another kind of information not usually perceived as such — the emotional force of events. In addition, new, historically significant persons and events were discovered when certain newspaper reports were transposed from the comic to the serious.[11] Women involved in strike events were sometimes treated in the press in the abstract as a homogeneous and stereotypical entity, "Woman," and as such were objects of indulgent humour without any claim to serious consideration. When, however, the reports were read from a feminist perspective, these women emerged as resolute, politicized individuals comprising an elite within both the CCF and the Communist Party of Canada (CPC). On being asked who on a list of CCF women of the thirties were working-class and who middle-class, one informant finally expostulated: "Working-class women in those days were intelligent human beings who had read enough and thought enough to know you had to change the system."[12]

It did seem, during the Great Depression of the thirties, that the capitalist system was breaking down, such was the depth of the economic crisis. In the spring and summer of 1935, the focus for unrest was a class

a life review. Effie Jones merged in memory the Mothers' Council with the Housewives League, which had launched her career in civic politics and was thus for her the more important of the two groups. Lil Stoneman telescoped the Mothers' Council with the Women's Labour League, of which, as secretary, she had been a leading member (tape 3601, WLHC). Jean Barman deals with the selectivity of memory in her working paper prepared for the Canadian Childhood History Project, "Accounting for Gender and Class in Retrieving the History of Canadian Childhood." On the "life review" (pp. 7-9), she cites, among others, Paul Thompson, *The Voice of the Past: Oral History* (Oxford: Oxford University Press, 1978), p. 113.

[10] On the question of re-examining available sources for new insights see Gerda Lerner, "New Approaches to the Study of Women in American History," in *Liberating Women's History: Theoretical and Critical Essays*, ed. Berenice A. Carroll (Chicago: University of Illinois Press, 1976), p. 353.

[11] For a discussion of the need for historians to abandon the study of Woman in the abstract, see Sheila Ryan Johansson, " 'Herstory' as History: A New Field or Another Fad?" in Carroll, pp. 402-03. For the effects of mockery and caricature on emerging women, see Rowbotham, p. 106. See *Vancouver Sun* report discussed on p. 57, fn. 66.

[12] Conversation with Hilda Kristiansen, 8 October 1985.

of single unemployed men who could not claim domicile, for they had not lived long enough in British Columbia. These were the men whom the Mothers' Council supported and befriended. The transients, as they were called, were mostly migrant workers attracted to Vancouver by the mild climate and the small hope, soon extinguished, that here conditions might be better. They had no home, unless a hobo jungle like the one behind the Canadian National Railway station could be called home, or the construction camps operated for a short time by the provincial government. With over 75,000 registered unemployed in British Columbia alone in June 1932, the federal government, fearful of uprisings across the country, accepted General McNaughton's plan to defuse incipient insurrection by isolating the men in relief camps. Thus in June 1933 the provincial road camps were incorporated into the national relief camp program of the Department of National Defence.[13]

But General McNaughton's plan did not work. The necessary funding for rehabilitation was not forthcoming from the federal government. The men were lonely, discontented, and starved for emotional and mental stimulation. Most of all they resented being paid twenty cents for a full day's work. Their Relief Camp Workers' Union, affiliated with the Workers' Unity League, protested camp conditions and claimed the camps had been militarized. When union organizers were expelled from the camps and blacklisted, the men began walking out.[14] In December 1934, 1,200 relief camp workers arrived in Vancouver and stayed for four weeks, demanding an end to the blacklist and re-instatement of those expelled. In April they staged another, and larger, walkout. Other unemployed men joined them. United in a disciplined group behind radical leaders, the unemployed now confronted the authorities as a powerful constituency, demanding real work with real wages and abolition of the camps.[15] Standing on street corners, holding out their tin cans

---

[13] Registered unemployed: "Province of British Columbia, History of Relief: October, 1930-December 1937," E. E. Winch Personal Papers, 55a.24, Angus MacInnis Memorial Collection (AMMC), UBCL. Relief camps: Marion Lane, "Unemployment During the Depression: The Problem of the Single Unemployed Transient in British Columbia, 1930-1938" (Graduating Essay, University of British Columbia, 1966), pp. 52-61. For a history and description of the camps, see "The Report of the Macdonald Commission," cited in full in Liversedge, ed. Hoar, pp. 125-45.

[14] Lane, pp. 75-85.

[15] For a first-hand account of December 1934 strike, see Jean Evans Sheils and Ben Swankey, *"Work and Wages!"* — *Semi-documentary Account of the Life and Times of Arthur H. (Slim) Evans* (Vancouver: Trade Union Research Bureau, 1977), p. 81. See also *Commonwealth*, 20 December 1934, p. 1, and "Relief Camp Workers' Appeal to the People of British Columbia and Citizens of Vancouver," Vancouver, March 1955, E. E. Winch Personal Papers, 55a.24, AMMC.

to collect money from passers-by, snarling traffic with their routine marches, the men were a presence that could not be ignored. Their numbers increased dramatically: the 9 April march of 5,000 men through downtown streets added, the *Vancouver Sun* observed, "a new chapter to the history of labour demonstration in Vancouver." The authorities, not least of all Mayor McGeer, were very much afraid of a popular revolt. It was, after all, only eighteen years since the Russian Revolution.[16] Both the mayor and Premier Pattullo insisted that unemployment was a federal responsibility and looked to Ottawa for financial assistance, but Prime Minister R. B. Bennett turned a deaf ear, taking refuge in the constitution: the men were a federal responsibility only while they were in the National Defence Camps. The strikers, having left the camps, were now a provincial responsibility and Vancouver must therefore look to Victoria for help, "for a municipality is a creation of the province."[17]

On 23 April 1935 a department store parade ended in a confrontation with the police and the reading of the Riot Act. Although in a private communication with Ottawa McGeer blamed the disturbance on the federal government's "ineffective policy of administering the unemployment situation," in his radio address a few days later he blamed the strike on communist leaders. It was a speech that could only contribute to the prevailing climate of fear; it did nothing to help solve the problem of how to feed the destitute strikers. On the following May Day 14,000 people marched in the parade and 20,000 gathered in Stanley Park for the rally. Public sympathy was with the strikers, as even Mayor McGeer acknowledged. For the left-wing strategists, the day was cause for jubilation, its success being in large part due to the co-operation of the CCF and the CPC on the issue of the unemployed. But Chief Constable Foster, reporting to Mayor McGeer, saw the day as "a real tragedy" because it had brought hopeful young men into contact with "foreigners of a low type" and "Communistic organizations intent upon destruction."[18]

16 *Vancouver Sun*, 10 April 1935, p. 2. Authorities: Documents cited in Liversedge, ed. Hoar, pp. 147-66, esp. pp. 147-49, Premier T. D. Pattullo to Sir George Perley, 25 and 27 March 1935.

17 Mayor McGeer and Bennett: Exchange of telegrams, 16-21 May 1935, from *Report of the Regina Riot Commission*, pp. 84-85, cited in Liversedge, ed. Hoar, pp. 162-64. Pattullo: "T. Dufferin Pattullo and the Little New Deal," in *Politics of Discontent*, ed. Ramsay Cook et al. (Toronto: University of Toronto Press, 1967), pp. 33-36; Premier Pattullo, "Your Government and the Problem of Relief," *Vancouver Sun*, 7 May 1935, p. 2.

18 For eyewitness accounts of the day's events see Acting Inspector Lester to Chief Constable Foster, 25 April 1935, in Liversedge, ed. Hoar, pp. 151-52, and Liver-

It was in this volatile political climate, with the three governments in a paralyzing stand-off and the strikers depending on public charity for food and shelter, that the left-wing women of Vancouver joined forces to form the Mothers' Day Committee, which eventually evolved into a permanent group, the Mothers' Council. The Committee originated among women participating in the events of a ten-day period from 23 April to 3 May. The Women's New Era League had called a conference late in April to discuss the relief camp strike. First formed in 1916 to help women make the best possible use of their newly won franchise, the League had been for nearly two decades an influential advocate of social legislation, notably the Pension Allowance Act (renamed the Children's Allowance Act). Susan Clark, its first president, was now its representative on the Vancouver Local Council of Women, a non-partisan federation of women's groups affiliated with the National Council of Women. The April conference brought together at the Hotel Georgia twenty-four delegates but announced itself as representing seventy-two organizations, since the delegate from the Local Council of Women represented fifty-seven of them. The other twenty-three delegates represented, among others, the Civilian Pensioned Mothers, the Women's Section of the Provincial Workers' Council, several church organizations and the Socialist Party. With Fanny Cowper of the New Era League in the chair and Peggy Harrison of the Women's Labour League secretary, the conference unanimously passed a resolution introduced by the Unemployment Relief Committee of the Local Council of Women urging the federal government to provide a works program and immediate temporary relief for the strikers. Vancouver school trustee Ada Crump announced that she would put the same resolution to the Provincial Parent-Teachers' Federation, also in conference that week. Because the New Era League conference coincided with the crisis over the reading of the Riot Act, the delegates elected an action committee of twelve to send a delegation to the mayor. The conference also discussed the need for unity among women

sedge's own memories, *ibid.*, pp. 74-76. Recalling events from a distance of thirty years, Liversedge telescopes the May Day rally and the Mothers' Day parade and rally held twelve days later. "Ineffective policy": McGeer to Sir George Perley, 23 April, in R. B. Bennett Papers, cited in Liversedge, ed. Hoar, p. 151. McGeer's speech: *Vancouver Sun*, 29 April 1935, pp. 1 and 5. May Day rally and Foster's report: Liversedge, ed. Hoar, pp. 157-58. A detailed account of the relief camp workers' strike is given in Victor Howard [formerly Victor Hoar], *"We Were the Salt of the Earth!" The On-to-Ottawa Trek and the Regina Riot* (Regina: Canadian Plains Research Centre, 1985).

and directed the action committee to meet again to consider further action.[19]

When the conference delegation visited Mayor McGeer the next day, 25 April, they requested that he demand immediate action from the federal government. Jumping at the chance to put pressure on Ottawa, McGeer wired Deputy Prime Minister Sir George Perley on the spot:

Public opinion is overwhelmingly opposed to any policy of forcing the men now on strike to return to camps without some definite indication that a work and wages program will be developed in immediate future. Public opposed to jailing these men for vagrancy.

If your government will not agree to call a conference through which some practical solution can be developed, I greatly fear the disorder that will accompany the widespread dissatisfaction and unrest that is arising.

While there is Communistic activity, the opposition to the existing relief system is by no means confined to that element.

The delegation in my office at the moment is representative of best citizenship of our city.[20]

The reading of the Riot Act had also sparked another very large popular demonstration in support of the relief camp strikers: the CCF parade and rally in the Denman Street Arena on 28 April. In this event, women in the CCF party committed themselves brilliantly, providing leadership, emotional energy, and their own kind of platform charisma.[21] The New Era League Conference action committee was doubtless given new impetus by the performance of socialist women in this great mass demonstration. Riding on a strong wave of political feeling in their own groups and in sympathetic non-political women's groups at this time, a nucleus of women from the CCF and Women's Labour League, some of whom were probably on the action committee, constituted themselves a Mothers' Day Committee which would carry out various activities on Mothers' Day in support of the relief camp strikers.[22] The fact that so

[19] Conference: *Vancouver Sun*, 26 April 1935, p. 4; *B.C. Workers' News*, 10 May 1935, p. 2. New Era League: Helen Gregory McGill Papers, Add Mss. 270, pp. 54-55, VCA. Susan Lane Clark; Mary Patricia Powell, "A Response to the Depression: the Local Council of Women of Vancouver," in *In Her Own Right: Selected Essays on Women's History in B.C.*, ed. Barbara Latham and Cathy Kess (Victoria, B.C.: Camosun College, 1980), p. 268. Powell lists the societies affiliated with the LCW on p. 277: one-third of the fifty-seven affiliates were church groups and branches of the Women's Christian Temperance Union.

[20] *Vancouver Sun*, 2 April 1935, p. 4.

[21] See below, p. 261.

[22] *Commonwealth*, 3 May 1935. Arthur Evans, leader of the On-to-Ottawa Trek, says the Committee was initiated by CCF women: Sheils and Swankey, p. 95; the *B.C. Workers' News*, 17 May 1935, p. 2, says it was initiated by the Women's Labour League.

many of the women knew one another through overlapping memberships, especially in the New Era League, the CCF Women's Central Group, and the Local Council of Women, suggests that the action committee may have *become* the Mothers' Day Committee or at least formed its nucleus. In any case, over the summer of 1935 the Committee evolved into a permanent group and by August had changed its name to the Mothers' Council.[23]

Not a great deal is known about the thirty-seven women who attended the first meeting of the Mothers' Day Committee on 3 May 1935. However, among those participating in their tag day the following week were women from the Local Council of Women, the New Era League, the Women's and Girls' Club, the Kitsilano Women's Club (Unemployed Section), the Women's Christian Temperance Union and, of course, the CCF Women's Central Group and the Women's Labour League. The original Committee almost certainly comprised women from these groups, all of which, except the Local Council of Women and the WCTU, belonged to the left or at least leaned that way. Women could also belong as individuals.[24] In the absence of record books, it is not possible to discuss the nature of the rank and file membership of the Mothers' Council. More is known about the leadership, which came largely from the CCF Women's Central Group and the CPC's Women's Labour League.

The CCF Women's Central Group was formed as early as the fall of 1934 to provide educational and social programs for CCF women as well as to co-ordinate their political activities. An offshoot of the CCF Education Committee, its main objective was to increase the political and social awareness, not just of women from local CCF clubs but of non-CCF women in the community as well. Membership in the Central Group was

[23] According to the research thus far, the Mothers' Council was first referred to by that name in the *Commonwealth*, 23 August 1935, p. 1.

[24] *Vancouver Sun*, 21 May 1938, p. 1; *Federationist*, 9 June 1938, p. 5. Socialists Dorothy Steeves, Susan Lane Clark, Helena Gutteridge and Laura Jamieson were very active in the Local Council of Women in these years: Powell, pp. 262, 272 and 275. Susan Clark, Helena Gutteridge and Mary Norton, also a socialist, were leading members of the New Era League: supra fn. 19; Susan Wade, "Helena Gutteridge: Votes for Women and Trade Unions," in Latham and Kess, p. 199; interview with Mary Norton, Vancouver, 21 February 1973, #141, Reynoldston Research and Studies, Oral History Programs, tape transcript, UBCL. In a report to the Toronto Branch of the Left Opposition, 24 September 1933, Earle Birney identified the Vancouver Women and Girls' Club as a Trotskyist organization which the "Stalinites" were trying to take over: Earle Birney Papers, University of Toronto. It is probably safe to say that the Kitsilano Women's Club with its Unemployed Women's Section was also a left-wing group. Conversations with Hilda Kristiansen, Vancouver, 8 October 1985, and Mildred Liversedge, Parksville, B.C., 15 September 1985, provided the names of a few individual members.

in addition to membership in a Vancouver or district CCF club. The women heard reports about what was going on in the legislature, House of Commons, city council and Vancouver School Board. They were encouraged to take part in discussion and were offered courses in public speaking.[25] Most importantly, they were provided with a role model of the socialist woman as a person who translated political and social awareness into action.

All of the women giving leadership to the CCF Women's Central Group were also active in the main body of the CCF. Mildred Osterhout (1900-   ), later Fahrni, had been a CCF candidate in the provincial election of 1933 and would win a place on the Vancouver School Board in the fall of 1935. On her weekly CCF broadcasts, "The Women's View," she sought to raise the political consciousness of her listeners as well as keep them informed on CCF policy and local issues. Journalist Elizabeth Kerr (1887-1978), under the name of Constance Errol, wrote a weekly column, also called "The Women's View," in the CCF newspaper the *Federationist*. An outspoken advocate for women and the unemployed, she was elected to the CCF Provincial Executive in 1938. One-time trade unionist and militant suffragist, Helena Gutteridge (1879-1960), emerged from political retirement in 1932 to re-dedicate herself to socialism by campaigning on the speakers' platform for CCF candidates in the 1933 provincial election. At the time of the relief camp workers' strike she was an invaluable member of the very important CCF Economic Planning Commission and would become its head the following year. Her fellow suffragist and friend, Susan Lane Clark (c. 1880s-1956), was also a veteran socialist campaigner and in 1937 won a two-year term on the Vancouver Parks Board. Sarah Colley (1880-1943) from New Westminster was on the roster of speakers who went out to explain party policy on unemployment to local CCF clubs. In fact all of these women were actively involved in the work of the CCF Unemployment Conference, Helena Gutteridge being secretary and Elizabeth Kerr head of the Women's Grievance Committee.[26] (The Conference consisted

---

[25] *Commonwealth*, 13 December 1934, p. 3; Circular letters, 12 November 1935 and 17 June 1936, E. E. Winch Personal Papers, 55a.29, AMMC.

[26] For biographical sketches of these women and for details not in these sketches see: Osterhout: *Commonwealth*, 25 October 1933, p. 3; 13 December 1935, p. 1; typescripts of broadcasts in private possession. Kerr: *Federationist*, 25 February 1937, p. 8 and 7 July 1938, p. 5. Gutteridge and Lane: Linda Hale, "Appendix: Votes for Women: Profiles of Prominent British Columbia Suffragists and Social Reformers," in Latham and Kess, pp. 288-89 and 292; planning commission: *Federationist*, 25 March 1937, p. 1. Colley: *Commonwealth*, 23 May 1935, p. 6 and 15 February 1935, p. 7. Unemployment Conference: *Commonwealth*, 2 August 1934,

of delegates from various CCF clubs and the CCF Provincial Council, who met frequently to take action on behalf of the unemployed.)

On 28 April, a few days after the reading of the Riot Act, the CCF staged a mass rally in the Denman Street Arena. The CCF Women's Central Group, led by Elizabeth Kerr, called a mass meeting in Moose Hall to make plans for a parade of women to the Arena rally. The organizing ability, the imagination and energy of the CCF women, as revealed in reports of the Moose Hall meeting and of the parade and rally, point to the political contribution they would be bringing to the Mothers' Council. The reports themselves supply evidence of the strong public emotions surrounding the whole question of the single unemployed transients.

Three hundred women attended the meeting, the CCF Women's Central Group, the Women's Labour League, the Parent-Teachers' Association and the New Era League playing a leading role. They decided that, in addition to the parade, they would also hold a tag day,[27] not to collect money, as was usually done, but to advertise the meeting. According to the report of the undercover agent who attended the Moose Hall meeting, a male CCF functionary addressed the women on the question of holding the tag day. The agent's report implies a passive audience of women getting their instructions from a male leader.[28] In contrast, the *Vancouver Sun* reporter reveals in his account women of energy and spirit who, far from being passive, give the impression that they themselves had everything in hand and were the initiators of action:

'It's up to the people to abolish the relief camps,' was the cry that went up from more than 300 women assembled under the auspices of the C.C.F. Women's Group in the Moose Hall on Thursday evening.

'We've had enough of commissions, delegations and petitions,' they shouted. 'Now we'll take over and act.'

*   *   *

'Abolish the camps: don't let the boys go back,' the women urged.

Not once were the strikers referred to as such or as men; always 'our boys.'

*   *   *

Shouts of 'let's go' greeted Ernest Cumber, Secretary of the Relief Camp

---

p. 1; 22 February 1935, p. 7; "Annual Report of the CCF Unemployment Conference," 24 July 1935, E. E. Winch Personal Papers, 55a.30, AMMC.

[27] Charitable organizations holding a tag day stationed their members on downtown sidewalks to solicit money from passers-by in return for a tag declaring the message or slogan of the organization. City by-laws allowed only three tag days a year.

[28] Liversedge, ed. Hoar, pp. 153-54.

Sarah Colley　　　　　　　　　　　*Helena Gutteridge*

Mothers' Council marching in May Day Parade, Georgia near Pender, 1930s

Effie Jones

Elizabeth Kerr

Women's demonstration, Stanley Park, 1935

Workers' Union, when he said he would like to have the pleasure of leading
the women down Granville Street and to the City Hall.[29]

The Commission referred to was the Macdonald Commission, finally
appointed by an intransigent federal government on 28 March 1935 to
study camp conditions, too late to stop the strike. In April there had been
delegations of strikers to see Mayor McGeer, three in as many days; the
first, led by Dorothy Steeves, represented the Action Committee of the
Relief Camp Workers' Union and the Canadian Labour Defence
League. A petition containing some 35,000 names had been presented,
with an accompanying brief, to Premier Pattullo by a delegation from
the B.C. Joint Committee on Unemployment; Sarah Colley had been
chosen to present the case for the impoverished mothers.[30] None of these
efforts had been to any avail, and now, like the miners' wives of Vancouver Island and Corbin, and the women of Versailles, the Vancouver
women at the Moose Hall meeting took action.

The *Sun* report also reveals the parental compassion felt by the assembled women for the strikers, a feeling shared by the people of Vancouver
generally. The relief camp workers had become "the boys" or "our boys,"
and almost always were referred to in this way by speakers addressing
mass rallies. Some of the older strikers were a little embarrassed at being
so fondly addressed, as Ronald Liversedge recalled thirty years later:

> Ma Boley, an old-time C.C.F.'er, a wonderful personality, coined the
> phrase, 'Our Boys'.... [He was surely referring to Sarah Colley.] While it
> came from the heart and actually described the vast majority of the camp
> workers, to those of us who were then in our late thirties, the phrase 'Our
> Boys' produced in us a certain self-consciousness.[31]

Whether or not Sarah Colley did introduce the phrase, it evokes the
aura of feeling surrounding many of the events of April and May 1935,
especially those planned by the women.

The following Saturday morning in downtown Vancouver, a large
contingent of women distributed 25,000 tags bearing the question, "Our

[29] 26 April 1935, pp. 1 and 4.

[30] The complete report of the Commission is in Liversedge, ed. Hoar, pp. 125-45.
Delegations: *Vancouver Sun*, 9 April 1935, pp. 1 and 12; *Commonwealth*, 12
April 1935, pp. 1 and 2. Petition and brief: "Annual Report of the CCF Unemployment Conference," 24 July 1935 and "Report of Delegation of Unemployed
Sponsored by the British Columbia Joint Committee on Unemployment...," in
private possession. The prime movers in the Committee were the CCF, represented
by their Unemployment Conference, and the Communist Party of Canada, represented by the Provincial Workers' Alliance.

[31] Liversedge, ed. Hoar, p. 64.

Boys, Are They Criminals?" This was a reminder that unemployed young men were being sent to jail for "tin-canning" or begging on the streets. The women also collected signatures on a petition demanding that the relief camps be closed.[32]

Then came Sunday's parade, stage-managed with a flair for political theatre by the CCF women. According to Victor Howard's narrative,

They [the camp men] had been told that they would set out first for the Arena, with the CCF women next.... But Sarah Colley now approached Smokey [Ernest] Cumber [secretary of the Relief Camp Workers' Union] and asked him whether the women could walk at the head of the column. Smokey said all right and off they went.

The RCMP had witnessed this exchange: 'Again the CCF leaders proved themselves masters of manoeuvres and sent Mother Colley to Cumber to ask him for the head of the line for the women. Cumber agreed.'[33]

The RCMP agent's interpretation, based as it is on a male view of docile womanhood, does not take into account that the CCF leadership included a number of forceful women whom one did not "send" to carry out one's bidding. The CCF Women's Central Group quite likely took the initiative in the arrangement with Cumber. Thus it was that two thousand Vancouver women, with Sarah Colley out in front, led the march from Cambie Street Grounds to the Denman Street Arena. Behind the women marched the contingent of relief camp workers and their sympathizers, 1,800 strong. Crowds lined the route and cheered as they passed. When they entered the Arena, "a storm of cheering broke as the women marched to seats on the floor in front of the rostrum." Then came the strikers, "the boys," in disciplined divisions, banners aloft. The assembled crowd numbered 16,000, the largest ever to attend an indoor meeting in Vancouver. Among those speaking from the platform were such CCF notables as Harold Winch, the fiery MLA, the eloquent Dr. Lyle Telford — and Sarah Colley, introduced as "the CCF Mother."[34]

The second main group providing leadership in the Mothers' Council was the Women's Labour League, comprising largely communist women, with branches in Vancouver, Vancouver Island and other parts of British Columbia during the thirties. The Labour Leagues originated in Britain after the general election of 1906 as women's unions affiliated with the British Labour Party. Transplanted in Canada before World War I, with

[32] *Commonwealth*, 3 May 1935, p. 7.

[33] RCMP report: Howard, p. 61.

[34] Parade and rally: *Vancouver Sun*, 29 April 1935, p. 1; "CCF Mother": *Commonwealth*, 3 May 1935, p. 3.

branches in Port Arthur, Fort William, Winnipeg and Toronto, a Canadian Federation of Women's Labour Leagues was formed at a convention in Ontario in 1924, with the aim of affiliating with the Trades and
Labour Congress and thus facilitating the unionization of women workers. However, the Congress refused to endorse the Women's Labour
Leagues because of their strong communist support. After the Sixth
Congress of the Communist International (Comintern) in Moscow in
1928, and at the suggestion of the Comintern, the Leagues affiliated with
the Workers' Unity League (WUL), the intention being that, in line
with the policy of the Comintern's Third Period (1928-35), they should
participate fully in the revolutionary labour movement launched by the
Communist Party in its dramatic turn to the left. In British Columbia the
response of the Leagues to this new directive was to encourage women
to set up union auxiliaries and to help establish a union for domestic
servants. The Leagues also supported the Party's efforts on behalf of the
unemployed, participating in Hunger Marches and Neighbourhood
Unemployment Committees. In Vancouver, throughout the depression,
the League was inventive and energetic in coming to the aid of the dis-
tressed. Wherever a family was threatened with eviction, the League was
on the picket line, even on occasion carrying back through the rear door
the furniture which the sheriff had just moved out the front. It interceded
on behalf of families having difficulty in getting relief and operated
summer camps for the children of needy working-class families, eventually establishing a permanent campsite on Indian Arm.[35]

Not a great deal is known of the Women's Labour League rank and
file in Vancouver or elsewhere in the province, but, like the CCF
Women's Central Group, the Vancouver League was sustained by a
spirited and committed leadership. Lil Stoneman, a former Saskatchewan
schoolteacher and wife of an unemployed worker, was recording secretary in 1935. The League's organizer, Annie Stewart (1893-1977), had
travelled throughout British Columbia in the late twenties and early

[35] Transplanted: Carol Bacchi, "Divided Allegiances: the Response of Farm and
Labour Women to Suffrage," in *A Not Unreasonable Claim: Women and Reform
in Canada, 1880s-1920s*, ed. Linda Kealey (Toronto: Women's Educational Press,
1979), p. 97. WLL, 1924 convention: John Manley, "Women and the Left in the
1930s: the Case of the Toronto CCF Women's Joint Committee," *Atlantis* 5
(Spring 1980): 118. Evolution of WLL: Sangster, "Canadian Women," esp. ch.
iii; cf. Avakumovic, p. 74 and *Canada's Party of Socialism*, p. 32. Eviction: interview with Elspeth Gardner, Vancouver, 6 March 1985. A branch of the WLL was
formed in Calgary in the late 1920s: "Memoirs," p. 46, Jean McDonald Papers,
M 724, Glenbow-Alberta Institute.

thirties, helping to establish new branches of the League — twenty-four in all. As a CPC organizer, in 1934 she visited Britannia Beach, Comox and Cumberland to encourage women in these mining communities to set up auxiliaries to the Mine Workers' Union of Canada. Annie Stewart also helped set up the Women's Auxiliary of the Vancouver Waterfront Workers. A stone-mason's daughter from Lancashire, she had started out soon after her arrival in 1911 as a children's nanny in a Vancouver household, an unlikely beginning for a future CPC organizer. Her great friend and co-worker, Elsie Munro (1887-1964), a little Scotswoman from Aberdeenshire, had been a cook in the British army during World War I and afterwards supervised the kitchens of the Scottish aristocracy for several years before immigrating to Canada. She married Peter Munro, who carried on a political courtship with her on park benches, declaring he would not marry her until she too became a socialist. The husbands of both women were leading members of the militant Street Railwaymen's Union (Charles Stewart was their long-time business agent), and all four were Party comrades.[36]

Communist women in the Mothers' Council did not all come from the Women's Labour League. Telephone operator Mildred Dougan (1905-   ), from a Vancouver Island pioneer farm family, thought the League was "too leftist," even for her, whose father had started out as a Nanaimo coal worker and retained strong working-class sympathies. She married Ronald Liversedge, one of the 1935 strike leaders, when he came back from fighting in the Spanish Civil War as a member of the Mackenzie-Papineau Battalion. Neither had one of the most politically talented of the communist women in Vancouver in the later thirties been a member of the Women's Labour League. Effie Jones, former school-teacher from Somerset and Wales, wife of a telephone lineman, joined the CCF in 1933 but left it five years later for the CPC because the CCF, as she put it, "wouldn't unite with anybody on anything." She was a member of the Mothers' Council from the beginning and during the 1938 sit-down strike, when she had either just made the transition to the CPC or was about to do so, emerged as one of the Council's leaders. However, it appears that once the strike was over she threw her main efforts into the newly incorporated Vancouver Housewives' League, a non-political consumers' group which soon expanded to become a pro-

[36] Lil Stoneman, WLHC; Annie Stewart: Conversation with Margaret North, Vancouver, 23 October 1985; *Pacific Tribune*, 23 February 1951, p. 2; *B.C. Workers' News*, 28 June 1935, p. 2. I am grateful to Mickey Beagle for this and other references to the women of the WLL in Vancouver.

vincial organization, influential in its efforts to combat rising prices during the early war years.[37]

As with the CCF Women's Central Group, the question arises as to what extent the activities of the Women's Labour League were generated by directives from CPC headquarters. Again it must be conceded that women were targeted as a special sector for party proselytizing. In his introduction to Ronald Liversedge's *Recollections of the On to Ottawa Trek*, Victor Hoar acknowledges the "radical imperative" of the Relief Camp Workers' Union and the Workers' Unity League, with both of which the League women worked closely. But he makes this cautionary observation:

It would be a mistake to assume that the single ambition of the communists was the embarrassment of any government, municipal, provincial or federal, which happened to get in their way. It would be another mistake to dismiss the rank and file of communists in this or any other protest movement of the era as agents of the Soviet Union. The Great Depression may have been induced by international economic upheavals, but we cannot afford to ignore the specific domestic tragedies, nor the conditions which inspired those tragedies. The radicals of Canada did not then, as they do not today, exist in a historical vacuum.[38]

These communist women did understand the political dimensions of working in the Women's Labour League and the Mothers' Council. This was what Lenin meant by "mass work." They were also aware of the "specific domestic tragedies" and the conditions which inspired those tragedies. When they looked about, they did not see "the masses." They saw their neighbours and fellow human beings. They saw families evicted from their homes, pregnant women deprived of milk for their unborn babies, fathers psychologically shattered because they couldn't support their families, mothers worn out by childbirth and the daily struggle to feed and clothe their children, young men with hopes as ragged as their

---

[37] Mildred Liversedge, 15 September 1985; Left the CCF: *Pacific Tribune*, 24 April 1985, p. 3. Housewives' League: Effie Jones, WLHC. "The Housewives League was started by some women and a man of the Liberal Party. They did nothing but they met socially. Well, the times called for something more than that. We could see that the only way was to get into this Housewives' League and make it work. That's what I did and quite a lot of my friends and outsiders." See also *Vancouver Province*, 30 July 1938, p. 28 and 16 November 1939, p. 8. *People's Advocate*, 9 September 1938, p. 2 and 16 September 1938, p. 1. In civic politics Effie Jones is best remembered for her imaginative 1947 mayoralty campaign in which, as "Low-Fare" Jones opposing a B.C. Electric transit fare increase, she came within 4,900 votes of defeating Charles "High-Fare" Jones and becoming mayor of Vancouver. *Vancouver Sun*, 16 April 1985, p. A 12.

[38] Liversedge, ed. Hoar, p. viii.

clothes, reduced to begging on the street and arrested and put in jail for doing it. Compassionate women, they heard the missionary call to political work and obeyed.

The CCF women were similarly motivated by deeply felt conviction. They too were "true believers." The CCF, having already elected seven members to the Legislature, was convinced that it would be forming the next government of British Columbia and was pursuing the achievement of the new co-operative society with religious enthusiasm and missionary zeal. Members felt they belonged not to a political party but to a movement dedicated to changing human hearts and minds. Speaking about the relief camp workers on her radio program, Mildred Osterhout appealed to her listeners: "Join us in this endeavour to wipe out the relief camps and institute a new order of society with freedom and justice for all." And she further admonished them: "You must accept your responsibility of educating through every means possible those who still walk in the darkness of individual Capitalist thinking." Helena Gutteridge was equally explicit. Defending the representation of political parties on city councils, she declared:

The CCF is not a party in the conventional sense, but a part of a worldwide movement of forward-thinking men and women who can visualize a world in which co-operative effort will replace the present cut-throat competition, and in which security and plenty will replace poverty and insecurity.[39]

Having already co-operated in the New Era League conference and in the CCF rally, left-wing women in Vancouver were ready to launch a specifically women's demonstration. The Mothers' Day Committee called its first mass meeting for 3 May to make plans for celebrating Mothers' Day in a manner appropriate to the concerns of all mothers in those troubled economic times. The Women's Labour League was quite explicit: "Such action will be something of real value instead of the usual bourgeois maudlin sentimentalism associated with Mother's Day."[40] Thus the Committee decided to act in a political way and to do so by employing a traditional form.

The Committee applied to city council for permission to hold a tag day to raise money. They were refused but went ahead anyway, and on 11 May collected nearly $1,000 for the camp boys. The following day, Mothers' Day, the Committee led 1,500 relief camp workers from Cambie

[39] Osterhout: typescript of broadcast, 4 April 1935; Gutteridge: *Federationist*: 16 September 1937, p. 4. See also Walter Young, *Anatomy of a Party: The National CCF, 1932-1961* (Toronto: University of Toronto Press, 1969), pp. 52-59.

[40] Sheils and Swankey, p. 96.

Street Grounds to Stanley Park. Their brigade of three hundred women
stepped out smartly at the head of the parade, marching in time to the
CCF Band and carrying a banner that read, "We the Mothers of Today
Demand Abolition of the Relief Camps." In front of the banner strode
four women pushing baby carriages. When the procession reached
Malkin Bowl in Stanley Park, the women marched to an area roped off
in the form of a huge heart and ranged themselves in outline around it.
The relief camp workers then marched inside the heart and filled it. Some
of them raised large placards bearing the letters which spelled out their
message to the mothers: "Mothers Abolish the Relief Camps." The whole
assembly sang "The Red Flag" and then broke up to sit on the grass and
listen to speakers, Mrs. Peggy Harrison of the Women's Labour League
presiding. Among the speakers was Sarah Colley, who emphasized that
this was not a political demonstration, but simply a mothers' protest, and
that governments should understand that the strikers were "Our Boys,"
not foreigners. "We Mothers are really aroused at the plight of the boys,"
she said, "and we'll keep right with them to the end of the road."[41]

Sarah Colley's statement poses a central question. Was the Mothers'
Day Committee/Mothers' Council, as its name implies, a traditional
women's auxiliary after all, assuming fundamentally a supportive, nurtur-
ing role? Sarah Colley makes it seem so. When she stood on that platform
and claimed that the Mothers' Day rally was simply a mothers' protest,
the audience probably found her statement quite credible. In his regular
Commonwealth column "Pertinent Portraits," Barry Mather said:

She has a strangely effective way of speaking. Maybe it's the more than wee
bit of Scotch accent that still clings to her tongue, although she has been
away from the old land now these many years. Maybe it's her simple sin-
cerity or the fact that she seems to have a knack of saying just the psychologically human thing at just the psychological moment.[42]

Evidently this stout, little, grey-haired woman was one of those comfort-
ing people who reached out and, to borrow a phrase from Dylan
Thomas, put her "arms round the griefs of the ages."

On the other hand, mothers carrying a banner demanding the abolition of the relief camps are patently engaged in political demonstration.
Sarah Colley was not so innocent as to be unaware that as "CCF

[41] *Vancouver Sun*, 13 May 1935, p. 5; *Commonwealth*, 10 May 1935, p. 5 and 17
May 1935, p. 1.
[42] 23 May 1935, p. 6. The collected portraits are in Barry Mather, *Pertinent Portraits: C.C.F. 1934*, ill. Fraser Wilson (Vancouver: The Boag Foundation, n.d.).
Sarah Colley's portrait is not included.

Mother" she was playing a most useful political role. In considering who should be the speaker for the Mothers' Day event, her colleagues surely thought of her as the obvious choice, for she had already filled the same role when she represented the impoverished mothers on the 1934 delegation of the B.C. Joint Committee on Unemployment and when she led the parade of 2,000 women to the CCF Arena Rally two weeks earlier.

In Alberta and Saskatchewan during the On-to-Ottawa Trek, women's committees were also set up, the word "Mother," observes Joan Sangster, again being used "as an organizing catchword."

In Regina after the Riot, a Mothers' Committee, led by Communist women ... was formed to visit the imprisoned Trekkers and lobby for their release. Some 'mothers' on the Committee ... were actually single unemployed women, but the Committee's name was less a statement of personnel and more an attempt to appeal, on an emotional level, to homemakers who were concerned about the future of their children.[43]

If the Mothers' Council considered Sarah Colley's motherliness an asset, they would not have been cynical, merely astute. They were not without their own maternal feelings, for most of them were mothers too. The Committee, having arranged for the strikers to be invited to Sunday dinner in homes throughout the city after the Mothers' Day rally, found that so many women had sent out invitations that there weren't enough willing strikers to go around. Some women even further opened their homes to the men, giving them a place to sleep and making them part of the family for a time. The Mothers' Day Committee and the large group of women they organized were touched by the tragedy of so many wasted young lives and were resolved to help in a practical and human way which, because of the economic source of the tragedy, coincided with their political task as socialists.

Quite aside from the ambivalence surrounding Sarah Colley as "CCF Mother," some of the work the Mothers' Council would undertake could without any ambiguity be labelled "women's work," by the standards of that earlier generation, at least. They raised money for the Regina Defence of the On-to-Ottawa trekkers who had been jailed, provided socks and underwear and cash for blacklisted men, held bazaars, dinners and picnics. Ronald Liversedge recalls with some nostalgia the 1938 Mothers' Day picnic the Council arranged for the boys. More than 4,000 gathered at Lumberman's Arch in Stanley Park to partake of the ample provisions, join in the community singing, play softball, and listen to one

[43] Sangster, "Canadian Women." Subsequent references to Sunday dinner, etc.: Sheils and Swankey, p. 95; interview with Elspeth Gardner.

of the boys, newly released from prison, urge solidarity and singleness of purpose.[44]

However, a distinction must be made between espousing the ideology of maternal feminism and giving expression to human compassion, surely universal among both men and women, and appealing to that feeling in others. These women did not see themselves as being endowed with special feminine qualities that made them uniquely qualified to nurture the world. They were not descended from suffragist and social reformer Nellie McClung, who declared, "Women were intended to guide and sustain life, to care for the race; not feed on it."[45]

True, a dedication to socialism does not necessarily prevent one from accommodating, however illogically, this main tenet of maternal feminism. The idea of Woman as a civilizing influence, the ultimate saviour of the world at the brink of nuclear holocaust, informs the thinking of many thoughtful people today. Thus it would not be surprising if some such strand of maternal feminism did linger on among women of the thirties. Helena Gutteridge, Mary Norton and Susan Lane Clark had been suffragists during the first decades of the century when this view of women provided one of the rationales for women's enfranchisement. These three were socialists, as were Sarah Colley and Elizabeth Kerr. All believed, along with younger socialist women like Mildred Osterhout and Grace MacInnis, who had grown up with the vote, that the liberation of women could only be accomplished when the new co-operative commonwealth had replaced capitalist society. The profound intellectual involvement of these women in Marxism, a central topic in the CCF education program of the thirties, precluded their espousing the apotheosis of the female of the species. Mildred Osterhout is a case in point. In one of her radio talks, "Raising your Son to be a Socialist," she makes it quite clear that the educative responsibility of mothers is a function of their social role as parents, not of an innate special feminine quality: "Our hope for the future lies in those of us who are teachers and who have the care of young children, facing up to the task of influencing them in the formation of social attitudes and behavior responses." Helena Gutteridge thought of the undeveloped potential of housewives and of how they could contribute to the work of the world, a point of view compatible with Marxism:

[44] Liversedge, p. 69. He does not recall the Mothers' Council as sponsors of the picnic, but this is made clear in the *Federationist*, 12 May 1938, p. 1 and *People's Advocate*, 12 May 1938, p. 5.

[45] "Gentle Lady," in Nellie McClung, *In Times Like These*, with an introduction by Veronica Strong-Boag (Toronto: University of Toronto, 1972), p. 64.

No matter how busy they may be with their families and homes, women are part of the larger community. They owe it to themselves to develop their abilities and to work for a better, peaceful world.

Both would have agreed with Grace MacInnis:

The first thing that any man or any woman needs in the line of liberation is to be liberated from the idea that they're just a man or just a woman. It's nice to be a woman if you're a woman, and nice to be a man, if you're a man. But there's something much better than being just either, and that's being a full human being. And I don't think that as long as you're clinging either to your masculinity or your femininity that you're making progress toward becoming a full human being.[46]

In her analysis of the ideologies of socialist and communist women during the latter half of the 1930s, Joan Sangster adopts the phrase 'militant mothering' to describe a blend of maternal feminism and various kinds of socialism — Fabian, Marxist, Leninist, Christian. Of the women in the CCF, she says:

Like the earlier 'maternal feminists' socialist women often saw women's political interests as an extension of their domestic maternal concerns; yet, in contrast to the earlier suffragists, the political outlook of socialist women, with its emphasis on class issues and militant action is better characterized as 'militant mothering'.[47]

It seems clear that, if the CCF women's emphasis was on "class issues and militant action," they should not have an epithet applied to them that describes a subordinate element in their ideology, if indeed a practical interest in domestic issues can be termed maternal feminism. The term 'militant mothering' is also a misnomer as applied to communist women of this time. With the Comintern's inauguration of the Popular Front policy in 1935, Party women were urged to go into the community and participate in women's organizations, seeking common ground in traditional women's concerns such as child care, consumer issues, education, war and peace. This tactic for establishing a base for proselytizing Joan Sangster labels "maternalism," maintaining that in its endeavour to politicize housewives by appealing to their special interests, the Party came "dangerously close" to asserting that a woman's place was in the home. But she also astutely observes that "the Party's invocation of maternalism always had an opportunistic edge to it: women's organization was encouraged, not simply for its intrinsic value to women's emancipation, but

---

[46] Osterhout, 3 July 1933. Gutteridge: *Pacific Tribune*, 8 March 1957, p. 12. MacInnis: interview with Anne Scotton, 164:1, UBCL.

[47] Sangster, "Canadian Women," p. 190.

because women were seen as crucial ingredients to a successful Popular Front coalition." She says further that the communist women "quite justly distinguished themselves from a 'bourgeois' mentality which confined women to the home, ignored class issues, and avoided militant action." It should be added that this political distancing, in which a sense of superiority was implicit, allowed communist women to exploit motherhood for its emotional value while being quite genuine in their community work and walking with confidence the moral tightrope of the true believer. The struggle of opposites inherent in this situation is immediately obvious to any student of Marxist dialectics, and Joan Sangster does conclude that "the Popular Front was a time of contradiction for the CPC's work among women."[48] But it is clear from the evidence adduced in her essay that if CPC women in the later thirties did not advance the cause of women according to the best tenets of Marx and Lenin, it was from revolutionary zeal in carrying out popular front policy, not from a change in ideology. In the case of the Vancouver communist women, the WLL's rejection of "the bourgeois maudlin sentimentalism associated with Mothers' Day" makes their position clear. In sum, for the Vancouver Mothers' Day Committee/Mothers' Council, maternal feminism, to the extent that it was present, was only an occasional coloured strand in the ideological fabric.

*   *   *

The Committee followed up their Mothers' Day demonstration by pressuring the mayor and city council to take action. Within the week a delegation from the Committee went to city hall and demanded a hearing. Council refusing to listen to them, they collared Mayor McGeer in the hallway. He told them that the city was not empowered to grant relief to the single unemployed transients. A woman objected that "it was the law of God that men should be fed." The mayor replied that the law of God wouldn't work in city council. When the delegates reported this to the next meeting of the Mothers' Committee, they decided that the Reverend Andrew Roddan, in whose church the mayor was scheduled to speak, should hear of this. The minister was a champion of the unemployed and often went down among the hoboes in their "jungles" to get to know them. His church brought food to them, setting up a kind of daily soup kitchen. Incensed at his refusal to cancel the service, the women attended First United Church in a body, filling all the pews. When McGeer rose to speak, they walked out en masse. A few days later, led by Sarah Colley

48 *Ibid.*, pp. 282, 288, 319, 323.

and Peggy Harrison, they simply marched to city hall, right past the guard and up to the fifth floor, where they demanded to see the mayor. He was not in. They waited an hour before being shown out of city hall.

Still determined that the boys should not go hungry, the women returned to the Majestic Hall where a decision was made to interview [Police] Chief Foster and remain in the police station until assurance was given that every boy had something to eat and a place to sleep. After more than two hours the assurance was made and the women dispersed.[49]

Early in June the Mothers' Day Committee decided to continue as a group to support the relief camp strikers. The men had just set out on their trek to Ottawa, where they intended to place their demands before Prime Minister Bennett. They did not reach their destination. On 1 July in Regina's Market Square, police and unemployed confronted one another, and the bloody battle which followed brought to an uneasy conclusion the relief camp workers' strike.

By August the Mothers' Day Committee had changed its name to the "Vancouver Mothers' Council." Its recognition as a public presence with some authority is evident from the reception accorded the women by Liberal MLA Gordon Wismer when a delegation visited him in August. They convinced him there was no justification for blacklisting the men and appealed to his compassion. He, in turn, gave them a letter to carry back to Acting Mayor Tisdall, urging him to "make representations to the proper authorities."[50] The Mothers' Council also made representations to Vancouver City Council, in the case of Ethel Evans, wife of the leader of the On-to-Ottawa Trek. Arthur Evans had been arrested after the 1 July battle in Regina and charged with acting "as an Officer of an unlawful association, to wit, the Relief Camp Workers' Union...." On this account his wife and small daughter were being denied relief. The Mothers' Council intervened on their behalf and after a two-month dispute with the Relief Department and city council were successful.[51]

After the unemployment crisis of the summer of 1935 had subsided, interest in the Mothers' Council waned, the non-left element withdrew, and probably the CCF as well, leaving a core of communist women to carry on until the second major crisis — the Post Office sit-down strike in

[49] *B.C. Workers' News*, 23 May 1935, p. 2. Both the church and police station incidents are described by Lil Stoneman, WLHC. See also *B.C. Workers' News*, 17 May 1935, p. 2: *Commonwealth*, 23 May 1935, p. 1.

[50] Decided to continue: *B.C. Workers' News*, 7 June 1935, p. 2. Changed its name, Wismer: *Commonwealth*, 23 August 1935, p. 1.

[51] Charged: Sheils and Swankey, p. 197. Obtained relief: *Commonwealth*, 15 November 1935, p. 8.

May 1938. It is not known why CCF women withdrew.[52] It seems likely
they had other priorities in the CCF. Certainly leading CCF women —
Mildred Osterhout, Helena Gutteridge, Elizabeth Kerr, Susan Lane Clark
— were at this time running for public office and/or emerging as committee and executive members in the CCF. During these three years, the
Mothers' Council was less a pressure group than a service and educational
organization. At first its declared concern was with "interesting women
in their own problems and those of the victims of the present system."
The Council invited speakers to address them on the subject of birth
control, unemployment and other contemporary issues, while continuing
to provide material support for the blacklisted men in the form of socks,
underwear and other clothing. Members also raised money for the
defence of the jailed Trekkers. In 1936, when, with a membership of
seventy-five, they applied for affiliation with the Local Council of
Women, their restated purpose was "to advance the economic, social and
cultural interests of the common people." As an affiliate, it was able to
work within the parent organization in support of the unemployed. The
Local Council of Women by this time had its own Unemployment Relief
Committee, on which Susan Clark was the socialist voice.[53]

The Mothers' Council did not, however, altogether abandon their
strategy of needling the community conscience through direct action. One
October Sunday morning in 1936, a parade of seventy unemployed men
led by thirty women could be seen filing into St. Andrew's Wesley United
Church. The Mothers' Council was confronting the church community
with the problem of the single unemployed. In the afternoon the men
attended the service at Four-Square Gospel Tabernacle on their own and
shared in its Harvest Festival, but in the evening the women were on duty
again, this time to lead 150 men into Christ Church Cathedral, where
they were welcomed by the Very Reverend Ramsay Armitage. On another occasion thirty city waitresses were thrown out of work by a city
bylaw that forbade white girls to work in Chinese restaurants. A Mothers'
Council committee accompanied the waitresses to city hall to demand
that the question be reopened. Thus the Mothers' Council maintained a

[52] This withdrawal is suggested by the establishment by CCF women in 1938 of a
new umbrella organization, the Women's Emergency Committee to Aid the Single
Unemployed.

[53] Declared concern: *Commonwealth*, 22 November 1935, p. 2. Speakers: *Commonwealth*, 26 November 1935, p. 2; *B.C. Workers' News*, 28 February 1936, p. 3;
27 August 1935, p. 2. Material support: *ibid.*, 6 December 1935, p. 2; 11 February
1935, p. 3; 21 February 1936, p. 3; 6 March 1936, p. 3. Affiliation: Vancouver
Local Council of Women Papers (VLCW), Minutes, 4 May 1936 and 14 September 1936, 4.16, UBCL.

working organization that would be ready to mobilize for action during the Post Office sit-down strike in the spring of 1938.[54]

In 1937 unemployment was down considerably from what it had been in 1936 or, indeed, any year since 1929. Although in 1938 the upward swing in the economy was not sustained (in British Columbia there was an increase of 7,000 in the number on relief), conditions were better than they had been for some years.[55] Nevertheless, the summer of 1938 was to bring a showdown in Vancouver between government and the unemployed — the Post Office sit-down strike.

A work scheme operated by the city in co-operation with the province was halted in the early spring after the province refused to continue to pay its share of the costs, thus virtually abandoning the single unemployed to the care of the city. When the provincial government also shut down its work project camps on 1 May, and the logging camps closed for an extended period because of an exceptionally dry summer, the time became ripe for a confrontation.[56] On 20 May the unemployed marched again in Vancouver, this time occupying three buildings: the Hotel Georgia, the Art Gallery and the Post Office. Mayor Miller said the sit-down strike was not a civic responsibility and left to spend the weekend with his family on Bowen Island.

The men bivouacked in the Post Office and the Art Gallery for a month (the group occupying the Hotel Georgia evacuated the building earlier when promised $500 for food). The success of this desperate strategy depended, of course, on their having access to a regular food supply. In this, the Mothers' Council played a crucial role, for clearly if the men had not been provided with food, they could not have held out. As in the 1935 strike, the traditional nurturing role assumed by the women was charged with political content. And, as before, they also took direct action. "You hold the fort and we'll see that you are fed," the Mothers' Council promised. They were as good as their word. The day after the men entered the buildings the women were preparing food in

54 Church parades: *B.C. Workers' News*, 23 October 1936, p. 3. Waitresses: *People's Advocate*, 1 October 1937, p. 1.

55 A DBS survey showed that "based on the 1926 average as 100, the 1938 index averaged 111.8 as compared with 114.1 in 1937 and 103.7 in 1936." *CAR*, 1937 and 1938, p. 394. See also pp. 395 and 509.

56 City work scheme: *Federationist*, 17 March 1938, p. 1. George S. Pearson, B.C. Minister of Labour, gave a summary of government policy and its application to provincial work camps in a radio address reported in the *Vancouver Sun*, 27 June 1938, p. 22.

the kitchen of the Disabled Veterans' Hall on Homer Street and having it delivered by truck to the men.[57]

But now the CCF women, seeing the need to reconstitute an organization like the original Mothers' Day Committee in order to draw on the resources of the whole community during this crisis, formed the Vancouver Women's Emergency Committee to Aid the Single Unemployed. In this they had the co-operation of the Mothers' Council, which for the duration of the strike worked under the new umbrella organization. The CCF women, some of whom were in public office, knew that it would be politically inappropriate and ineffectual for them to approach the Mothers' Council and ask to be re-admitted. The communist women doubtless recognized that, despite their own worthy work for the unemployed, the CCF women had more public credibility than they. Although the Council was now part of a larger group, it provided a good deal of impetus for the new enterprise. Indeed, the women's part in the Post Office sit-down strike is remembered under the rubric of the Mothers' Council, even by CCF women who participated. The Council had, after all, established a public presence in the crisis of 1935 and remained on the scene, however reduced in numbers and influence, to take visible direct action on behalf of the unemployed over the longer period, 1935 to 1938.[58]

With Betty Kerr as chairperson and Effie Jones secretary, the new Committee, composed for all practical purposes of the CCF Women's Central Group and the Mothers' Council, appealed to women throughout Vancouver to come to the aid of the strikers. Volunteers from the Liberal Women's Association, the Imperial Order of the Daughters of the Empire, the Society for the Prevention of Cruelty to Animals and a number of church groups responded and subsequently assembled with the left-wing women and labour union people at the Ukrainian Labour Temple to be part of the work crew preparing food. Largely anonymous helpers, these volunteers were probably also assigned to canvassing business for donations of food. It is not likely that people from non-left organizations, nor even from the Relief Project Workers' Union, were on the executive of the Emergency Committee. The men certainly counted on the women for help and kept them in touch with developments. The Women's Emergency Committee met daily in an office next door to CCF headquarters to plan ways of mobilizing more support for the men, both

[57] *People's Advocate*, 27 May 1938, p. 1.
[58] WEC: *ibid.*, p. 6. Impetus: Effie Jones, WLHC; Mildred Liversedge, 15 September 1985; interview with Hilda Kristiansen, 3 April 1983.

practical and political. The Relief Project Workers' Union sent its men out to gather donations of food, but the women conducted their own campaign as well, visiting Vancouver storekeepers and cafe owners with soliciting sheets. The food thus gathered was delivered to their new headquarters, the Ukrainian Labour Temple on East Pender Street, where forty or fifty women at a time were on duty preparing salads and sandwiches and other simple meals. The men then delivered the food by truck to the Post Office.[59]

Two weeks later, when the mayor announced in council that the policy of the authorities was to wait out the strike, Helena Gutteridge underlined the political importance of the women's work with this rejoinder: "If you think you are going to starve them [the sit-downers] out, you are mistaken, because the women intend to see that these boys are fed." The strikers too recognized just how vital were the efforts of the women to the success of Operation Sit-Down: at their sports day and concert in the Post Office lobby, they singled out the head of the Mothers' Council, Mrs. Mildred Lusk, from among the guests and presented her with a bouquet of flowers.[60]

After the strike had been in progress for nearly two weeks, it became necessary to decide just how long to continue supporting the strikers. The Women's Emergency Committee called a special meeting of women in St. Andrew's Wesley Church. With Laura Jamieson, former Burnaby juvenile court judge, in the chair, the 150 women heard Dorothy Steeves, CCF MLA, declare that "the authorities expected the people of Vancouver to get tired feeding the men, but that the people must not get tired till the matter had been settled." She urged "a short range policy of assistance for the men, and a long range one of pressure on governments for a works program, immediately." The meeting decided to keep up a steady supply of food for the men and appointed a contact committee to involve more women in canvassing work. The meeting also passed a resolution, moved by Helena Gutteridge, asking that a federal works scheme be inaugurated without delay and that the men participating in it be paid at union rates. Mayor Miller, as special guest, also spoke. Completely out of touch with the prevailing sympathy for the strikers throughout the city, he observed that the men had lost public support by

[59] Secretary: Mrs. E. Jones to Chief Constable Foster, 17 June 1938, VCPD, File 28, Loc. 75 (F) 2, VCA. Volunteers: *Federationist*, 9 June 1938, p. 5. Food: *Vancouver Sun*, 21 May 1938, p. 1; 25 May 1938, p. 1; 28 May 1938, p. 3. The Relief Project Workers' Union replaced the Relief Camp Workers' Union.

[60] Gutteridge: *People's Advocate*, 3 June 1938, p. 6. Lusk: *Post Office Sitdowners' Gazette*, vol. 1, no. 2, E. E. Winch Personal Papers, 55a.25, AMMC.

their action in taking over a public building and declaring that "they could set [sic] there for all summer as far as he was concerned." Cries of "No, No!" and "Sit down!" interrupted him, and the chair had to ask for order before he could continue.[61]

With the new impetus from this meeting, the Women's Emergency Committee sponsored a mass meeting at Powell Street grounds where 5,000 people gathered on 12 June to hear Harold Winch, Dr. Lyle Telford, Mildred Osterhout and Laura Jamieson urge them to support the single unemployed in their effort to obtain work and wages. Mildred Lusk, president of the Mothers' Council, chaired the meeting.[62]

Mayor Miller saw the sit-down strike as a communist strategy for fomenting unrest and accused the Mothers' Council of being led by communists. The women wrote to city council, refuting the charge and deploring the easy resort to the red smear to discredit any and all persons or groups seeking to help the unemployed.[63] Certainly local communists were to be found leading many groups, especially since a united front was by then the declared policy of the CPC. Implementation of that policy meant that party members, "the vanguard," considering themselves more politically advanced than other people, sought membership in a wide range of political and non-political organizations and worked with other communists as the "party fraction" in any given group. They even joined the CCF to try to influence it — "infiltrated," in other words. To this Sarah Colley took strong objection:

They [the communists] are a hindrance to our progress and should be dealt with accordingly. Why doesn't the Communist party mind their business and leave the CCF alone, as the CCF is decidedly the people's front, having proven so in the past. We have nothing to fear if we stick by the policy of the CCF.[64]

Nevertheless, as vice-president of the CCF Women's Central Group, Sarah Colley would have been working with Betty Kerr in the Women's Emergency Committee and the Mothers' Council, and, for all her opposition to the united front, would also have been working alongside communist women.

On the other hand, the Women's Labour League had been dwindling in membership for several years. At their 1935 convention they disaffili-

61 *Federationist*, 2 June 1938, p. 1; *People's Advocate*, 3 June 1938, pp. 1 and 6.

62 *Vancouver Sun*, 13 June 1938, p. 9.

63 Miller: *Vancouver Sun*, 6 July 1938, p. 3. Deploring: *Federationist*, 14 July 1938, p. 2.

64 *Federationist*, 5 April 1937, p. 6. On party fractions see Avakumovic, p. 34.

ated with the Workers' Unity League, then disbanding, to seek a broader sphere of action. The following year they applied to affiliate with the Vancouver Local Council of Women, and after some delay were accepted.[65] In joining the VLCW, a "bourgeois" organization, they were implementing the new popular front policy officially adopted by the Seventh Congress of the Communist International in July and August 1935. Lil Stoneman, secretary of the Vancouver Women's Labour League, recalls how their popular front policy evolved:

Becky Buhay [a Communist Party organizer] came from Toronto.... We had meetings and we decided they [the Women's Labour League] weren't getting any bigger. And it did broaden out. And in fact we were accepted in the Local Council of Women, to our big surprise. And I think it was Mrs. Stewart who went on to the platform. There was to be a National Council [of Women] meeting here and we [herself and another woman] were invited to the evening and the government officials came. Professor Weir came, whom I'd known in Saskatchewan years before. He was the Minister of Education here. He gave me a big kiss.[66]

For Lil Stoneman, secretary of the Women's Labour League, that kiss was the accolade. She and her friends were now members in good standing in a "broad" organization. Here was the popular front in action.

With the CCF, however, the CPC from 1935 on sought a united front; that is, an alliance with a workers' social reform party, for that is how they characterized the CCF, in contrast to their own perception of themselves as the revolutionary party of Marxism. The British Columbia CCF in convention in July 1937 decided to reject the overtures of the Communist Party to form an alliance on the grounds that the CCF itself was the united front of the farmer-labour-socialist movement. But the hard truth was that, similar though their programs were in many respects, the two parties were rivals for the support of the working class. Indeed, according to one CCF historian, "the aim of the Communists was not co-operation with the CCF for the achievement of socialism, but the absorption of the CCF by the Communist Party."[67]

[65] Dwindling: Lil Stoneman, WLHC and Mildred Liversedge. According to Tom McEwen, Annie Stewart and a few other women wanted to keep the League going (interview by Sue Lockhart, September 1975). Disaffiliated: *B.C. Workers' News*, 29 November 1935, p. 3. WUL disbanding: Paul A. Phillips, *No Power Greater: A Century of Labour in British Columbia* (Vancouver: B.C. Federation of Labour and Boag Foundation, 1967), pp. 110-12. VLCW: Minutes, 4 May 1936, 2 November 1936, 4 October 1937, 4.16.

[66] WLHC interview.

[67] *Federationist*, 28 January 1937, p. 7. Young, p. 263. For the convention decision see the *Federationist* editorial, 8 July 1937, p. 4, cited by Dorothy Steeves, *The*

Vancouver CCF women acted in violation of their party's policy during the Post Office sit-down strike when they formed their own united front with CPC women. There was ample precedent for shared discussion and even common action in the Western Women's Conferences (1924-32) where women from various labour parties were able to meet, until 1929, with communist women and to consult and sometimes act together on behalf of working-class women. In Toronto in 1936, the Women's Joint Committee was an explicitly united front organization of CCF and communist women. In Vancouver CCF women leaders were far from hostile to the Communist Party. Betty Kerr had even, the year before while on a visit to the Soviet Union, sent a message to "all progressive parties in British Columbia" urging them to "weld themselves together in the face of the coming provincial election." The CCF women were well aware of the delicate political balance that had to be achieved in a partnership with CPC women. Even though Annie Stewart, Effie Jones and Elsie Munro scarcely fitted the stereotype of Communist Party manipulators employing devious stratagems for their own political ends, for CCF women the protection of their autonomy was a central concern in the formation of the Women's Emergency Committee and in the central role assigned to themselves at their mass meeting in St. Andrew's Wesley Church. Rather than allowing themselves to be manipulated, Betty Kerr, Helena Gutteridge, Sarah Colley and other CCF women were doing the pragmatic thing demanded of them by the situation, for a split among left-wing women would feed no strikers. By working with CPC women, who also were genuinely interested in the welfare of the unemployed, they were achieving that "unity of purpose expressive of ideals higher than that of personalities or factions" which was the declared aim of the CCF Women's Central Group.[68]

*   *   *

On the morning of 19 June 1938 the single unemployed were forcibly evicted from the Post Office by tear gas and truncheons. Members of the Women's Emergency Committee were immediately summoned for help. "We tore up sheets to make bandages and set up a first-aid station in the Ukrainian Labour Temple," recalls Mildred Liversedge. "We got all the

---

Compassionate Rebel: Ernest Winch and the Growth of Socialism in Western Canada (Vancouver: J. J. Douglas Ltd., 1977), p. 116. For the decision of the CCF provincial executive, see Minutes, 16 January 1937, 46.1, AMMC.

[68] WWC: Sangster, "Canadian Women," p. 167. WJC: Manley, pp. 100-18. Kerr: *People's Advocate*, 21 May 1937, p. 3. Unity of purpose: 11 February 1937, p. 6.

men to lie outside on the lawn. They were vomiting; it took all day for them to recover."[69]

In the following days the Women's Emergency Committee also took it upon themselves to be among the mediators between the strikers and the provincial government. At midnight on Eviction Day a delegation of one hundred men, the first of several contingents, marched onto the midnight boat, en route to Victoria to put their case to the Premier. A cheering crowd of six or seven thousand gathered at Pier D to see them off, lustily singing "Hold the Fort."

Cheers were given frequently. There were cheers for Steve Brodie, the post office leader who went to hospital, cheers for the Mothers' Council and the Women's Emergency Committee. There were cheers for the Communist Party, but rather weak.

Biggest cheer of all went to Harold Winch, M.L.A., who appeared on the ramp to deliver a parting speech.[70]

After the boat sailed, the crowd surged up the street to the Post Office and threatened a disturbance. Once again Harold Winch found the words to subdue them, and again violence was averted. But the word went out to the rest of Vancouver and British Columbia that the city had suffered great property losses, was in the control of the mob or was terrorized by the police. Little wonder that Victoria awaited in trepidation the arrival of contingents of relief camp workers.[71]

[69] Summoned: Mildred Liversedge; Effie Jones, WLHC. Mildred Liversedge says she was one of the women gassed during the Vancouver longshoremen's strike in 1935. The incident is described in *"Man Along the Shore!" — the Story of the Vancouver Waterfront*, consultant and writer, Ben Swankey (Vancouver: ILWU Local 500 Pensioners, n.d.), p. 84: "The Longshoremen's Women's Auxiliary established a first-aid post in the Longshoremen's Hall to treat the injured. Police smashed the windows and hurled tear gas bombs inside."

[70] *Vancouver Sun*, 20 June 1938, p. 5.

[71] Control of mob, trepidation: *Vancouver Sun*, 21 June 1938, p. 1. The following two paragraphs are also based on this *Sun* report, which is an example of how the serious political actions of women can be so frivolously treated as to radically diminish those actions and make the women invisible to history. The reporter assigned to accompany the women dealt with the purpose of the delegation in one sentence. For the rest of his report he exploited the perceived anomaly inherent in a group of married women engaged in a democratic political activity as earnest as seeking to speak with the elected head of their government. They were "staid." They were disarming. They were so disarming they wrapped a CPR policeman around their collective little finger: he sent stewards for pillows and blankets (for the women could not afford staterooms), and before he knew what he was doing he was arranging the pillows for them on the floor of the foyer where they could stretch out comfortably. They even managed to "wangle" a cup of tea before disembarking. Ten mothers asleep on the foyer floor of the *Princess Joan* does present a comical image, as would ten fathers, ten seagulls, ten of any creature

The Women's Emergency Committee sent ten women to Victoria on the next midnight boat to see the Premier and demand work and wages and immediate relief for the single unemployed. It is clear that it was still functioning as an umbrella group in which the Mothers' Council, sending four of the ten delegates, was predominant. For the Women's Emergency Committee, Hilda Kristiansen of the CCF balanced Ethel Evans. Betty Kerr from the CCF Women's Central Group was one of the co-ordinators of the enterprise with Mothers' Council president, Mildred Lusk. Other delegates represented the Ukrainian Farmer-Labour Association, the Women's Auxiliary of the Pacific Coast Fishermen's Union, and the Women's Labour League. Sarah Colley, whose opposition to the Communist Party has been noted, was not part of the delegation. The fact that Maurice Rush,[72] secretary of the Young Communist League, accompanied the women suggests that since 1935 the Mothers' Council had moved further to the left.

"TEN VANCOUVER MOTHERS JOIN VICTORIA TREK," announced the *Vancouver Sun* over a two-column front-page story. The contingent of one hundred men who had gone to Victoria the night before met them when they disembarked. The women fell into their accustomed place, leading the procession of men up Belleville and Government Streets, the whole company singing "Hold the Fort." Premier Pattullo refused to see the women, but, significantly, chose to account for his refusal: "The mothers' council, I understand, applied for a meeting with me but I had them informed to submit their suggestions in writing. I am not granting interviews to every organization that come[s] along."

In the end Pattullo did see them, although not until the next day. Always enterprising, always persistent, the women appealed to the Victoria Ministerial Association, one of whose members agreed to intercede with the Premier on their behalf. In the meantime, the women addressed a meeting of three hundred in Victoria's Central Park. Then they sailed home, leaving Betty Kerr and Mildred Lusk to carry on. These two, supported by seven members of the newly-formed Victoria Women's Emergency Committee and two men, the Reverend Bryce Wallace and CCF MLA Sam Guthrie, met the Premier and Minister of Labour George Pearson the next afternoon. The Premier was adamant: he would not

---

lined up in a row. But to the *Vancouver Sun* reporter the mothers were comic because women didn't customarily take political responsibility, much less behave in so unconventional a manner.

[72] Now Provincial Secretary of the British Columbia Communist Party.

change his policy and demonstrations would serve no purpose. The women threw the ball into his court by asking what the men would do if the women stopped providing them with food. But the Premier was willing to deal with them only on the most superficial level and countered by asking in turn "why they should stop such worthy work." "We didn't gain anything," reported Betty Kerr after the meeting, "but we told the Premier and Mr. Pearson a few things they didn't know."[73]

Returning to Vancouver, the Women's Emergency Committee continued to make their presence felt. In the 1935 relief camp workers' strike, the Mothers' Council had sent delegations to see the mayor. Since then, Helena Gutteridge had been elected to city council. With their own socialist representative on the inside, the Women's Emergency Committee found a new way to challenge the mayor and his Non-Partisan Association aldermen. The Committee had written to city council condemning alleged police brutality in the eviction of the sit-downers. Helena Gutteridge would have known when the city clerk was to read the letter; thus it was no accident that thirty women from the Committee were in the gallery that afternoon. The ensuing encounter was reported as follows:

Ald. Gutteridge demanded an investigation.

Ald. H. L. Corey stated the matters were under investigation.

Said Ald. Fred Crone: 'People looking for publicity. . . . '

'Making a hullabaloo about nothing,' interrupted Mayor G. C. Miller.

'Boo!' cried a loud contralto from the gallery of the council chamber. The gallery was jammed with women.

. . . Sergeant-at-Arms Alex. McKay galloped upstairs and stood, looking perplexedly at the rows of women.

'I'll clear the chamber if you can't behave as [sic] ladies,' the Mayor said, as boos and jeers were heard. 'You can boo me at your meetings, but can't here.'

'I've given you the facts privately, now I'll do it publicly,' Ald. de Graves told Ald. Guttridge [sic]. He praised the police for moderation at the Post Office, Art Gallery, Police Station and CPR dock on Eviction Sunday.

'The police were called filthy names. I never saw anything like their forbearance,' he said.

'If they hadn't beaten the men in the post office, nothing would have hap-

---

[73] *Daily Colonist*, 22 June 1938, p. 16. Worthy work: *Federationist*, 30 June 1938, p. 5. Didn't gain: *Vancouver Sun*, 22 June 1938, p. 16.

pened,' declared Ald. Guttridge [*sic*]. 'I want to know if they were instructed to do it. . . . '

The women left the gallery.[74]

Whether or not one approves of such strategies or considers them effective, it must be acknowledged that they are characteristic, not of the traditional women's auxiliary, but of a political direct action group.

Pattullo eventually had to make concessions, providing temporary relief to single, able-bodied men, whether domiciled in British Columbia or not, and assigning non-transients to temporary work projects. In the fall the men continued to roam the province looking for work, continued to confront governments with their demands for work and wages. The Women's Emergency Committee, having served its purpose, presumably ceased functioning; at any rate, by the end of the summer of 1938 nothing more is heard of it in the press. The Mothers' Council was left to carry on as the women's advocate for the unemployed during the fall of 1938. As before, the Council also continued to come to the aid of impoverished families. Gradually, over the next year, the Council petered out. It seems likely that some of its energies were transferred to the Vancouver Housewives' League in which Effie Jones was then much involved and Annie Stewart, a charter member.[75] With unemployment no longer a problem, the Mothers' Council may have been replaced by the Housewives' League as a popular front organization alert to the new problems of wartime Canada.[76]

[74] *Vancouver Sun*, 28 June 1938, p. 9. The mayor's second remark is interpolated from the Vancouver *Daily Province*, 28 June 1938, p. 8.

[75] Concessions: *Vancouver Sun*, 8 July 1938, p. 1; 9 July 1938, p. 1; *Federationist*, 14 July 1938, p. 1. Council carries on: *People's Advocate*, 19 August 1938, p. 6; *Commonwealth*, 27 October 1938, p. 1. Stewart: *Pacific Tribune*, 23 February 1951, p. 2.

[76] Effie Jones made the Housewives' League known across Canada, even in high places. In the winter of 1940-41, price controls had been imposed by the Canadian government on certain commodities, including some foods. According to a first-hand account, the chairman of the Combines Investigation Board, which worked with the Wartime Prices and Trade Board, addressed a class in economics at Queen's University. A student asked him why the government didn't leave food prices to the free market to encourage farmers to produce as much as possible for the war effort. The answer came without hesitation: "Should we do that, within the hour there would be a telegram from Mrs. Effie Jones of the Vancouver Housewives' League." Interview with Emil Bjarnason, 5 September 1985. According to Sara Diamond (p. 295), Women's Auxiliaries of the International Woodworkers of America in British Columbia "united with consumer groups to lobby Ottawa for price controls, milk subsidies, rent controls, low-cost housing, farm subsidies and a peacetime price regulation agency."

The Mothers' Council had done their best. They had exploited the received idea of motherhood and embraced a new one with such genuine conviction that thousands rallied with them around the struggles of the unemployed. They had been sensitive to the political dynamics of the time, in their protean way changing shape and structure in order to pursue their own united front policy and draw in as many non-left sympathizers as possible. They had accepted the work of feeding the strikers, understanding that the political dimensions of that work demanded it be performed with energy and imagination. They had paraded and demonstrated, addressed mass meetings and confronted the authorities to make them listen, and when these measures failed, adopted militant tactics. But despite their efforts and those of every other concerned citizen group and of every government, no solution was found until the following year when Canada went to war. Then there was work for everyone, no matter where they were domiciled, though many were killed doing it.

"A Palace for the Public": Housing Reform and the 1946 Occupation of the Old Hotel Vancouver*

JILL WADE

On 26 January 1946 thirty veterans led by a Canadian Legion sergeant-at-arms occupied the old Hotel Vancouver to protest against the acute housing problem in Vancouver. The incident climaxed two years of popular agitation over the city's increasingly serious accommodation shortages. In the end, this lengthy, militant campaign achieved some concrete housing reforms for Vancouver's tenants. The struggle and its results provide an excellent case study by which to examine the interaction between protest and housing reform in mid-twentieth century urban Canada.

In the past, historians of Canadian housing have not concerned themselves with the interrelations of protest and reform. Rather, some have concentrated upon specific instances of improvements in housing: the activities of the Toronto Housing Company and the Toronto Public Housing Commission between 1900 and 1923; the distinctive urban landscape of homes and gardens in pre-1929 Vancouver; the establishment of the St. John's Housing Corporation in the forties; the reconstruction of Richmond following the 1917 Halifax explosion; and the array of federal programs undertaken between 1935 and 1971.[1] Other historians have

* I would like to thank Douglas Cruikshank, Robin Fisher, Logan Hovis and Allen Seager for their helpful comments during this paper's preparation.

[1] Shirley Campbell Spragge, "The Provision of Workingmen's Housing: Attempts in Toronto, 1904-1920" (M.A. thesis, Queen's University, 1974); *idem*, "A Confluence of Interests: Housing Reform in Toronto, 1900-1920," in *The Usable Urban Past: Planning and Politics in the Modern Canadian City*, eds. Alan F. J. Artibise and Gilbert A. Stelter, Carleton Library, no. 119 (Toronto: Macmillan of Canada in Association with the Institute of Canadian Studies, Carleton University, 1979), pp. 247-67; Lorna F. Hurl, "The Toronto Housing Company, 1912-1923: The Pitfalls of Painless Philanthropy," *Canadian Historical Review* 65 (March 1984): 28-53; Deryck William Holdsworth, "House and Home in Vancouver: The Emergence of a West Coast Urban Landscape, 1886-1929" (Ph.D. dissertation, University of British Columbia, 1981); *idem*, "House and Home in Vancouver: Images of West Coast Urbanism, 1886-1929," in *The Canadian City*, eds. Gilbert A. Stelter and Alan F. J. Artibise, Carleton Library, no. 109 (Toronto: Macmillan of Canada in Association with the Institute of Canadian Studies, Carleton University, 1979), pp. 186-211; Jane Lewis and Mark Shrimpton, "Policy-Making in New-

288

BC STUDIES, nos. 69-70, Spring-Summer 1986

emphasized more negative aspects of housing reform and living conditions: the inequalities of capitalist society that assign the least satisfactory accommodation to low-income people; the control of the reform process by an interconnected state and business community; and the residual role of the federal government in residential construction.[2] Still others have explored the relationship of class structure to home ownership and tenancy.[3] But, despite recent British and American attempts to link working class agitation and state intervention in housing, Canadian historians have not investigated the impact of popular protest upon the implementation of federal housing programs.[4]

foundland during the 1940s: The Case of the St. John's Housing Corporation," *Canadian Historical Review* 65 (June 1984): 209-39; John Weaver, "Reconstruction of the Richmond District in Halifax: A Canadian Episode in Public Housing and Town Planning, 1918-1921," *Plan Canada* 16 (March 1976): 36-47; and David G. Bettison, *The Politics of Canadian Urban Development*, vol. 1 (Edmonton: University of Alberta Press for the Human Resources Research Council of Alberta, 1975).

[2] Allan Moscovitch, "Housing: Who Pays? Who Profits?" in *Inequality: Essays on the Political Economy of Social Welfare*, eds. Allan Moscovitch and Glenn Drover (Toronto: University of Toronto Press, 1981), pp. 314-47; Alvin Finkel, "The Construction Industry," in *Business and Social Reform in the Thirties* (Toronto: James Lorimer, 1979), pp. 100-16; Terry Copp, "Housing Conditions," in *The Anatomy of Poverty: The Condition of the Working Class in Montreal, 1897-1929* (Toronto: McClelland & Stewart, 1974), pp. 70-87; Michael J. Piva, "Public Health and Housing," in *The Condition of the Working Class in Toronto, 1900-1921*, Cahiers d'Histoire de l'Université d'Ottawa, no. 9 (Ottawa: University of Ottawa Press, 1979), pp. 125-42; Marc H. Choko, *Crises du logement à Montréal (1860-1939)* (Montréal: Editions coopératives Albert Saint-Martin, 1980); John T. Saywell, "The Search for a Solution, 1914-1974," in *Housing Canadians: Essays on the History of Residential Construction in Canada*, ed. John T. Saywell, Discussion Paper, no. 24 (Ottawa: Economic Council of Canada, 1975), pp. 150-216; Albert Rose, *Canadian Housing Policies (1935-1980)* Toronto: Butterworths, 1980); and John C. Bacher, "The Origins of a Non-Policy: The Development of the Assumption of a Housing Responsibility by the Canadian Federal Government" (M.A. thesis, McMaster University, 1980).

[3] Michael J. Doucet, "Working Class Housing in a Small Nineteenth Century Canadian City: Hamilton, Ontario, 1852-1881," in *Essays in Canadian Working Class History*, eds. Gregory S. Kealey and Peter Warrian (Toronto: McClelland & Stewart, 1976), pp. 83-105; R. Harris, G. Levine and B. S. Osborne, "Housing Tenure and Social Classes in Kingston, Ontario, 1881-1901," *Journal of Historical Geography* 7 (July 1981): 271-89; A. Gordon Darroch, "Occupational Structure, Assessed Wealth and Homeowning during Toronto's Early Industrialization, 1861-1899," *Histoire sociale/Social History* 16 (November 1983): 381-410; Michael B. Katz, Michael J. Doucet and Mark J. Stern, "Property: Use Value and Exchange Value," in *The Social Organization of Early Industrial Capitalism* (Cambridge, Mass.: Harvard University Press, 1982), pp. 131-57.

[4] Seán Damer, "State, Class, and Housing: Glasgow, 1885-1919," in *Housing, Social Policy, and the State*, ed. Joseph Melling (London: Croom Helm, 1980), pp. 73-112; Joseph Melling, "Clydeside Housing and the Evolution of State Rent Control, 1900-1939," in *Housing, Social Policy, and the State*, pp. 139-67; Manuel Castells,

This case study, which examines the background, the actors, the ferment and the reforms associated with Vancouver's mid-forties shelter problem, asserts that on occasion protest has succeeded in bringing about measures to improve the accommodation of the Canadian people. As well, the study raises and answers a number of questions about the interaction between protest and housing reform. Were the changes substantial and lasting, or remedial and temporary? Did all protest groups share a commitment to fundamental reform? How responsive were governments to popular demands? And, finally, did the housing protests represent a struggle between the working class and the state and capital?

Vancouver's wartime and post-war housing question was a local manifestation of a larger problem affecting much of urban Canada. By 1940, supply shortages, insufficient replacement of substandard housing and overcrowding associated with the depression had created an enormous unsatisfied need for accommodation across the country. These difficulties exacerbated pre-depression urban blight in the older cities. Wartime conditions heightened the problem: the migration of workers and their families to industrial areas; the federal government controls on materials and manpower; the demobilization of 620,000 armed forces personnel between June 1945 and June 1946; and the arrival of some 43,000 war brides.[5] In 1944 an Advisory Committee on Reconstruction report on housing and planning (the Curtis report) calculated that the actual accumulated urban housing demand in 1944-45 would amount to

"The Industrial City and the Working Class: The Glasgow Rent Strike of 1915," in *The City and the Grassroots: A Cross-Cultural Theory of Urban Social Movements* (Berkeley and Los Angeles: University of California Press, 1983), pp. 27-37. In Canada, Marc H. Choko has written "Le Mouvement des squatters à Montréal, 1946-1947," *Cahiers d'Histoire* 2 (Printemps 1982): 27-39. Unfortunately, Choko has not conclusively demonstrated a connection between the squatters' movement and the introduction of federal programs. For the squatters' movement, see also Merrily Weisbord, *The Strangest Dream: Canadian Communists, the Spy Trials, and the Cold War* (Toronto: Lester & Orpen Dennys, 1983), pp. 179-80.

5 Canada, Department of Reconstruction and Supply, *Manpower and Material Requirements for a Housing Program in Canada*, by O. J. Firestone (Ottawa: King's Printer, 1946), p. 15; and O. J. Firestone, *Residential Real Estate in Canada* (Toronto: University of Toronto Press, 1951), p. 437. For a summary of the 1940s housing problem in Canada and of federal government reaction, see Catherine Jill Wade, "Wartime Housing Limited, 1941-1947: Canadian Housing Policy at the Crossroads" (M.A. thesis, University of British Columbia, 1984); and idem, *Wartime Housing Limited, 1941-1947: An Overview and Evaluation of Canada's First National Housing Corporation*, U.B.C. Planning Papers, Canadian Planning Issues, no. 13 (Vancouver: School of Community and Regional Planning, University of British Columbia, 1984).

500,000 dwelling units and maintained that low-income tenants experienced the greatest need.[6]

The federal government reacted to the wartime problem with unprecedented direct intervention in the housing field. In 1941 it created a crown company, Wartime Housing Limited (WHL), to build war workers' housing. The Wartime Prices and Trade Board (WPTB) instituted rent controls and housing registries in heavily congested urban centres. The Board and other agencies also regulated prices, materials, labour, and permits in the construction industry. The National Housing Administration of the Department of Finance introduced a Home Conversion Plan to renovate and to sublet rental accommodation. After 1944 WHL and the Veterans Land Act Administration (VLA) constructed veterans' rental housing. The WPTB set up an Emergency Shelter Administration that mainly converted vacant buildings into temporary accommodation.

As well, Ottawa first reduced and then reasserted its market-oriented, indirectly interventionist pre-war programs. In order to conserve the materials and manpower supply, the government initially curtailed its mortgage-financing function under the 1938 National Housing Act (NHA) and eliminated the 1936 Home Improvement Plan (HIP). But, in 1944, a new NHA once again increased opportunities for home ownership and provided financial aid to limited dividend companies for medium-cost rental housing construction. An Interdepartmental Housing Committee attempted to co-ordinate the various federal activities until, following its establishment in 1946, Central Mortgage and Housing Corporation (CMHC) gradually consolidated under its control all the direct and indirect programs excepting VLA operations.

In Vancouver, the mid-forties housing situation developed more from wartime than from pre-war conditions. The city experienced a less acute problem during the depression than other Canadian urban centres. Housing stock expansion before the Great War and during the 1920s diminished the effects of the depression's construction lag.[7] Moreover, while doubling up and overcrowding increased between 1931 and 1941, particularly in the downtown area, they were not as extensive as in other principal cities. (Table 1) The physical condition of Vancouver's housing

[6] Canada, Advisory Committee on Reconstruction, Subcommittee on Housing and Community Planning [chaired by C. A. Curtis], *Final Report of the Subcommittee, March 24, 1944* [hereafter referred to as Curtis *Report*] (Ottawa: King's Printer, 1946), pp. 137-43.

[7] Wade, "Wartime Housing Limited: Canadian Housing Policy at the Crossroads," pp. 25, 28.

TABLE 1

Housing Conditions in Selected Larger Canadian Cities,
1941 (by Percentage)

Selected larger cities (1)	Doubled-up households (2)	Overcrowded households (3)	Substandard dwellings (4)	Owner-occupied dwellings (5)
Halifax	17.2 (9.2)	26.1	43	36.5 (35.2)
Montreal	7.5 (6.4)	24.4	27	11.5 (14.9)
Toronto	19.1 (8.4)	12.4	29	43.8 (46.5)
Hamilton	12.4 (7.8)	10.7	28	44.0 (48.0)
Winnipeg	15.1 (7.3)	19.0	36	43.9 (47.0)
Regina	10.0 (4.5)	24.0	43	38.7 (50.3)
Calgary	12.1 (5.2)	18.5	38	44.6 (51.7)
Edmonton	7.6 (4.3)	22.2	46	46.3 (53.0)
Vancouver	8.5 (5.1)	13.2	27	50.1 (51.0)
Victoria	10.5 (4.9)	11.1	26	45.8 (46.8)

Sources: Column 2: Canada, Department of Munitions and Supply, "Preliminary Report on the Housing Situation in Canada and Suggestions for Its Improvement," by Lesslie R. Thomson (Ottawa, 1942), p. 56B, table 5. 1931 percentages are in parentheses.

Column 3: Canada, Dominion Bureau of Statistics, *Eighth Census of Canada, 1941,* vol. 9: *Housing* (Ottawa: King's Printer, 1949), p. 182, table 36.

Column 4: Canada, Advisory Committee on Reconstruction, Subcommittee on Housing and Community Planning [chaired by C. A. Curtis], *Final Report of the Subcommittee, March 24, 1944* [hereafter referred to as Curtis *Report*], p. 105, table 24. Substandard dwellings were in need of external repairs and lacking or with shared use of toilets and bathing facilities.

Column 5: Curtis *Report*, p. 244, table 57. 1931 percentages are in parentheses.

ranked about the same as, or better than, that of other major centres: the highest incidence of deteriorated and insanitary accommodation occurred in the overcrowded downtown area.[8] (Table 1) The percentage of owner-occupied dwellings remained about the same between 1931 and 1941 while it generally dropped elsewhere. (Table 1) Moreover, the 1931 Canadian census confirmed Deryck Holdsworth's characterization of Vancouver as an urban landscape of homes and gardens contrasting

[8] Burrard Inlet, Burrard Street, Clark Drive, and 6th Avenue bordered the downtown area; see Vancouver, Building, Civic Planning, and Parks Committee, [A Survey of the Housing Situation in Vancouver], (Vancouver, 1937), City of Vancouver Archives [CVA], PD 447; and Vancouver Housing Association, "Housing Vancouver: A Survey of the Housing Position in Vancouver" (Vancouver, 1946), pp. 1-4.

with older industrial cities in Europe and North America:[9] 80 percent of Vancouver's population lived in single houses.[10] By 1941, 75.2 percent of all housing types still consisted of detached dwellings.[11]

The city's problem in the forties resulted mainly from a huge population increase amounting to 44,000 people between 1939 and 1944.[12] This growth may be attributed to a heavy inward movement of workers and their families attracted by the expansion of wartime shipbuilding and aircraft industries, to an influx of armed forces dependents, and to an uninterrupted migration from the prairie provinces. Later, in 1945-46, demobilization greatly affected the housing situation. As federal officials expected, significantly more discharged personnel than the city's 30,000 enlistments settled in the area.[13] In August 1945 they calculated that 8,500 veterans were already in the city.[14] Service men and women continued to return well into 1946, with several hundred frequently arriving on the same day.[15] In addition, 240 British war brides had reached Vancouver by June 1945, and officials expected another 2,400 before the year's end.[16]

Housing statistics for the early 1940s revealed serious congestion. In 1942 the vacancy rate for all types of accommodation dropped below

[9] Holdsworth, "House and Home in Vancouver: Emergence of a West Coast Urban Landscape," xi, p. 33.

[10] Canada, Dominion Bureau of Statistics, *Seventh Census of Canada, 1931: The Housing Accommodation of the Canadian People* (Ottawa: King's Printer, 1935), chart 5, p. 19, and table 10, p. 30.

[11] Canada, Dominion Bureau of Statistics, *Vancouver Housing Atlas* (Ottawa: King's Printer, 1944), p. 2.

[12] "A Memorandum Respecting the Housing Situation in the Vancouver-New Westminster Area Prepared by the Emergency Shelter Administration, Vancouver, B.C.," 1 May 1945, Department of Finance Records, RG 19, ser. E3, vol. 4017, Public Archives of Canada, Ottawa [PAC]; see also chapter 4 in Patricia E. Roy, *Vancouver: An Illustrated History* (Toronto: James Lorimer and National Museum of Man, National Museums of Canada, 1980).

[13] "Memorandum Respecting the Housing Situation in Vancouver," p. 1, RG 19, ser. E3, vol. 4017, PAC. In 1951 veterans headed 24 percent of British Columbia households, a higher percentage than in any other province; see Canada, Dominion Bureau of Statistics, *Ninth Census of Canada, 1951*, vol. 10 (Ottawa: Queen's Printer, 1953), p. 425, table XVII.

[14] L. F. Stevenson to D. Gordon, 31 July 1945, p. 3, Central Mortgage and Housing Corporation Records, RG 56, vol. 17, file 105-10, PAC.

[15] For example, 800 Seaforth Highlanders were released on a single day; see *Vancouver Sun*, 9 October 1945, p. 13.

[16] [Wartime Housing Limited Report to 2nd Interdepartmental Housing Committee Meeting, 6 June 1945] "Re: Vancouver #2-100 Houses," RG 19, ser. E3, vol. 4017, [unclassified document no. 13], PAC.

.257 percent; in mid-1945, it reached .004 percent.[17] The local WPTB housing registry statistics also indicated the critical situation. In 1943, when it handled an average 1,600 requests per month, the registry failed to house 10,500 of its 19,709 applicants.[18] In December 1945 it sought to accommodate an all-time high of 4,143 families, of which 3,483 belonged to service personnel.[19] In mid-1945 federal officials estimated the housing demand until December 1946 at 25,000 units.[20]

Federal initiatives somewhat alleviated Vancouver's housing situation in the early 1940s. The 1938 NHA and HIP stimulated residential construction and renovations and repairs until 1941, and the Home Conversion Plan prompted some additional alterations activity after 1943.[21] Still, although Vancouverites benefited from a WPTB registry, from rent controls, and from a local emergency shelter administration, the Board's materials and manpower regulations depressed new construction between 1942 and 1945.[22] Before 1944 WHL built 750 units in North Vancouver and about 300 in Richmond but none in Vancouver itself.[23] VLA did not initiate its veterans' housing program until V-E Day. Thus increasing congestion and insufficient federal response combined to produce an acute need for accommodation.

Early in 1944 the threat of mass evictions in a period of serious accommodation shortages ignited public agitation about Canada's (and Vancouver's) housing problem. According to the October 1943 WPTB rental regulations,[24] landlords could give notices-to-vacate to their tenants only between April 30 and September 30; the Board banned winter evictions. Consequently, large numbers of notices accumulated for 1 May 1944.

[17] Canada, Department of Munitions and Supply, "Preliminary Report on the Housing Situation in Canada, p. 64B, table 6; and Vancouver Housing Association, "Housing Vancouver," p. 3.

[18] *Sun*, 11 April 1944, p. 13.

[19] *Ibid.*, 5 December 1945, p. 13.

[20] "Memorandum Respecting the Housing Situation in Vancouver," p. 3, RG 19, ser. E3, vol. 4017, PAC.

[21] Annual Summaries of the Building Reports, 1938-1946, Building Reports, Building Department, Department of Permits and Licences, Vancouver, vol. 125-A-1, files 2 and 3, CVA.

[22] Operated by two paid staff members and many volunteers, the Vancouver registry assisted tenants between 1942 and 1946; see *Sun*, 7 October 1942, p. 17, 19 October 1942, p. 17, and 19 December 1942, p. 3; and *Vancouver Daily Province*, 7 October 1942, p. 11. For the decline in new construction, see Annual Summaries of the Building Reports, 1942-1945.

[23] Wade, *Wartime Housing Limited: Overview and Evaluation*, pp. 8-9.

[24] Canada, Wartime Prices and Trade Board, *Canadian War Orders and Regulations*, vol. 3 (1943), order no. 294.

Given the low vacancy rates in cities across Canada, tenants faced with eviction could not find alternative shelter. In addition, many of the tenants were the dependents of servicemen fighting overseas. MPs in the House of Commons brought the problem to the government's attention beginning in February.[25] Finally, in May, the federal government responded to the evictions situation not by altering the rental regulations but by expanding the WHL operations to furnish housing for soldiers' families.[26]

In Vancouver the evictions issue marked the beginning of two years of active protest. A variety of groups pressed the federal government to act on the housing problem. No formal organization united them, although their membership often overlapped, and some groups were even bitter opponents in the broader political context. The objectives of the organizations differentiated them. On the one hand, the veterans' associations and the Citizens' Rehabilitation Council of Greater Vancouver sought an immediate remedy for the servicemen's and veterans' housing emergency; they were temperorarily reform-minded. On the other hand, the Co-operative Commonwealth Federation (CCF), the Labor Progressive Party (LPP) and the Vancouver Housing Association (VHA) wanted a comprehensive program to solve the long- and short-range aspects of the housing problem.

Veterans' organizations, such as the provincial command and the local branches of the Canadian Legion, the Army and Navy Veterans of Canada, the Canadian Corps Association, the War Amputations Association, and the co-ordinating Vancouver Veterans' Council, supported by women's auxiliaries to various regiments, urged quick resolution of the housing emergency. In August 1944 a delegation representing these groups made several recommendations to city council: imposition of an evictions freeze for soldiers' dependents; use of vacant dwellings for temporary accommodation; provision of more WHL houses; construction of government-assisted housing developments by limited dividend companies; and conversion of the old Hotel Vancouver to a veterans' hostel.[27] Within a year, veterans' organizations had adopted other demands: a

[25] Canada, Parliament, House of Commons, *Debates*, vol. 1 (1944): 561-63, vol. 2 (1944): 1865-66, and vol. 3 (1944): 2130.

[26] Minutes, Meeting of WHL Board of Directors, 10 May 1944, p. 10, Defence Construction Ltd. Records, RG 83, vol. 70, Minutes: vol. 1, PAC. See also "Report for Interdepartmental Housing Committee by Mr. Jas. A. Hall Representing Wartime Housing Limited," Privy Council Office Records, RG 2, ser. 18, vol. 9, file H-13, PAC.

[27] *Sun*, 4 August 1944, p. 17.

federal housing ministry; a low-income housing program; new controls and priorities on building materials; a ceiling on real estate prices; and training of skilled building tradesmen.[28]

Veterans held the just belief that the rehabilitation of discharged service personnel required government assistance in housing as well as in employment, health care and education. Canadians (including elected members of government and government officials) generally shared this view. To some extent the leaders of veterans' organizations used the morality issue to arouse ex-service men and women to act on the evictions issue.[29] As well, some veterans took advantage of the housing controversy for their own political purposes. Jack Henderson, the president of the Canadian Legion's provincial command, ran as a Non-Partisan Association-endorsed candidate for school board in the 1944 civic elections and as a Liberal candidate in Vancouver East in the 1945 federal general election.[30] James Sinclair was known as the Liberal "soldier M.P." for North Vancouver.[31] Many LPP members also participated in veterans' organizations to pursue their party's political objectives.[32]

The Citizens' Rehabilitation Council of Greater Vancouver concerned itself with the immediate problem of re-establishing demobilized armed forces personnel. It represented a diversity of interests in the city — business, professional, social welfare, labour, government, veterans and church.[33] Not surprisingly, membership sometimes overlapped with other groups like the veterans' organizations. In June 1944 a local housing registry official explained the veterans' shelter problem to the Council, whose members quickly set up a housing committee chaired by former Conservative cabinet minister H. H. Stevens.[34] The Council endorsed rehabilitation not only out of "a sense of gratitu[de]" to veterans but "because Canada's future stability and progress depend[ed] upon the

[28] *Ibid.*, 20 March 1946, p. 2.

[29] "Veterans Picket Line Planned for Evictions" [unidentified newspaper clipping], 25 August 1944, Newspaper Clippings, M4289-3, CVA.

[30] *Sun*, 22 November 1944, p. 10, and 27 October 1944, p. 15.

[31] "Housing Set-Up Scored," [unidentified newspaper clipping], 28 July 1944, Newspaper Clippings, M4289-3, CVA.

[32] *Sun*, 31 December 1945, p. 3.

[33] Meeting of the Rehabilitation Section of the Co-ordinating Council for War Work and Civilian Services, 22 February 1944, Frank E. Buck Papers, box 11, file 13, Special Collections Division, University of British Columbia Library. See also "The Citizens Rehabilitation Council of Greater Vancouver: Summary of Activities, 1940-1948," Buck Papers, box 11, file 15.

[34] Richard Wilbur, *H. H. Stevens, 1878-1973* (Toronto: University of Toronto Press, 1977), p. 213.

combined effort of government and people in removing causes of dis-satisfaction and unrest."[35] Its role was conciliatory and cautionary. It assisted in the resolution of differences over legal agreements between Vancouver City Council and WHL, and it warned the prime minister and others of the potential danger for social unrest in the city's housing situation.[36]

The 1944 Curtis report and the 1944 report of the British Columbia Post-War Rehabilitation Council influenced organizations that sought a comprehensive housing policy. The Curtis report recommended a national housing and planning program to provide for town planning, home ownership, home improvement, slum clearance, low-rental projects and co-operative and rural housing.[37] This program would require two sepa-rate Dominion housing and planning administrations, federal financial assistance, municipal and provincial administrations, sensitivity to com-munity concerns, and public, private and co-operative ownership of housing. In particular, it would recognize the accommodation needs of low- and moderate-income Canadians. The section of the Post-War Rehabilitation Council report dedicated to planning and housing[38] called for a provincial planning and housing authority, enabling legislation for regional planning and housing authorities, federal subsidies or loans for municipal housing schemes, and adjustments to NHA to subsidize low-rental projects. Both the LPP and the CCF used the Curtis report and the provincial post-war rehabilitation report to press for resolution of the long-term housing problem.[39]

The LPP advocated policies on housing not very much different from those of the CCF.[40] In particular, it supported low-rental housing pro-jects assisted by federal funding, local housing authorities, slum clearance

[35] A. W. Cowley to W. L. M. King, 22 June 1945, RG 2, ser. 18, vol. 9, file H-13, PAC.

[36] "City Ready to Back Housing Plan: Seeks Better Terms," [unidentified newspaper clipping], 1 August 1944, Newspaper Clippings, M4289-3, CVA.

[37] Curtis *Report*, pp. 9-22.

[38] British Columbia, Post-War Rehabilitation Council, *Reports of the Post-War Rehabilitation Council; The Interim Report (1943) and Supplementary Report (1944)* (Victoria: King's Printer, 1945), p. 150.

[39] For the CCF, see *CCF News*, 13 April 1944, p. 2, 24 August 1944, p. 3, and 30 September 1945, p. 3. CCF MLAs C. G. MacNeil, D. G. Steeves and H. E. Winch sat on the British Columbia Post-War Rehabilitation Council. For the LPP, see *Pacific Advocate*, 13 October 1945, pp. 12-13, and 25 January 1946, housing supplement, passim.

[40] Ivan Avakumovic, *The Communist Party in Canada: A History* (Toronto: Mc-Clelland & Stewart, 1975), pp. 103, 135, 176, 273. After it was made illegal in 1940, the Communist Party regrouped as the LPP.

and a federal housing ministry.[41] But, unlike the CCF, the LPP employed more aggressive and militant tactics, especially at the local level. In 1944 and 1945 party members like John McPeake and Elgin Ruddell were instrumental in forming the "5000 Homes Now" Committee and the Citizens' Emergency Housing Committee.[42] Both groups took a spirited offensive on the housing issue, and Ruddell was later active in the VHA.[43] The LPP initiated public rallies and picket lines at homes of soon-to-be-evicted tenants. As well, LPP members had gained the leadership of major British Columbia unions and the Vancouver Labor Council during the early 1940s.[44] All of these organizations agitated for improvements in housing conditions.[45] Some union leaders, including McPeake of the International Union of Mine, Mill, and Smelter Workers and Harold Pritchett of the International Woodworkers of America, also led protest activities.[46]

At its provincial and national conventions, in its election manifestos, and in its publications, the CCF committed itself to a comprehensive, planned and need-oriented program very much like the one recommended by the Curtis report.[47] This program recognized the relationship between housing and planning, called for dominion, provincial and municipal housing authorities, required federal funding, advocated low-rental

[41] *Pacific Advocate*, 25 November 1944, p. 4, and 18 January 1946, pp. 1, 3.

[42] The "5000 Homes Now" Committee emerged from the Consumers' Council in March 1944 but was disbanded the following September; see *Sun*, 1 March 1944, p. 13, and 20 September 1944, p. 15. The Citizens' Emergency Housing Committee formed the next summer; see *ibid.*, 15 June 1945, p. 26.

[43] *Ibid.*, 5 January 1946, p. 27.

[44] Irving Martin Abella, *Nationalism, Communism, and Canadian Labour: The CIO, the Communist Party, and the Canadian Congress of Labour, 1935-1956* (Toronto: University of Toronto Press, 1973), pp. 80, 177-78.

[45] For example, see *Sun*, 26 July 1944, p. 13, and 27 June 1945, p. 13; *Main Deck*, 11 August 1943, p. 4; *'756' Review*, November 1944, p. 1, February 1945, p. 4, and June 1945, p. 3; Minutes, Building, Civic Planning, and Parks Committee, Vancouver City Council, 26 A, vol. 9, 22 May 1944, p. 337, 5 June 1944, p. 339, and 9 April 1945, p. 382, and vol. 10, 9 July 1945, p. 3, CVA; M. A. Knight, Britannia Mine and Mill Workers' Union, to W. L. M. King, 13 June 1945, and telegram, E. Leary, Vancouver Labor Council, to W. L. M. King, 13 July 1945, RG 19, vol. 716, file 203-17, PAC; and G. W. Caron, Boilermakers and Iron Shipbuilders' Union, to W. L. M. King, 6 July, RG 19, ser. E3, vol. 4018, PAC.

[46] "Friends Assist Evictee," [unidentified newspaper clipping], 19 August 1944, Newspaper Clippings, M4289-3, CVA.

[47] The League for Social Reconstruction developed a housing program proposal preliminary to both the CCF's policy and the Curtis report; see League for Social Reconstruction, Research Committee, *Social Planning for Canada*, introd. F. R. Scott et al. (Toronto: University of Toronto Press, 1975), pp. 451-63; and Humphrey Carver, *Compassionate Landscape* (Toronto: University of Toronto Press, 1975), p. 51.

housing and slum clearance, supported private home ownership and co-operative housing, and proposed research into new materials and methods of construction.[48]

Unlike the LPP, the CCF relied less upon militant tactics and more upon its elected members at all three government levels to advance its housing program — Helena Gutteridge in Vancouver, Dorothy Steeves, Laura Jamieson, Grace MacInnis and Grant MacNeil in Victoria, and Angus MacInnis in Ottawa. CCF women most vigorously promoted improvements in housing.[49] Gutteridge generated a storm of housing reform activity while a city council member between 1937 and 1939.[50] As chairperson of the city's special committee on housing, she helped to prepare the 1937 survey of Vancouver's housing conditions and attempted to attract support from community, housing and labour organizations for low-rental housing under the 1938 NHA.[51] Beginning in the mid-1930s, Steeves continually raised the housing issue in the provincial legislature and later served as a member of the British Columbia Post-War Rehabilitation Council.[52] Jamieson established co-operative houses for single working women during the war.[53] Grace MacInnis presented the party's housing policy in her writings and in speeches to public meetings, to CCF-sponsored eviction rallies, and to the Legislature.[54]

Despite the similarity of LPP and CCF solutions to the housing problem, the two political parties could not act together on the issue. At the

[48] *Federationist*, 25 March 1943, p. 4, and 22 April 1943, p. 4; *CCF News*, 18 January 1945, p. 4, 16 May 1945, p. 3, 30 September 1945, p. 3, and 22 August 1946, p. 1.

[49] Women played active roles in most European and North American housing reform movements; see Eugenie Ladner Birch and Deborah S. Gardiner, "The Seven-Percent Solution: A Review of Philanthropic Housing, 1870-1910," *Journal of Urban History* 7 (August 1981): 406, 412-14, 429-31; Spragge, "Confluence of Interests," pp. 247, 255-56; and Damer, "State, Class, and Housing," pp. 103-04.

[50] See Susan Wade, "Helena Gutteridge: Votes for Women and Trade Unions," in *In Her Own Right: Selected Essays on Women's History in B.C.*, eds. Barbara Latham and Cathy Kess (Victoria: Camosun College, 1980), pp. 187-203.

[51] Vancouver, Building, Civic Planning, and Parks Committee, [Survey of the Housing Situation]. The 1938 NHA Part II made available but never actually advanced loans to limited dividend companies and to municipal housing authorities for low-rental housing programs.

[52] *Province*, 18 March 1936, p. 6; *Sun*, 2 November 1938, p. 3; and British Columbia, Post-War Rehabilitation Council, *Reports*, pp. 166, 199.

[53] Laura E. Jamieson, "Co-op Living in Vancouver," *Canadian Forum* 23 (April 1943): 18-19; and *Federationist*, 1 July 1943, p. 3.

[54] *CCF News*, 17 February 1944, p. 1, 16 March 1944, p. 5, 22 February 1945, p. 1, 12 April 1945, p. 3, 7 February 1946, p. 6, 5 September 1946, p. 3, and 22 May 1947, p. 2; and *Sun*, 11 March 1944, p. 5, and 11 July 1945, p. 13.

national level, the LPP wished to form a popular left-wing front with the CCF, but the social democrats rejected such a coalition. Bitter feelings extended from the national struggle into the local housing controversy. For example, CCF member E. S. Scanlon withdrew from the "5000 Homes Now" Committee because the LPP had infiltrated the organization and made it "a political football," while McPeake denied Scanlon's charges and asserted that the group was "broadly representative" of the public; in addition, Angus MacInnis refused to participate in the "5000 Homes Now" meetings.[55]

Like the two left-wing political parties, the VHA directed its efforts toward resolving the long-term housing problem. It was the local wing of the Housing and Planning Association of Canada, which represented Canada's national low-rental housing and slum clearance lobby. Upon its formation in 1937, the Vancouver group began a survey of the city's housing conditions, but the war postponed completion of the study until 1946.[56] Although influenced by the Curtis report, the VHA emphasized low-rental housing and slum clearance more than the rest of the comprehensive housing program.[57] It demanded the consolidation of all housing and planning activities in one federal ministry and the creation of local authorities for the construction and the administration of low-rental projects. As well, it advocated that, if the dominion government refused to take the initiative, the municipalities should approach provincial governments to request federal financial assistance.[58] Although, on the whole, concerns about low-rental housing needs motivated the VHA membership, the participation of some individual members furthered their professional or political interests. For politicians like Helena Gutteridge, Grace MacInnis and Elgin Ruddell, the VHA complemented and reinforced CCF and LPP positions on housing.[59] In addition, the VHA incidentally advanced the professional careers and concerns of some of its members like Frank Buck, a faculty member at the University of British Columbia and a member of the Town Planning Commission, Jocelyn Davidson, a local CMHC officer, and later Leonard Marsh, the

[55] *Sun,* 31 March 1944, p. 15, and 13 April 1944, p. 11.

[56] *Ibid.,* 5 January 1946, p. 27; and *Vancouver News-Herald,* 11 December 1937, p. 2.

[57] Vancouver Housing Association, "Housing Vancouver," pp. 51-56.

[58] The VHA waited until 1947 to launch a campaign urging city council to ask Ottawa for funds and legislation to create a local housing authority for a low-rental project; see *Sun,* 25 March 1947, p. 9.

[59] *News-Herald,* 11 December 1937, p. 2; and *Province,* 31 January 1947, p. 5.

research adviser for the Curtis report and a University of British Columbia professor after the war.[60]

A great many community groups supported the drive for action led by the veterans, the Rehabilitation Council, the LPP, the CCF and the VHA. Most prominent were women's organizations, churches, professional groups, social welfare associations and service clubs.[61] Frequently these groups also participated in the housing campaign through their representatives on the Rehabilitation Council or the VHA.[62]

Newspapers and journals brought the housing issue to public attention and demanded and offered solutions. The *Sun*, the *Daily Province* and the *News-Herald* in Vancouver published stories, editorials and articles on all aspects of the housing situation. Similarly, articles in popular magazines like *Maclean's* and *Saturday Night*, professional and business journals like *Canadian Business* and the Royal Architectural Institute of Canada *Journal*, and political and labour publications like the *CCF News*, the *Pacific Advocate* (*Tribune*) and the Trades and Labor Congress *Journal* covered housing conditions and very often suggested answers to difficulties.[63] Some government officials blamed the 1944-45 agitation over evictions on inflammatory press coverage.[64] In fact the local press and popular and serious journals together increased public awareness of the housing problem and generated constructive responses to it.

[60] Michael Bliss, Preface to *Report on Social Security for Canada*, by Leonard Marsh (Ottawa, King's Printer, 1943; reprint ed., Toronto: University of Toronto Press, 1975), ix-x; and Michael Horn, "Leonard Marsh and the Coming of a Welfare State in Canada," *Histoire sociale/Social History* 9 (May 1976): 197-204.

[61] These community groups included First United Church, Local Council of Women, University Women's Club of Vancouver, Women's Voluntary Services, Lions' Ladies Club, Women's Christian Temperance Union, Vancouver Council of Jewish Women, Canadian Daughters League, B'nai B'rith Women, Vancouver Business and Professional Women's Club, Catholic Women's League of Canada, B.C. Mainland Canadian Association of Social Workers, Family Welfare Bureau, Kinsmen Club of Vancouver, and Soroptimist Club. See the representatives from these groups in RG 19, vol. 716, file 203-17, PAC, and in minutes, Building, Civic Planning, and Parks Committee, 26 A, vol. 9, 6 March 1945, pp. 375-76, and vol. 10, 20 May 1946, p. 73, 11 June 1946, p. 78, and 10 June 1947, p. 189.

[62] Minutes, Meeting of the Rehabilitation Section of the Co-ordinating Council for War Work and Civilian Services, 22 February 1944, Buck Papers, box 11, file 13.

[63] See J. David Hulchanski, *Canadian Town Planning and Housing, 1940-1950: A Historical Bibliography* (Toronto: Centre for Urban and Community Studies, University of Toronto, 1979); and Allan Moscovitch with Theresa Jennisson and Peter Findlay, *The Welfare State in Canada: A Selected Bibliography, 1840 to 1978* (Waterloo: Wilfrid Laurier University Press, 1983).

[64] "Responsibility for Shelter," memorandum from D. Gordon, 7 December 1944, Wartime Prices and Trade Board Records, RG 64, ser. 1030, box 708, file 25-14-17-1, PAC.

Public protests about the housing question went to federal, provincial and municipal governments. The Prime Minister and the ministers of Finance, Munitions (Reconstruction) and Supply, National Defence, and Pensions and National Health (Veterans Affairs), the WPTB chairman, and the Interdepartmental Housing Committee received letters, resolutions, telegrams and delegations of officials from Vancouver organizations.[65] The same groups also sent letters and delegations to the provincial government and the city council, which in turn exerted pressure upon the dominion government.[66] In addition, CCF MLAs made demands upon the British Columbia Legislative Assembly, and federal ministers requested action from each other.[67] Moreover, internal reports went directly from the Emergency Shelter Administration and the housing registry in Vancouver to top WPTB officials.[68] Finally, federal officials and ministers directly confronted the local housing issue by reading critical editorials in Vancouver newspapers.[69] The protests ultimately reached federal Finance minister J. L. Ilsley and Munitions and Supply minister C. D. Howe for decision-making on emergency housing policy.[70]

Between 1944 and 1946 the agitation of many Vancouver protest groups induced the federal government to respond with an evictions freeze, with WHL housing, and with the old Hotel Vancouver hostel and the Renfrew Heights subdivision. The militant campaign for a suspension of evictions commenced in the summer of 1944 and concluded successfully a year later. At first the Rehabilitation Council, labour and veterans'

65 For these representations, see RG 19, vol. 716, file 203C-17, and vol. 2730, file 200-2, PAC. As well, see *Sun*, 29 July 1944, p. 7, 1 June 1945, p. 3, 13 June 1945, p. 1, and 25 June 1945, p. 10.

66 For representations to the province, see *Sun*, 10 March 1944, p. 1, 27 June 1945, p. 1, 2 March 1946, p. 14, 19 March 1946, p. 5, and 10 April 1946, p. 2. For representations to the city, see Minutes, Building, Civic Planning, and Parks Committee, 26 A, vol. 9, 6 March 1945, pp. 375-76; and *Sun*, 10 March 1944, p. 1, 6 June 1944, p. 5, 4 August 1944, p. 17, and 1 December 1944, p. 1. For representations from province to dominion, see *Sun*, 26 July 1944, p. 13, and 10 July 1945, p. 7; and R. L. Maitland to D. Gordon, 20 July 1944, RG 64, ser. 1030, box 701, file 25-2, vol. 1, PAC.

67 *Sun*, 11 March 1944, p. 5, and 18 July 1943, p. 1; and the 1944-46 correspondence between Ian Mackenzie, Veterans Affairs (Pensions and National Health) minister, and J. L. Ilsley, Finance minister, in RG 19, vol. 716, file 203C-17, PAC.

68 For housing registry reports, see RG 64, ser. 1040, box 215, file G.05.02, PAC. See also "Memorandum Respecting the Housing Situation in Vancouver," RG 19, ser. E3, vol. 4017, PAC.

69 For Donald Gordon's encounter with a critical *Vancouver Sun* editorial, see RG 19, vol. 716, file 203C-17, PAC.

70 Minutes, special Wartime Prices and Trade Board meeting, 23 July 1945, RG 64, ser. 1030, box 700, file 25-1-3, PAC; and *Sun*, 27 July 1945, p. 1.

organizations, and city council sent resolutions requesting a freeze to the federal government,[71] but as the evictions grew in number and as the government failed to react to representations, the LPP and the veterans adopted more aggressive tactics. In mid-July the LPP organized a street rally outside the home of an evicted serviceman's wife.[72] Shortly afterwards, picketing Legion members halted the eviction of a widow whose son was serving overseas.[73] When over 2,000 households received notices-to-vacate between May and October 1945, protesters used the street rally and the picket line with greater effectiveness.[74] Both the LPP and the CCF organized rallies frequently attended by several hundred neighbours and activists.[75] For two weeks in July 1945 an Anti-Evictions Committee stopped all evictions by posting eight picketers at five houses for nine or twelve hours a day.[76] On July 25, as social tension mounted in Vancouver and in other cities faced with the evictions problem, the WPTB issued a suspension order applicable to congested areas across Canada.[77] Information appended to the order noted that the Board took protest wires from Vancouver into special consideration before implementing the freeze.

In 1944 and 1945 protesters were instrumental in procuring 1,200 WHL houses for Vancouver. Fearful of social unrest, Rehabilitation Council representatives attended negotiations between city council and WHL for the construction of 200 dwellings and convinced the city to conclude two separate agreements with the crown company despite un-

[71] *Sun*, 26 July 1944, p. 13, 29 July 1944, p. 7, and 4 August 1944, p. 17. Under pressure from protest groups like the LPP, the provincial government urged the WPTB and J. L. Ilsley to deal with the evictions situation; see R. L. Maitland to D. Gordon, 20 July 1944, RG 64, ser. 1030, box 701, file 25-2, vol. 1; and R. L. Maitland to Ilsley, 7 September 1944, RG 64, ser. 1030, box 701, file 25-2, vol. 2.

[72] *Sun*, 18 August 1944, p. 1, and 19 August 1944, p. 17.

[73] "Veterans' Picket Line Planned for Evictions," [unidentified newspaper clipping], 25 August 1944, and "Eviction of Widow Halted by Legion," [unidentified newspaper clipping], 28 August 1944, Newspaper Clippings, M4289-3, CVA.

[74] "Memorandum Respecting the Housing Situation in Vancouver," RG 19, ser. 3, vol. 4017, PAC; and minutes, special Wartime Prices and Trade Board meeting, 23 July 1945, app. A, p. 2, RG 64, ser. 1030, box 700, file 25-1-3, PAC. 769 notices-to-vacate were issued for 1 May 1945, and 1,976 notices from May to October.

[75] For examples of LPP rallies, see *Sun*, 5 June 1945, p. 3, 14 July 1945, p. 3, 17 July 1945, p. 8, and 18 July 1945, p. 13. For examples of CCF rallies, see *ibid.*, 10 July 1945, p. 3, 11 July 1945, p. 13, and 13 July 1945, p. 8.

[76] *Ibid.*, 23 July 1945, p. 1.

[77] Canada, Wartime Prices and Trade Board, *Canadian War Orders and Regulations*, vol. 7 (1945), order no. 537. The evictions problem seriously affected Toronto (3,500 notices-to-vacate between June and October 1945) and to a lesser extent other cities like Winnipeg, Montreal and Hamilton.

favourable financial terms.[78] The Rehabilitation Council subsequently pressed the federal government for 5,000 government-built, low-income houses. Finally, impelled by increasingly militant eviction protests, the government offered an additional 1,000 WHL units to Vancouver's mayor on the very day of the WPTB's freeze announcement.[79]

During the winter months of 1945-46, agitation over the housing problem culminated in the old Hotel Vancouver controversy. The protesters recognized that the hotel would soon stand empty in the midst of severe housing shortages. In 1939 the present Hotel Vancouver had replaced the structure erected in stages since 1901 at Georgia and Granville.[80] A Canadian National Railway-Canadian Pacific Railway (CPR) agreement applying to both buildings ordered the demolition of the original premises if it remained unsold by 1946.[81] But Vancouver's citizens had long regarded the hotel as "a palace for the public."[82] They as much as Winston Churchill, Babe Ruth, Charlie Chaplin or R. B. Bennett had used and enjoyed the Spanish Grill, the Peacock Alley shops, the Crystal Ballroom and the roof-top garden.[83] Before the war they tried unsuccessfully to preserve the hotel as a civic auditorium, a museum and a library, or a provincial government office building. During wartime the Department of National Defence leased the building and converted it first to a recruiting centre and later to offices and barracks. Between 1944

[78] For the Rehabilitation Council's participation, see *Sun*, 11 July 1944, p. 1, 4 August 1944, p. 17, 5 December 1944, p. 11, and 20 March 1945, p. 9. See also the agreements between the Corporation of the City of Vancouver, H.M. the King in right of Canada, and Wartime Housing Limited, 25 September 1944 and 1 July 1945, located in City Clerk's Department, City of Vancouver. For the city's dissatisfaction about WHL's terms, see *Sun*, 1 August 1944, p. 13.

[79] For the Rehabilitation Council's drive for 5,000 houses, see *Sun*, 29 May 1945, p. 9, and 1 June 1945, p. 3. For the announcement of WHL's offer, see *ibid.*, 25 July 1945, p. 1, and 26 July 1945, p. 2; a WHL official visited Mayor J. W. Cornett on the 25th, and C. D. Howe wired the offer to Cornett the next day. For the agreement for 1,000 houses, see agreement between the Corporation of the City of Vancouver, H.M. the King in right of Canada, and Wartime Housing Limited, 1 September 1945, located in City Clerk's Department, City of Vancouver.

[80] For architectural descriptions of the old hotel, see "The New C.P.R. Hotel, Vancouver," *Architectural Review* 42 (August 1917): 29-40; and "The New Hotel Vancouver," *American Architect* 110 (13 September 1916): 153-58, 161. In 1945-46 the hotel remained structurally sound despite its obsolete wiring and plumbing; see A. Haggert to F. Jones, 22 October 1945, Vancouver City Clerk's Records, ser. 1, Operational Files, Special Committee Files, 28-C-1, CVA.

[81] P. C. 460, 5 March 1938, with appended agreement, RG 19, vol. 716, file 203C-17, vol. 1, PAC.

[82] *Province*, 19 February 1901, p. 1.

[83] *Ibid.*, magazine section, 10 February 1940, p. 3, and 21 August 1948, pp. 22-23.

and 1946 many citizens believed that the old hotel could still benefit the community as a temporary veterans' hostel.

Discussions about the hostel plan occupied federal and local government officials after March 1945, when Vancouver's Emergency Shelter administrator, Leigh F. Stevenson, formally recommended the scheme to his superiors in Ottawa.[84] The major federal participants included J. L. Ilsley, his parliamentary assistant and Victoria MP R. H. Mayhew and Emergency Shelter co-ordinator Eric Gold. Mayor J. W. Cornett and a special committee of three aldermen represented the City of Vancouver. The Rehabilitation Council executive and CPR president D. C. Coleman took part in the official debate to a lesser degree. Eventually Veterans Affairs minister Ian Mackenzie, who was MP for the federal riding in which the hotel stood, acted as conciliator in the final resolution of the dispute. Formal discussion covered several issues: the allocation of responsibility for leasing, refurbishing, financing and managing the hotel; the municipal property tax revenue; and the building's suitability as family accommodation.

Negotiations were unnecessarily protracted, apparently irresolvable and occasionally maladroit. City and federal officials bargained by letter and telegram and by face-to-face meetings in May, July and December.[85] No agreement seemed possible. According to the Finance Department, the city or some local agency should lease the old hotel from the CPR, repair, maintain and manage the premises, pay for a predetermined percentage of the operating expenses and forgo the CPR's property tax revenue. The federal government would provide furniture and equipment. The city refused to surrender its tax revenue. It also argued that it lacked the administrative machinery necessary to operate a hostel. Furthermore, no local organization was willing to assume the management responsibilities and the financial risks inherent in the venture. In addition, WHL declined the city's request to take over the hotel because it offered inadequate family housing facilities, and the federal government rejected an army-run operation. Ottawa complained about Vancouver's procrastination. The city and the Rehabilitation Council faulted the federal government for suddenly announcing the termination of its lease with the CPR while Mayhew conducted talks with them in Vancouver. Alderman H. L.

---

[84] L. F. Stevenson to D. G. Mackenzie, 16 March 1945, and "Vancouver Hotel," memorandum by Eric Gold, 14 February 1946, RG 19, vol. 716, file 203C-17, vol. 1, PAC.

[85] Federal records for the negotiations are located in RG 19, vol. 716, PAC, and the city's records may be found in the Special Committee Files, 28-C-1 and 28-C-4, CVA.

Old Hotel Vancouver, ca. 1927

Labor Progressive Party veterans picketing Old Hotel Vancouver, January 1946

Corey's "flying trip"[86] to Ottawa and Montreal in mid-January produced no offer from the Finance Department and the CPR satisfactory to the city. As the date of the lease's termination, 1 February, approached and as no local sponsor came forth, city council prepared to drop the old Hotel Vancouver plan.[87]

Public agitation in support of the hotel's conversion mushroomed between May 1945 and January 1946. Community organizations, veterans' groups, trade unions, several British Columbia MPs, and, in particular, the Rehabilitation Council bombarded the federal government with representations.[88] Finally, at New Year's, veterans with LPP affiliation began to picket the old hotel.[89] A few days later, Canadian Legion member Bob McEwen, who had recently organized a successful campaign to speed up the war brides' passage to Canada and who now required a home for his own war bride, set up a campsite and an information picket on the neighbouring courthouse lawn.[90] On 8 January a LPP delegation to city council precipitated Corey's eastern trip.[91]

At last, on the afternoon of Saturday, 26 January, members of the New Veterans Branch of the Canadian Legion resolved to occupy the old Hotel Vancouver.[92] Led by sergeant-at-arms Bob McEwen, a "shock troop" walked into the hotel lobby and informed two lone army guards that they were taking possession of the building. They wired the news to Prime Minister Mackenzie King. The "occupying force" drew up strict house rules to govern behaviour and organized committees to handle food, billeting, recreation and hygiene. They hung a 15′x3′ banner on the hotel's Granville Street wall reading "Action at Last / Veterans! Rooms for You. Come and Get Them." By Saturday evening, 100 ex-service men and women and their dependents had registered at the hotel. A "gay holiday spirit" pervaded the building as they danced to jukebox music in the Spanish Grill. By Tuesday, 1,400 people were registered,

---

[86] *Province*, 18 January 1946, p. 1.

[87] *Ibid.*, 23 January 1946, pp. 1, 6.

[88] The representations may be found in RG 19, vol. 716, file 203C-17, PAC.

[89] *Sun*, 31 December 1945, p. 3.

[90] *Ibid.*, 5 January 1946, pp. 1-2.

[91] *Province*, 8 January 1946, p. 20; and minutes, Finance Committee, 8 January 1946, in Special Committee Files, 28-C-4, CVA.

[92] *Sun*, 26 January 1946, p. 1. For newspaper accounts of the occupation, see the *Sun*, the *Province* and the *News-Herald* from 28 January to 1 February 1946; and the *Pacific Advocate*, 1 February 1946. See also Paddy Sherman, *Bennett* (Toronto: McClelland & Stewart, 1966), p. 51.

although the majority were not staying on the premises. The old Hotel Vancouver had become a veritable "palace for the public."

Federal and civic authorities made no attempt to eject the veterans from the hotel. As Ian Mackenzie pointed out to J. L. Ilsley, public opinion sided with the occupation.[93] MP James Sinclair told the veterans that their action was "the right thing to do."[94] The British Columbia Command of the Canadian Legion and the provincial CCF leader, Harold Winch, endorsed the New Veterans Branch's "sitdown." Granville Street restaurants offered free evening meals to the militants and sent in sandwiches and coffee. Vancouver newspapers sympathetically reported the "invasion" and treated lightly complaints that one occupation committee member belonged to the LPP. Three factors account for public support. First, Vancouverites believed that the veterans' wartime service should reward them with "homes as well as jobs — some would go so far as to say homes before jobs."[95] Secondly, the public's own experience of the worsening housing situation probably aroused a compassionate response to the veterans' predicament. Finally, since 1939 the community had wanted to find some socially useful purpose for the old hotel.

The occupation forced a quick resolution of the hostel problem. Mackenzie arrived in a snowy Vancouver on Monday morning's train and, as federal representative, began serious negotiations with the veterans, the city council, the Rehabilitation Council and the CPR. The next day he announced a hotel conversion plan. The CPR and the Rehabilitation Council signed an agreement on Thursday the 31st. All parties endorsed the settlement. The city contributed a $24,000 annual sum and received its tax revenue from a specially created hostel maintenance fund. The federal government conceded an annual amount of $70,000 and assured the Rehabilitation Council of a future $30,000 grant. The Board of Trade, the city council and the government sanctioned the release of locally raised civil defence money to the hostel fund. With its financial risk minimized, the Rehabilitation Council agreed to lease the building and to operate the hostel. On 1 February the veterans vacated the old hotel.

Popular protest did bring about improvements in Vancouver's living conditions. The old Hotel Vancouver occupation created a veterans'

---

[93] Telegram, I. Mackenzie to J. L. Ilsley, 29 January 1946, RG 19, vol. 716, file 203C-17, vol. 1, PAC.

[94] *Province*, 28 January 1946, p. 2.

[95] *Ibid.*, 29 January 1946, p. 4.

hostel operated until 1948 by the Rehabilitation Council. The "hotel coup" also led to the Renfrew Heights subdivision. Cognizant of the city's persistent accommodation shortages, the Rehabilitation Council approached the federal government in 1946 about permanent rental housing for the hostel tenants.[96] Subsequently, lengthy and difficult negotiations between the Department of Reconstruction and Supply and the Vancouver city council produced a 1947 agreement making possible CMHC's construction of a 600-unit garden suburb at Boundary Road and Grandview Highway.[97] Many veterans and their families moved directly from the hotel to the new subdivision known as Renfrew Heights. Thus the popular pressure of 1944-46 resulted in a hostel and a rental housing development for veterans as well as an evictions freeze and 1,200 WHL houses.

How fundamental or permanent were these improvements? The measures signified a temporary, directly interventionist program distinct from the federal government's long-term housing policy of market-related, indirect participation. As C. D. Howe, the minister responsible for housing, clearly stated in 1947, the government had no intention of applying its emergency remedies on a permanent basis.[98] Eventually CMHC sold its WHL and Renfrew Heights houses to its tenants. The Hotel Vancouver hostel and rent controls disappeared within a few years. These temporary reforms accompanied other more lasting programs fostering home ownership, stimulating the housing market and creating employment. Indeed, the federal government had introduced its business-oriented 1944 NHA at the same time as popular agitation in Vancouver had demanded and won short-term changes.

Not all of the Vancouver protest groups were committed to fundamental reform. Veterans' organizations and the Rehabilitation Council concerned themselves with the immediate needs of returned service personnel. With wartime public opinion behind them, they forced concessions like the hostel from Ottawa. The CCF, the LPP and the VHA, which did desire more substantial change, exercised less influence on the

---

[96] *Sun*, 9 November 1946, p. 3; and "The Citizens Rehabilitation Council of Greater Vancouver: Summary of Activities, 1940-1948," Buck Papers, box 11, file 15.

[97] Agreement between the City of Vancouver and H.M. the King in right of Canada represented by Wartime Housing Limited, 31 December 1947, located in the Legal Department, City of Vancouver. See also newspaper clippings on Renfrew Heights, M7913, CVA.

[98] C. D. Howe, "Meeting Canada's Housing Needs," *Public Affairs* 10 (October 1947): 217-21.

federal government. Even in 1949, when it finally amended NHA to permit the subsidization of public housing, the government failed to develop the planned, comprehensive and need-oriented solution to the housing problem recommended by the left-wing parties and by housing associations like the VHA.

However grudging and slow their responses, the federal and the Vancouver governments did eventually react to public pressure. But what were the reasons for their reluctance in bringing about even temporary reforms? The national Finance Department's hesitancy in resolving the old Hotel Vancouver question originated in its opposition towards expanding federal participation in the direct provision of housing.[99] WPTB officials who refused to take "drastic action" on the evictions issue until July 1945 were satisfied with the functioning of their rent control system and preferred to shift responsibility for housing supply to other agencies like WHL.[100] And, while WHL exhibited a notable eagerness to build more houses, it complicated matters by offering financial terms unfavourable to Vancouver. The city council declined to shoulder the financial or administrative burden of a national housing problem. Still, in the end, active protest forced the hand of the federal and the civic governments.

The Vancouver housing protests of 1944-46 did not constitute a strictly working-class movement against state and capital.[101] The LPP and the CCF may have represented the interests of labour, but the Canadian Legion acted on behalf of ex-service personnel from both the working and the middle classes, and the Rehabilitation Council, which supported housing reform out of its concern for the legitimate needs of returning service men and women as well as its fears of social unrest,[102] spoke for business, professional, labour, veterans' and community groups. While not class-specific, the Vancouver protests of the mid-forties expressed a triumph of popular will. In this one instance, at least, popular pressure brought about measures, however temporary, to improve the accommodation of the Canadian people.

[99] Wade, *Wartime Housing Limited: Overview and Evaluation*, pp. 25-26, 40-41.

[100] O. Lobley to D. Gordon, 24 August 1944, p. 1, and E. R. Gold to D. Gordon, 5 August 1944, RG 64, ser. 1030, box 701, file 25-2, vol. 1.

[101] By contrast, the momentous 1915 Glasgow rent strikes, which invite comparison with Vancouver, denoted a strictly class-based movement of workers in the neighbourhood and in the workplace; see Damer, "State, Class, and Housing," pp. 73-75, 101-06.

[102] A. W. Cowley to W. L. M. King, 22 June 1945, RG 2, ser. 18, vol. 9, file H-13, PAC; "Memorandum Respecting the Housing Situation in Vancouver," p. 8, RG 19, ser. E3, vol. 4017, PAC; telegram, I. Mackenzie to J. L. Ilsley, 19 September 1944, and J. Clark to I. Mackenzie, 21 September 1944, RG 19, vol. 716, file 203C-17, PAC.

A Half Century of Writing on Vancouver's History*

PATRICIA ROY

At the time of Vancouver's Golden Jubilee, Walter N. Sage, a historian at the University of British Columbia, wrote a historical sketch, "Vancouver: The Rise of a City," in the *Dalhousie Review*.[1] This article, published in distant Halifax, was probably the first attempt by a professional historian to present an overview of the city's history. So new was Vancouver that Sage wrote of "old timers" who remembered the first clearings, and so imbued was he by their spirit of optimism that, despite the Depression, he suggested the city was "preparing for another boom." He also noted the "small but growing City Archives." Sage may have planned to write a large-scale study himself. In 1932-33 the Canadian Club of Vancouver granted him $250 to collect and copy material for a history of Vancouver.[2] The resulting six bound volumes of typescripts demonstrate the physical impediments to historical research before the easy availability of copying machines, the lack then of accessible manuscript sources and, especially, the narrow focus of historical interest. The collection includes extracts from *British Columbia Magazine, circa* 1911, biographies from R. E. Gosnell's *History of British Columbia* and newspaper stories about anti-Asian disturbances of 1886-87 and 1907.

In the meantime, the indefatigable Major J. S. Matthews, the more or less self-appointed city archivist, began collecting and interpreting selected

---

* I wish to thank the editors of this volume, Jean Barman and Robert McDonald, for their helpful suggestions. However, I am wholly responsible for any sins of omission and for all judgements on the literature.

[1] Vol. XVII (April 1937), pp. 49-54. In 1946 Sage took the city's story up to that date. Though noting the "sterner days" of Wars and Depression, his outlook was still optimistic. For example, his few paragraphs on the Depression referred to grain exports and the new city hall but not to demonstrations of the unemployed. Indeed, he concluded by suggesting that "if Vancouverites will only look back on the sixty years of progress since 1886 they can look towards the future with calmness and confidence." W. N. Sage, "Vancouver: 60 Years of Progress," *Journal of Commerce Year Book* 13 (1946): 97-115.

[2] A set of the volumes was deposited in the Library of the University of British Columbia. The W. N. Sage Papers in the Special Collections Division of that Library provide information on the origins of the volumes.

BC STUDIES, nos. 69-70, Spring-Summer 1986

fragments of Vancouver's history. While Matthews' many publications are most kindly described as antiquarian miscellanies, the opinionated major did make Vancouver residents realize they had a history worth preserving.

If Sage could see Vancouver in 1986, its physical expansion might not startle him; the growth of its historiography undoubtedly would. Indeed, the Centennial will be marked by the publication of an assortment of neighbourhood and specialized studies, a major bibliographical guide compiled by Linda Hale and published by the Vancouver Historical Society,[3] and, of course, this volume. Despite the apparent proliferation of material, it is safe to say that no aspect of Vancouver's history has been completely and systematically examined and that many subjects remain virtually unexplored.

Until the late 1950s, academic interest in Vancouver's history was limited even though *The British Columbia Historical Quarterly (BCHQ)*, founded in 1937, provided scholars with an attractive place in which to publish their findings. Significantly, except for articles by its editor and provincial archivist, W. Kaye Lamb, on trans-Pacific shipping and a complementary study of the Trans-Pacific Mail service to Australia by a columnist for *Harbour and Shipping*, most writers on Vancouver subjects concentrated on the pre-railway era. For example, Judge F. W. Howay, at one time the province's leading historian, contributed several articles to the *BCHQ* on economic and social developments on Burrard Inlet in the 1860s and 1870s.[4] Younger scholars were similarly fascinated by the pioneer era.[5] One M.A. graduate even wrote on newspapers published in Vancouver before the arrival of the CPR!

The fading of the *BCHQ* in the 1950s paradoxically paralleled a rising interest in British Columbia history as epitomized by the publication in

[3] Linda Hale, comp., *Vancouver Centennial Bibliography*, 4 vols. (Vancouver: Vancouver Historical Society, 1986).

[4] Lamb, "Empress Odyssey: A History of the Canadian Pacific Service to the Orient, 1913-1945," *British Columbia Historical Quarterly* [hereafter *BCHQ*] 11 (January 1948): 1-78, "Empress to the Orient," *BCHQ* 4 (January 1940): 29-56 and *BCHQ* 4 (April 1940): 79-110 and "The Pioneer Days of the Trans-Pacific Service," *BCHQ* 1 (July 1937): 143-64; J. H. Hamilton, "The All-Red Route, 1893-1958: A History of the Trans-Pacific Mail Service between British Columbia, Australia and New Zealand," *BCHQ* 20 (January-April 1956): 1-126; Howay, "Coal Mining on Burrard Inlet," *BCHQ* 4 (January 1940): 1-20, "Early Settlement on Burrard Inlet," *BCHQ* 1 (April 1937): 101-14 and "Early Shipping in Burrard Inlet," *BCHQ* 1 (January 1937): 1-20.

[5] For example, Helen R. Boutilier, "Vancouver's Earliest Days," *BCHQ* 10 (April 1946): 151-70; Bessie Lamb, "From 'Tickler' to 'Telegram': Notes on Early Vancouver Newspapers," *BCHQ* 12 (July 1945): 175-99.

1958 of a provincial centennial volume, *British Columbia: A History* by Margaret A. Ormsby.[6] Ormsby's stage was the entire province but in a few paragraphs she vividly depicted the development of Vancouver as a metropolis. While Ormsby was familiar with Maurice Careless's now classic article on metropolitanism and the literature from which it developed,[7] she was not the first to apply metropolitan themes to Vancouver. Indeed, Sage, who is chiefly recorded in Canadian historiography as an early proponent of the frontier thesis,[8] implicitly accepted metropolitanism in his Vancouver article. Since then, despite its complexities and inexactness,[9] or more likely because of them, and because of its adaptability to the whiggish idea of the city getting bigger and better, metropolitanism has provided historians of Vancouver with a convenient, if not always rigorous, theme.

A good example of the subsumption of the concept is *Vancouver: From Milltown to Metropolis*,[10] whose author, Alan Morley, extensively quoted Ormsby's comments on Vancouver's metropolitan role. In a sense, Morley also serves as a bridge between the preoccupation with pioneers and a growing interest in the city's later years. Morley, a journalist, first demonstrated his interest in Vancouver's history in a series of pioneer stories published in 1940 in the Vancouver *Sun*; fully a third of his book deals with the years before incorporation. It is tempting to dismiss Morley's work as a chronicle of "facts" and anecdotes, but a careful reading reveals that Morley is telling the story of Vancouver "flowering into a metropolis" (p. 189).

In 1970, about a year after the publication of a second edition of Morley's book, another Vancouver writer, Eric Nicol, contributed *Vancouver*[11] to "The Romance of Canadian Cities Series." Nicol, a highly acclaimed humorist and essayist, strains to sustain humour throughout Vancouver's history. Like Morley, his approach is anecdotal; he develops his stories more fully but presents less information, and he lacks the in-

---

[6] Toronto: Macmillan, 1958. A revised edition was published in 1971.

[7] "Frontierism, Metropolitanism, and Canadian History," *Canadian Historical Review* [hereafter *CHR*] 35 (March 1954): 1-21.

[8] "Some Aspects of the Frontier in Canadian History," Canadian Historical Association, *Annual Report*, 1928, pp. 62-72.

[9] See Donald F. Davis, "The 'Metropolitan Thesis' and the Writing of Canadian Urban History," *Urban History Review* [hereafter *UHR*] XIV (October 1985): 95-113.

[10] Vancouver: Mitchell Press, 1969 (second edition). The first edition was published in 1961.

[11] New York: Doubleday, 1970.

sightful observations about the nature of the city's growth that occasionally appear in Morley's work. The books do complement each other:
Morley focuses on economic and political matters; Nicol is more interested in the kind of social history commonly known as manners. More
informative than either Morley or Nicol is *The Vancouver Book*,[12] edited
by Chuck Davis, which appeared in 1976. Somewhat of a cross between
an encyclopedia and an almanac, its short essays touch on almost every
aspect of activity within the city. Its sketches and maps of city neighbourhoods are especially valuable.

Recent histories have relied as much on illustrations as on prose. In
Vancouver's First Century, Anne Kloppenborg and her former colleagues
in the City's Social Planning Department produced a rich scrapbook of
historical photographs.[13] Another exceptionally handsome volume, *Vancouver: The Way It Was*,[14] is remarkable for the detailed watercolour
sketches of historic Vancouver scenes by its author, Michael Kluckner,
and for its numerous well-chosen historical photographs. Organized by
neighbourhoods and incidents, the text is fact-filled but somewhat dis-
jointed.

Photographs are also a feature of *Vancouver: An Illustrated History*[15]
by Patricia E. Roy. Unfortunately, the captions, which were concocted
in Toronto, are not always accurate. The main text, the first attempt at
a book-length academic overview of the city's history, reflects the accessibility of Vancouver's abundant historical record and synthesizes a number
of scholarly articles and theses, written mainly in the 1960s and 1970s.
Though somewhat constrained by the format of "The History of Canadian Cities" series in which it appears, the volume explores Vancouver's
metropolitan aspirations and achievements and its relations with the
provincial government.

Roy's book was influenced by several articles on early Vancouver by
Norbert MacDonald. The importance of the CPR in directing the city's
early growth is extensively documented in "The Canadian Pacific Railway
and Vancouver's Development to 1900."[16] His earlier essay, "A Critical

[12] North Vancouver: J. J. Douglas, 1976.

[13] Anne Kloppenborg *et al.*, eds., *Vancouver's First Century: A City Album, 1860-
1960* (Vancouver: J. J. Douglas, 1977). A second edition, carrying the subject up
to 1985, was published in 1985.

[14] Vancouver: Whitecap, 1984.

[15] Toronto: James Lorimer, 1980.

[16] *BC Studies* [hereafter *BCS*] 35 (Autumn 1977): 3-35. [Reprinted in W. P. Ward
and R. A. J. McDonald, eds., *British Columbia: Historical Readings* (Vancouver:
Douglas & McIntyre, 1981), pp. 396-425.]

Growth Cycle for Vancouver, 1900-1914," is a useful narrative follow-up.[17] MacDonald came to his interest in Vancouver with the idea of comparing it with Seattle. An early result was a study of the responses of the two cities to the Klondike Gold Rush,[18] but his most stimulating work is "Population Growth and Change in Seattle and Vancouver, 1880-1960."[19]

While Norbert MacDonald has delineated the general outlines of the city's early decades and raised some interesting comparative questions, his colleague, Robert A. J. McDonald, has intensively analyzed the city's early business elites and their role in developing the city. One of his first articles, "City-Building in the Canadian West: A Case Study of Economic Growth in Early Vancouver, 1886-1893,"[20] suggests that "the outline of Vancouver's role as a metropolitan centre for the resource economy of British Columbia was clearly discernible by 1893." Attributing this to what he calls internal factors, namely the "railroad and real estate interests," rather than to more outward-looking businessmen such as "wholesale merchants, lumbermen or salmon canners," McDonald emphasizes that "the growth-producing regional connections that later propelled Vancouver to metropolitan status were not yet the principal agents of city expansion" (p. 28). In a subsequent article, covering a broader time period and concentrating particularly on the changing relationships of Vancouver and Victoria,[21] he has shown how, beginning in the 1890s, the expansion of the provincial economy and strengthening of continental rather than maritime ties led to "Vancouver's triumph over Victoria" (p. 39). The geographer, L. D. McCann, has explored the same theme in a more generalized and theoretically focused essay.[22]

[17] *BCS* 17 (Spring 1973): 26-42. The two articles have been revised and combined as " 'C.P.R. Town': The City-Building Process in Vancouver, 1860-1914," in G. A. Stelter and A. F. J. Artibise, eds., *Shaping the Urban Landscape: Aspects of the Canadian City-Building Process* (Ottawa: Carleton University Press, 1982), pp. 382-412.

[18] *CHR* XLIX (September 1968): 234-46.

[19] *Pacific Historical Review* 39 (October 1970): 297-321. [Reprinted in J. Friesen and H. K. Ralston, eds., *Historical Essays on British Columbia* (Toronto: McClelland & Stewart, 1976), pp. 201-27.] Also see his forthcoming *Distant Neighbors: A Comparative History of Seattle and Vancouver* (Lincoln: University of Nebraska Press).

[20] *BCS* 43 (Autumn 1979): 3-28.

[21] "Victoria, Vancouver, and the Economic Development of British Columbia, 1886-1914," in A. F. J. Artibise, ed., *Town and City* (Regina: Canadian Plains Research Centre, 1981), pp. 31-55. [Reprinted in Ward and McDonald, *British Columbia*, pp. 369-95.]

[22] "Urban Growth in a Staple Economy: The Emergence of Vancouver as a Regional Metropolis, 1886-1914," in L. J. Evenden, ed., *Vancouver: Western Metropolis* (Victoria: University of Victoria, 1978), pp. 17-41. This volume consists of a

Vancouver's dominance of its hinterland is also implicit in a variety of works on transportation such as histories of the Union Steamship Company and the Canadian Pacific's coastal fleet and an article on Premier Richard McBride's railway policies.[23] A very detailed study of John Hendry, a railway promoter and lumberman, illustrates the metropolitan ambitions of one Vancouver resident and sheds light on the relation between business and government in the early twentieth century,[24] a theme examined in several articles on the British Columbia Electric Railway Company that also provide some information about urban transportation.[25] Metropolitan ambitions were not confined to the white business community. As Paul Yee's studies of Chinese business records demonstrate, members of Vancouver's Chinese community also organized trade throughout the province.[26] Studies of individual companies and businessmen are still rare. Nevertheless, several locally based firms such as the forest giant MacMillan-Bloedel, Canadian Pacific Air Lines and Woodward's Department Stores have commissioned histories of themselves or their founders. To these, Donald Gutstein's *Vancouver, Ltd.*,[27] which is less sympathetic to business, offers some contrast.

The role of businessmen also appears in several studies of recreational facilities. William McKee has argued that the parks system that evolved

number of essays, mainly but not exclusively contemporary, on the general theme suggested by its title.

[23] Gerald Rushton, *Echoes of the Whistle: An Illustrated History of the Union Steamship Company* (Vancouver: Douglas & McIntyre, 1980); Norman R. Hacking and W. Kaye Lamb, *The Princess Story: A Century and a Half of West Coast Shipping* (Vancouver: Mitchell Press, 1974); Patricia E. Roy, "Progress, Prosperity and Politics: The Railway Policies of Richard McBride," *BCS* 47 (Autumn 1980): 3-28.

[24] Phyllis Veazey, "John Hendry and the Vancouver, Westminster and Yukon Railway: 'It Would Put Us on Easy Street,'" *BCS* 59 (Autumn 1983): 44-63.

[25] Patricia E. Roy, "Regulating the British Columbia Electric Railway: The First Public Utilities Commission in B.C.," *BCS* 11 (Fall 1971): 3-20; "The Fine Art of Lobbying and Persuading: The Case of the B.C. Electric Railway," in David S. Macmillan, ed., *Canadian Business History: Selected Studies* (Toronto: McClelland & Stewart, 1972), pp. 125-43; "Direct Management from Abroad: The Formative Years of the British Columbia Electric Railway," *Business History Review* 47 (Summer 1973): 239-59.

[26] In addition to the paper in this volume see "Business Devices from Two Worlds: The Chinese in Early Vancouver," *BCS* 62 (Summer 1984): 44-67.

[27] Donald MacKay, *Empire of Wood: the MacMillan Bloedel Story* (Vancouver: Douglas & McIntyre, 1982): Ronald A. Keith, *Bush Pilot with a Briefcase* (Toronto: Doubleday, 1972); Douglas E. Harker, *The Woodwards* (Vancouver: Mitchell Press, 1976); Donald Gutstein, *Vancouver, Ltd.* (Toronto: James Lorimer, 1975).

from 1886 to 1929 was "a product of local businessmen,"[28] while David Breen and Kenneth Coates have demonstrated the importance of businessmen in establishing the Pacific National Exhibition,[29] and Robert McDonald has used controversies relating to the uses of Stanley Park to explore class differences in Vancouver.[30]

Nevertheless, historians have neither exhausted the possibilities of examining Vancouver's businesses and businessmen nor fully studied the history of organized labour. Since 1899, when the Vancouver Trades and Labor Council was founded, Vancouver has been the centre for much of the activity of organized labour in the province — a fact underscored, for example, in Stuart Jamieson's now classic essay, "Regional Factors in Industrial Conflict."[31] Surprisingly, despite the availability of records, no one has written a full study of the Council, though it is mentioned in general studies of the labour movement in western Canada. A few unions have sponsored the writing of their own histories. One of the best is *That Long Distance Feeling: A History of the Telecommunications Union*, by Elaine Bernard.[32] This book is especially valuable for its references to the effects of technological change on workers and on the place of women in the workplace. In "Union Maids: Organized Women Workers in Vancouver, 1900-1915,"[33] Star Rosenthal undertook a pioneer study of that long-ignored subject, women in the workforce. The marginality of that place is well demonstrated in Deborah Nilsen's essay on prostitution. The developing interest in women's studies has also led to the publication of several essays on women in organizations as diverse as the Waitresses' Union and the University Women's Club.[34]

---

[28] "The Vancouver Park System, 1886-1929: A Product of Local Businessmen, *UHR* 3-78 (February 1979): 33-49.

[29] *Vancouver's Fair: An Administrative & Political History of the Pacific National Exhibition* (Vancouver: University of British Columbia Press, 1982).

[30] " 'Holy Retreat' or 'Practical Breathing Spot'?: Class Perceptions of Vancouver's Stanley Park, 1910-1913," *CHR* LXV (June 1984): 127-53.

[31] "Regional Factors in Industrial Conflict: The Case of British Columbia," *Canadian Journal of Economics and Political Science* XXXVIII (August 1962): 405-16. [Reprinted in Friesen and Ralston, *Historical Essays*, pp. 238-42 and Ward and McDonald, *British Columbia*, pp. 500-14.]

[32] Vancouver: New Star, 1982.

[33] *BCS* 41 (Spring 1979): 36-55.

[34] Deborah Nilsen, "The 'Social Evil': Prostitution in Vancouver, 1900-1920," in Barbara Latham and Cathy Kess, eds., *In Her Own Right: Selected Essays in Women's History in British Columbia* (Victoria: Camosun College, 1980), pp. 205-28. Three other essays in the same volume are of interest: Marie Campbell, "Sexism in British Columbia Trade Unions," pp. 147-86; Susan Wade, "Helena Gutteridge: Votes for Women and Trade Unions," pp. 187-203; and Tami Adil-

Historians have focused characteristically on dramatic incidents such as
the severe labour unrest around the time of the First World War[35] or the
events that led to Mayor G. G. McGeer's reading of the Riot Act and
the departure of the On-To-Ottawa-Trek in 1935. The "Red Scare,"
which McGeer exploited politically, also provides the background for
R. C. McCandless' study of the waterfront strike of 1935. Unrest, of
course, did not end in 1935. Good evidence of this may be found in
Steve Brodie's recollections of the 1938 Sit Downers' Strike.[36]

Closely related to labour unrest was the question of relief for the unemployed and others unable to provide for themselves. In "Public Welfare: Vancouver Style, 1910-1920,"[37] Diane Matters sketches the various
resources available to the needy, including women and children, around
the time of the First World War, while in "Vancouver: A 'Mecca' for
the Unemployed,"[38] Patricia Roy shows how the city tried to cope with
periodic influxes of unemployed men before 1930. Irene Howard's
refreshing essay in this volume documents how left-wing women helped
the unemployed men in the 1930s; Mary Patricia Powell has described
how the more broadly based Local Council of Women showed support

man, "Evlyn Farris and the University Women's Club," pp. 147-66. See also
Gillian Weiss, "The Brightest Women of Our Land: Vancouver Clubwomen,
1919-1928," in Barbara K. Latham and Roberta J. Pazdro, *Not Just Pin Money:
Selected Essays on the History of Women's Work in British Columbia* (Victoria:
Camosun College, 1984), pp. 199-209, and, in the same volume, Marilyn Barber,
"The Gentlewomen of Queen Mary's Coronation Hostel," pp. 141-58.

[35] Vancouver incidents are included in such general studies of labour in Western
Canada as Paul Phillips, *No Power Greater: A Century of Labour in B.C.* (Vancouver: B.C. Federation of Labour, 1967); A. Ross McCormack, *Reformers, Rebels
and Revolutionaries: The Western Canadian Radical Movement, 1899-1919*
(Toronto: University of Toronto Press, 1977); David J. Bercuson, *Fools and Wise
Men: The Rise and Fall of the One Big Union* (Toronto: McGraw-Hill Ryerson,
1978); and Martin Robin, *Radical Politics and Canadian Labour, 1880-1930*
(Kingston: Queen's University, Industrial Relations Centre, 1968). One article
that focuses mainly on Vancouver is Patricia E. Roy, "The British Columbia Electric Railway and Its Street Railway Employees: Paternalism in Labour Relations,"
BCS 16 (Winter 1972-73): 3-24.

[36] Ronald Liversedge, ed., *Recollections of the On To Ottawa Trek*, ed. by Victor
Howard (Toronto: McClelland & Stewart, 1973); "Vancouver's 'Red Menace' of
1935: The Waterfront Situation," *BCS* 22 (Summer 1974): 56-70. Some of the
strikers' own recollections may be found in ILWU Local 500 Pensioners, *'Man
Along the Shore': The Story of the Vancouver Waterfront* (Vancouver, 1975);
Steve Brodie, *Bloody Sunday Vancouver — 1938* (Vancouver: Young Communist
League, 1974).

[37] *Journal of Canadian Studies* 14 (Spring 1979): 3-15.

[38] Artibise, ed., *Town and City*, pp. 393-413.

for unemployed men while concentrating on the problems of unemployed women.[39]

Although Vancouver had many difficulties in providing adequate social welfare services, Margaret Andrews has demonstrated early Vancouver's great pride in its public health program and great interest in public health matters during the Influenza Epidemic of 1918-19. A related study examines the patterns of practice of Vancouver doctors, 1886-1920.[40] Andrews is sympathetic to the medical profession. In contrast, in their essay in this volume, Veronica Strong-Boag and Kathryn McPherson contend that in obstetrical matters doctors did not always know best. Though writing from different points of view, all of these authors on medical subjects allude to a recurring theme in studies of Vancouver's history, namely the population's transient nature. Important as this basic theme is, few historians have systematically examined it.

Some of the documentation for such a study may well exist in the records of the Vancouver School Board. However, despite the importance of education and some of the Board's innovations, historians have given the schools relatively short shrift. Specific exceptions are "house" histories of the first fifty years of the high schools and of the University of British Columbia.[41] Vancouver schools, however, receive more than passing mention in such provincial studies as F. H. Johnson's *History of Public Education in British Columbia*,[42] Jean Barman's *Growing Up British in British Columbia: Boys in Private School*[43] and essays on public schooling by Timothy Dunn, on kindergartens by Gillian Weiss and on schools for juvenile delinquents by Diane Matters.[44] As well, a national survey,

---

[39] "A Response to the Depression: The Local Council of Women of Vancouver," in Latham and Kess, *In Her Own Right*, pp. 255-78.

[40] "The Best Advertisement a City Can Have: Public Health Services in Vancouver, 1886-1888," *UHR* XII (February 1984): 19-27; "Epidemic and Public Health: Influenza in Vancouver, 1918-1919," *BCS* 34 (Summer 1977): 21-44; "Medical Attendance in Vancouver, 1886-1920," *BCS* 40 (Winter 1978-79): 32-56.

[41] [K. A. Waites, ed.] *The First Fifty Years: Vancouver High Schools, 1890-1940* [Vancouver: Vancouver Board of School Trustees, 1940]; H. T. Logan, *Tuum Est: A History of the University of British Columbia* (Vancouver: The University of British Columbia, 1958).

[42] Vancouver: University of British Columbia Publications Centre, 1964.

[43] Vancouver: University of British Columbia Press, 1984.

[44] Timothy A. Dunn, "The Rise of Mass Public Schooling in British Columbia, 1900-1929," in J. Donald Wilson and David C. Jones, eds., *Schooling and Society in Twentieth Century British Columbia* (Calgary: Detselig, 1980), pp. 23-51; Gillian Weiss, "An Essential Year for the Child: The Kindergarten in British Columbia," in Wilson and Jones, *Schooling and Society*, pp. 139-61; Diane L. Matters, "The Boys' Industrial School: Education for Juvenile Offenders," in Wilson and Jones,

Neil Sutherland's *Children in English-Canadian Society*, includes considerable Vancouver material.[45] Recently, Sutherland has turned his interests specifically to Vancouver. The charming essay in this volume is an early result.

With their emphasis on the everyday experiences of ordinary people, these recollections of childhood fit the current historical fashion of looking at working-class life.[46] In a fundamental article that is also important for its methodology, Eleanor Bartlett has constructed statistical series for Vancouver from 1900 to 1929 showing that "inflation often outweighed the benefits" of rapid growth for most working men (p. 60).[47] The fullest expression of interest in working-class life is the Centennial volume, *Working Lives*. This generously illustrated book includes brief notes on a variety of activities from childbirth to funerals, on occupations as diverse as canning salmon and banking, and on working-class organizations. Four analytical essays tie the sometimes eclectic vignettes together. Anecdotal evidence of working-class life in the first half of the twentieth century can be found in such volumes as Rolf Knight's *Along the #20 Line* and the *Sound Heritage* volume, *Opening Doors*, a collection of interviews with long-time residents of the East End, including Strathcona, Vancouver's immigrant neighbourhood.[48]

Historical studies of Vancouver's ethnic communities, especially its highly visible Asian population, have often concentrated on specific incidents. For example, there are several books on the *Komagata Maru* incident of 1914,[49] which saw over 300 would-be Sikh immigrants denied entry to Canada, but study of the East Indian community has been the almost exclusive preserve of sociologists.[50] The East Asian community has

   Schooling and Society, pp. 53-70; and Indiana Matters, "Sinners or Sinned Against?: Historical Aspects of Female Juvenile Delinquency in British Columbia," in Latham and Pazdro, *Not Just Pin Money*, pp. 265-77.

[45] Toronto: University of Toronto Press, 1976.

[46] The Working Lives Collective, *Working Lives: Vancouver, 1886-1986* (Vancouver: New Star, 1985).

[47] *BCS* 51 (Autumn 1981): 3-62.

[48] *Along the No. 20 Line: Reminiscences of the Vancouver Waterfront* (Vancouver: New Star, 1980); *Sound Heritage* VIII (Victoria: Provincial Archives of British Columbia, 1979).

[49] The best is Hugh Johnston, *The Voyage of the Komagata Maru: The Sikh Challenge to Canada's Colour Bar* (Delhi: Oxford University Press, 1979).

[50] Though now somewhat dated, a bibliographical essay by Norm Buchignani, "A Review of the Historical and Sociological Literature on East Indians in Canada," *Canadian Ethnic Studies* IX (1977): 86-108 is still useful. Despite its title, James G. Chadney, *The Sikhs of Vancouver* (New York: AMS Press, 1984) is largely a survey of the community in 1972-73.

received more attention because it is larger and older and because the Japanese presence, in particular, led to several incidents of international and national consequence. Since Canada's Chinese and Japanese communities before World War II were largely concentrated in the Vancouver area, general histories such as *From China to Canada*,[51] edited by Edgar Wickberg, and Ken Adachi's *The Enemy That Never Was*[52] inevitably include considerable Vancouver material.[53] Moreover, because the 1907 Anti-Asian Riot created an international incident, that particular subject has even attracted the attention of a Japanese scholar.[54] Vancouver's other ethnic communities, in contrast, have had a relatively low profile both in fact and in historiography. The native Indians, for example, are virtually non-existent in historical studies of Vancouver, though Rolf Knight's *Indians at Work*[55] offers a fleeting glimpse of them in various workplaces.

The distinctiveness of Vancouver's neighbourhoods is clearly revealed in two essays in this collection. From her analysis of school board election results and census data, Jean Barman suggests that while Vancouver had neighbourhoods with distinctive demographic characteristics, Vancouver voters, at least in the interwar years, demonstrated a sense of community that transcended local areas. Using descriptions of housing and the residents' comments, Deryck Holdsworth's essay reaches a similar conclusion.[56] While the homes of workingmen and of business and professional men might differ in size and architectural splendour and be in different neighbourhoods, the owners of "cottages" and "castles" shared

[51] Toronto: McClelland & Stewart, 1982.

[52] Toronto: McClelland & Stewart, 1976.

[53] A comprehensive though now somewhat dated review of the literature on East Asians is Patricia E. Roy, " 'White Canada Forever': Two Generations of Studies," *Canadian Ethnic Studies* XI (1979): 97-109.

[54] Masako Iino, "Japan's Response to the Vancouver Riot of 1907," *BCS* 60 (Winter 1983-84): 28-47.

[55] Vancouver: New Star, 1978. Despite its title, Irene Howard, *Vancouver's Svenskar: A History of the Swedish Community in Vancouver* (Vancouver: Vancouver Historical Society, 1970), focuses more on the province than on the city.

[56] Holdsworth has published several studies of housing styles: "House and Home in Vancouver: Images of West Coast Urbanism, 1886-1929," in G. A. Stelter and A. F. J. Artibise, eds., *The Canadian City: Essays in Urban History* (Toronto: McClelland & Stewart, 1977), pp. 186-211, and, with E. G. Mills, "The B. C. Mills Prefabricated System: The Emergence of Ready-Made Buildings in Western Canada," *Occasional Papers in Archaeology and History*, no. 14 (Ottawa: Canadian Historic Sites, 1975), pp. 127-69. Some of Vancouver's most interesting historic buildings are described in Harold Kalman, *Exploring Vancouver 2* (Vancouver: University of British Columbia Press, 1978).

both a "sense that they were part of a distinctive place" and a pride in home ownership. As John Weaver has shown, the tendency toward single family residential neighbourhoods was reinforced by zoning regulations and the business interests that influenced it.[57]

Rapid population growth after World War II challenged the ideal of individual home ownership. The seriousness of the post-war housing shortage is vividly illustrated in Jill Wade's essay in this volume on the occupation of the "old" Hotel Vancouver, which led the federal government to develop new housing. Since the 1950s, as the demography of city residents changed and real estate prices rose sharply, the owner-occupied single family home has become less and less a feature of Vancouver's landscape. As yet, however, no historian has made any comprehensive study of this phenomenon.

Civic government is another subject that historians have not yet fully explored, although David Ricardo Williams' forthcoming biography of Gerry McGeer should go some way towards filling the gap.[58] Collectively, the existing historiography offers only an episodic view. Robert McDonald's thoughtful analysis of the role of business leaders in civic government indicates that before 1914, small rather than large businessmen — that is, contractors, real estate men and merchants rather than representatives of large corporations such as the CPR or the major mill owners — controlled civic government. His essay also notes the weakness of the urban reform movement but does not take the subject past 1914.[59] Indeed, civic politics from 1914 until the mid-1930s, when the paradox of the introduction of party politics at city hall stimulated the creation of the long dominant Non-Partisan movement, are largely an unknown subject. In her essay, "The CCF, NPA and Civic Change: Provincial Forces Behind Vancouver Politics, 1930-1940," Andrea Smith shows that in the 1930s provincial politicians rather than local businessmen dominated the NPA and abolished the ward system.[60]

Despite its primary concern of examining models of party development at the municipal level, Fern Miller's study of civic political parties provides considerable useful material on local politics 1936-71 and on the

[57] "The Property Industry and Land Use Controls: The Vancouver Experience, 1910-1945," *Plan Canada* 19 (September-December 1979): 211-25. [Reprinted in Ward and McDonald, *British Columbia*, pp. 426-48.]

[58] Vancouver: Douglas & McIntyre, 1986.

[59] "The Business Elite and Municipal Politics in Vancouver," *UHR* XI (February 1983): 1-14.

[60] *BCS* 53 (Spring 1982): 45-65.

changing nature of the city.[61] Paul Tennant's overview of "Vancouver Civic Politics, 1929-1980"[62] does touch on the earlier period but deals chiefly with 1968-72, which Tennant describes as a turning point in civic politics because of the emergence of new parties, notably TEAM and COPE, and the appearance of professionals rather than businessmen as the majority on city council. Some of the aldermen who participated in much of this activity were unusually articulate and have published such relevant books as *Vancouver*,[63] by the geographer Walter Hardwick; *Vancouver Tomorrow: A Search for Greatness*[64] and *Cities, Citizens and Freeways*,[65] by the urban planners Warnett Kennedy and V. Setty Pendakur respectively; and *A Socialist Perspective for Vancouver*,[66] by Harry Rankin, a lawyer and founder of COPE, the left-wing civic political group.

Traditionally, historians looked at Vancouver subjects primarily for their own sake. Many institutions and organizations, for example, have published or encouraged the publication of their own histories. Most of them are primarily for the benefit of members but some, such as Peter Moogk's history of local defences[67] and R. H. Roy's history of the Seaforth Highlanders,[68] have more than parochial interest. Imaginative readers of the histories of such groups as the Vancouver Club, the Royal Vancouver Yacht Club and the Georgian Club can glean insight into the social lives of Vancouver's upper classes.[69] Similarly, a variety of books

---

[61] "Vancouver Civic Political Parties: Developing a Model of Party-System Change and Stabilization," *BCS* 25 (Spring 1975): 3-31.

[62] *BCS* 46 (Autumn 1980): 3-27. Useful supplements are two earlier articles of which Tennant was a co-author: with Robert Easton, "Vancouver Civic Party Leadership: Backgrounds, Attitudes and Non-Civic Party Affiliation," *BCS* 2 (Summer 1969): 19-29 and with David Zirnhelt, "The Emergence of Metropolitan Government in Greater Vancouver," *BCS* 15 (Autumn 1972): 3-28.

[63] Don Mills, Ontario: Collier-Macmillan, 1974.

[64] Vancouver: Mitchell Press, 1975.

[65] Vancouver: Transportation Development Agency, 1972.

[66] Vancouver: Progress, 1974.

[66] Peter N. Moogk, *Vancouver Defended: A History of the Men and Guns of the Lower Mainland Defences, 1859-1949* (Surrey: Antonson, 1978).

[68] Reginald H. Roy, *The Seaforth Highlanders of Canada, 1919-1965* (Vancouver: Seaforth Highlanders, 1969).

[69] Paul L. Bissley, *The History of the Vancouver Club* (Vancouver: Vancouver Club, 1971); G. A. Cran and Norm Hacking, *Annals of the Royal Vancouver Yacht Club, 1903-1965* (Vancouver: Royal Vancouver Yacht Club, 1965); and Mrs. R. H. Tupper, *The History of the Georgian Club* (Vancouver, 1961).

such as Ivan Ackery's recollections of his life as a theatre manager and the history of the Vancouver Canucks help document popular culture.[70]

More recently, as some of the studies already mentioned suggest and as some of the essays in this volume confirm, scholars have begun to take a more sophisticated approach and have examined Vancouver subjects in a broader comparative perspective or as case studies designed to test more universal theories. For example, in his essay in this volume, James Huzel, a demographic historian, uses local data to study the relationship between law, crime and society in Vancouver and to use Vancouver "as a test case within the extensive debate on the impact of economic condition on crime."

Finally, Robert McDonald's examination of the concept of class as it applied to working-class Vancouver before World War I pulls together two strands that have informed the historiography of Vancouver: learning more about Vancouver and using Vancouver as a case study. Yet McDonald does not abandon the framework that sees Vancouver as existing in metropolitan relationship with a hinterland. At the same time he draws on a historical literature that has investigated a number of themes such as ethnic relations, labour conflict, transiency, neighbourhood differences and the role of women. Most significantly, he challenges the conventional wisdom that Vancouver workers were unusually militant and radical. The existence of such a challenge suggests that the historiography of Vancouver is beginning to come of age. Perhaps some day a historian will qualify metropolitanism as a concept to interpret Vancouver's past. That, however, will be difficult to do until much more is known about all aspects of the city's history.

If W. N. Sage, the only historian to publish for Vancouver's Golden Jubilee, could see the variety of historical studies available for the Centennial, he would be surprised. He might be disappointed that his collection of typescript documents had been little used, but he should be pleased to see that the metropolitan concept was still popular. Though he might mourn the demise of the *British Columbia Historical Quarterly*, surely he would be cheered by the fact that a replacement journal, *BC Studies*, has published a number of articles on Vancouver since its founding in 1969 and is the vehicle for this Centennial collection. And he might even chuckle when he noticed that whereas he and his contemporaries concentrated on the pioneer era before the railway, few historians since have taken their studies past his time, the 1930s. The Centennial,

---

[70] Ivan Ackery, *Fifty Years on Theatre Row* (Vancouver: Hancock, 1980); Denny Boyd, *The Vancouver Canucks Story* (Toronto: McGraw-Hill Ryerson, 1973).

the resulting lively interest in writing neighbourhood histories, and the publication of a very practical guide to the writing of Vancouver's history[71] may mean that we will not have to wait for a Sesquicentennial or rely only on political scientists for analyses of the rapidly changing city of the 1940s and beyond.

[71] *Exploring Vancouver's Past: An Informal Guide to Researching Local and Family History* (Vancouver: Vancouver Centennial Commission, 1984).

Contributors

Jean Barman teaches history and history of education at the University of British Columbia. She is the author of *Growing Up British in British Columbia: Boys in Private School.*

Deryck Holdsworth is an urban historical geographer who is currently an Associate Editor of the Historical Atlas of Canada project based in Toronto. Most recently, he edited *Reviving Main Street.*

Irene Howard is a Vancouver writer specializing in local history. Her publications include *Vancouver's Svenskar: A History of the Swedish Community in Vancouver* and *Bowen Island, 1870-1972.* She is currently researching the life and times of Helena Gutteridge.

James Huzel is a member of the history department at the University of British Columbia specializing in European social history. He has published on rural labour, urban population change and the social impact of welfare policy in England.

Robert A. J. McDonald teaches western Canadian history at the University of British Columbia. He has published several articles on early Vancouver and co-edited *British Columbia: Historical Readings.*

Kathryn McPherson is completing a doctorate in history at Simon Fraser University. She has written on the history of Canadian medicine and has a special interest in the development of the nursing profession.

Patricia Roy teaches Canadian history at the University of Victoria. The author of *Vancouver: An Illustrated History*, she has published widely on various aspects of British Columbia's past.

Veronica Strong-Boag teaches Canadian history and women's studies at Simon Fraser University. She is the author of numerous publications on Canadian women's history and, most recently, was a member of the collective that produced *Working Lives: Vancouver 1886-1986.*

Neil Sutherland teaches history of education at the University of British Columbia. The author of *Children in English-Canadian Society: Framing the Twentieth-Century Consensus,* he is currently completing a successor volume on Canadian childhood after the First World War.

Jill Wade, who has published previously in *BC Studies,* is a doctoral student in history at Simon Fraser University. Her major research interest is Vancouver housing policy between 1930 and 1955.

Paul Yee, an archivist with the City of Vancouver, recently completed his master's degree in history at the University of British Columbia. An earlier article in *BC Studies,* as well as the essay in this volume, are taken from his thesis research on Chinese business in early Vancouver.